"Our mission is to improve decision making, stimulate research and inform debate within government and the wider community by providing a quality statistical service"

Economic Trends

**No 484
February 1994**

Editor: ALAN HYDE

London: HMSO

© *Crown copyright 1994*
First published February 1994

Proposals for reproduction of tables or contents should be addressed to Copyright Section, CSO Press and Publications Branch, Room D.134, Government Buildings, Cardiff Road, Newport, Gwent, NP9 1XG. Telephone 0633 812915 or Fax 0633-812863.

Central Statistical Office

The Central Statistical Office is the government agency responsible for preparing the United Kingdom's national accounts, for the collection of data from businesses, and for the compilation of a wide range of official statistics - including the retail prices index and the overseas trade figures.

CSO began life in 1941 on the orders of Winston Churchill who wanted better statistics to manage the war-time economy. It remained part of the Cabinet Office until mid-1989, when it became a separate government department responsible to the Chancellor of the Exchequer. In November 1991 it became a Government Executive Agency.

Today, anyone can benefit from the following:

  * A range of statistical publications. The *Monthly Digest, Economic Trends* and *Social Trends* are among the best known. Details from HMSO bookshops (071-873 0011).

  * Public inquiry services in London (071-270 6363/6364) and Newport (0633 812973). Call London for details of how to subscribe to CSO first releases, how to phone 'talking' release notices, or how to receive release notices by Fax. Call Newport for inquiries on business statistics and details of *Business Monitors*. Call either with general inquiries about government statistics.

  * A wide range of data on disk. See page 4 for details.

Government Statistical Service

A service of statistical information and advice is provided to Government by specialist staffs employed in the statistics division of individual Departments. Statistics are made generally available through their publications and further information and advice on them can be obtained from the Department concerned.

The sources of the series published in this volume and further information about them are shown in the index. Current telephone numbers of these sources as well as general information about *Economic Trends* can be obtained from the Central Statistical Office, Great George Street, London SW1P 3AQ. Telephone: 071-270 6363/6364.

Enquiries about orders and subscriptions for *Economic Trends* and other Central Statistical Office publications should be made to:

HMSO, PO Box 276, London SW8 5DT
(Telephone: 071-873 8499 for subscriptions; 071-873 9090 for orders)

ISBN 0 11 620633 0
ISSN 0013-0400

Contents

	Page
Introduction	4
Symbols and definitions used	4
Important change to Economic Trends	5
Economic Update	8

Tables and charts

	Page
Main economic indicators for the United Kingdom	11
National accounts aggregates	12
Gross domestic product: by category of expenditure	14
Personal disposable income and consumption	16
Real consumers' expenditure - component categories	16
Retail sales, new registrations of cars and credit business	18
Gross domestic product and shares of income and expenditure	20
Income, product and spending per head	20
Gross domestic fixed capital formation	22
Indicators of fixed investment by manufacturing industry	24
Indicators of fixed investment in dwellings	26
Value of physical increase in stocks and work in progress at 1990 market prices	28
Stock ratios	28
Inland energy consumption	30
Index of output of the production industries	32
Index numbers of output at constant factor cost	34
Engineering and construction: output and orders	36
Motor vehicle production and steel production and consumption	38
Output per person employed	40
National employment and unemployment	42
Regional unemployment rates	44
Labour force survey economic activity	46
Labour force survey economic activity by age	48
Labour force survey economic activity by age: not seasonally adjusted	49
Average earnings	50
Prices	52
Visible trade	54
Measures of UK competitiveness in trade in manufactures	56
Balance of payments: current account	58
Sterling exchange rates and UK official reserves	60
Monetary aggregates	62
Counterparts to changes in M4	64
General government receipts and expenditure	66
Financial transactions of the public sector	66
Summary capital accounts and financial surplus or deficit	68
Appropriation account of industrial and commercial companies	70
Capital account and financial surplus/deficit of industrial and commercial companies	72
Financial transactions including net borrowing requirement of industrial and commercial companies	72
UK banks' lending to UK residents	74
UK banks' loans, advances and acceptances to UK residents	74
Interest rates, security prices and yields	76
A selection of asset prices	78
Number of property transactions in England and Wales	79
Cyclical indicators for the UK economy	80
Measures of variability of selected economic series	84

Articles

	Page
International economic indicators	85
Taxes and Social Security contributions: an international comparison 1981-1991	92
Testing for bias in initial estimates of the components of GDP	104
Seasonal adjustment of the number of property transactions in England and Wales	117
Index of sources	122
Release dates of economic statistics as at 28 February 1994	128

Other

Articles published in recent Economic Trends	inside front cover

Introduction

Economic Trends brings together all the main economic indicators. It contains three regular sections of tables and charts illustrating trends in the UK economy.

'Economic Update' is a feature giving an overview of the latest economic statistics. The content and presentation will vary from month to month depending on topicality and coverage of the published statistics. The accompanying table on main economic indicators is wider in coverage than the table on selected monthly indicators appearing in previous editions of *Economic Trends*. Data included in this section may not be wholly consistent with other sections which will have gone to press earlier.

The main section is based on information available to the CSO on the date printed at the foot of this page and shows the movements of the key economic indicators. The indicators appear in tabular form on left hand pages with corresponding charts on facing right hand pages. Colour has been used to aid interpretation in some of the charts, for example by creating a background grid on those charts drawn to a logarithmic scale. Index numbers in some tables and charts are given on a common base year for convenience of comparison.

The section on cyclical indicators shows the movements of four composite indices over 20 years against a reference chronology of business cycles. The indices group together indicators which lead, coincide with and lag behind the business cycle, and a short note describes their most recent movements. The March, June, September and December issues carry further graphs showing separately the movements in all of the 27 indicators which make up the composite indices.

An article on international economic indicators appears monthly and an article on regional economic indicators appears every March, June, September and December. Occasional articles comment on and analyse economic statistics and introduce new series, new analyses and new methodology.

Quarterly articles on the national accounts and the balance of payments appear in a separate supplement to *Economic Trends* entitled *UK Economic Accounts* which is published every January, April, July and October.

Economic Trends is prepared monthly by the Central Statistical Office in collaboration with the statistics divisions of Government Departments and the Bank of England.

Notes on the tables

1. Some data, particularly for the latest time period, are provisional and may be subject to revisions in later issues.

2. The statistics relate mainly to the United Kingdom; where figures are for Great Britain only, this is shown on the table.

3. Almost all quarterly data are seasonally adjusted; those not seasonally adjusted are indicated by NSA.

4. Rounding may lead to inconsistencies between the sum of constituent parts and the total in some tables.

5. A line drawn across a column between two consecutive figures indicates that the figures above and below the line have been compiled on different bases and are not strictly comparable. In each case a footnote explains the difference.

6. 'Billion' denotes one thousand million.

7. There may sometimes be an inconsistency between a table and the corresponding chart, because the data may be received too late to update the chart. In such cases it should be assumed that the table is correct.

8. There is no single correct definition of *money*. Consequently, several definitions of money stock are widely used:

M0 the narrowest measure consists of notes and coin in circulation outside the Bank of England and bankers' operational deposits at the Bank.

M2 comprises notes and coin in circulation with the public *plus* sterling retail deposits held by the UK private sector with UK banks and building societies.

M4 comprises notes and coin in circulation with the public, together with all sterling deposits (including *certificates of deposit*) held with UK banks and building societies by the rest of the private sector.

The Bank of England also publish data for liquid assets outside M4.

9. Symbols used:
   .. not available
   - nil or less than half the final digit shown
   + alongside a heading indicates a series for which measures of variability are given in the table on page 84
   † indicates that the data has been revised since the last edition; the period marked is the earliest in the table to have been revised
   * average (or total) of five weeks.

The Editor would welcome readers' suggestions for improvements to *Economic Trends*.

Central Statistical Office, 14 February 1994

CSO Databank

The data in this publication can be obtained in computer readable form via the CSO Databank service which provides macro-economic times series data on magnetic tape and High Density floppy disk. For more details about availability and prices, or to place your order you can telephone, write or fax to: Databank Marketing, Room 56/5, Central Statistical Office, Government Buildings, Great George Street, London, SW1P 3AQ (telephone: 071 270 6081, fax: 071 270 6019). For further information on the CSO Databank content and technical details you can telephone or write to: The Databank Service, Room 52/4, Central Statistical Office, Great George Street, London SW1P 3AQ (telephone: 071 270 6386 or 6387). The CSO does not offer direct on-line access for these data, but a list of host bureaux offering such a facility is available on request from the CSO.

Important change to Economic Trends

As part of our ongoing programme of improvements to *Economic Trends*, we shall be introducing a new decimal-based numbering system for the tables from the March 1994 edition onwards. This will enable tables to be grouped into six distinct sub-sections, each based upon a common economic theme, similar to the numbering system used in other CSO monthly publications.

Indexes to the new numbering system appear below.

Please note that this system will also be introduced into the 1994 edition of the *Economic Trends Annual Supplement*. As a result, its publication will be delayed until April.

New number to current number

		Current number
1. SUMMARY		
1.1	Selected monthly indicators	1
2. UK ECONOMIC ACCOUNTS		
2.1	National accounts aggregates	2
2.2	Gross domestic product: by category of expenditure	3
2.3	Gross domestic product and shares of income and expenditure	7
2.4	Income, product and spending per head	8
2.5	Personal disposable income and consumption	4
2.6	Real consumers' expenditure - component categories	5
2.7	Gross domestic fixed capital formation	9
2.8	Index numbers of output at constant factor cost	16
2.9	Summary capital accounts and financia surplus or deficit	35
2.10	Appropriation account of industrial and commercial companies	36
2.11	Capital account and financial surplus/deficit of industrial and commercial companies	37
2.12	Financial transactions including net borrowing requirement of industrial and commercial companies	38
2.13	Balance of payments: current account	29
2.14	Visible trade (on a balance of payments basis)	27
2.15	Measures of UK competitiveness in trade and manufactures	28
3. PRICES		
3.1	Prices	26
4. LABOUR MARKET		
4.1	Average earnings	25
4.2	National employment and unemployment	20
4.3	Regional unemployment rates	21
4.4	Labour force survey: Economic activity	22
4.5	Labour force survey: Economic activity seasonally adjusted	23
4.6	Labour force survey: Economic activity by age	24
4.7	Output per person employed	19
5. SELECTED OUTPUT AND DEMAND INDICATORS		
5.1	Index of output of production industries	15
5.2	Engineering and construction: output and orders	17
5.3	Motor vehicle production and steel production and consumption	18
5.4	Indicators of fixed investment by manufacturing industry	10
5.5	Indicators of fixed investment in dwellings	11
5.6	Number of property transactions in England and Wales	43
5.7	Stock changes	12
5.8	Stock ratios	13
5.9	Retail sales, new registrations of cars, and credit business (Great Britain)	6
5.10	Inland energy consumption	14
6. SELECTED FINANCIAL STATISTICS		
6.1	Sterling exchange rates and UK official reserves	30
6.2	Monetary aggregates	31
6.3	Counterparts to changes in M4	32
6.4	General government receipts and expenditure	33
6.5	Financial transactions of the public sector	34
6.6	UK banks' lending to UK residents	39
6.7	UK banks' loans, advances and acceptances to UK residents	40
6.8	Interest rates, security prices and yields	41
6.9	A selection of asset prices	42

Current number to new number

		New number
1	Selected monthly indicators	1.1
2	National accounts aggregates	2.1
3	Gross domestic product: by category of expenditure	2.2
4	Personal disposable income and consumption	2.5
5	Real consumers' expenditure - component categories	2.6
6	Retail sales, new registrations of cars, and credit business (Great Britain)	5.9
7	Gross domestic product and shares of income and expenditure	2.3
8	Income, product and spending per head	2.4
9	Gross domestic fixed capital formation	2.7
10	Indicators of fixed investment by manufacturing industry	5.4
11	Indicators of fixed investment in dwellings	5.5
12	Stock changes	5.7
13	Stock ratios	5.8
14	Inland energy consumption	5.10
15	Index of output of production industries	5.1
16	Index numbers of output at constant factor cost	2.8
17	Engineering and construction: output and orders	5.2
18	Motor vehicle production and steel production and consumption	5.3
19	Output per person employed	4.7
20	National employment and unemployment	4.2
21	Regional unemployment rates	4.3
22	Labour force survey: Economic activity	4.4
23	Labour force survey: Economic activity seasonally adjusted	4.5
24	Labour force survey: Economic activity by age	4.6
25	Average earnings	4.1
26	Prices	3.1
27	Visible trade (on a balance of payments basis)	2.14
28	Measures of UK competitiveness in trade and manufactures	2.15
29	Balance of payments: current account	2.13
30	Sterling exchange rates and UK official reserves	6.1
31	Monetary aggregates	6.2
32	Counterparts to changes in M4	6.3
33	General government receipts and expenditure	6.4
34	Financial transactions of the public sector	6.5
35	Summary capital accounts and financial surplus or deficit	2.9
36	Appropriation account of industrial andcommercial companies	2.10
37	Capital account and financial surplus/deficit of industrial and commercial companies	2.11
38	Financial transactions including net borrowing requirement of industrial and commercial companies	2.12
39	UK banks' lending to UK residents	
40	UK banks' loans, advances and acceptances to UK residents	6.7
41	Interest rates, security prices and yields	6.8
42	A selection of asset prices	6.9
43	Number of property transactions in England and Wales	5.6

SNAPSHOT OF BRITAIN

Do you need economic and social statistics on different parts of the United Kingdom? If so, there are few better sources than Regional Trends.

Here's what the press have said about this famous publication ...

'... provides a fascinating insight into the differing lifestyles of particular regions...' - *Financial Times*

'... essential to Government planners, scientific researchers or businessmen seeking a profile of an area in which to test their market...' - *Daily Telegraph*

'... includes district statistics... providing an intriguing insight into small pockets of the country...' *The Times*

'... the definitive reference book on how parts of Britain differ...' - *Daily Telegraph*

'...*Regional Trends*' 200 pages provide a highly readable snapshot of social and economic conditions in Britain...' - *Daily Star*

'... myths exploded by the latest statistics from Regional Trends...' - *The Guardian*

'...contains some information to confirm stereotyped images of lifestyle around Britain's regions-but also some to challenge them...' - *Financial Times*

From HMSO and through good booksellers.

Regional Trends

Published for the Central Statistical Office by HMSO.
Price £26 net
ISBN 0 11 620 596 2

ECONOMIC UPDATE - FEBRUARY 1994

(includes data up to 18 February 1994)

Summary

- The **retail prices index** rose by 2.5 per cent in the year to January 1994.

- **Retail sales volume** rose by 0.8 per cent in the three months to January 1994 compared with the three months to October 1993.

- **Manufacturing output** rose by 0.5 per cent between 1993 Q3 and 1993 Q4.

- **UK claimant unemployment**, seasonally adjusted, rose by 15,500 in January 1994.

Activity

The CSO's **coincident cyclical indicator** has increased steadily from its trough in 1992 Q2. At the beginning of 1994, the **shorter leading index** is continuing to rise, while the **longer leading index** has begun to rise once again after faltering last year. Chart 1 shows the longer and shorter leading indicators (advanced by their average lead) compared with the GDP reference cycle.

Chart 1
Leading cyclical indicators

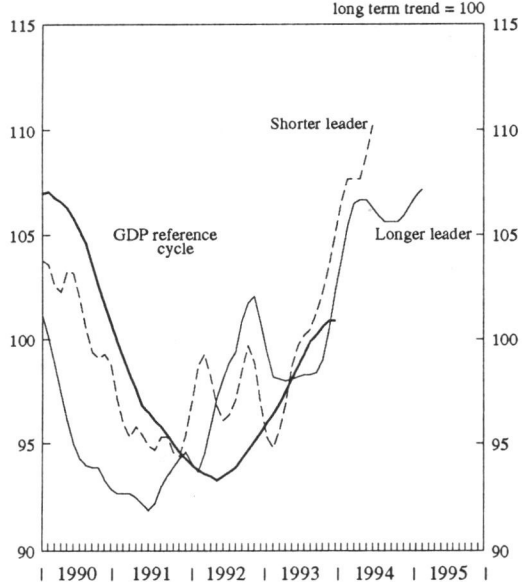

Output and expectations

2. The **index of industrial production**, seasonally adjusted, was 1.3 per cent higher in the fourth quarter of 1993 than the third quarter. Within this there were substantial variations in growth. **Manufacturing output** rose by 0.5 per cent, **mining and quarrying** (including oil and gas extraction) rose 7.6 per cent and **electricity, gas and water** rose by 1.7 per cent. Mining and quarrying was buoyed by several recent new oil and gas fields reaching full production and further new fields starting. Chart 2 shows that manufacturing output has risen less strongly than overall production since the recent troughs in the respective series.

Chart 2
Output of the production industries

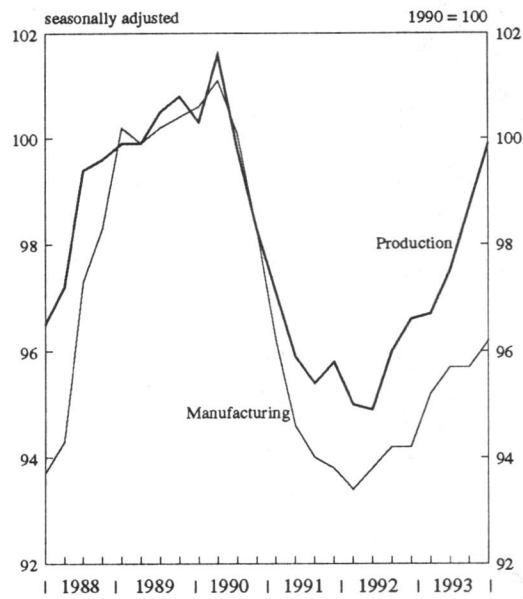

3. The **CBI Quarterly Industrial Trends Enquiry in manufacturing** revealed that the **output expectations** balance in the next 4 months, seasonally adjusted, rose from 16 per cent in December 1993 to 18 per cent in January 1994.

Indicators of domestic demand

4. The recent run of figures suggests a continued upward trend for total retail sales. In the three months to January 1994, the **volume of retail sales** was 0.8 per cent higher than in the three months to October 1993 and 3.8 up on a year earlier.

5. The latest figures on **net lending to consumers**, shown in chart 3, show a slight downturn in borrowing by consumers in 1993 Q4. On the broader coverage net

lending, seasonally adjusted, fell from £714 million in 1993 Q3 to £634 million in 1993 Q4, but remains well above the levels of 1992.

Chart 3
Net lending to consumers
(broader coverage)

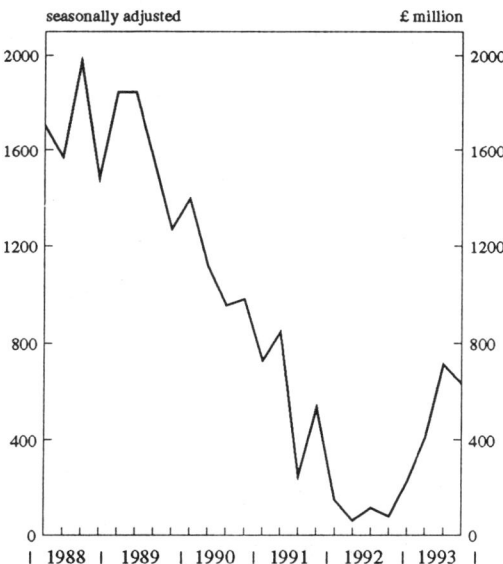

Chart 4
Retail prices index

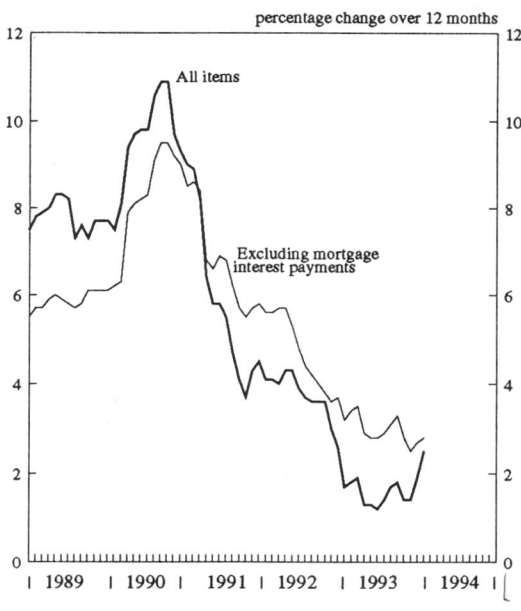

Prices and wages

6. The 12-month rate of increase of the **retail prices index** (RPI) rose from 1.9 per cent in December 1993 to 2.5 per cent in January 1994. The increase in the headline rate was mainly due to a smaller fall in mortgage interest rates in January 1994 than in January 1993. **Excluding mortgage interest payments**, the 12-month rate rose from 2.7 per cent in December 1993 to 2.8 per cent in January 1994. Chart 4 shows the progression of retail price changes since 1989.

7. The rate of increase in the price of manufacturing output continued to fall, while input prices fell sharply. The **output price index for manufactured products** (home sales), seasonally adjusted and excluding food, beverages, tobacco and petroleum, rose by an annualised 1.9 per cent in the three months to January 1994 compared with the three months to October 1993. Over the same period the **input prices** (all manufacturing), seasonally adjusted, fell by an annualised 7.4 per cent.

8. **Expectations of price increases** also remain subdued in January. The CBI Quarterly Industrial Trends Enquiry for manufacturing implied a balance of 2 per cent, seasonally adjusted by the CSO, expecting to raise prices in the next four months.

9. Underlying average earnings growth remained stable in December 1993. The annual rise in underlying **whole economy average earnings** for Great Britain remained at 3 per cent in December 1993, for the fourth consecutive month. The underlying increase for manufacturing remained at 4¼ per cent and for services at 2½ per cent. Underling average earnings for the whole economy, services and manufacturing are shown in chart 5.

Chart 5
Underlying average earnings in GB

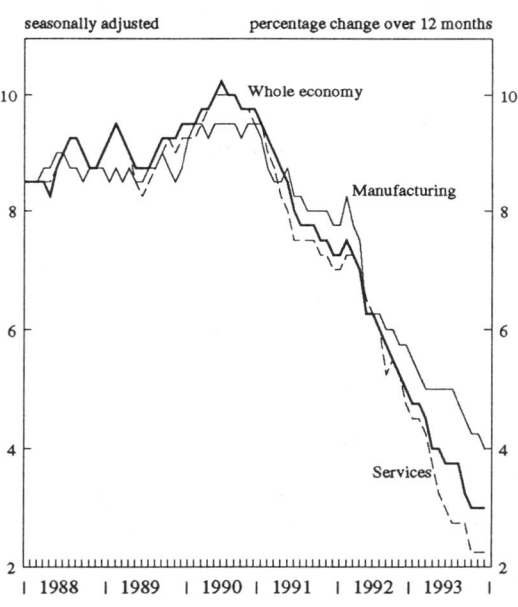

Labour market and productivity

10. **UK claimant unemployment**, seasonally adjusted, rose in January by 15,500 to 2.788 million, or 9.9 per cent of the workforce. The rise was due to a fall in the outflow from the unemployment register, while there was a small

rise in the inflow onto the register. Chart 6 shows that inflows to the register has fallen since 1992, while outflows have risen. Erratic figures are not unusual, especially over holiday periods. The January rise follows an exceptionally large fall in the previous month. In the three months to January the average monthly fall was 21,500; similar to the fall of 21,400 in the three months to October 1994.

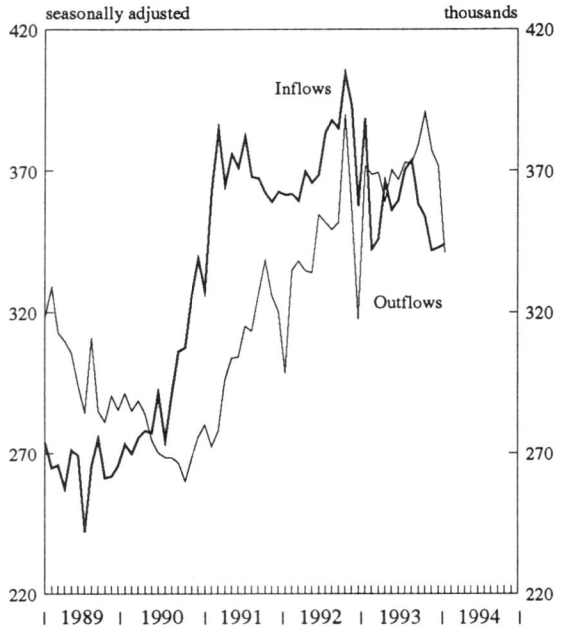

Chart 6
Unemployment - inflows and outflows

11. **Manufacturing employment** is estimated to have fallen by 3,000 in the fourth quarter of 1993 compared with the third quarter.

12. In the three months to December 1993, **productivity in manufacturing** was 3.2 per cent above the level in the three months to December 1992. **Unit wage costs in manufacturing** was 0.8 per cent above that level.

Monetary indicators

13. The annual growth of narrow money (**M0**), seasonally adjusted, fell from 5.8 per cent in December 1993 to 5.3 per cent in January, but remained outside the Government's monitoring range of 0-4 per cent. The annual growth of broad money (**M4**), seasonally adjusted, provisionally rose from 5.4 per cent in December 1993 to 5.5 per cent in January, to remain well within the monitoring range of 3-9 per cent.

Government finances

14. The **public sector borrowing requirement (PSBR)** in January 1994 showed a repayment of £1.6 billion, which was lower than the repayment of £3.7 billion in January 1993. For the first ten months of 1993-94 the **PSBR** was £30.2 billion against £21.5 billion in the same period last year. Excluding privatisation proceeds the figures were £33.6 billion and £27.8 billion respectively. The budget forecast for 1993-94 was for a deficit of £50.0 billion.

Balance of payments

15. The deficit on the **balance of UK visible trade** worsened, in the three months to November 1993. It averaged £3.0 billion; above the £2.5 billion in the three months to August 1993. On a trend basis the visible deficit appears to be flattening. The balance of UK visible trade and its trend is shown in chart 7. The **volume of total exports, excluding oil and erratics**, fell by 2 per cent in the three months to November 1993 compared with the three months to August 1993. On the same basis **imports** rose by 3 per cent. Latest estimates in the trend for trade volumes (excluding oil and erratics) suggest a small decrease in exports and a small increase in imports.

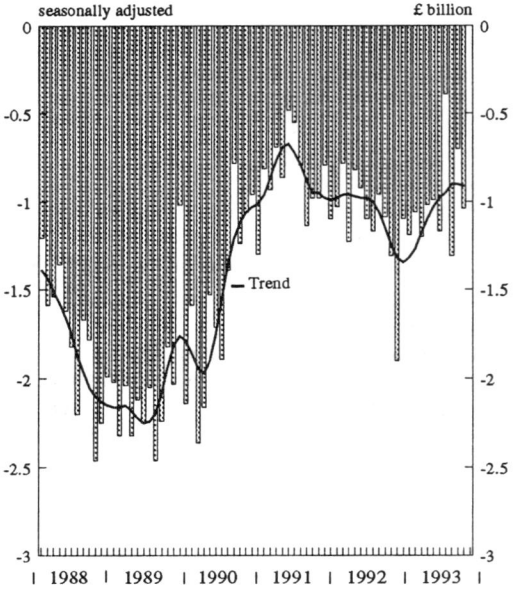

Chart 7
Balance of UK visible trade

1 Main Economic indicators for the United Kingdom

seasonally adjusted unless otherwise stated

		1992	1993	1993 Q1	1993 Q2	1993 Q3	1993 Q4	1993 Oct	1993 Nov	1993 Dec	1994 Jan	% Change Latest 3 months avg over previous 3 months
Output in constant prices (1990 = 100 unless otherwise stated)												
Gross domestic product at factor cost	DJDD	97.2	99.1	98.2	98.8	99.4	100.1	..	..	..	..	0.7
Industrial production	DVZI	95.6	98.2	96.7	97.5	98.7	99.9	100.0	100.2	99.6	..	1.3
Oil and gas extraction	DVZT	108.8	127.7	112.6	120.8	132.1	145.3	138.7	147.1	150.1	..	10.0
Manufacturing	DVZK	93.9	95.7	95.2	95.7	95.7	96.2	96.3	96.4	95.9	..	0.5
Construction	DVJO	86.9	..	85.3	85.1	85.3	..	..	..	..	..	0.2
Car production (thousands)	FFAO	107.7	114.6	106.9	117.6	119.4	114.6	108.9	112.3	122.7	100.8	-4.4
GB housing completions (thousands)	CTPA	170.2	174.0	43.0	43.7	42.6	44.7	15.6	14.6	14.5	..	4.9
Domestic demand												
Retail sales volume (1990 = 100)	FAAM	99.5	103.0	101.9	102.4	103.4	104.3	104.0	104.4	104.3	105.0	0.8
GB new registrations of cars ('000s)	DKBY	1 595.2	1 761.3	424.6	433.2	451.0	452.5	157.6	160.7	134.2	..	0.3
Manufacturing investment (£m 1990 prices)	DECV	11 907	..	2 988	2 909	2 966	..	..	..	..	..	2.0
Manufacturing stockbuilding (£m 1990 prices)	DHBM	-2 171	..	-719	290	-736	..	..	..	..	..	
Prices & wages (12 monthly % change)												
Retail prices index[1]	FRAN	3.7	1.6	1.8	1.3	1.7	1.6	1.4	1.4	1.9	2.5	
Retail prices index[1] (less MIPS)[2]	CDKQ	4.7	3.0	3.4	2.8	3.1	2.7	2.8	2.5	2.7	2.8	
Producer output prices (less FBTP)[3] (1990 = 100)	EUAA	2.2	2.6	2.3	2.3	2.7	3.1	3.2	3.1	2.8	2.7	
Producer input prices (1990 = 100)	EUAB	-0.2	4.4	6.5	6.6	5.6	-0.7	0.4	-1.3	-1.3	-2.6	
GB underlying average earnings	DNEM	..	..	4.25	3.75	3.25	3.00	3.00	3.00	3.00	..	
Foreign trade (1990 = 100 volumes unless otherwise stated)												
Non EC visible trade balance (£ million)	ENRX	-9 749	-9 539	-3 130	-2 156	-2 427	-1 826	-378	-773	-675	..	
Non EC exports of goods (excl oil & erratics)	ENUA	96.8	106.6	101.8	106.4	107.1	111.0	117.0	104.5	111.4	..	3.5
Non EC imports of goods (excl oil & erratics)	ENTS	105.3	117.2	114.2	115.0	117.6	122.1	121.5	120.9	124.0	..	4.0
Non EC import unit value (excl oil)[4]	ENXR	0.7	8.1	8.3	9.3	11.4	3.5	4.8	3.4	2.2	..	
Non EC export unit value (excl oil)[4]	ENXS	3.4	10.9	11.0	7.4	12.7	12.4	11.6	13.3	12.2	..	
Non EC terms of trade (excl oil)	ENUY	104.0	106.7	105.6	103.2	107.7	110.4	109.2	111.0	111.3	..	2.5
Labour market and productivity (1990 = 100 unless otherwise stated)												
UK claimant unemployment (thousands)	BCJD	2 766.5	2 903.5	2 966.7	2 922.9	2 914.1	2 812.4	2 852.0	2 813.0	2 772.1	2 787.6	-3.5
Vacancies (thousands)	DPCB	117.1	127.9	121.3	122.3	127.6	140.2	134.4	140.9	145.4	141.8	9.9
GB employment in manufacturing (thousands)	DMGR	4 359	4 193	4 197	4 203	4 188	4 182	4 183	4 187	4 176	..	-0.1
Whole economy productivity	DMBE	102.8	..	105.7	106.2	106.5	..	..	..	..	..	0.2
Manufacturing productivity	DMOB	106.3	112.2	111.6	112.0	112.4	113.0	113.1	113.1	112.8	..	0.6
Unit wage costs - whole economy	DJDO	111.7	..	112.3	112.1	112.3	..	..	..	..	..	0.2
Unit wage costs manufacturing	DMGH	108.6	107.4	107.2	106.4	107.7	108.3	108.1	108.2	108.5	..	0.5
Financial markets[1]												
Sterling ERI(1985 = 100)	AJHV	88.4	80.2	78.5	80.2	81.0	81.0	80.4	81.0	81.7	82.5	
Average exchange rate /US $	AJFA	1.7665	1.5015	1.4771	1.5340	1.5047	1.4914	1.5037	1.4806	1.4904	1.4940	
Average exchange rate /DM	AJPH	2.7513	2.4830	2.4141	2.4843	2.5221	2.5100	2.4629	2.5174	2.5494	2.6039	
FTSE (100 share)	AJNO	2 561.06	2 959.88	2 842.60	2 847.41	2 966.04	3 183.47	3 125.15	3 111.59	3 313.68	3 431.29	
3 month inter-bank rate[5]	HSAJ	7.13	5.31	6.00	5.88	5.88	5.31	5.63	5.31	5.31	5.38	
3 month interest on US Treasury bills[6]	AJIA	3.06	2.98	2.90	3.03	2.92	2.98	3.03	3.11	2.98	2.95	
Monetary conditions/government finances												
M0 (year on year percentage growth)	EUAC	2.3	4.8	4.4	4.2	5.0	5.4	5.4	5.1	5.8	5.3	
M4 (year on year percentage growth)	EUAD	5.3	3.9	3.5	3.6	3.7	4.9	4.3	4.9	5.4	5.5	
PSBR (nsa)[1] (£ million)[7]	ABEN	36 547	..	11 270	13 367	10 765	7 664	2 565	3 013	2 086	-1 636	
Net lending to consumers (£ million)(narrower)	RLMJ	362	2 889	400	525	919	1 045	312	290	443	..	

		1992 Dec	1993 Jan	1993 Feb	1993 Mar	1993 Apr	1993 May	1993 Jun	1993 Jul	1993 Aug	1993 Sep	1993 Oct	1993 Nov	1993 Dec	1994 Jan
Activity and expectations															
Coincident indicator (1990 = 100)	DKBP	96.2	96.9	97.6	98.3	99.1	99.5	100.3	101.2	102.0	102.4	103.1	104.0	104.6	..
Shorter leading indicator (1990 = 100)	DKBS	98.7	99.7	100.2	100.5	101.3	102.3	103.5	105.0	106.6	107.7	107.7	107.7	108.8	110.2
Longer leading indicator (1990 = 100)	DKBR	103.9	105.6	106.6	106.9	106.9	106.5	106.1	105.8	105.8	105.8	105.9	106.1	106.3	106.6
CBI output expectations balance[8]	ETCV	–	5	9	10	10	14	9	2	16	18	11	16	16	18
CBI optimism balance[8]	DKDK	..	13	..	..	17	..	..	11	..	..	14	..	..	28
CBI price expectations balance[8]	ETDQ	3	1	11	7	6	7	6	3	3	5	1	5	-5	2
GB housing starts (thousands)	CTOZ	13.4	15.1	15.3	16.7	15.3	14.9	15.2	14.2	15.0	16.0	16.2	17.3	15.2	..
New engineering orders (1990 = 100)	FEAL	98	84	91	105	85	97	93	87	104	94	86	93	..	..

1 not seasonally adjusted
2 MIPS: mortgage interest payments
3 FBTP : food, beverages, tobacco and petroleum
4 12 monthly percentage change
5 last Friday of the period
6 last working day
7 annual figure is for the financial year 1992/3
8 seasonally adjusted by CSO

2 National accounts aggregates

	£ million		Index numbers (1990 = 100)					Implied gross domestic product deflator[4]	
	At current prices		Value indices at current prices		Volume indices at 1990 prices				
	Gross domestic product at market prices[1]	Gross domestic product at factor cost	Gross domestic product at market prices[2]	Gross domestic product at factor cost	Gross national disposable income at market prices[3]	Gross domestic product at market prices	Gross domestic product at factor cost +	At market prices	At factor cost[5]
	CAOB	CAOM	DJCL	CAON	DJCR	FNAO	DJDD	DJDT	DJCM
1987	423 381	360 675	76.8	75.3	92.7	92.8	92.7	82.8	81.3
1988	471 430	401 428	85.5	83.8	97.7	97.5	97.3	87.8	86.2
1989	515 957	441 759	93.6	92.2	99.7	99.6	99.4	94.0	92.8
1990	551 118	478 886	100.0	100.0	100.0	100.0	100.0	100.0	100.0
1991	573 645	494 824	104.1	103.3	98.4	97.8	97.7	106.5	105.8
1992	595 477	514 741	108.0	107.5	98.6	97.2	97.2	111.1	110.6
1993	..	..	..	..	..	..	99.1	..	..
1989 Q4	133 065	114 110	96.6	95.3	99.7	99.8	99.8	96.7	95.5
1990 Q1	135 409	116 084	98.3	97.0	99.7	100.4	100.4	97.9	96.6
Q2	136 952	119 167	99.4	99.5	100.3	100.9	100.7	98.5	98.8
Q3	139 703	121 982	101.4	101.9	100.8	99.8	99.8	101.6	102.1
Q4	139 054	121 653	100.9	101.6	99.2	98.9	99.1	102.0	102.5
1991 Q1	140 470	122 659	102.0	102.5	98.7	98.1	98.1	103.9	104.4
Q2	142 969	122 860	103.8	102.6	98.7	97.6	97.6	106.3	105.1
Q3	144 052	123 657	104.6	103.3	97.8	97.5	97.5	107.2	106.0
Q4	146 154	125 648	106.1	105.0	98.6	97.7	97.5	108.5	107.7
1992 Q1	146 334	126 151	106.2	105.4	98.0	96.8	96.9	109.7	108.8
Q2	148 601	128 501	107.9	107.3	98.1	97.0	97.0	111.2	110.7
Q3	149 739	129 654	108.7	108.3	99.2	97.4	97.4	111.6	111.2
Q4	150 803	130 435	109.5	108.9	99.1	97.7	97.7	112.1	111.5
1993 Q1	153 402	132 879	111.3	111.0	99.0	98.2	98.2	113.4	113.0
Q2	155 648	134 505	113.0	112.3	100.0	98.9	98.8	114.2	113.8
Q3	157 709	136 281	114.5	113.8	100.7	99.5	99.4	115.0	114.5
Q4	..	..	..	..	..	..	100.1	..	..

Percentage change, quarter on corresponding quarter of previous year[6]

1989 Q4	7.8	8.5	7.8	8.5	0.3	0.9	1.2	6.9	7.2
1990 Q1	7.8	8.0	7.8	8.0	-0.2	1.1	1.3	6.6	6.6
Q2	7.7	9.7	7.7	9.7	0.4	1.3	1.4	6.3	8.1
Q3	7.4	9.4	7.4	9.4	1.4	0.1	0.3	7.3	9.1
Q4	4.5	6.6	4.5	6.6	-0.6	-0.9	-0.7	5.5	7.4
1991 Q1	3.7	5.7	3.7	5.7	-1.0	-2.2	-2.2	6.1	8.1
Q2	4.4	3.1	4.4	3.1	-1.6	-3.2	-3.1	7.9	6.4
Q3	3.1	1.4	3.1	1.4	-3.0	-2.3	-2.4	5.5	3.8
Q4	5.1	3.3	5.1	3.3	-0.6	-1.2	-1.6	6.4	5.0
1992 Q1	4.2	2.8	4.2	2.8	-0.7	-1.3	-1.3	5.5	4.2
Q2	3.9	4.6	3.9	4.6	-0.6	-0.6	-0.7	4.6	5.3
Q3	3.9	4.8	3.9	4.8	1.4	-0.2	-0.1	4.1	5.0
Q4	3.2	3.8	3.2	3.8	0.5	-0.1	0.2	3.2	3.6
1993 Q1	4.8	5.3	4.8	5.3	1.0	1.4	1.4	3.4	3.9
Q2	4.7	4.7	4.7	4.7	1.9	1.9	1.9	2.8	2.8
Q3	5.3	5.1	5.3	5.1	1.5	2.2	2.1	3.0	3.0
Q4	..	..	..	..	..	..	2.5	..	..

1 These series are affected by the abolition of domestic rates and the introduction of the Community Charge. For details, see notes in the UK National Accounts article in the latest edition of *UK Economic Accounts*.
2 "Money GDP."
3 Also known as real national disposable income (RNDI).
4 Based on the sum of expenditure components of GDP at current and constant prices.
5 Also known as the Index of total home costs.
6 These estimates of change are based in some cases on less rounded figures than in the table.

Source: Central Statistical Office

CSO STATFAX
For the most up-to-date data on gross domestic product, poll the following number from your fax machine:
0336 416045
Calls charged at 36p per minute cheap rate, 48p per minute at all other times

Gross domestic product (average measure)

1990 = 100 seasonally adjusted log scale

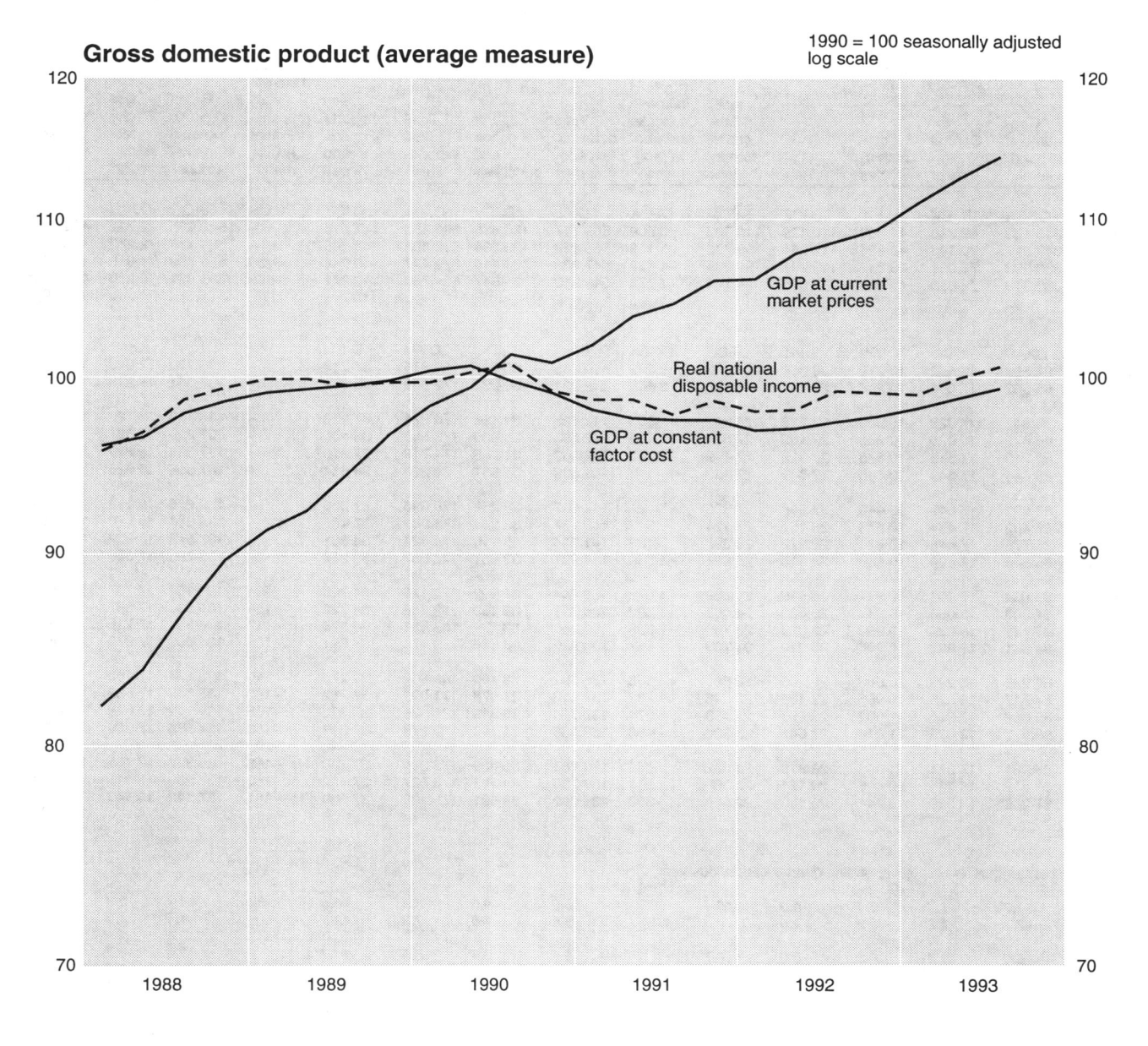

Gross domestic product (average measure) and real national disposable income

Percentage change on year earlier

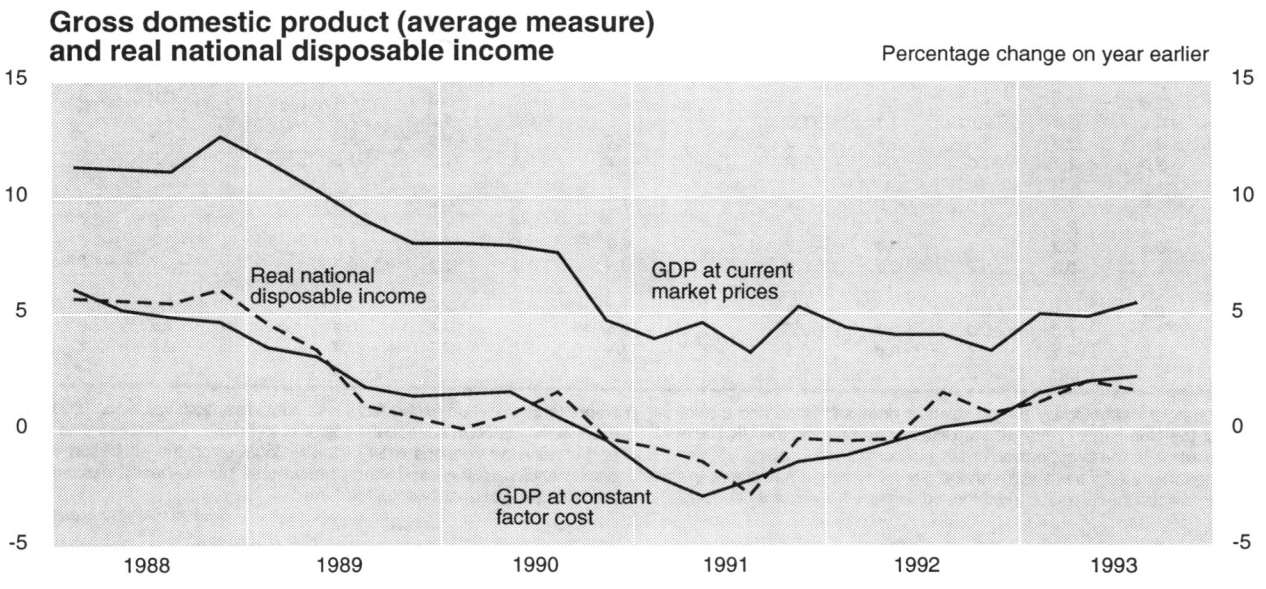

3 Gross domestic product: by category of expenditure

£ million, 1990 prices

	Domestic expenditure on goods and services at market prices										Statistical discrepancy (expenditure adjustment)[4]	Gross domestic product at market prices[1]	less Factor cost adjustment[3]	Gross domestic product at factor cost[4]
	Consumers' expenditure+[1]	General government final consumption			Gross domestic fixed capital formation+	Value of physical increase in stocks and work in progress+[2]	Total domestic expenditure[1]	Exports of goods and services+	Total final expenditure[1]	less Imports of goods and services+				
		Central government	Local authorities	Total										
	CCBH	DJDK	DJDL	DJCZ	DFDM	DHBK	DIEL	DJCV	DJDA	DJCY	GIXS	CAOO	DJCU	CAOP
1989	345 406	68 836	41 303	110 139	110 503	3 669	569 717	126 836	696 553	147 615	–	548 938	72 712	476 226
1990	347 527	70 108	42 826	112 934	106 776	–1 118	566 119	133 284	699 403	148 285	–	551 118	72 232	478 886
1991	339 993	71 950	43 847	115 797	96 265	–4 722	547 333	132 114	679 447	140 248	–430	538 769	71 049	467 720
1992	339 610	72 678	43 957	116 635	94 741	–1 773	549 213	135 547	684 760	148 271	–668	535 821	70 250	465 571
1993	..	..	..	..	..	..	..	..	..	..	..	..	..	474 665
	CAAB	DIAV	DIAW	DIAT	DECU	DGBA	DIAY	DJDG	DIAU	DJDJ			DIAS	
1988 Q3	84 690	16 592	10 276	26 868	26 288	1 322	139 168	30 707	169 875	34 719	–	135 156	17 943	117 213
Q4	85 562	17 046	10 215	27 261	26 629	3 469	142 921	30 032	172 953	36 602	–	136 351	18 248	118 103
1989 Q1	85 847	17 023	10 259	27 282	28 343	953	142 425	31 496	173 921	37 133	–	136 788	18 120	118 668
Q2	86 472	16 925	10 260	27 185	27 551	1 485	142 693	31 000	173 693	36 468	–	137 225	18 327	118 898
Q3	86 243	17 545	10 378	27 923	27 449	1 345	142 960	31 759	174 719	37 350	–	137 369	18 239	119 130
Q4	86 844	17 343	10 406	27 749	27 160	–114	141 639	32 581	174 220	36 664	–	137 556	18 026	119 530
1990 Q1	86 992	17 547	10 443	27 990	27 628	27	142 637	33 259	175 896	37 630	–	138 266	18 112	120 154
Q2	87 409	17 484	10 673	28 157	27 124	547	143 237	33 264	176 501	37 487	–	139 014	18 433	120 581
Q3	86 778	17 448	10 824	28 272	26 397	–133	141 314	33 110	174 424	36 881	–	137 543	18 029	119 514
Q4	86 348	17 629	10 886	28 515	25 627	–1 559	138 931	33 651	172 582	36 287	–	136 295	17 658	118 637
1991 Q1	85 834	17 902	10 917	28 819	24 669	–1 078	138 244	31 932	170 176	34 908	–84	135 184	17 707	117 477
Q2	84 806	18 086	10 944	29 030	24 063	–1 692	136 207	33 159	169 366	34 726	–104	134 536	17 657	116 879
Q3	84 712	18 039	10 990	29 029	23 750	–1 535	135 956	33 475	169 431	34 923	–117	134 391	17 715	116 676
Q4	84 641	17 923	10 996	28 919	23 783	–417	136 926	33 548	170 474	35 691	–125	134 658	17 970	116 688
1992 Q1	84 227	18 223	10 983	29 206	23 817	–858	136 392	33 460	169 852	36 273	–145	133 434	17 443	115 991
Q2	84 717	18 525	10 956	29 481	23 548	–733	137 013	34 078	171 091	37 262	–160	133 669	17 589	116 080
Q3	85 089	17 905	11 002	28 907	23 450	274	137 720	33 819	171 539	37 222	–175	134 142	17 579	116 563
Q4	85 577	18 025	11 016	29 041	23 926	–456	138 088	34 190	172 278	37 514	–188	134 576	17 639	116 937
1993 Q1	85 981	17 871	11 048	28 919	24 032	–766	138 166	35 082	173 248	37 766	–155	135 327	17 735	117 592
Q2	86 432	18 765	10 406	29 171	23 386	241	139 230	34 597	173 827	37 424	–153	136 250	18 015	118 235
Q3	87 268	18 699	10 444	29 143	23 560	–369	139 602	35 591	175 193	37 900	–151	137 142	18 140	119 002
Q4	..	..	..	..	..	..	..	..	..	..	..	..	..	119 836

Percentage change, quarter on corresponding quarter of previous year

1988 Q3	7.7	–1.7	0.4	–0.9	10.4		6.9	–0.5	5.5	8.8		4.7	5.0	4.6
Q4	7.1	1.7	–0.2	1.0	7.0		8.5	1.8	7.3	19.2		4.5	5.3	4.4
1989 Q1	5.0	–0.2	–0.3	–0.2	10.7		5.5	5.4	5.5	14.7		3.2	3.1	3.3
Q2	4.7	0.2	0.2	0.2	5.1		4.6	1.4	4.0	8.0		3.0	3.6	2.9
Q3	1.8	5.7	1.0	3.9	4.4		2.7	3.4	2.9	7.6		1.6	1.6	1.6
Q4	1.5	1.7	1.9	1.8	2.0		–0.9	8.5	0.7	0.2		0.9	–1.2	1.2
1990 Q1	1.3	3.1	1.8	2.6	–2.5		0.1	5.6	1.1	1.3		1.1	0.0	1.3
Q2	1.1	3.3	4.0	3.6	–1.5		0.4	7.3	1.6	2.8		1.3	0.6	1.4
Q3	0.6	–0.6	4.3	1.2	–3.8		–1.2	4.3	–0.2	–1.3		0.1	–1.2	0.3
Q4	–0.6	1.6	4.6	2.8	–5.6		–1.9	3.3	–0.9	–1.0		–0.9	–2.0	–0.7
1991 Q1	–1.3	2.0	4.5	3.0	–10.7		–3.1	–4.0	–3.3	–7.2		–2.2	–2.2	–2.2
Q2	–3.0	3.4	2.5	3.1	–11.3		–4.9	–0.3	–4.0	–7.4		–3.2	–4.2	–3.1
Q3	–2.4	3.4	1.5	2.7	–10.0		–3.8	1.1	–2.9	–5.3		–2.3	–1.7	–2.4
Q4	–2.0	1.7	1.0	1.4	–7.2		–1.4	–0.3	–1.2	–1.6		–1.2	1.8	–1.6
1992 Q1	–1.9	1.8	0.6	1.3	–3.5		–1.3	4.8	–0.2	3.9		–1.3	–1.5	–1.3
Q2	–0.1	2.4	0.1	1.6	–2.1		0.6	2.8	1.0	7.3		–0.6	–0.4	–0.7
Q3	0.4	–0.7	0.1	–0.4	–1.3		1.3	1.0	1.2	6.6		–0.2	–0.8	–0.1
Q4	1.1	0.6	0.2	0.4	0.6		0.8	1.9	1.1	5.1		–0.1	–1.8	0.2
1993 Q1	2.1	–1.9	0.6	–1.0	0.9		1.3	4.8	2.0	4.1		1.4	1.7	1.4
Q2	2.0	1.3	–5.0	–1.1	–0.7		1.6	1.5	1.6	0.4		1.9	2.4	1.9
Q3	2.6	4.4	–5.1	0.8	0.5		1.4	5.2	2.1	1.8		2.2	3.2	2.1
Q4	..	..	..	..	..		..	..	..	..		..	..	2.5

1 These series are affected by the abolition of domestic rates and the introduction of the Community Charge. For details, see notes in the UK National Accounts article in the latest edition of *UK Economic Accounts*.
2 Includes quarterly alignment adjustment. For explanation see notes in the UK National Accounts article in the latest edition of *UK Economic Accounts*.
3 Represents taxes on expenditure less subsidies, both valued at 1990 prices.
4 GDP is estimated in seasonally adjusted form only. Therefore whilst seasonally and unadjusted versions exist of the residual error, the attribution of statistical discrepancies to the expenditure-based and income-based estimates can be made only in seasonally adjusted form.

Source: Central Statistical Office

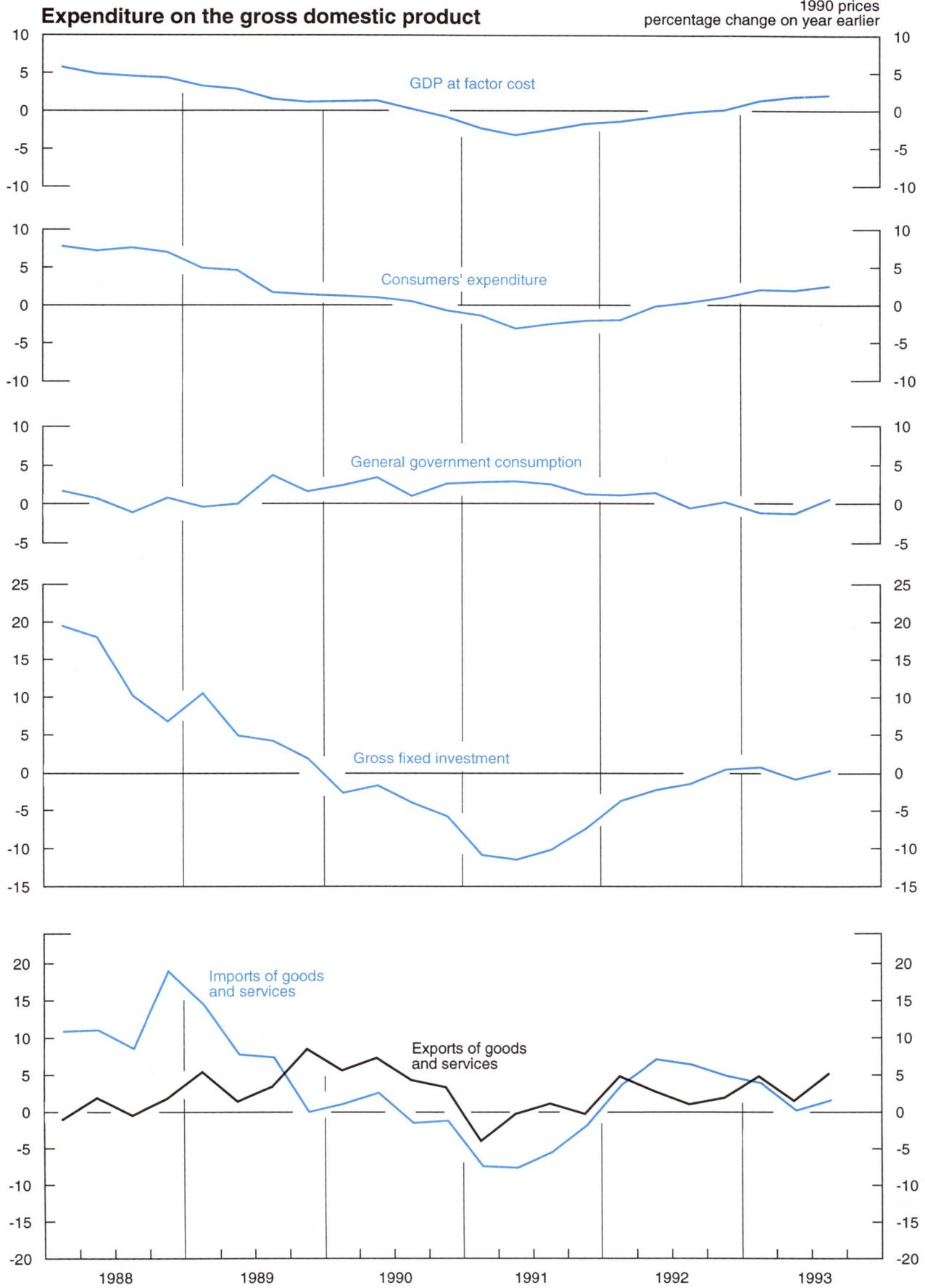

4 Personal disposable income and consumption

	£ million, current prices					£ million, 1990 prices		Real personal disposable income at 1990 prices (1990=100)
	Personal income before tax		Total personal disposable income[2,3]	Consumers' expenditure[3] +	Personal saving ratio[4] (percentage)+	Real personal disposable income[5] +	Total consumers' expenditure[3]	
	Total[1]	of which: Wages, salaries and forces' pay						
	AIIQ	AIJB	AIIW	AIIX	AIIZ	CECP	CAAB	CECR
1989	442 421	249 103	352 905	327 363	7.2	372 356	345 406	98.0
1990	487 391	275 016	380 092	347 527	8.6	380 092	347 527	100.0
1991	516 582	288 054	406 069	365 057	10.1	378 189	339 993	99.5
1992	550 649	300 005	437 551	382 426	12.6	388 563	339 610	102.2
1989 Q3	112 105	62 977	89 461	82 213	8.1	93 855	86 243	98.8
Q4	114 206	64 809	90 980	84 248	7.4	93 791	86 844	98.7
1990 Q1	117 911	66 647	93 928	85 928	8.5	95 100	86 992	100.1
Q2	120 360	68 344	93 031	86 179	7.4	94 368	87 409	99.3
Q3	123 826	69 761	95 945	87 138	9.2	95 558	86 778	100.6
Q4	125 294	70 264	97 188	88 282	9.2	95 066	86 348	100.0
1991 Q1	126 584	71 120	98 442	89 105	9.5	94 835	85 834	99.8
Q2	128 719	71 637	101 227	90 779	10.3	94 574	84 806	99.5
Q3	130 159	72 392	102 773	92 046	10.4	94 591	84 712	99.5
Q4	131 120	72 905	103 627	93 127	10.1	94 189	84 641	99.1
1992 Q1	136 203	74 939	106 513	93 556	12.2	95 892	84 227	100.9
Q2	137 061	75 121	109 239	95 017	13.0	97 397	84 717	102.5
Q3	138 009	74 717	110 526	96 104	13.0	97 858	85 089	103.0
Q4	139 376	75 228	111 273	97 749	12.2	97 416	85 577	102.5
1993 Q1	141 670	76 258	113 504	98 972	12.8	98 606	85 981	103.8
Q2	142 498	76 406	113 554	100 287	11.7	97 866	86 432	103.0
Q3	142 957	76 965	113 934	101 909	10.6	97 565	87 268	102.7

1 Before providing for depreciation and stock appreciation.
2 *Equals* total personal income before tax *less* payments of taxes on income, social security contributions and other current transfers, before providing for depreciation, stock appreciation and additions to tax reserves.
3 This series is affected by the abolition of domestic rates and the introduction of the community charge. For details, see notes in the UK National Accounts article in the latest edition of *UK Economic Accounts*.
4 Personal savings as a percentage of personal disposable income.
5 Personal disposable income revalued by the implied consumers' expenditure deflator (1990 = 100).

Source: Central Statistical Office

5 Real consumers' expenditure - component categories

£ million, 1990 prices

	Durable goods	Food	Alcoholic drink and tobacco	Clothing and footwear	Energy products	Other goods	Rent, rates and water charges	Other services[1]	Total+
	CCBW	CCCA	FCCD	FCCE	CCCG	CCCM	CCCN	CCCJ	CAAB
1989	36 815	42 281	30 433	20 662	22 305	38 485	38 426	115 999	345 406
1990	34 745	41 816	30 272	20 876	22 422	39 566	38 915	118 915	347 527
1991	30 472	41 870	29 437	20 535	23 209	38 563	39 328	116 579	339 993
1992	30 553	42 469	28 682	20 629	22 980	38 796	39 683	115 818	339 610
1989 Q3	9 099	10 508	7 590	5 095	5 543	9 631	9 616	29 161	86 243
Q4	9 120	10 525	7 565	5 123	5 708	9 850	9 651	29 302	86 844
1990 Q1	9 054	10 479	7 572	5 325	5 414	9 940	9 679	29 529	86 992
Q2	8 872	10 521	7 603	5 298	5 641	9 911	9 713	29 850	87 409
Q3	8 561	10 369	7 573	5 236	5 742	9 876	9 747	29 674	86 778
Q4	8 258	10 447	7 524	5 017	5 625	9 839	9 776	29 862	86 348
1991 Q1	7 933	10 459	7 472	5 186	5 775	9 733	9 799	29 477	85 834
Q2	7 491	10 443	7 285	5 121	5 985	9 598	9 820	29 063	84 806
Q3	7 670	10 478	7 394	5 145	5 637	9 638	9 842	28 908	84 712
Q4	7 378	10 490	7 286	5 083	5 812	9 594	9 867	29 131	84 641
1992 Q1	7 398	10 473	7 202	5 004	5 657	9 572	9 890	29 031	84 227
Q2	7 505	10 603	7 266	5 122	5 613	9 745	9 908	28 955	84 717
Q3	7 735	10 657	7 087	5 184	5 810	9 754	9 930	28 932	85 089
Q4	7 915	10 736	7 127	5 319	5 900	9 725	9 955	28 900	85 577
1993 Q1	8 020	10 793	7 144	5 258	5 650	9 979	9 976	29 161	85 981
Q2	8 231	10 601	7 197	5 279	5 663	10 078	9 994	29 389	86 432
Q3	8 495	10 563	7 200	5 355	5 885	10 169	10 017	29 584	87 268

1 Including the adjustments for international travel, etc. and final expenditure by private non-profit-making bodies.

Source: Central Statistical Office

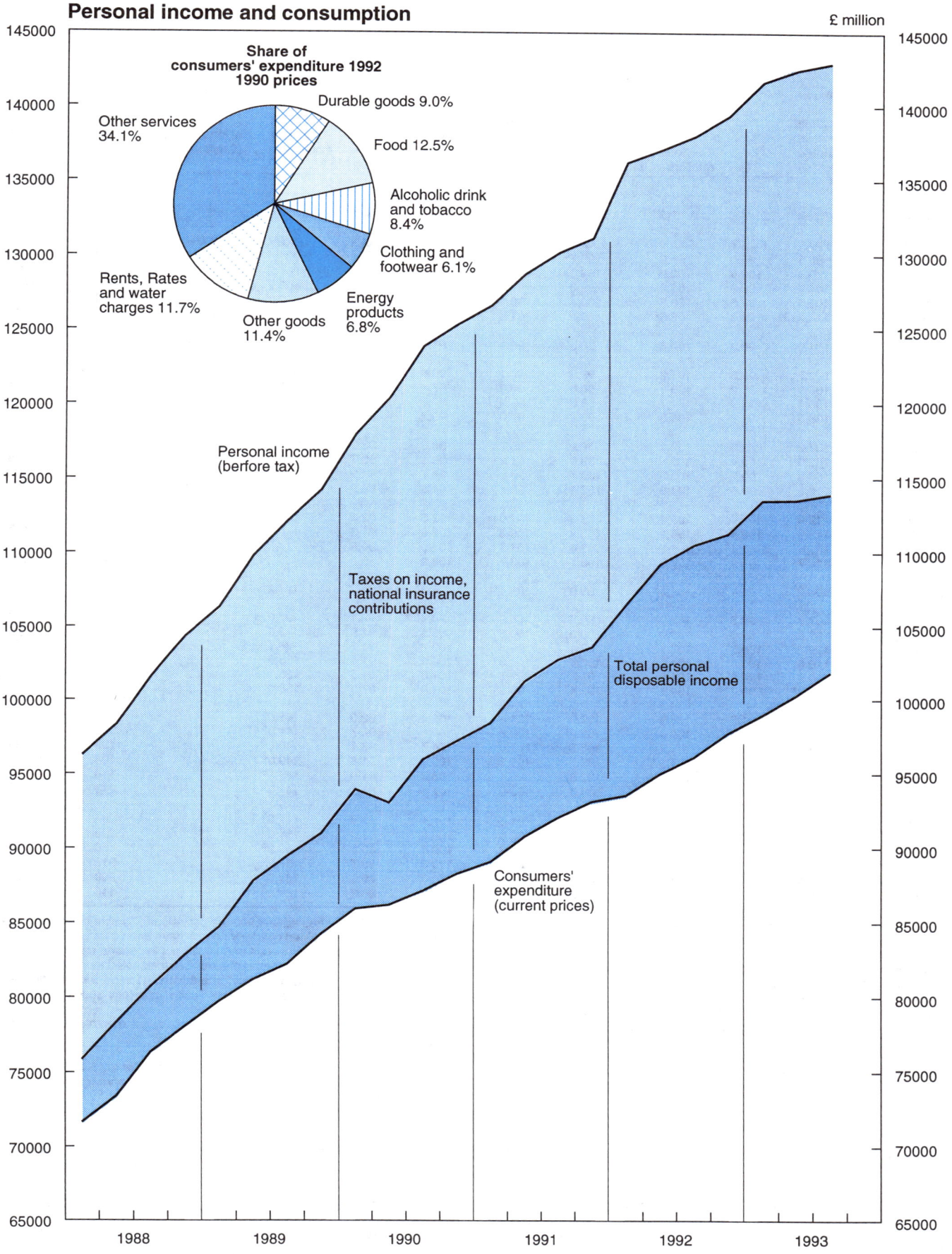

6 Retail sales, new registrations of cars and credit business (Great Britain)

	Value of retail sales per week: total (average 1990=100)	Volume of retail sales per week+ (average 1990=100)						New registrations of cars+ (seasonally adjusted, thousands) 4,5	Total consumer credit: Net lending (£ million) 1,2	Net lending (£ million)	
		Total	Food retailers+	Mixed retail businesses+	Clothing and footwear retailers+	Household goods retailers+	Other non-food retailers+			Credit business: (Narrower coverage) Agreements with consumers[3]	Finance houses and other specialist credit grantors: Agreements with businesses
Sales in 1990 £ million	129 324	129 324	47 517	22 090	12 752	22 473	24 492				
	FAAL	FAAM	FAAN	FAAO	FAAP	FAAQ	FAAR	DKBY	RLMH	RLMJ	RLMG
1989	93.5	99.3	99.0	99.7	97.9	101.8	97.8	2 304.5	6 518	3 248	1 628
1990	100.0	100.0	100.0	100.0	100.0	100.0	100.0	2 005.2	4 450	3 531	223
1991	104.7	98.9	101.2	99.0	97.6	98.8	94.9	1 600.2	2 360	1 060	−778
1992	108.5	99.5	103.3	100.4	98.1	99.4	91.8	1 599.0	401†	362	−327
1993	114.7	103.0	106.5	105.5	101.6	107.2	90.7	..	1 983	2 889	678
1990 Q4	101.0	98.9	100.6	98.5	96.1	97.5	98.8	453.9	981	899	−56
1991 Q1	102.7	99.6	101.2	99.3	98.1	100.6	96.3	420.2	728	485	−164
Q2	103.9	98.2	100.9	98.6	96.9	97.4	93.8	373.0	849	477	−38
Q3	105.6	98.9	101.7	98.8	97.9	97.9	94.7	419.3	246	202	−161
Q4	106.5	98.8	101.0	99.2	97.3	99.2	94.6	387.7	537	−104	−415
1992 Q1	107.2	98.6	102.1	98.9	95.7	98.6	93.2	381.7	149	142	130
Q2	108.0	99.4	103.4	99.6	97.9	98.1	93.7	386.6	60	5	128
Q3	108.8	99.7	103.3	100.7	99.0	99.7	91.9	405.0	114†	−11	−330
Q4	110.5†	100.5†	104.8†	102.4†	99.7†	101.6†	89.9†	424.7	78	226	−255
1993 Q1	112.9	102.0	105.9	103.3	101.0	103.6	92.3	437.4	226	400	−35
Q2	113.9	102.4	106.1	103.8	100.3	106.8	91.3	..	409	525	452
Q3	115.8	103.4	106.6	106.4	101.4	108.9	90.8	..	714	919	61
Q4	116.7	104.2	107.6	108.1	103.7	109.9	89.0	..	634	1 045	200
1992 Jun	108.2*	99.4*	103.1*	98.9*	97.4*	98.8*	94.3*	124.2	..	−56	77
Jul	107.7	98.8	103.0	98.5	96.9	98.4	92.1	127.0	..	83	86
Aug	108.8	99.8	100.6	100.9	100.6	99.9	91.9	143.8	..	−69	−203
Sep	109.8*	100.3*	103.8*	102.4*	99.5*	100.6*	91.7*	136.1	..	−25	−213
Oct	110.6	100.8	104.9	102.4	100.3	100.9	91.5	135.5	..	72	−112
Nov	110.6	100.6	104.8	101.3	99.6	101.8	91.5	136.1	..	17	−99
Dec	110.2*†	100.2*†	104.7*†	103.4*†	99.3*†	101.9*†	87.5*†	156.0	..	137	−44
1993 Jan	112.1	101.7	105.9	102.9	101.3	102.4	92.0	141.0[6]	..	150	−89
Feb	112.8	102.0	105.9	103.2	100.8	103.6	92.7	144.0[6]	..	54	31
Mar	113.5	102.2	105.9	103.8	101.0	104.7	92.1	140.0[6]	..	196	23
Apr	113.3	102.1	105.8	102.1	101.1	105.9	91.8	140.0[6]	..	194	−12
May	113.3	101.8	105.9	103.6	95.1	106.8	91.0	147.0[6]	..	118	49
Jun	114.9	103.3	106.4	105.3	103.9	107.4	91.2	147.0[6]	..	213	415
Jul	115.2	103.1	106.0	106.1	101.5	108.4	91.0	147.0[6]	..	204	417
Aug	115.9	103.4	106.8	106.0	100.0	108.8	91.6	154.0[6]	..	225	−342
Sep	116.2	103.7	106.9	106.9	102.3	109.4	90.0	149.0[6]	..	490	−14
Oct	116.5	104.0	107.1	107.4	103.0	110.3	89.7	157.0[6]	..	312	85
Nov	117.0	104.4	107.7	108.7	103.3	110.0	89.5	164.0[6]	..	290	29
Dec	116	104.2	108.0	108.2	104.6	109.5	88.0	..[6]	..	443	86

1 Net lending equals changes in amounts outstanding adjusted to remove distortions arising from revaluations of debt such as write-offs.
2 Covers all institutions providing finance for consumers; including loans by banks on personal accounts and on bank credit cards and charge cards, by insurance companies, non-bank credit companies and retailers, but excluding loans for house purchase.
3 Since end 1985, covers lending by finance house and other specialist credit grantors, on bank credit cards (VISA and Mastercard only) and unsecured loans by building societies (since the end of 1986). Before end 1985 included loans by retailers but excluded loans on bank credit cards and block discounted agreements with finance houses and other specialist credit grantors. Prior to January 1991 loans greater than £15 000 were excluded.
4 Seasonally adjusted figures within 1992 are provisional. To obtain a more stable series the seasonally adjusted quarterly figures have been derived directly from the corresponding unadjusted series and so will not in general equal the sum of the figures shown for the relevant months. As the unadjusted monthly series for car new registrations is relatively "noisy", the advantage in deriving the quarterly seasonally adjusted series from the less "noisy" quarterly series will tend to be greater than usual.
5 The annual and quarterly figures shown are totals, not monthly averages as previously shown.
6 Provisional.

Sources: Central Statistical Office; Department of Transport

CSO STATFAX
For the most up to date data on the retail sales index and credit business, poll the following numbers from your fax machine:
0336 416043 (RSI), 0336 416044 (credit business)
Calls charged at 36p per minute cheap rate, 48p per minute at all other times

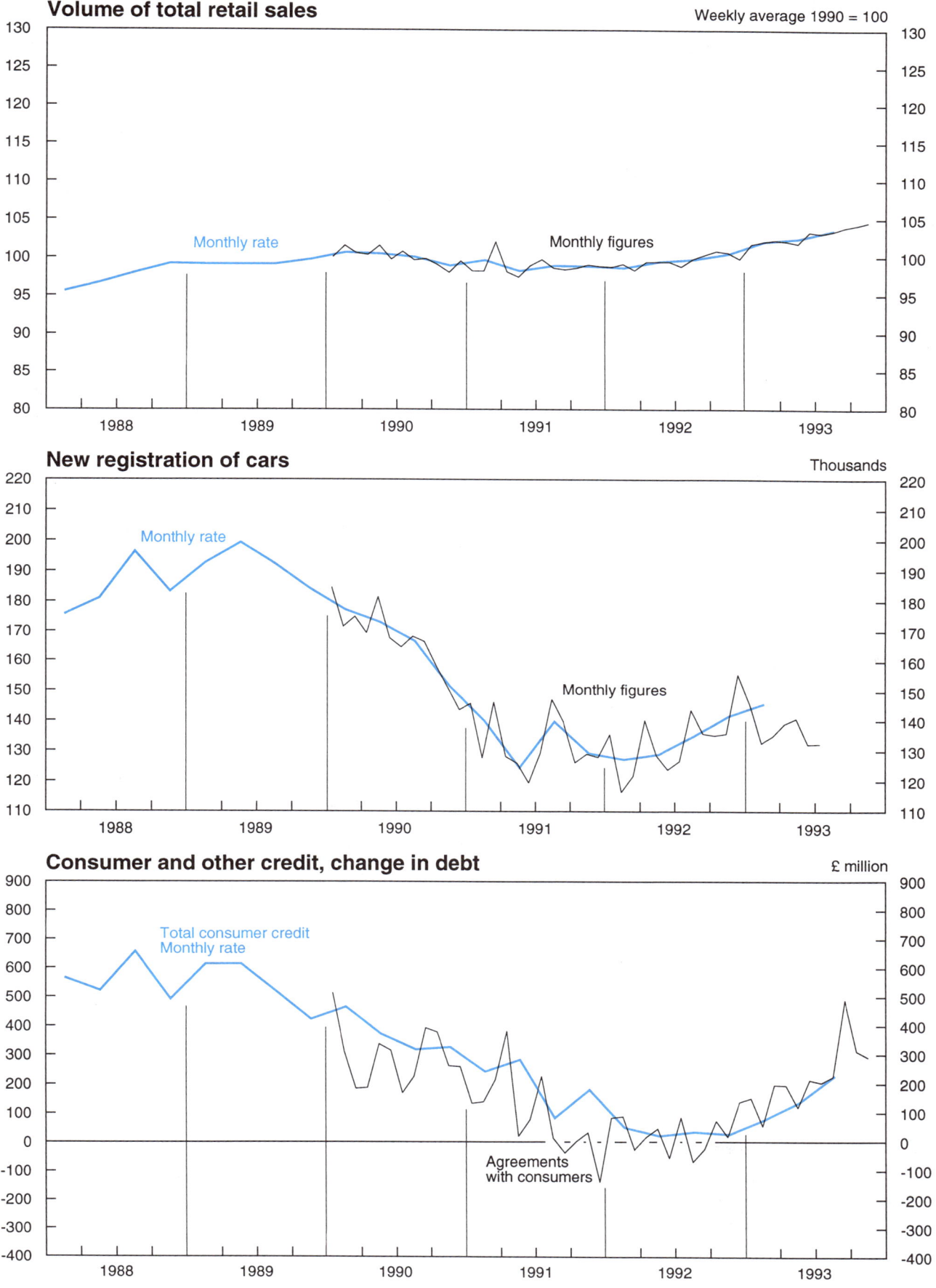

7 Gross domestic product and shares of income and expenditure

	Gross domestic product at current factor cost		Total final expenditure (current market prices)[1] (£mn)	Percentage share of total final expenditure						Percentage share of gross domestic product (income-based)				
	Expenditure-based (£ mn)	Income-based (£ mn)		Consumers' expenditure[1]	General government consumption	Gross fixed investment			Exports	Income from employment	Gross trading profits[2]		Income from self-employment[2]	Other income[4]
						General government	Public corporations	Private sector			Companies	Other[3]		
	DJBA	DJBE	DIAB	FBBD	FBBE	FBBF	FBBG	FBBH	FBBI	FBBJ	FBBK	FBBL	FBBM	FBBN
1989	441 759	441 759	658 765	49.7	15.5	1.5	0.8	13.6	18.4	64.2	13.6	1.5	12.1	8.5
1990	478 886	478 886	699 403	49.7	16.1	1.8	0.7	12.7	19.1	65.2	12.4	0.8	12.6	9.0
1991	495 279	494 834	714 875	51.1	17.4	1.7	0.5	11.3	18.8	66.3	12.0	0.4	11.7	9.6
1992	515 480	514 891	745 380	51.3	17.8	1.7	0.6	10.1	18.8	66.3	12.0	0.4	11.4	9.9
														FBBO
1990 Q3	121 982	121 982	175 961	49.5	16.3	1.8	0.8	12.6	18.8	65.6	13.0	0.8		21.6
Q4	121 653	121 653	174 930	50.5	16.8	1.9	0.7	12.1	19.2	64.6	12.0	0.5		21.3
1991 Q1	122 747	122 669	174 881	51.0	17.1	1.6	0.7	11.9	18.3	66.9	12.3	0.5		21.6
Q2	122 969	122 868	177 786	51.1	17.5	1.6	0.5	11.5	18.9	66.6	12.0	0.3		21.4
Q3	123 781	123 659	179 941	51.2	17.5	1.8	0.5	10.9	19.1	66.9	11.7	0.4		21.5
Q4	125 782	125 638	182 267	51.1	17.4	1.7	0.5	10.8	18.8	65.0	11.9	0.3		20.9
1992 Q1	126 309	126 188	182 629	51.2	17.8	1.8	0.5	10.4	18.8	67.5	10.8	0.3		21.5
Q2	128 678	128 542	185 585	51.2	18.0	1.7	0.5	10.2	18.8	66.3	12.0	0.4		21.3†
Q3	129 848	129 693	186 758	51.5	17.7	1.6	0.6	10.0	18.5	65.8	12.6	0.4		21.2
Q4	130 645	130 468	190 408	51.3	17.7	1.7	0.6	10.0	18.9	65.7	12.7	0.6		21.1
1993 Q1	133 054	132 968	194 640†	50.8	17.4	1.8	0.7	9.5	20.2	65.4	13.1	0.5		20.9
Q2	134 679	134 608	196 443	51.1	17.4	1.5	0.5	9.6	19.6	64.9	13.8	0.6		20.7
Q3	136 454	136 393	199 185	51.2	17.2	1.5	0.5	9.6	20.2	64.6	14.2	0.5		20.6

1 This series is affected by the abolition of domestic rates and the introduction of the community charge. For details, see notes in the UK National Accounts article in the latest edition of *UK Economic Accounts*.
2 After providing for stock appreciation.
3 Gross trading surplus of public corporations and general government enterprises.
4 Rent income, and imputed charge for consumption of non-trading capital.

Source: Central Statistical Office

8 Income, product and spending per head

£

	At current prices				At 1990 prices		
	Gross national product at factor cost	Gross domestic product at factor cost	Consumers' expenditure[1]	Personal disposable income[1]	Gross domestic product at factor cost (average estimate)	Consumers' expenditure	Personal disposable income
	CAQA	CAQB	FBCC	FBCD	CAQC	FBCF	FBCH
1989	7 777	7 718	5 720	6 166	8 320	6 035	6 506
1990	8 370	8 341	6 053	6 621	8 341	6 053	6 621
1991	8 589	8 583	6 332	7 044	8 113	5 898	6 561
1992	8 999	8 898	6 610	7 564	8 049	5 870	6 717
							CAIU
1990 Q3	2 144	2 124	1 517	1 671	2 081	1 511	1 664
Q4	2 130	2 116	1 535	1 690	2 063	1 502	1 653
1991 Q1	2 123	2 131	1 548	1 710	2 041	1 491	1 647
Q2	2 132	2 132	1 575	1 757	2 028	1 472	1 641
Q3	2 151	2 144	1 596	1 782	2 023	1 469	1 640
Q4	2 183	2 177	1 613	1 795	2 021	1 466	1 632
1992 Q1	2 199	2 184	1 619	1 844	2 008	1 458	1 660
Q2	2 237	2 222	1 643	1 889	2 008	1 465	1 684
Q3	2 276	2 240	1 661	1 910	2 014	1 470	1 691
Q4	2 287	2 252	1 687	1 921	2 019	1 477	1 682
1993 Q1	2 296	2 292	1 707	1 957	2 028	1 483	1 701
Q2	2 333	2 318	1 728	1 956	2 038	1 489	1 686
Q3	2 364	2 347	1 754	1 961	2 049	1 502	1 679

1 This series is affected by the abolition of domestic rates and the introduction of the community charge. For details, see notes in the UK National Accounts article in the latest edition of *UK Economic Accounts*.

Source: Central Statistical Office

Shares of income and expenditure

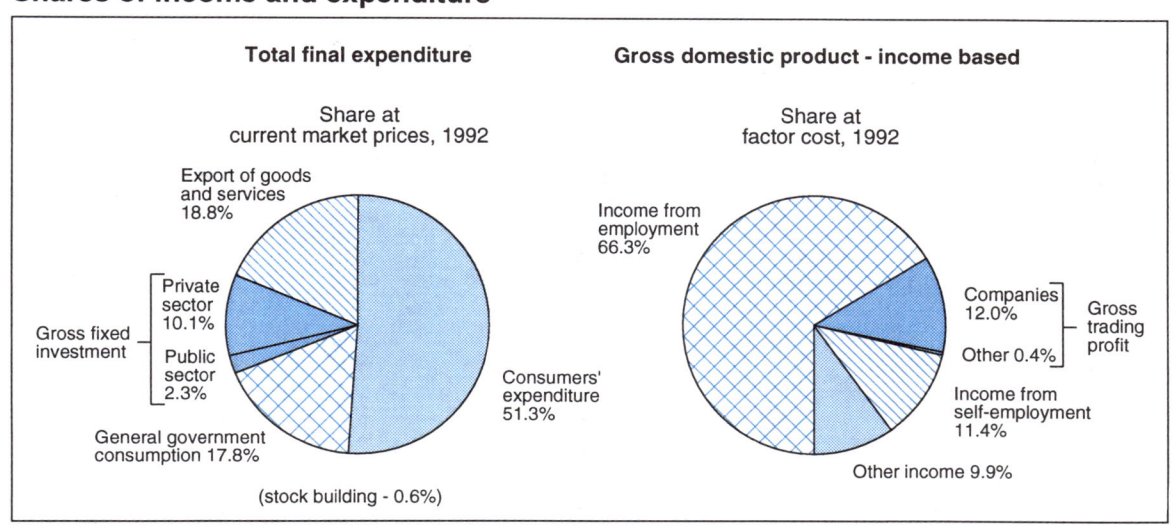

Income, product and spending per capital

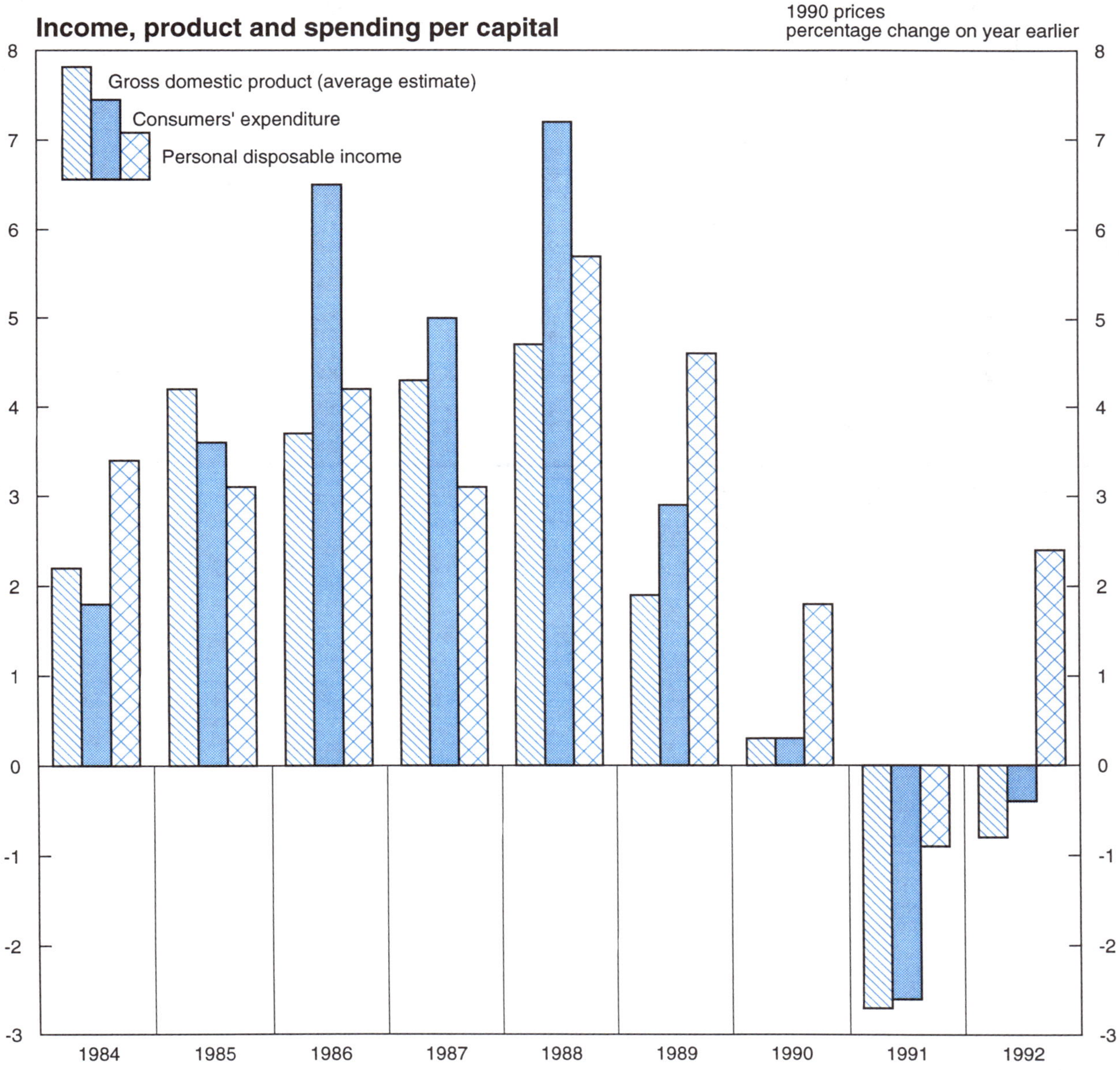

1990 prices
percentage change on year earlier

- Gross domestic product (average estimate)
- Consumers' expenditure
- Personal disposable income

9 Gross domestic fixed capital formation

£ million, 1990 prices

	Analysed by sector[1]			Analysed by type of asset						Total gross domestic fixed capital formation+
	Private sector	General government	Public corporations	Dwellings			Other new building and works[2]	Vehicles, ships and aircraft	Plant and machinery	
				Private	Public	Total				
	DFEB	DFED	DFDA	DFEA	DFEC	DFEG	DFCV	DEBP	DEBO	DECU
1986	67 877	9 163	6 645	16 681	3 489	20 170	27 510	8 493	27 512	83 685
1987	78 013	9 027	5 220	17 957	3 771	21 728	31 600	9 846	29 086	92 260
1988	92 043	7 579	5 104	21 303	3 506	24 809	35 775	10 372	33 770	104 726
1989	94 778	10 054	5 671	19 686	4 136	23 822	37 525	11 231	37 925	110 503
1990	89 162	12 659	4 955	16 530	4 227	20 757	38 991	10 266	36 762	106 776
1991	79 697	12 688	3 880	13 942	2 836	16 778	37 522	8 008	33 957	96 265
1992	76 552	13 765	4 424	14 671	2 732	17 403	37 154	7 306	32 878	94 741
1990 Q3	21 945	3 122	1 330	4 214	965	5 179	9 688	2 527	9 003	26 397
Q4	21 058	3 268	1 301	3 956	902	4 858	9 887	2 248	8 634	25 627
1991 Q1	20 664	2 826	1 179	3 700	726	4 426	9 581	2 120	8 542	24 669
Q2	20 084	3 016	963	3 406	734	4 140	9 272	2 180	8 471	24 063
Q3	19 374	3 494	882	3 444	684	4 128	9 525	1 630	8 467	23 750
Q4	19 575	3 352	856	3 392	692	4 084	9 144	2 078	8 477	23 783
1992 Q1	19 233	3 624	960	3 702	747	4 449	9 198	1 900	8 270	23 817
Q2	19 226	3 336	986	3 522	635	4 157	9 342	1 803	8 246	23 548
Q3	18 965	3 251	1 234	3 591	692	4 283	9 266	1 736	8 165	23 450
Q4	19 128	3 554	1 244	3 856	658	4 514	9 348	1 867	8 197	23 926
1993 Q1	18 535	4 072	1 425	3 551	777	4 328	9 299	2 182	8 223	24 032
Q2	18 831	3 556	999	3 705	682	4 387	9 039	1 868	8 092	23 386
Q3	18 838	3 581	1 141	3 578	748	4 326	9 054	1 936	8 244	23 560

Percentage change, quarter on corresponding quarter of previous year

1990 Q3	-5.8	16.3	-9.8	-8.6	-9.3	-8.7	3.2	-12.3	-5.3	-3.8
Q4	-7.2	7.8	-8.8	-5.1	-26.2	-9.9	5.3	-20.9	-9.5	-5.6
1991 Q1	-10.5	-16.4	1.2	-10.5	-48.7	-20.3	1.2	-26.8	-12.1	-10.7
Q2	-13.0	4.5	-16.9	-19.4	-22.2	-19.9	-6.8	-15.9	-10.0	-11.3
Q3	-11.7	11.9	-33.7	-18.3	-29.1	-20.3	-1.7	-35.5	-6.0	-10.0
Q4	-7.0	2.6	-34.2	-14.3	-23.3	-15.9	-7.5	-7.6	-1.8	-7.2
1992 Q1	-6.9	28.2	-18.6	0.1	2.9	0.5	-4.0	-10.4	-3.2	-3.5
Q2	-4.3	10.6	2.4	3.4	-13.5	0.4	0.8	-17.3	-2.7	-2.1
Q3	-2.1	-7.0	39.9	4.3	1.2	3.8	-2.7	6.5	-3.6	-1.3
Q4	-2.3	6.0	45.3	13.7	-4.9	10.5	2.2	-10.2	-3.3	0.6
1993 Q1	-3.6	12.4	48.4	-4.1	4.0	-2.7	1.1	14.8	-0.6	0.9
Q2	-2.1	6.6	1.3	5.2	7.4	5.5	-3.2	3.6	-1.9	-0.7
Q3	-0.7	10.2	-7.5	-0.4	8.1	1.0	-2.3	11.5	1.0	0.5

1 Including purchases *less* sales of land and existing buildings.
2 Including transfer costs of land and buildings.

Source: Central Statistical Office

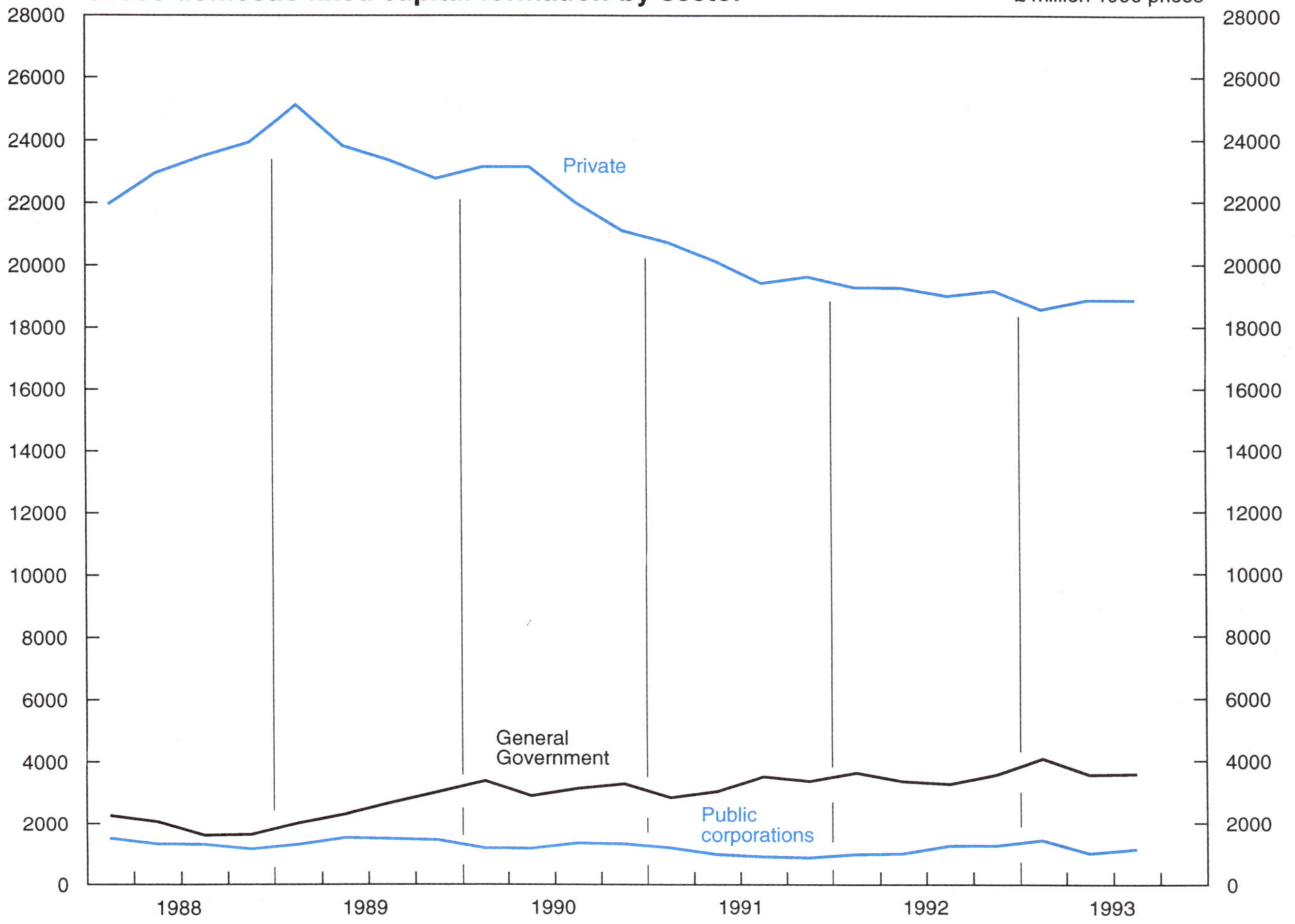

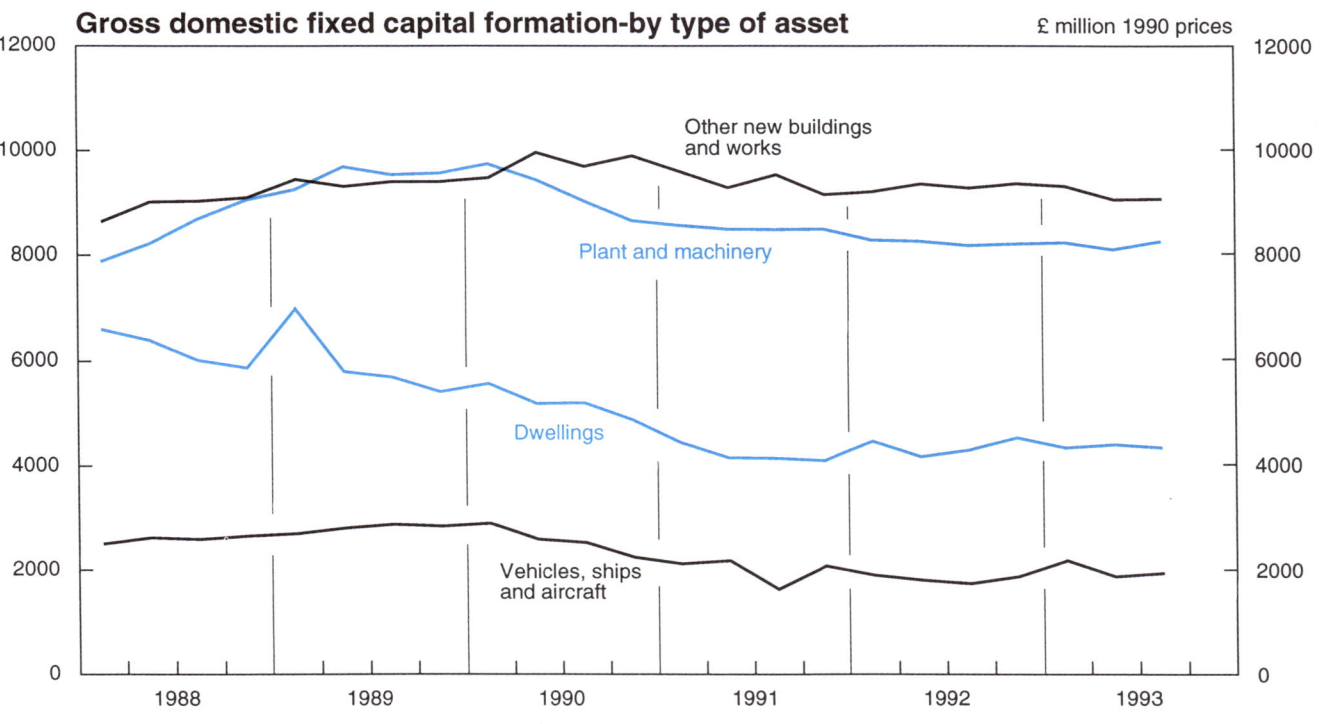

10 Indicators of fixed investment by manufacturing industry

	Gross fixed investment by manufacturing industry (including leased assets) (revised definition)							New orders received by contractors for private industrial work(GB) (£ million, 1985 prices)
	Plant and machinery			New building and works				
	Gross fixed investment		CBI Intentions Inquiry: balance[1] (NSA)	Gross fixed investment		CBI Intentions Inquiry: balance[1] (NSA)	Total+ (£ million, 1990 prices)	
	Total (£ million, 1990 prices)	Change on year earlier (percentage)		Total (£ million, 1990 prices)	Change on year earlier (percentage)			
	DFQP			DFQQ			DECV	DPBT
1988	11 169	35.6		1 837	58.1		13 846	2 495
1989	11 996	7.4		2 044	11.3		14 984	2 385
1990	11 531	-3.9		1 907	-6.7		14 227	2 338
1991	10 333	-10.4		1 900	-0.4		12 803	2 099
1992	9 677	-6.3		1 583	-16.7		11 907	1 446
			FBAD			FBAG		
1988 Q1	2 666	41.5	20	440	69.9	1	3 318	665
Q2	2 869	42.4	32	466	54.8	6	3 542	578
Q3	2 879	36.3	19	480	56.9	-6	3 577	587
Q4	2 755	23.7	21	451	52.4	-4	3 409	666
1989 Q1	2 949	10.6	21	490	11.4	-9	3 663	599
Q2	3 020	5.3	18	546	17.2	-1	3 834	630
Q3	3 019	4.9	3	524	9.2	-7	3 775	594
Q4	3 008	9.2	-3	484	7.3	-10	3 712	562
1990 Q1	3 042	3.2	-8	527	7.6	-23	3 791	632
Q2	2 920	-3.3	-8	620	13.6	-23	3 741	707
Q3	2 851	-5.6	-7	327	-37.6	-22	3 359	524
Q4	2 718	-9.6	-15	433	-10.5	-26	3 336	475
1991 Q1	2 657	-12.7	-31	463	-12.1	-33	3 251	392
Q2	2 631	-9.9	-34	501	-19.2	-35	3 258	763
Q3	2 537	-11.0	-30	503	53.8	-35	3 195	474
Q4	2 508	-7.7	-7	433	0.0	-24	3 099	471
1992 Q1	2 355	-11.4	-16	405	-12.5	-34	2 908	457
Q2	2 387	-9.3	-10	426	-15.0	-30	2 989	337
Q3	2 420	-4.6	-9	394	-21.7	-30	2 978	341
Q4	2 515	0.3	-18	358	-17.3	-35	3 032	310
1993 Q1	2 376	0.9	-7	449	10.9	-23	2 988	440
Q2	2 349	-1.6	-8	397	-6.8	-20	2 909	374
Q3	2 384	-1.5	-3	395	0.3	-20	2 966	383[†]

1 Percentage of firms expecting to authorise more in next 12 months *less* percentage expecting to authorise less.

Sources: *Central Statistical Office; Confederation of British Industry; Department of the Environment*

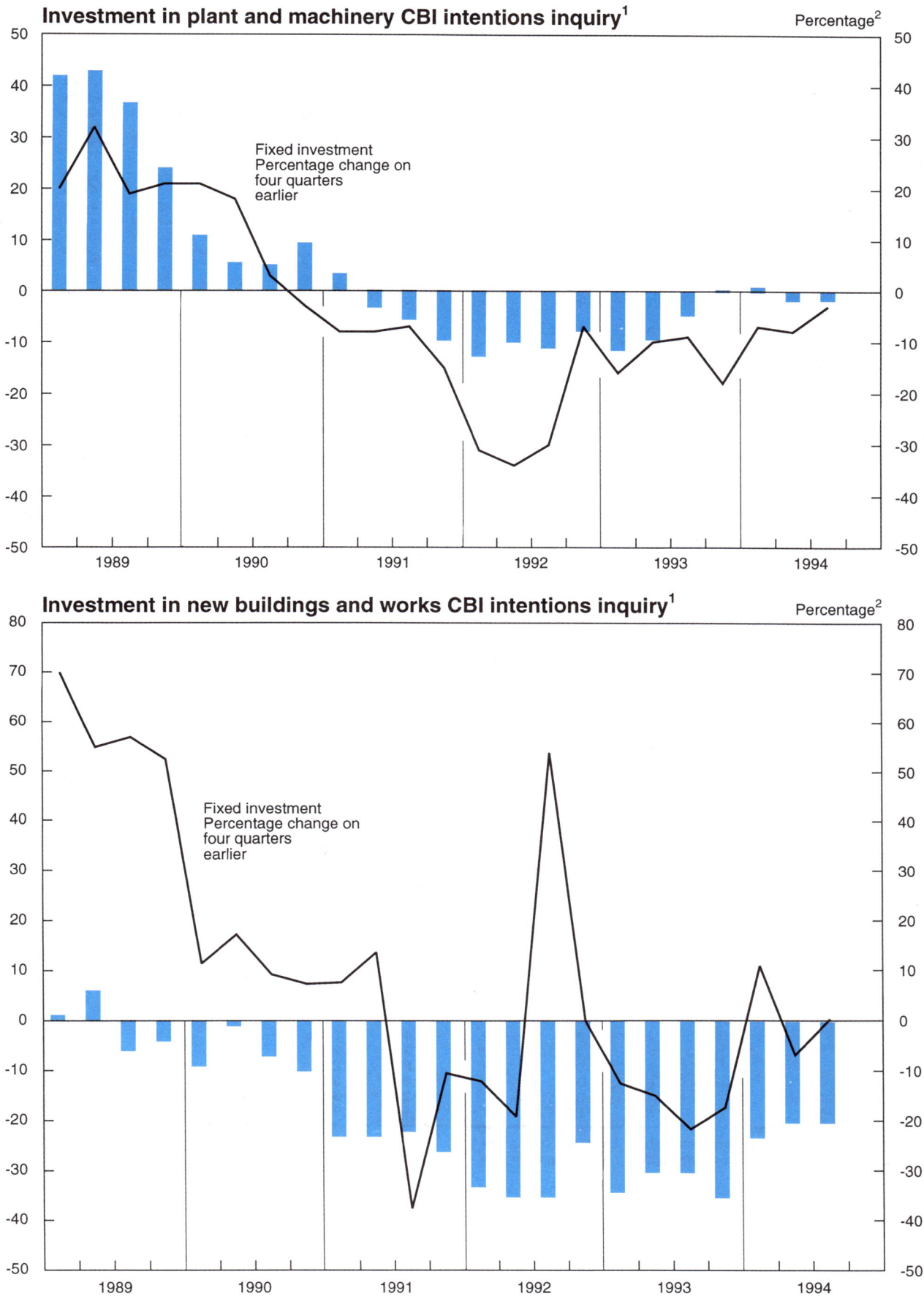

11 Indicators of fixed investment in dwellings

			Housing starts (GB)+			Housing completions (GB)+			Building societies		
	Fixed investment in dwellings (£ million, 1990 prices)	Orders received by contractors for new houses (GB) (£ million, 1985 prices)	Private enterprise (thousands)	Housing associations (thousands)	Local authorities new towns and government departments (thousands)	Private enterprise (thousands)	Housing associations (thousands)	Local authorities new towns and government departments (thousands)	Commitments on new dwellings (£ million, current prices)	Advances on new dwellings (£ million, current prices)	Average price of new dwellings: mortgages approved[1,2]
	DFEG	FCAS	FCAT	CTOQ	CTOU	FCAV	CTOS	CTOW	AHLO	AHLS	FCAX
1987	21 728	6 011	196.8	12.9	19.9	183.7	12.6	20.1	3 703	3 488	51 290
1988	24 809	6 143	221.4	14.5	16.4	199.5	12.8	19.7	4 832	4 696	64 615
1989	23 822	4 684	169.9	15.9	15.2	179.6	13.9	17.6	4 479	4 221	74 976
1990	20 757	3 348	135.4	18.6	8.6	159.0	16.8	16.5	3 902	3 774	78 917
1991	16 778	3 326	135.0	22.4	4.1	151.7	19.7	10.3	4 017	3 769	76 443
1992	17 403	3 373	120.1	33.8	2.6	140.0	25.6	4.6	3 385	3 353	73 093
1993	..	..	143.1	41.3	2.0	137.3	34.5	2.2	3 318	3 241	74 854
1989 Q2	5 784	1 210	44.9	4.2	4.3	45.9	3.1	4.3	1 163	1 084	74 799
Q3	5 673	1 049	39.4	4.1	4.0	44.0	3.8	4.2	1 150	999	75 566
Q4	5 392	1 075	37.4	3.7	3.3	42.7	3.4	4.6	1 136	1 108	76 716
1990 Q1	5 551	971	35.6	4.3	2.7	40.8	3.5	4.6	1 087	1 058	79 196
Q2	5 169	854	33.0	4.8	2.2	39.0	4.4	4.3	888	923	79 051
Q3	5 179	804	33.0	4.7	2.0	39.3	4.0	4.2	915	896	79 355
Q4	4 858	719	33.8	4.8	1.6	39.9	5.2	3.4	1 012	897	78 154
1991 Q1	4 426	781	31.1	5.1	1.3	35.2	4.8	3.1	929	900	76 414
Q2	4 140	840	34.0	5.5	1.2	38.9	5.5	3.0	1 047	937	76 640
Q3	4 128	892	35.4	5.7	0.9	38.6	5.1	2.3	1 033	959	76 412
Q4	4 084	813	34.5	6.1	0.7	39.0	4.3	1.9	1 008	973	76 056
1992 Q1	4 449	862	31.5	8.0	0.7	36.5	4.9	1.8	930	893	74 442
Q2	4 157	831	31.0	7.8	0.6	35.2	5.3	1.1	871	871	73 349
Q3	4 283	880	29.5	9.1	0.7	35.9	7.2	1.0	804	870	71 969
Q4	4 514	800	28.1	8.9	0.6	32.4	8.2	0.7	780	719	72 383
1993 Q1	4 328	978	34.0†	12.5	0.6	34.4†	8.2	0.4	855	823	74 022
Q2	4 387	1 054	34.9	10.1	0.4	34.3	8.6	0.8†	827	789	75 360
Q3	4 326	1 040	35.5	9.1†	0.6†	33.9	8.1†	0.6	787	818	75 012
Q4	..	..	38.7	9.6	0.4	34.7	9.6	0.4	849	811	74 862
1991 Dec	..	277	11.1	2.1	0.2	13.0	1.2	0.5	319	315	75 294
1992 Jan	..	269	11.4	2.4	0.2	12.7	1.7	0.7	317	306	75 559
Feb	..	310	9.9	2.5	0.2	11.3	1.5	0.5	304	302	73 927
Mar	..	283	10.2	3.1	0.3	12.5	1.7	0.6	309	285	73 924
Apr	..	291	10.1	2.9	0.2	11.7	1.5	0.4	283	308	73 316
May	..	271	10.5	2.1	0.2	11.3	1.7	0.4	292	276	75 357
Jun	..	269	10.4	2.8	0.2	12.2	2.1	0.3	296	287	71 868
Jul	..	290	10.5	2.9	0.2	11.8	2.3	0.3	309	299	72 267
Aug	..	282	9.7	3.0	0.2	13.2	2.5	0.3	260	344	71 604
Sep	..	309	9.3	3.2	0.3	10.9	2.4	0.4	235	227	71 707
Oct	..	257	9.3	2.6	0.2	10.7	2.6	0.3	242	238	73 929
Nov	..	275	8.8	3.1	0.2	10.4	2.8	0.2	250	226	71 772
Dec	..	268	10.0	3.2	0.2	11.3	2.8	0.2	288	255	71 150
1993 Jan	..	294	10.7	4.1	0.3	10.8†	2.1	0.1	274	266	73 475
Feb	..	349	11.3	3.8	0.2	11.6	2.6	0.1	297	275	73 752
Mar	..	334	12.0†	4.6	0.1	12.0	3.5	0.2	284	282	74 101
Apr	..	389	11.6	3.6	0.1	11.7	3.4	0.2	292	264	75 019
May	..	300	11.6	3.2	0.1	11.9	2.7	0.3	261	264	76 320
Jun	..	364	11.7	3.3	0.2	10.7	2.5	0.3†	274	261	75 604
Jul	..	327	11.2	2.8†	0.2	11.1	2.5†	0.2	255	255	75 216
Aug	..	361	12.1	2.7	0.2†	11.3	2.8	0.2	248	248	74 536
Sep	..	373†	12.2	3.6	0.2	11.5	2.8	0.2	284	315	75 476
Oct	..	361	13.0	3.0	0.2	11.8	3.7	0.1	248	266	74 881
Nov	..	359	13.4	3.8	0.1	11.3	3.1	0.2	303	259	75 021
Dec	..	..	12.3	2.8	0.1	11.6	2.8	0.1	298	286	74 507

1 Mortgages with building societies by private owners. The series covers only dwellings on which building societies have approved mortgages during the period. The cost of land is included.
2 The Abbey National ceased to operate as a building society in July 1989, but to ensure continuity in the data its results are included in the building society sector.

Sources: Central Statistical Office;
Department of the Environment;
Scottish Development Department;
Building Societies Association

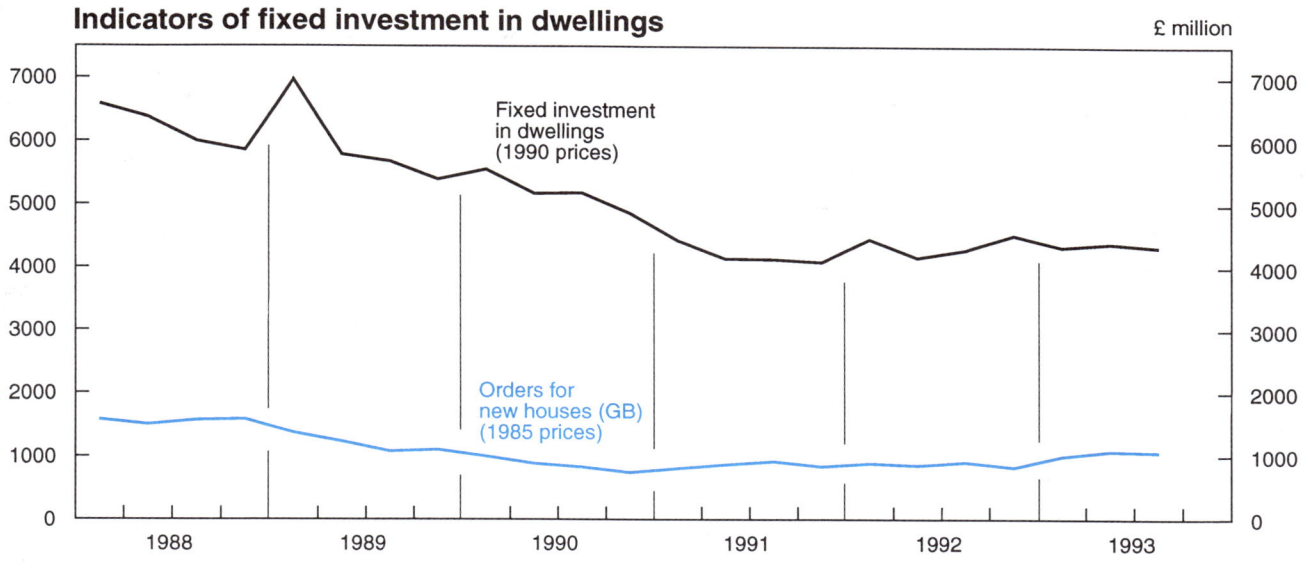

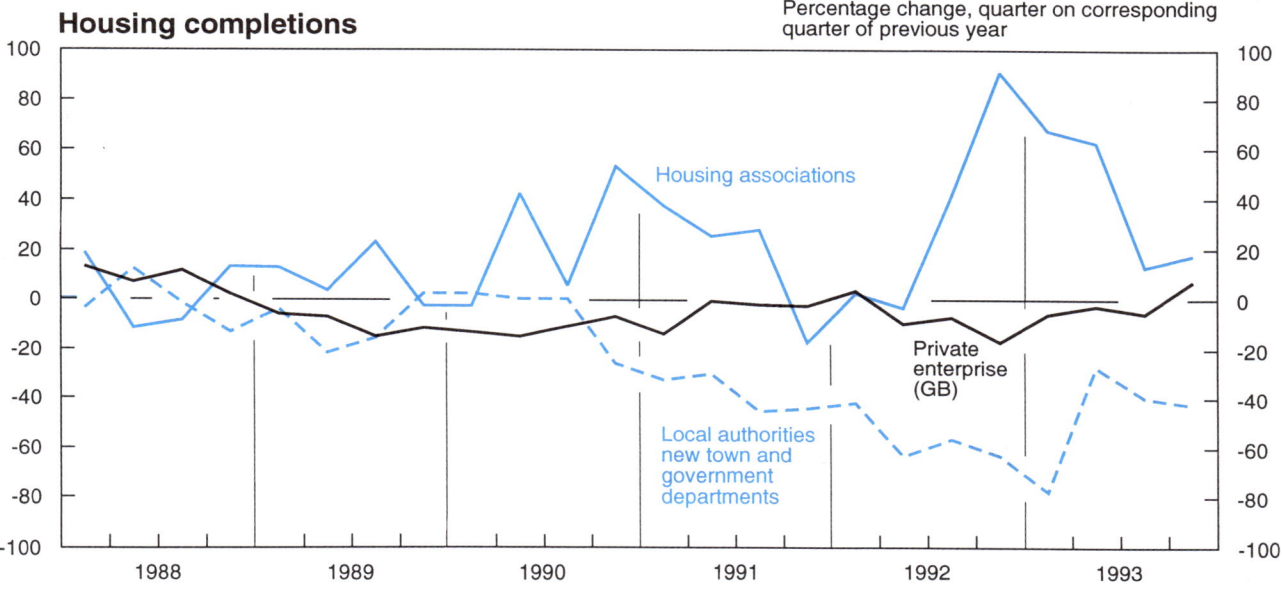

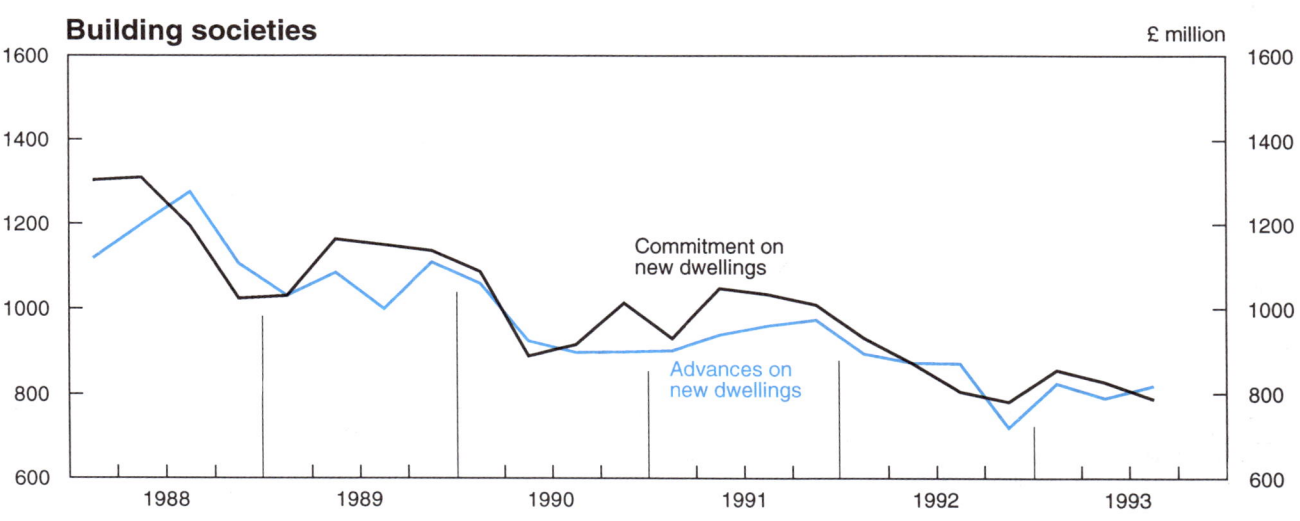

12 Value of physical increase in stocks and work in progress at 1990 market prices[1]

£ million

	Mining and quarrying	Manufacturing industries (revised definition)				Electricity, gas and water supply	Distributive trades		Other industries[3]	Total value of physical increase in stocks
		Materials and fuel	Work in progress	Finished goods	Total		Wholesale[2]	Retail[2]		
Level of stocks held at end-December 1992	1014	14669	15620	17258	47547	2817	17772	14996	30355	114501
Seasonally adjusted	DGGZ	DGAX	DGAY	DGAW	DHBM	DGGY	DHBO	DHBN	DHBR	DGBA
1988 Q4	64	163	368	313	845	−7	232	353	1 982	3 469
1989 Q1	86	82	−137	337	282	125	212	−25	273	953
Q2	94	−57	−92	156	7	1	91	370	922	1 485
Q3	12	59	29	70	159	−99	357	60	856	1 345
Q4	23	−135	−170	57	−248	−89	191	−53	62	−114
1990 Q1	−33	−52	−144	−221	−418	−58	131	92	313	27
Q2	7	16	−376	−52	−412	−32	−53	5	1 032	547
Q3	−39	−123	−474	157	−440	−7	−355	−19	727	−133
Q4	−38	−107	−517	−20	−644	−32	−275	103	−673	−1 559
1991 Q1	157	−285	−186	−276	−748	−38	−134	−332	17	−1 078
Q2	−23	−270	−627	−283	−1 180	165	−118	−102	−434	−1 692
Q3	38	−131	−401	−472	−1 004	54	−74	−27	−522	−1 535
Q4	52	−175	−144	−315	−632	19	−287	57	374	−417
1992 Q1	−24	−102	−904	14	−992	185	−183	631	−475	−858
Q2	32	−44	−192	38	−197	−341	−181	−336	290	−733
Q3	54	−191	−383	51	−523	−63	36	108	662	274
Q4	−15	−169	−193	−98	−459	117	234	236	−569	−456
1993 Q1	−49	12	−282	−450	−719	214	−29	−35	−148	−766
Q2	87	−32	−216	538	290	6	−160	−194	212	241
Q3	30	−146	−368	−223	−736	−158	425	349	−279	−369

1 Estimates are given to the nearest £ million but cannot be regarded as accurate to this degree.
2 Wholesaling and retailing estimates exclude the motor trades.
3 Quarterly alignment adjustment included in this series. For description see notes.

Source: Central Statistical Office

13 Stock ratios

	Manufacturers' stocks[1] to manufacturing production				Retail stocks[1] to retail sales[2,3]	Total stocks[1,4] to gross domestic product (expenditure-based)[2]
	Materials and fuel	Work in progress	Finished goods	Total stocks		
	FDCC	FDCD	FDCE	FDCB	FDCF	FDCA
1988 Q3	102	103	96	101	97	96
Q4	103	105	97	102	98	98
1989 Q1	101	102	98	100	98	98
Q2	101	101	99	101	101	99
Q3	101	101	100	101	101	100
Q4	100	100	100	100	100	100
1990 Q1	99	99	98	99	100	99
Q2	99	96	97	97	100	99
Q3	99	94	99	97	100	100
Q4	100	92	101	98	102	99
1991 Q1	100	93	101	98	99	99
Q2	100	90	101	96	100	98
Q3	99	88	97	95	99	97
Q4	98	87	95	93	99	96
1992 Q1	98	82	96	91	104	97
Q2	97	80	96	90	101	96
Q3	95	77	96	88	101	95
Q4	93	75	95	87	102	95
1993 Q1	93	73	90	84	100	93
Q2	89	71	94	84	99	92

1 Measured at 1990 prices; end-December 1989=100.
2 Measured at 1990 prices; 4th quarter 1989=100.
3 Classes 64-65 excluding activity headings 6510 and 6520, retail distribution of motor vehicles and parts, and filling stations.
4 Including quarterly alignment adjustment. For details of adjustments see notes section in the UK National Accounts article in the latest edition of *UK Economic Accounts*.

Source: Central Statistical Office

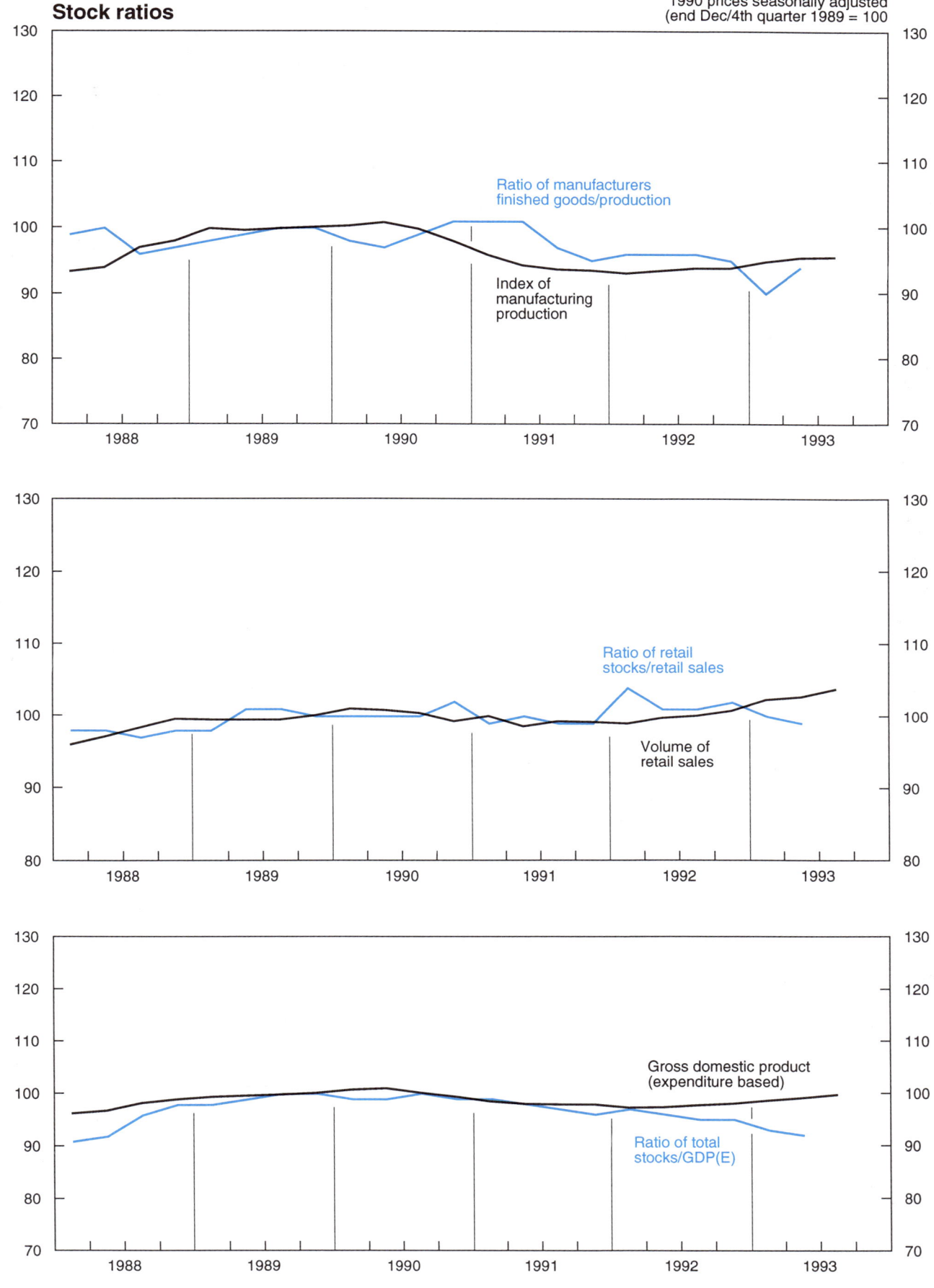

14 Inland energy consumption

Annual rates, temperature corrected

	Primary fuel input (million tonnes of coal or coal equivalent)						
			Natural gas (excl. flared or re-injected)	Primary electricity (not temperature corrected)			
	Coal[1]	Petroleum		Nuclear	Hydro[2] (NSA)	Net imports (NSA)	Total
	FDAI	FDAJ	FDAK	FDAL	FDAM	FDAW	FDAH
1983	111.6	105.9	75.6	18.1	2.4	–	313.6
1984	78.5	134.7	77.3	19.5	2.1	–	312.1
1985	103.6	113.2	81.2	22.1	2.1	–	322.3
1986	110.6	110.6	81.6	21.3	2.4	1.7	328.3
1987	114.3	108.0	84.4	19.8	2.1	4.8	333.3
1988	112.0	116.2	84.5	22.9	2.4	5.2	343.3
1989	109.7	119.3	85.8	25.9	2.3	5.2	348.2
1990	110.5	124.6	89.1	24.1	2.6	4.9	355.8
1991	108.0	120.5	89.9	25.8	2.4	6.7	353.3
1992	101.7	122.6	91.5	29.0	2.9	6.8	354.3
1988 Q3	108.8	115.1	83.4	24.9	2.4	5.7	340.4
Q4	111.2	119.8	85.8	26.0	2.5	4.5	349.7
1989 Q1	108.3	118.1	85.2	26.6	2.4	5.2	345.8
Q2	109.3	118.7	84.1	26.4	2.6	6.5	347.6
Q3	109.5	121.0	85.5	25.3	2.5	5.8	349.6
Q4	109.8	120.6	87.0	24.2	2.4	3.5	349.4
1990 Q1	115.3	128.0	90.8	24.0	2.4	–	360.6
Q2	104.2	130.7	85.9	23.1	2.6	5.8	352.2
Q3	110.3	129.9	85.5	23.8	2.6	6.7	358.9
Q4	111.2	114.0	89.0	26.7	2.6	7.0	350.5
1991 Q1	108.3	117.5	90.1	25.9	2.3	7.0	351.1
Q2	110.0	123.9	90.4	24.3	2.2	6.2	358.1
Q3	106.6	125.0	89.8	27.3	2.2	6.7	357.5
Q4	106.4	118.7	89.1	25.9	2.3	7.0	349.2
1992 Q1	104.0	128.4	87.9	27.1	2.4	7.0	357.0
Q2	106.3	125.5	88.6	28.0	2.5	6.6	357.5
Q3	100.8	118.2	88.4	27.3	2.6	6.6	343.7
Q4	96.6	111.4	94.4	31.0	2.7	7.0	343.1
1993 Q1	93.0	126.5	96.9	30.8	2.5	7.0	356.7
Q2	86.2	122.9	100.3	30.4	2.5	6.6	348.8
Q3	82.8	118.7	102.0	34.0	2.5	6.7	346.5

Percentage change, quarter on corresponding quarter of previous year

	FDAP	FDAQ	FDAR	FDAS	FDAT	FDAX	FDAO
1988 Q3	-6.0	3.6	-2.3	33.1	6.8	23.1	0.8
Q4	-3.7	8.2	1.4	37.7	14.5	-12.3	3.8
1989 Q1	-5.9	4.2	1.1	38.4	4.4	1.4	1.9
Q2	-0.8	2.4	1.2	21.1	10.7	15.2	2.8
Q3	0.6	5.2	2.4	3.2	5.9	0.9	2.7
Q4	-1.2	0.7	1.5	0.3	-0.8	-23.8	–
1990 Q1	5.5	8.4	6.6	-9.8	-0.3	-100.0	4.0
Q2	-4.6	10.1	2.0	-12.5	-0.4	-11.2	1.3
Q3	1.9	7.4	–	-5.9	2.4	15.5	2.7
Q4	2.8	-5.2	2.3	2.7	5.7	100.0	0.4
1991 Q1	-6.1	-8.2	-0.8	7.9	-4.3	–	-2.6
Q2	6.5	-5.2	-2.5	5.2	-13.7	7.3	1.4
Q3	-3.4	-3.8	5.1	14.7	-15.4	0.1	-0.4
Q4	-4.3	4.1	0.1	-3.2	-14.5	-0.3	-0.4
1992 Q1	-5.4	9.3	-2.4	4.6	3.0	0.6	-0.9
Q2	-3.4	1.3	-2.0	15.2	10.2	6.3	-0.2
Q3	-5.4	-5.5	-1.6	0.1	14.9	-0.6	-3.9
Q4	-9.2	-6.1	6.0	19.9	16.6	0.3	-1.7
1993 Q1	-10.7	-1.4	10.3	13.4	6.1	-0.7	-0.1
Q2	-18.9	-2.1	13.2	8.5	-0.5	0.8	-2.4
Q3	-17.9	0.4	15.3	24.7	-4.2	0.4	0.8

1 Annual data includes adjustment for net foreign trade and stock change in other solid fuels.
2 Estimated annual out-turn.

Source: Department of Trade and Industry

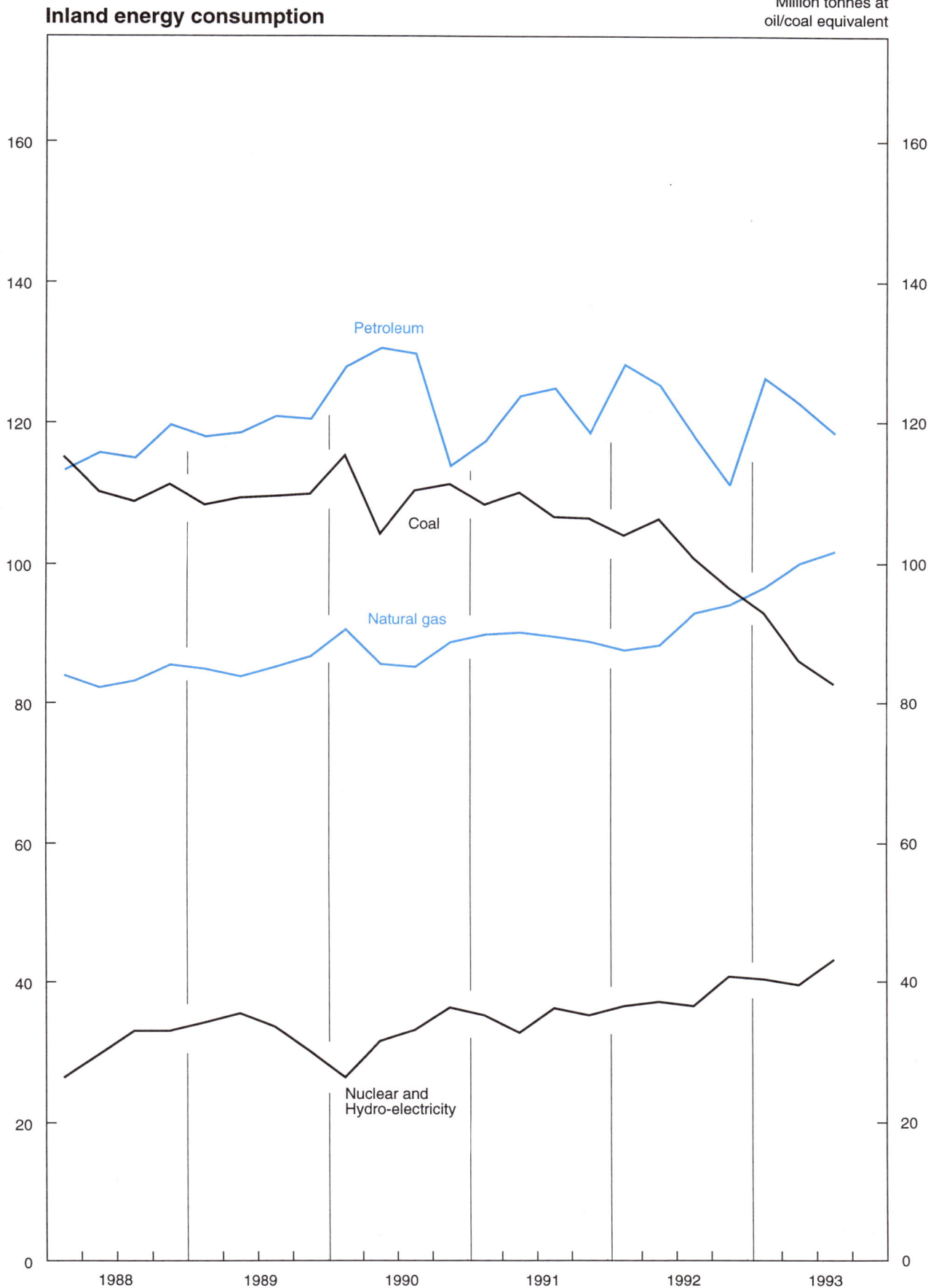

15 Index of output of the production industries[1]

1990 = 100

	Total production industries+	Mining and quarrying	Electricity, gas and water supply	Total manufacturing industries+	By market sector		
					Consumer goods industries	Investment goods industries	Intermediate goods industries
1990 weights	1 000	77	79	844	298	229	473
	DVZI	DVZJ	DVZS	DVZK	DVJP	DVJV	DVJZ
1986	90.1	133.8	95.1	85.6	87.7	81.8	95.7
1987	93.7	134.1	97.6	89.6	92.6	83.1	99.5
1988	98.2	123.4	97.7	95.9	97.7	90.0	102.4
1989	100.3	104.3	97.3	100.2	100.0	98.6	101.3
1990	100.0	100.0	100.0	100.0	100.0	100.0	100.0
1991	96.0	101.0	105.9	94.7	95.2	94.1	97.5
1992	95.6	104.8	105.4	93.9	96.2	91.4	97.4
1988 Q3	99.4	120.3	101.2	97.3	99.4	91.0	103.4
Q4	99.6	115.2	98.9	98.3	99.1	94.2	102.6
1989 Q1	99.9	102.7	94.1	100.2	100.4	97.6	101.0
Q2	99.9	99.2	99.7	99.9	99.9	97.5	100.8
Q3	100.5	107.0	97.5	100.2	99.7	100.1	101.2
Q4	100.8	108.4	97.9	100.4	100.0	99.3	102.1
1990 Q1	100.3	103.3	94.1	100.6	100.4	99.7	100.4
Q2	101.6	108.8	100.2	101.1	100.9	101.3	102.2
Q3	99.8	93.4	102.7	100.1	100.0	100.6	99.3
Q4	98.3	94.5	103.0	98.3	98.7	98.4	98.1
1991 Q1	97.1	98.7	104.9	96.2	96.3	96.9	97.7
Q2	95.9	95.1	110.2	94.6	95.4	94.3	97.0
Q3	95.4	103.4	102.6	94.0	94.5	93.0	97.2
Q4	95.8	106.6	106.1	93.8	94.7	92.1	98.3
1992 Q1	95.0	103.4	103.9	93.4	95.6	90.4	96.9
Q2	94.9	99.8	102.3	93.8	96.3	90.4	96.3
Q3	96.0	105.6	106.2	94.2	96.3	91.7	98.0
Q4	96.6	110.5	109.2	94.2	96.5	93.1	98.6
1993 Q1	96.7	106.3†	103.4	95.2	97.1	94.0	97.8
Q2	97.7	109.8	106.2	95.8†	97.5†	94.7†	99.2†
Q3	98.7	117.3	111.7	95.8†	97.8†	94.1	101.5†
1991 Jun	97.2	107.5	114.1	94.6	95.4	93.8	99.9
Jul	96.2	104.1	105.3	94.6	95.3	93.7	97.9
Aug	95.0	102.2	102.1	93.6	94.0	92.4	96.8
Sep	95.2	103.9	100.3	93.9	94.3	92.7	96.9
Oct	95.8	108.8	107.3	93.5	94.5	90.6	99.1
Nov	96.2	104.9	106.7	94.5	95.0	93.8	98.2
Dec	95.3	106.1	104.3	93.5	94.7	91.7	97.4
1992 Jan	94.5	106.6	102.7	92.6	94.9	89.8	96.5
Feb	95.5	104.8	105.2	93.8	95.9	90.5	97.8
Mar	95.0	98.9	103.8	93.8	95.9	91.0	96.4
Apr	95.7	103.6	105.5	94.1	96.0	91.1	97.8
May	94.2	99.2	102.5	93.0	95.8	89.1	95.8
Jun	94.8	96.6	99.0	94.3	97.0	91.1	95.4
Jul	95.3	100.0	105.0	94.0	96.1	91.2	96.9
Aug	96.1	106.3	105.4	94.3	96.3	92.0	98.0
Sep	96.7	110.3	108.3	94.3	96.6	91.9	99.0
Oct	97.6	112.6	112.1	94.8	96.3	94.7	99.9
Nov	96.4	109.0	108.8	94.1	95.7	92.8	98.8
Dec	95.8	109.9	106.8	93.5	97.3	91.7	97.1
1993 Jan	96.2	105.2	102.9	94.8†	96.8	94.0	96.9
Feb	97.4	111.4	102.6	95.6	97.2†	94.4	99.0
Mar	96.6	102.5	104.6	95.3	97.4	93.6	97.6†
Apr	96.9	104.1	103.5	95.6	97.1	94.9†	97.6†
May	98.5	107.9	106.8	96.9	98.4	96.0	99.9
Jun	97.6	117.3	108.4	94.8	97.1	93.0	100.1
Jul	98.7†	117.6†	109.3	96.0	98.0	94.5	101.2
Aug	98.6	119.6	111.8	95.4	97.3	94.2	101.5
Sep	98.7	114.8	113.9	95.8	98.1	93.5	101.6
Oct	99.7	121.2	116.7†	96.2	97.8	94.6	103.4
Nov	100.2	126.6	113.8	96.5	98.5	94.2	104.1

1 The figures contain, where appropriate, an adjustment for stock changes.

Source: Central Statistical Office

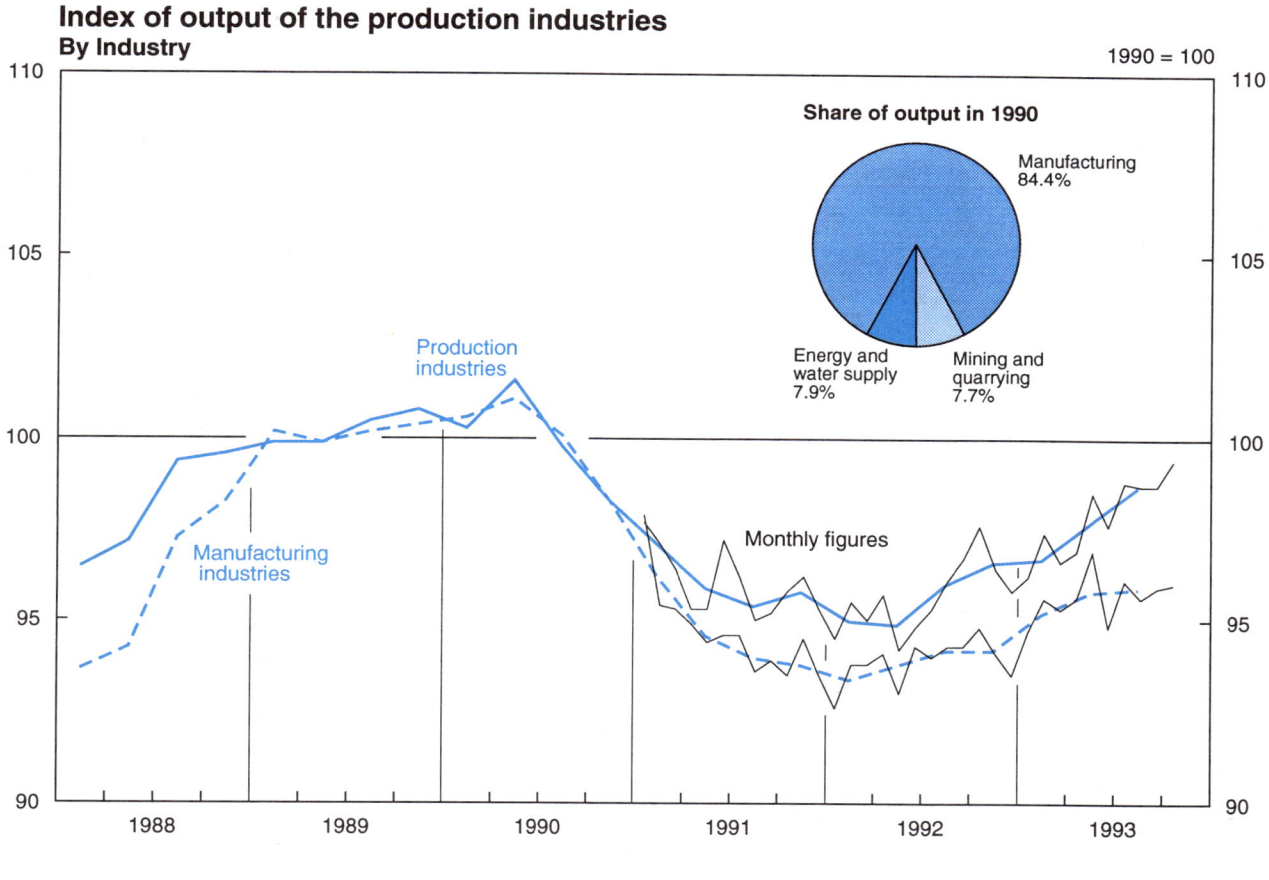
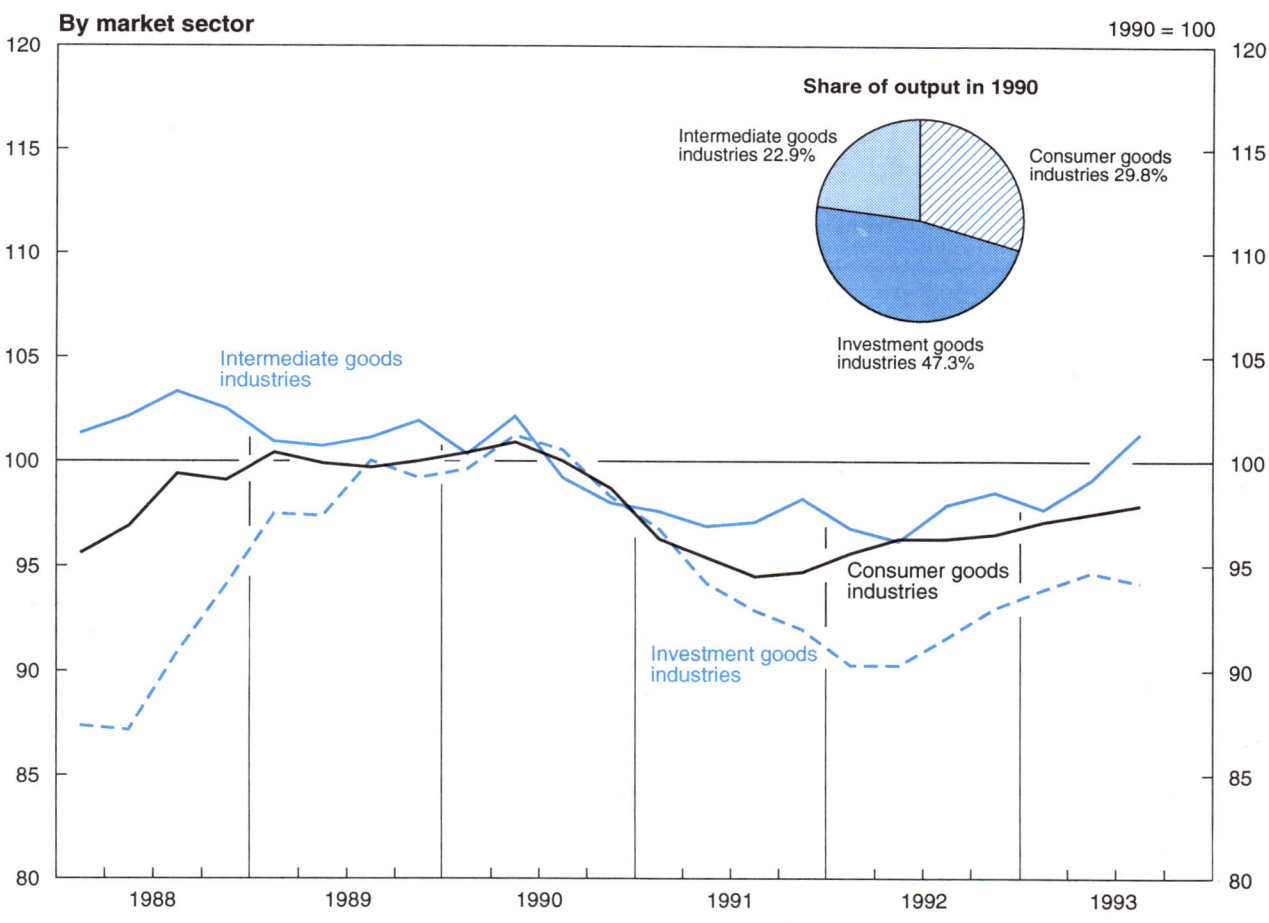

16 Index numbers: Gross domestic product: at constant factor cost

1990 = 100

	Agriculture, hunting forestry and fishing	Production industries[1]	Construction	Service industries						Gross domestic product[2]	Gross domestic product excluding oil and gas extraction[2]
				Distribution; hotels and catering; repairs	Transport, storage and communication	Other services	Financial and business services	Government and other services	Total services		
1990 weights	19	281	72	142	84	403	186	217	629	1,000	983
	CKAP		DVJO	CKAQ	CKAR	CKAS	CKJB	CKJC	CKCE	DJDD	CKJL
1987	93.5	93.7	84.9	91.4	89.6	94.0	90.9	96.6	92.8	92.7	91.9
1988	92.1	98.2	92.3	96.9	94.2	98.0	96.6	99.1	97.2	97.3	96.8
1989	96.7	100.3	97.6	100.8	99.1	98.8	97.8	99.6	99.3	99.4	99.4
1990	100.0	100.0	100.0	100.0	100.0	100.0	100.0	100.0	100.0	100.0	100.0
1991	103.9	96.1	92.1	95.3	97.3	100.3	100.0	100.5	98.8	97.7	97.6
1992	106.1	95.6	86.9	93.9	98.8	100.2	98.7	101.5	98.6	97.2	97.0
1993	..	..	..	96.8	..	..	..	..	100.7	99.1	98.6
1988 Q3	91.6	99.4	92.3	97.3	93.8	98.7	97.8	99.4	97.7	97.9	97.5
Q4	92.2	99.6	94.2	99.1	96.2	98.9	97.9	99.8	98.6	98.6	98.4
1989 Q1	95.9	99.9	96.4	100.4	97.7	98.7	97.3	99.9	99.0	99.1	99.1
Q2	95.4	99.9	98.0	100.8	98.6	98.8	97.7	99.7	99.2	99.3	99.4
Q3	98.3	100.5	97.6	100.9	100.1	98.5	97.7	99.2	99.3	99.5	99.4
Q4	97.2	100.8	98.6	100.9	100.0	99.1	98.6	99.4	99.6	99.8	99.7
1990 Q1	97.8	100.3	100.7	101.6	101.2	99.8	100.0	99.7	100.4	100.4	100.3
Q2	99.3	101.6	101.0	101.0	100.3	100.1	100.2	100.0	100.3	100.7	100.5
Q3	100.6	99.8	100.4	99.7	99.3	99.9	99.7	100.1	99.8	99.8	100.0
Q4	102.2	98.3	97.9	97.8	99.2	100.2	100.1	100.2	99.5	99.1	99.2
1991 Q1	103.7	97.1	94.5	96.8	95.9	100.1	100.0	100.1	98.8	98.1	98.1
Q2	104.8	95.9	92.7	95.2	97.2	100.2	99.9	100.4	98.7	97.6	97.7
Q3	103.0	95.4	91.4	95.0	97.5	100.4	100.1	100.7	98.8	97.5	97.3
Q4	104.1	95.8	89.8	94.3	98.4	100.5	99.9	101.0	98.8	97.5	97.3
1992 Q1	104.0	95.0	88.4	93.3	98.5	100.0	98.7	101.1	98.3	96.9	96.7
Q2	105.1	94.9	87.2	93.8	98.5	100.2	98.7	101.4	98.5	97.0	96.9
Q3	108.1	96.0	86.4	94.1	98.9	100.2	98.7	101.6	98.6	97.4	97.1
Q4	107.1	96.6	85.5	94.5	99.4	100.5	98.9	101.8	99.0	97.7	97.3
1993 Q1	104.1	96.7	85.3	95.6	99.7	101.5	100.6	102.2	99.9	98.2	98.0
Q2	99.3	97.7	85.1	96.4	100.0	102.0	101.3	102.7	100.5	98.8	98.4
Q3	100.6	98.7	85.3	97.3	100.3	102.4	101.9	102.9	101.0	99.4	98.9
Q4	..	..	..	98.1	..	..	..	..	101.4	100.1	99.3

Percentage change, quarter on corresponding quarter of previous year

1988 Q3	-0.2	5.2	6.9	5.3	2.4	4.1	6.3	2.4	4.2	4.6	5.1
Q4	-0.6	4.4	5.9	5.5	5.0	3.8	6.1	1.8	4.3	4.4	4.9
1989 Q1	3.7	3.6	6.0	5.2	3.9	2.1	2.5	1.7	3.0	3.3	4.0
Q2	3.5	2.7	7.0	5.4	6.2	1.3	1.9	0.7	2.8	2.9	3.7
Q3	7.3	1.2	5.7	3.7	6.7	-0.2	-0.1	-0.2	1.6	1.6	1.9
Q4	5.5	1.2	4.6	1.8	3.9	0.2	0.7	-0.3	1.0	1.2	1.3
1990 Q1	2.1	0.3	4.5	1.2	3.6	1.1	2.8	-0.2	1.5	1.3	1.2
Q2	4.1	1.7	3.1	0.1	1.7	1.4	2.6	0.3	1.1	1.4	1.2
Q3	2.4	-0.7	2.9	-1.2	-0.8	1.4	2.0	0.9	0.5	0.3	0.6
Q4	5.2	-2.5	-0.7	-3.1	-0.8	1.1	1.5	0.8	-0.1	-0.7	-0.4
1991 Q1	6.0	-3.2	-6.1	-4.7	-5.3	0.2	0.0	0.5	-1.6	-2.2	-2.1
Q2	5.5	-5.6	-8.3	-5.7	-3.1	0.1	-0.3	0.4	-1.6	-3.1	-2.8
Q3	2.4	-4.4	-8.9	-4.7	-1.8	0.5	0.4	0.6	-1.0	-2.4	-2.6
Q4	1.8	-2.6	-8.2	-3.6	-0.7	0.3	-0.3	0.7	-0.7	-1.6	-2.0
1992 Q1	0.3	-2.1	-6.5	-3.6	2.7	-0.1	-1.3	1.0	-0.5	-1.3	-1.4
Q2	0.3	-1.0	-5.9	-1.5	1.3	0.0	-1.2	1.0	-0.2	-0.7	-0.8
Q3	5.0	0.6	-5.5	-1.0	1.4	-0.2	-1.4	0.9	-0.1	-0.1	-0.2
Q4	3.0	0.9	-4.8	0.3	1.0	0.0	-0.9	0.9	0.2	0.2	0.0
1993 Q1	0.1	1.8	-3.5	2.5	1.2	1.5	2.0	1.1	1.7	1.4	1.3
Q2	-5.6	2.9	-2.4	2.8	1.5	1.9	2.6	1.3	2.0	1.9	1.5
Q3	-6.9	2.8	-1.3	3.4	1.5	2.2	3.2	1.3	2.4	2.1	1.8
Q4	..	..	..	3.8	..	..	..	..	2.4	2.5	2.1

Source: Central Statistical Office

1 The latest data for the index of production are presented in Table 15. The figures given in this table are consistent with the figures for the output measure of gross domestic product.
2 Embraces an implicit discrepancy compared with the sum of the previous columns, because the GDP aggregate takes account of other information based on incomes and expenditure.

CSO STATFAX

For the most up-to-date data on the index of production, poll the following number from your fax machine:

0336 416041

Calls charged at 36p per minute cheap rate, 48p per minute at all other times

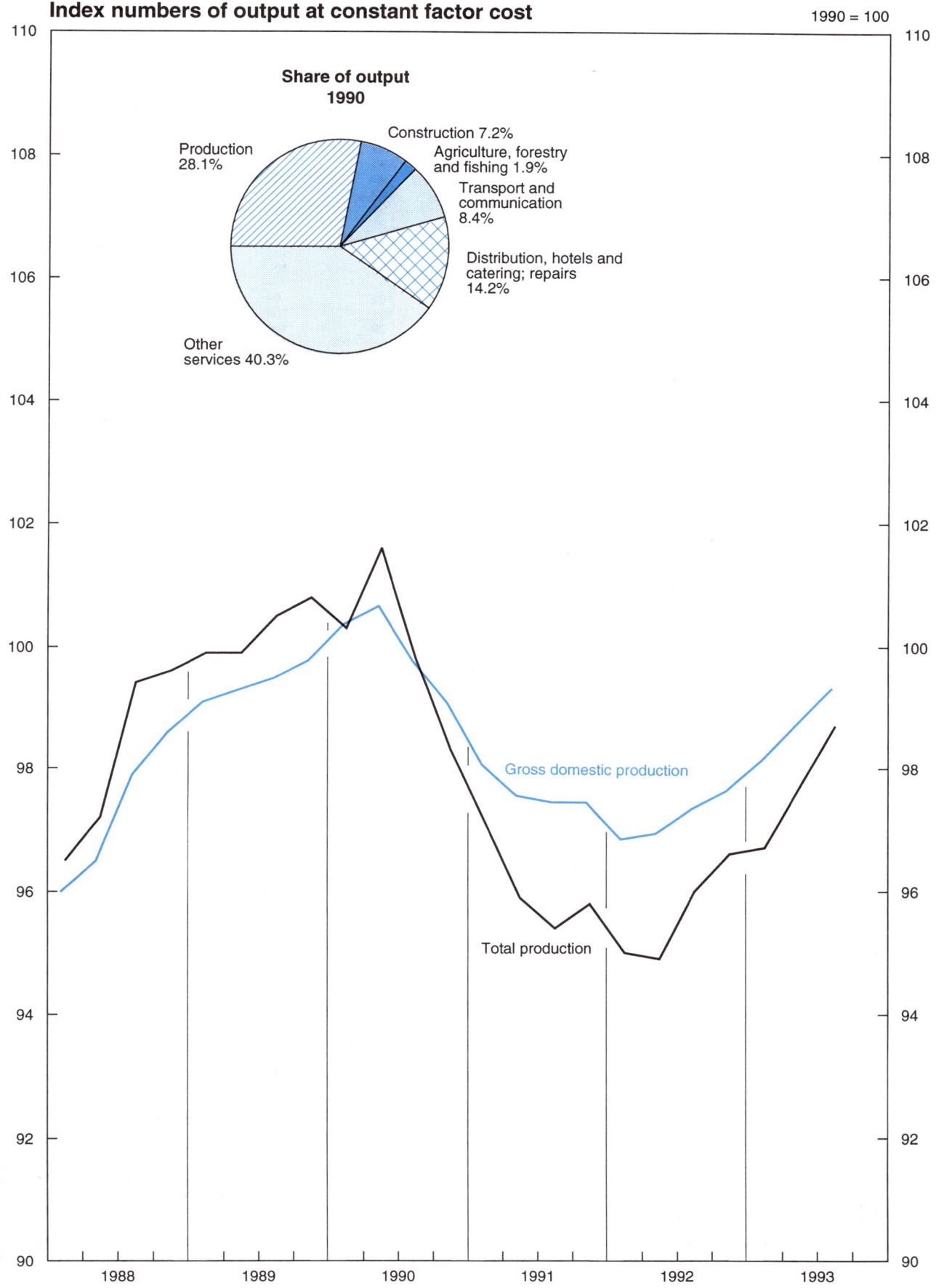

17 Engineering and construction: output and orders

Volume index numbers

	Engineering industries[1,2]							Construction (GB)	
	Home market		Export		Total				
	Orders on hand end of period (average 1990 = 100)	New orders[3] (1990 average monthly sales = 100)	Orders on hand end of period (average 1990 = 100)	New orders[3] (1990 average monthly sales = 100)	Sales[3] (1990 average monthly sales = 100)	Orders on hand end of period (average 1990 =100)	New orders[3] (1990 average monthly sales = 100)	Gross output+[4] (1985 = 100)	Orders received (1985 = 100)
	FEAV	FEAN	FEAX	FEAP	FEAJ	DKCJ	FEAL	FEAQ	FEAZ
1988	95	98	86	91	93	92	96	124.6	134.0
1989	103	103	99†	102	98	102	102	133.1	129.2
1990	95	97	96	98	100	95	97	135.5	111.5
1991	82	86	90	95	94	85	89	126.0	103.4
1992	78	85	103	108†	91	88	93†	119.8	98.9
1989 Q3	104	100	101	107	98	103	102	132.9	121.0
Q4	103	99	99†	96†	100	102	98	134.4	122.3
1990 Q1	100	98	98	99	102	99	98	137.2	118.0
Q2	102	105	104	112	101	103	107	137.0	120.0
Q3	101	97	100	91	99	100	95	134.5	107.3
Q4	95	86	96	92	97	95	88	133.4	100.6
1991 Q1	88	83	88	85	96	88	84	128.9	97.3
Q2	85	87	88	97	94	86	90	125.9	109.6
Q3	84	88	88	99	92	86†	92	125.2	103.7
Q4	82	85	90	102	92	85	91†	123.9	103.0
1992 Q1	80	85	92	104	91	85	91	122.0	111.4
Q2	78	83	93	101	90	84	89	120.2	90.8
Q3	76	83	94	101	92	83	89	119.0	99.9
Q4	78	90	103	124	92	88	101	118.0	93.4
1993 Q1	75†	85	108	109	92	88	93	117.6	113.9
Q2	75	86†	107	104	93	87	92	116.8	100.6
Q3	73	87	110	110	94	88	95	117.1[5]	110.5
1991 May	86	89†	87	92	93	87†	90†	..	122.8
Jun	85	86	88	104†	95	86	92	..	111.0
Jul	86†	95	88	102	93	87	97	..	110.8
Aug	86	91	88	98	92	87	93	..	106.6
Sep	84	79	88	96	92	86	85	..	93.6
Oct	84	86	88	98	90	85	90	..	108.8
Nov	83	86	90	112	93	86	95	..	106.1
Dec	82	83	90	96	92	85	87	..	94.2
1992 Jan	82	87	91†	104	89	85	92	..	99.9
Feb	81	80	93	116	91	86	92	..	125.8
Mar	80	87	92	93	93	85	89	..	108.6
Apr	80	86	92	96	90	85	89	..	91.9
May	79	77	94	109	89	84	88	..	96.7
Jun	78	85	93	98	91†	84	89	..	83.9
Jul	79	88	93	102	91	84	92	..	106.7
Aug	78	87	93	98	94	84	91	..	98.1
Sep	76	75	94	104	91	83	85	..	94.9
Oct	76	91	100	143	93	86	108	..	93.0
Nov	77	91	101	109	92	87	97	..	104.2
Dec	78	88	103	119	92	88	98	..	83.0
1993 Jan	75	79	103	95	93	86	84	..	112.0
Feb	75	88	101	95	94	85	91	..	112.7
Mar	75	89	108	138	90	88	105	..	117.0
Apr	75	81	106	94	92	87	85	..	100.8
May	75	91	106	109	96	87	97	..	97.0
Jun	75	85	107	109	91	87	93	..	104.0
Jul	74	85	105	93	94	86	87	..	109.8
Aug	73	89	110	133	94	88	104	..	98.8
Sep	73	88	110	104	95	88	94	..	122.8
Oct	72	86	107	88	95	86	86	..	115.9
Nov	73	87	107	105	92	86	93	..	116.7

1 Mechanical, instrument and electrical engineering (SIC Classes 32, 33, 34 and 37).
2 The figures are derived from the Monthly Sales Inquiry (MSI). From October 1993, the MSI has been conducted using an improved sample design which means that estimates for smaller businesses are based on actual data and not on general assumptions about their similarity to larger businesses. This has led us to revise the previously published data in the light of these new estimates in order to produce consistent series using the latest available information.
3 Net of cancellations.
4 This index is based on a gross output series which includes repair and maintenance estimates, unrecorded output by self-employed workers and small firms and output by the direct labour departments of the public sector. The index has been revised from 1980 onwards using improved estimates of unrecorded output and following improvements to the coverage of the Department's register.
5 Provisional.

Sources: Central Statistical Office;
Department of the Environment

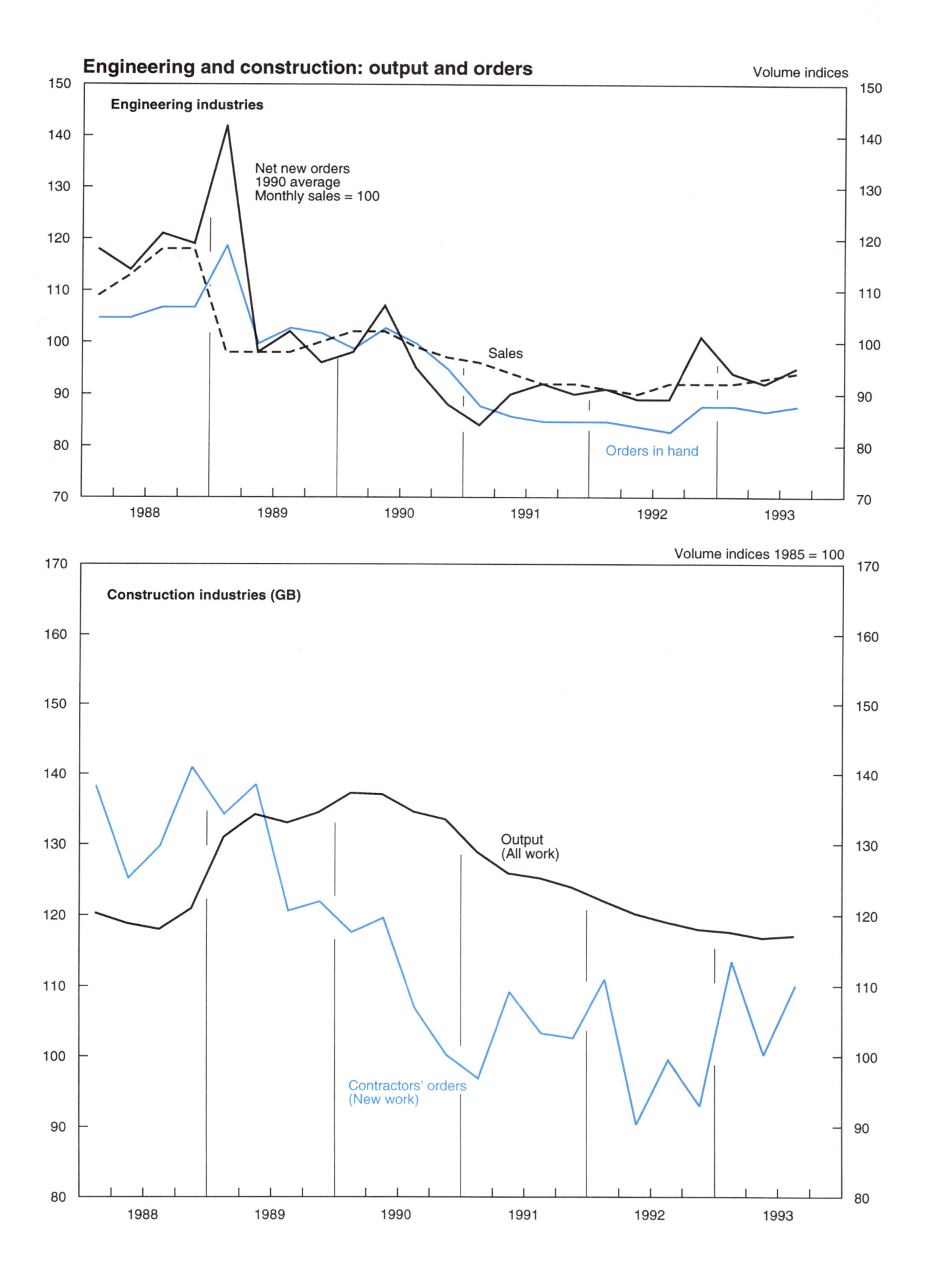

Engineering and construction: output and orders

Engineering industries

Volume indices

Net new orders
1990 average
Monthly sales = 100

Sales

Orders in hand

Construction industries (GB)

Volume indices 1985 = 100

Output
(All work)

Contractors' orders
(New work)

18 Motor vehicle production[1] and steel production and consumption

	Passenger cars+		Commercial vehicles+		Crude steel production[2] (thousand tonnes)	Finished steel consumption (thousand tonnes)
	Total production (thousands)	Of which for export (thousands)	Total production (thousands)	Of which for export (thousands)		
	FFAO	FFAP	FFAQ	FFAR	FFAM	FFAN
1984	75.7	16.0	18.7	4.2	15 076	11 340
1985	87.3	17.3	22.2	5.5	15 716	11 560
1986	84.9	15.6	19.1	4.1	14 723	11 840
1987	95.2	18.8	20.6	5.1	17 414	12 330
1988	102.2	17.8	26.4	7.0	18 950	14 480
1989	108.3	23.4	27.2	8.0	18 740	14 700
1990	108.0	33.8	22.5	8.0	17 841	14 070
1991	103.1	50.4	18.1	9.2	16 475	12 170
1992	107.7	49.1	20.7	10.9	16 212	11 440
1993	114.6	44.4	16.1	7.6	16 618	..
1988 Q4	107.5	19.5	29.0	7.7	4 727.3	3 700
1989 Q1	110.3	23.1	28.1	7.9	4 854.0	3 670
Q2	108.0	23.1	27.2	7.9	4 740.6	3 910
Q3	108.6	24.5	25.9	8.1	4 912.0	3 660
Q4	106.1	22.9	27.6	7.9	4 282.6	3 530
1990 Q1	97.8	26.3	20.8	6.1	4 539.8	3 600
Q2	101.1	23.9	26.0	8.5	4 543.9	3 680
Q3	112.3	36.3	23.5	8.6	4 758.5	3 460
Q4	120.6	48.8	19.8	8.7	4 075.7	3 330
1991 Q1	106.1	51.3	18.1	8.5	3 912.8	3 290
Q2	109.9	57.2	16.2	7.9	4 267.5	2 980
Q3	100.8	49.0	16.2	8.0	4 222.2	2 920
Q4	95.5	44.4	21.8	12.5	4 101.3	2 980
1992 Q1	105.4	43.4	20.7	12.5	4 134.0	3 060
Q2	110.2	45.0	22.2	11.5	4 078.1	2 870
Q3	110.0	51.4	22.1	11.0	4 353.2	3 020
Q4	105.1	56.7	17.8	8.5	3 650.6	2 490
1993 Q1	104.3†	43.8†	17.8†	9.3†	4 028.6	2 730
Q2	119.5	47.8	14.8	6.0	4 249.6	2 800
Q3	121.7	45.6	13.6	5.9	4 166.4	..
Q4	113.1	40.4	18.2	9.1	4 118.4	..
1991 Dec	100.5	47.3	22.2	12.6	1 229.6	..
1992 Jan	100.3	43.3	18.5	11.2	1 546.0*	..
Feb	106.9	42.2	19.8	12.3	1 303.2	..
Mar	108.9	44.6	23.8	13.9	1 284.8	..
Apr	113.0	46.7	22.0	11.2	1 572.5*	..
May	107.9	43.9	21.3	11.2	1 278.8	..
Jun	109.7	44.4	23.3	12.2	1 226.8	..
Jul	118.5	47.6	22.9	10.7	1 592.5*	..
Aug	94.1	41.2	22.6	11.8	1 311.2	..
Sep	117.4	65.4	21.0	10.6	1 449.5*	..
Oct	109.9	58.8	18.9	8.5	1 204.8	..
Nov	95.1	54.7	16.4	8.6	1 176.8	..
Dec	110.2	56.5	18.1	8.2	1 269.0*	..
1993 Jan	93.0†	42.6†	17.8	9.2†	1 220.4	..
Feb	102.9	44.3	17.2†	9.8	1 249.2	..
Mar	116.9	44.4	18.3	8.9	1 559.0*	..
Apr	117.0	52.5	15.0	6.3	1 301.2	..
May	120.8	43.6	15.1	5.9	1 288.4	..
Jun	120.5	47.4	14.4	6.0	1 660.0*	..
Jul	126.3	42.1	13.4	4.4	1 315.6	..
Aug	110.9	46.4	8.7	3.9	1 266.8	..
Sep	127.7	48.3	18.8	9.4	1 584.0*	..
Oct	109.5	45.8	18.4	8.7	1 324.8	..
Nov	108.3	38.2	19.3	11.5	1 305.6†	..
Dec	121.5	37.2	17.1	7.2	1 488.0*	..

1 Annual and quarterly figures are monthly averages.
2 The totals are for 'usable steel' in accordance with the system used by the EC and the International Iron and Steel Institute. Figures are based on weekly averages.

Sources: Central Statistical Office; British Iron & Steel Producers Association

Production of passenger cars Thousands

Total

of which:
For export

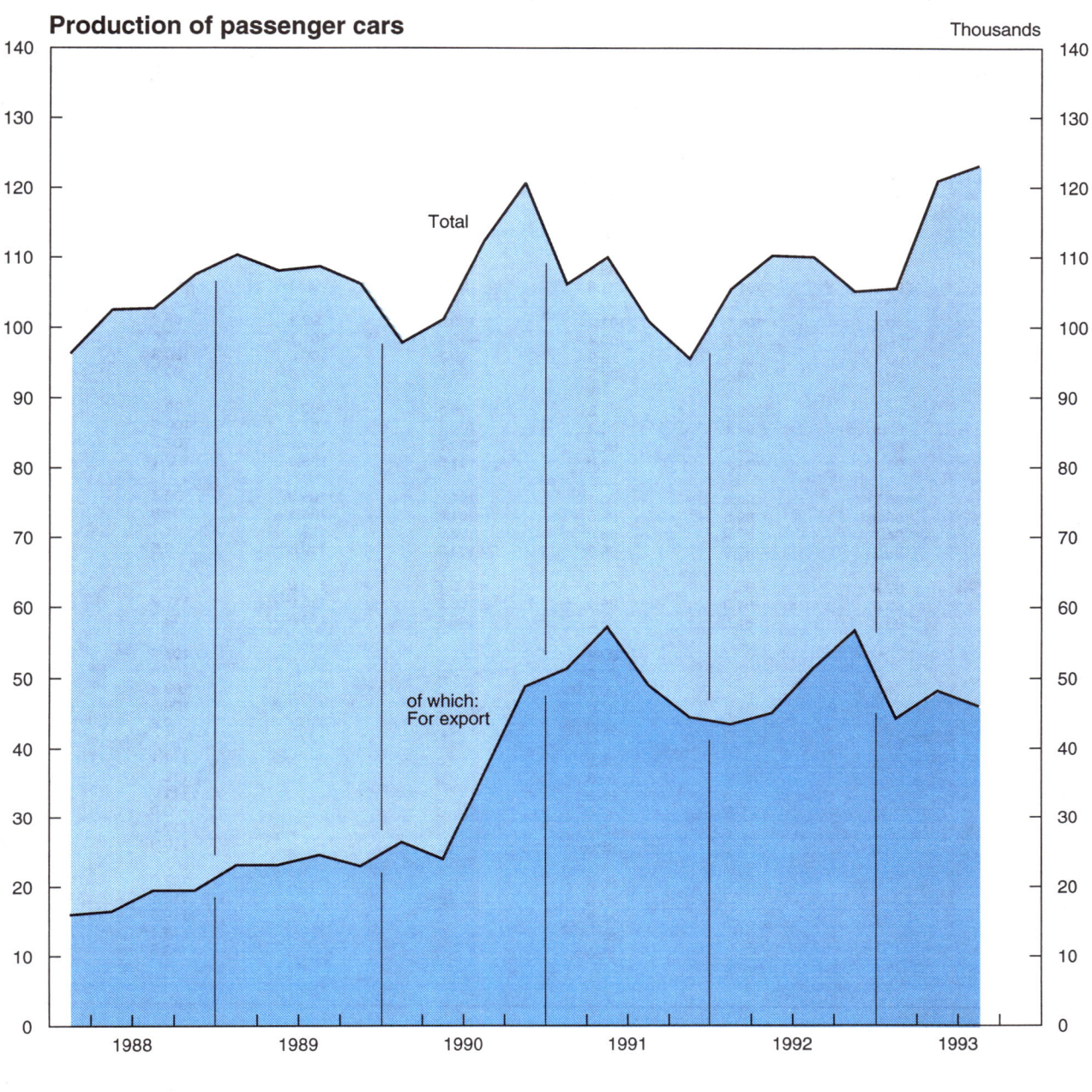

Production of commercial vehicles Thousands

Total

of which:
For export

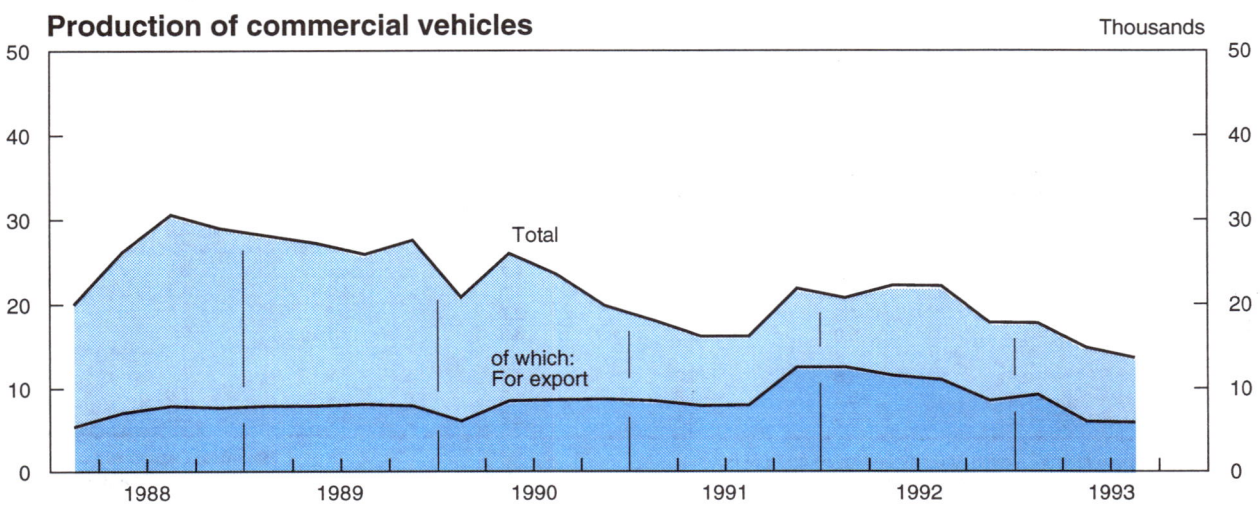

19 Output per person employed

1990 = 100

	Workforce[1]			Output per person employed[2]			Output per hour in manufacturing industries
	Whole economy	Total production industries	Manufacturing industries[3]	Whole economy	Total production industries	Manufacturing industries	
	DMBC	DMWA	DMWB	DMBE	DMOA	DMOB	DMGI
1987	93.9	101.6	100.7	98.7	92.2	89.0	88.8
1988	96.9	102.4	102.0	100.3	95.9	94.0	93.5
1989	99.3	102.2	102.1	100.1	98.2	98.1	97.7
1990	100.0	100.0	100.0	100.0	100.0	100.0	100.0
1991	97.2	93.6	93.4	100.5	102.6	101.4	102.4
1992	94.6	88.4	88.4	102.8	108.3	106.3	107.2
1989 Q3	99.5	102.1	102.1	100.0	98.5	98.1	97.8
Q4	99.9	101.7	101.8	99.9	99.1	98.6	98.6
1990 Q1	100.1	101.2	101.2	100.3	99.1	99.4	99.3
Q2	100.3	100.5	100.4	100.4	101.1	100.6	100.5
Q3	100.1	99.8	99.9	99.7	100.0	100.3	100.2
Q4	99.5	98.5	98.5	99.6	99.8	99.7	99.9
1991 Q1	98.5	96.5	96.3	99.6	100.6	99.9	100.8
Q2	97.5	94.4	94.2	100.1	101.6	100.5	101.7
Q3	96.8	92.4	92.2	100.7	103.2	102.0	102.9
Q4	96.1	91.2	91.0	101.5	105.0	103.1	104.0
1992 Q1	95.7	90.2	90.1	101.2	105.3	103.7	104.4
Q2	95.3	89.5	89.5	101.8	106.1	104.8	105.1
Q3	94.1	87.9	88.0	103.5	109.2	107.1	108.0
Q4	93.2	85.9	86.0	104.8	112.5	109.5	111.2
1993 Q1	92.9	85.1	85.3	105.7	113.6	111.6	113.0
Q2	93.0	84.9	85.4	106.2	115.0	112.2	114.0
Q3	93.3	84.5	85.2	106.5	116.8	112.5	114.2
1992 Aug	..	..	87.8	..	..	107.4	108.4
Sep	..	..	87.5	..	..	107.8	109.1
Oct	..	..	86.7	..	..	109.4	110.9
Nov	..	..	85.9	..	..	109.5	111.0
Dec	..	..	85.3	..	..	109.6	111.6
1993 Jan	..	..	85.3	..	..	111.1	112.2
Feb	..	..	85.3	..	..	112.1	113.3
Mar	..	..	85.3	..	..	111.7	113.5
Apr	..	..	85.4	..	..	112.0	114.3
May	..	..	85.3	..	..	113.7	114.9
Jun	..	..	85.6	..	..	110.8	112.8
Jul	..	..	85.4	..	..	112.6	113.5
Aug	..	..	85.0	..	..	112.4	114.4
Sep	..	..	85.2	..	..	112.5	114.6
Oct	..	..	85.0	..	..	113.1†	115.7†
Nov	..	..	85.0	..	..	113.5	116.8

Percentage change, quarter on corresponding quarter of previous year

	DMDN	DMGJ	DMGK	DMDQ	DMGL	DMGM	DMGN
1989 Q3	2.2	−0.3	−	−0.6	1.5	3.0	3.1
Q4	1.9	−0.7	−0.4	−0.7	2.0	2.6	3.4
1990 Q1	1.4	−1.4	−1.2	−0.1	1.7	1.5	2.2
Q2	1.1	−1.8	−1.8	0.3	3.6	3.0	3.3
Q3	0.6	−2.2	−2.2	−0.3	1.5	2.2	2.4
Q4	−0.4	−3.1	−3.2	−0.3	0.7	1.1	1.3
1991 Q1	−1.6	−4.6	−4.8	−0.7	1.6	0.5	1.5
Q2	−2.7	−6.0	−6.2	−0.4	0.4	−0.1	1.2
Q3	−3.3	−7.4	−7.7	1.1	3.3	1.7	2.7
Q4	−3.4	−7.5	−7.6	1.9	5.3	3.4	4.1
1992 Q1	−2.8	−6.5	−6.5	1.7	4.6	3.8	3.6
Q2	−2.3	−5.2	−5.0	1.8	4.4	4.3	3.4
Q3	−2.7	−4.9	−4.6	2.7	5.8	5.0	5.0
Q4	−3.0	−5.8	−5.5	3.3	7.1	6.2	6.9
1993 Q1	−2.9†	−5.6	−5.3	4.4	7.9	7.7	8.2
Q2	−2.4	−5.1	−4.6	4.3	8.4	7.0	8.4
Q3	−0.8	−3.9	−3.1	2.9	6.9	5.1	5.7

1 Comprises employees in employment, the self-employed and HM Forces.
2 The ratios do not take into account part-time working or hours of work.

Sources: Department of Employment;
Central Statistical Office

Output per person employed 1990 = 100

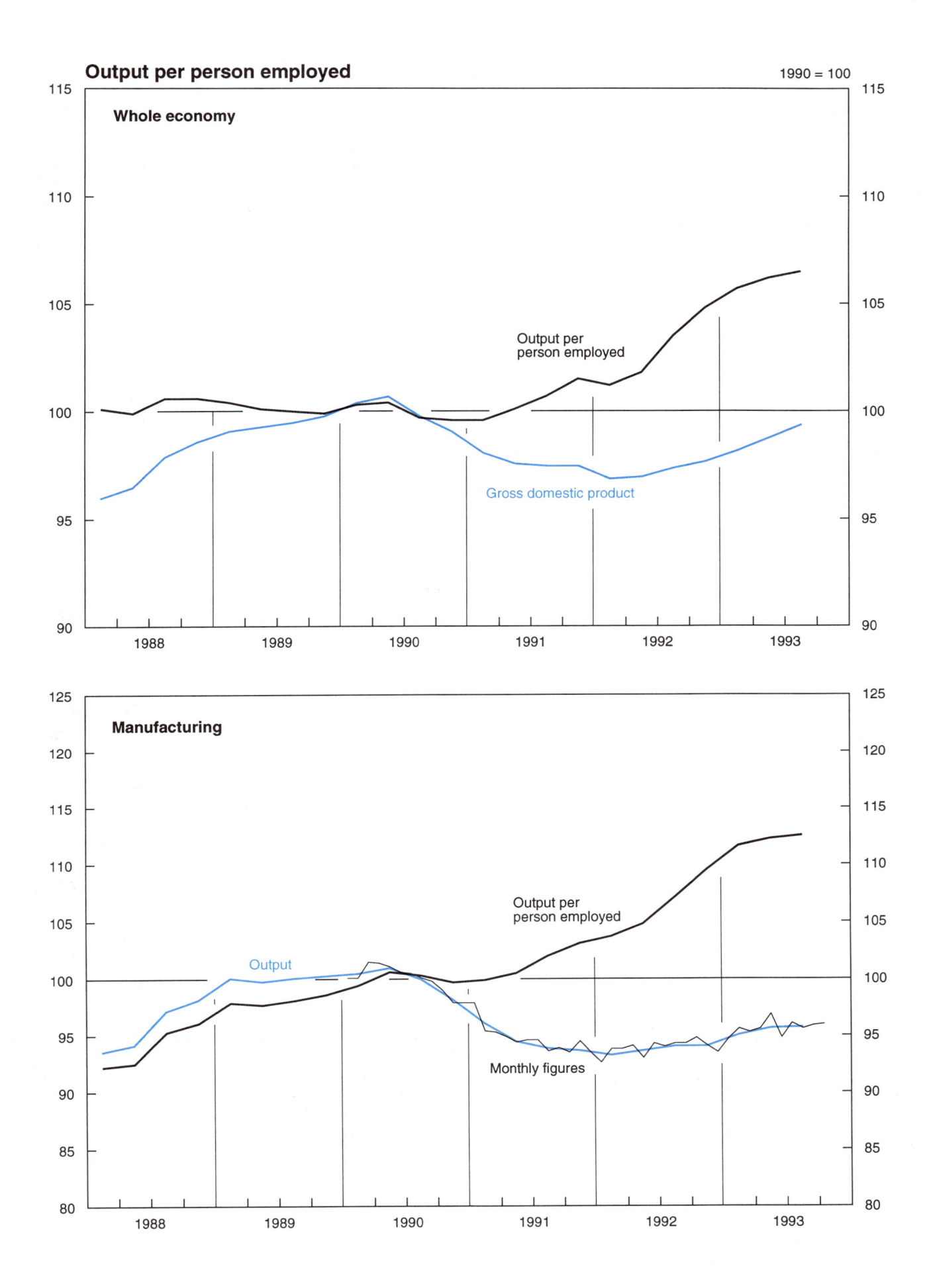

Whole economy

- Output per person employed
- Gross domestic product

Manufacturing

- Output per person employed
- Output
- Monthly figures

20 National employment and unemployment [1]

	Workforce[2,3] (thousands)	Workforce in employment[2,3,4] (thousands)	Employees in employment[2,3,4] (thousands)	Unemployed[5] + Total (thousands)	Unemployed[5] + Percentage of workforce[6]	Vacancies at job centres+[7] (thousands)	Employees in employment (GB) (thousands) Manufacturing industry	Employees in employment (GB) (thousands) Production industry	Total unemployed[5] (thousands) (NSA)
	DYDD	DYDC	BCAJ	BCJD	BCJE	DPCB	BCHK	DYCP	BCJA
1987	28 077	25 084	21 586	2 806.5	10.0	235.4	5 068	5 567	2 953.4
1988	28 347	25 922	22 266	2 274.9	8.1	248.6	5 109	5 587	2 370.4
1989	28 480	26 693	22 670	1 784.4	6.3	219.5	5 101	5 558	1 798.7
1990	28 549	26 937	22 913	1 662.7	5.8	173.6	5 018	5 461	1 664.5
1991	28 338	26 044	22 251	2 287.4	8.1	118.0	4 623	5 054	2 291.9
1992	28 180	25 457	21 839	2 766.5	9.8	117.1	4 419	4 815	2 778.6
1993	27 826	24 914	21 335	..	..	..	4 212	4 564	..
1989 Q4	28 512	26 872	22 841	1 660.4	5.9	210.8	5 083	5 530	1 635.8
1990 Q1	28 482	26 884	22 858	1 611.0	5.7	194.4	5 050	5 494	1 687.0
Q2	28 549	26 937	22 913	1 602.5	5.6	191.7	5 018	5 461	1 626.3
Q3	28 506	26 831	22 856	1 652.5	5.7	167.7	4 965	5 405	1 623.6
Q4	28 495	26 642	22 703	1 784.8	6.1	140.8	4 861	5 298	1 670.6
1991 Q1	28 426	26 336	22 450	1 991.5	6.7	137.7	4 734	5 169	1 959.7
Q2	28 338	26 044	22 251	2 227.7	7.6	110.7	4 623	5 054	2 198.5
Q3	28 296	25 845	22 105	2 410.1	8.3	108.3	4 538	4 963	2 367.5
Q4	28 234	25 684	21 969	2 520.4	8.8	115.1	4 485	4 899	2 426.0
1992 Q1	28 276	25 628	21 943	2 635.0	9.3	118.0	4 444	4 851	2 673.9
Q2	28 180	25 457	21 839	2 708.1	9.6	116.6	4 419	4 815	2 736.5
Q3	27 904	25 063	21 479	2 805.0	9.8	115.9	4 309	4 701	2 774.0
Q4	27 924	24 951	21 365	2 917.8	10.2	118.1	4 190	4 571	..
1993 Q1	27 822	24 881	21 336	2 966.7	10.7	121.3	4 201	4 571	..
Q2	27 826	24 914	21 335	2 922.9	..	122.3	4 212	4 564	..
Q3	27 931	25 005	21 434	2 914.1	..	127.6	4 185	4 530	..
Q4	..	..	..	2 810.4	..	140.2	..	..	..
1991 Oct	..	..	..	2 484.8	8.8	109.8	4 511	4 932	2 426.0
Nov	..	..	..	2 526.3	8.9	113.2	4 492	4 909	2 471.8
Dec	..	..	..	2 550.1	9.0	122.2	4 485	4 899	2 551.7
1992 Jan	..	..	..	2 611.3	9.3	117.9	4 455	4 866	2 673.9
Feb	..	..	..	2 645.8	9.4	118.4	4 452	4 858	2 710.5
Mar	..	..	..	2 647.9	9.4	117.6	4 444	4 851	2 707.5
Apr	..	..	..	2 689.8	9.6	116.6	4 428	4 832	2 736.5
May	..	..	..	2 712.0	9.7	117.1	4 418	4 817	2 707.9
Jun	..	..	..	2 722.5	9.7	116.1	4 419	4 815	2 678.2
Jul	..	..	..	2 758.3	9.8	119.1	4 374	4 769	2 774.0
Aug	..	..	..	2 815.7	10.0	117.1	4 330	4 723	2 845.5
Sep	..	..	..	2 841.0	10.1	111.5	4 309	4 701	2 847.4
Oct	..	..	..	2 868.1	10.2	113.5	4 266	4 656	2 814.4
Nov	..	..	..	2 912.8	10.3	117.4	4 225	4 610	2 864.1
Dec	..	..	..	2 972.4	10.6	123.4	4 190	4 571	2 983.3
1993 Jan	..	..	..	2 992.3	10.6	120.3	4 193	4 570	3 062.1
Feb	..	..	..	2 966.8	10.6	120.5	4 197	4 571	3 042.6
Mar	..	..	..	2 941.0	10.5	123.2	4 201	4 571	2 996.7
Apr	..	..	..	2 939.9	10.5	123.5	4 202	4 566	3 000.5
May	..	..	..	2 916.8	10.4	123.6	4 196	4 552	2 916.6
Jun	..	..	..	2 912.0	10.4	119.7	4 212	4 564	2 865.0
Jul	..	..	..	2 916.3	10.4	127.6	4 201	4 551	2 929.3
Aug	..	..	..	2 921.9	10.4	128.0	4 177	4 523	2 960.0
Sep	..	..	..	2 904.1	10.3	127.3	4 185	4 530	2 912.1
Oct	..	..	..	2 852.0	10.1	134.4	4 175	4 518	2 793.6
Nov	..	..	..	2 813.0	10.0	140.9	4 168	4 508	2 769.4
Dec	..	..	..	2 766.2	9.8	145.4	..	..	2 782.7

1 Unemployment figures do not include students registered for temporary employment during a current vacation.
2 The workforce consists of the workforce in employment and the unemployed (claimants); the workforce in employment comprises employees in employment, the self-employed, HM Forces and participants in work-related government training programmes. See *Employment Gazette* August 1988, page S6.
3 For all dates, individuals with two jobs as employees of different employers are counted twice.
4 Annual estimates relate to mid-year. Figures for the four quarters relate to March, June, September and December.
5 Unadjusted unemployment figures have been affected by changes in the coverage. The seasonally adjusted figures however, as given in this table, are estimated on the current basis, allowing for the discontinuities, and are therefore recommended for the purposes of assessing trends. The seasonally adjusted figures now relate only to claimants aged 18 or over in order to maintain the consistent series, available back to 1971 (1974 for the regions), allowing for the effect of the change in benefit regulations for under 18 year olds from September 1988. (See page 660 of the December 1988 *Employment Gazette*. See also page 422 of the October 1986 edition for the list of previous discontinuities taken into account.)
Note: Quarter figures relate to January, April, July and October.
6 The denominator used to calculate unemployment rates is the workforce - see footnote 2.
7 Vacancies notified to job centres and remaining unfilled.
Note: Quarter figures relate to the average of the three months in each quarter.

Source: Department of Employment

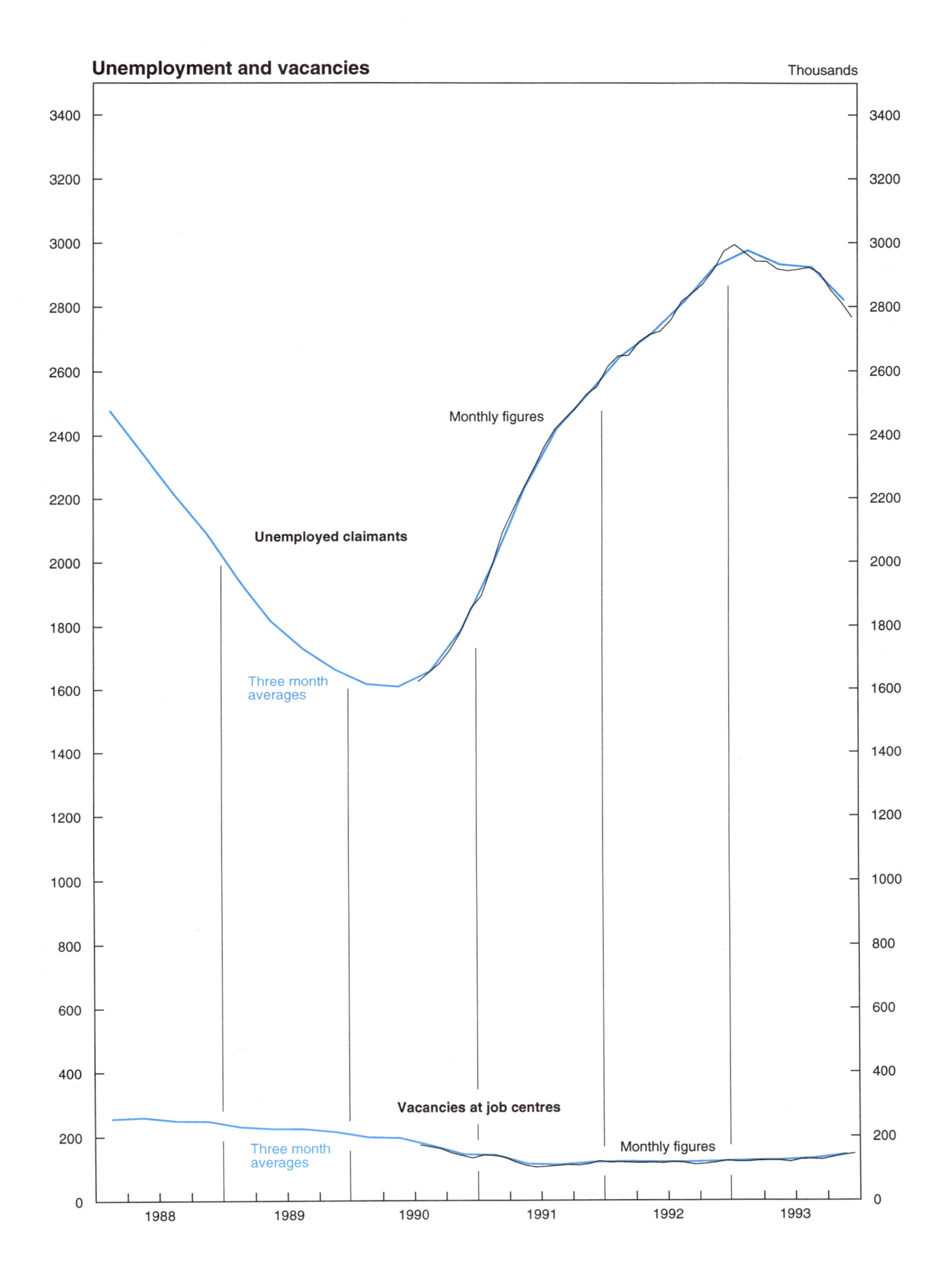

Unemployment and vacancies

Thousands

Unemployed claimants

Monthly figures

Three month averages

Vacancies at job centres

Three month averages

Monthly figures

21 Regional unemployment rates [1]

Percentages

	North	Yorkshire and Humberside	East Midlands	East Anglia	South East	South West	West Midlands
	DPBH	DPBI	DPBJ	DPBK	DPBL	DPBM	DPBN
1987 Q1	15.0	12.2	9.8	8.2	8.0	9.0	12.5
Q2	14.7	11.9	9.5	7.8	7.6	8.6	12.0
Q3	14.0	11.3	9.0	7.3	7.1	8.1	11.3
Q4	13.4	10.7	8.4	6.7	6.7	7.6	10.7
1988 Q1	12.8	10.2	7.9	6.1	6.1	7.1	10.0
Q2	12.3	9.8	7.5	5.6	5.7	6.6	9.5
Q3	11.8	9.2	7.0	5.1	5.2	6.1	8.8
Q4	11.3	8.8	6.7	4.7	4.9	5.7	8.2
1989 Q1	11.0	8.2	6.1	4.0	4.4	5.0	7.5
Q2	10.3	7.6	5.6	3.6	4.0	4.6	6.8
Q3	9.7	7.3	5.3	3.5	3.9	4.4	6.4
Q4	9.2	7.0	5.1	3.4	3.7	4.2	6.1
1990 Q1	8.8	6.7	4.9	3.3	3.7	4.0	5.8
Q2	8.5	6.5	4.9	3.4	3.6	4.0	5.6
Q3	8.6	6.6	5.0	3.6	3.8	4.3	5.7
Q4	8.8	6.9	5.4	4.1	4.4	4.8	6.0
1991 Q1	9.3	7.5	5.9	4.7	5.2	5.5	6.8
Q2	10.0	8.4	6.8	5.5	6.4	6.6	8.0
Q3	10.5	9.0	7.5	6.1	7.2	7.4	8.8
Q4	10.7	9.3	8.0	6.5	7.9	8.0	9.4
1992 Q1	10.9	9.6	8.6	7.1	8.5	8.7	10.0
Q2	11.0	9.7	8.9	7.5	9.0	9.1	10.3
Q3	11.2	9.9	9.1	7.7	9.3	9.4	10.5
Q4	11.5	10.2	9.4	8.2	9.9	9.8	10.9
1993 Q1	12.1	10.7	9.9	8.7	10.4	10.2	11.4

	North West	Wales	Scotland	Great Britain	Northern Ireland	United Kingdom
	DPBO	DPBP	DPBQ	DPAJ	DPBR	BCJE
1987 Q1	13.4	13.0	13.7	10.7	17.4	10.9
Q2	13.0	12.4	13.6	10.3	17.2	10.5
Q3	12.4	11.9	13.0	9.8	17.0	10.0
Q4	11.8	11.4	12.4	9.3	16.8	9.5
1988 Q1	11.3	10.6	12.0	8.7	16.1	8.9
Q2	10.8	10.3	11.5	8.2	15.8	8.4
Q3	10.2	9.7	11.0	7.7	15.6	7.9
Q4	9.9	9.4	10.8	7.4	15.3	7.6
1989 Q1	9.4	8.3	10.2	6.8	15.2	7.0
Q2	8.8	7.6	9.6	6.2	14.9	6.5
Q3	8.4	7.2	9.1	6.0	14.6	6.2
Q4	8.0	6.8	8.8	5.7	14.2	5.9
1990 Q1	7.7	6.6	8.4	5.5	13.6	5.7
Q2	7.6	6.4	8.2	5.4	13.4	5.6
Q3	7.5	6.5	8.0	5.5	13.2	5.7
Q4	7.8	6.9	8.0	5.9	13.1	6.1
1991 Q1	8.3	7.6	8.0	6.5	13.0	6.7
Q2	9.0	8.5	8.4	7.5	13.3	7.6
Q3	9.6	9.2	8.9	8.2	13.5	8.3
Q4	10.0	9.4	8.9	8.6	13.7	8.8
1992 Q1	10.5	9.7	9.1	9.2	13.8	9.3
Q2	10.7	9.7	9.2	9.5	13.9	9.6
Q3	10.7	9.9	9.5	9.7	14.3	9.8
Q4	10.9	10.2	9.6	10.1	14.3	10.2
1993 Q1	11.2	10.6	9.8	10.5	14.3	10.7

Note: Figures shown are at January, April, July and October respectively.

1 The seasonally adjusted figures now relate only to claimants aged 18 or over in order to maintain the consistent series, available back to 1971 (1974 for the regions), allowing for the effect of the change in benefit regulations for under 18 year olds from September 1988. (See page 660 of the December 1988 Employment Gazette. See also page 422 of the October 1986 edition for the list of previous discontinuities taken into account). The denominators used to calculate unemployment rates are the sum of the appropriate mid-year estimates of employees in employment and the unemployed, the self-employed, HM Forces and participants in work-related government training programmes. Recent figures are based on mid-1990 estimates.

Source: Department of Employment

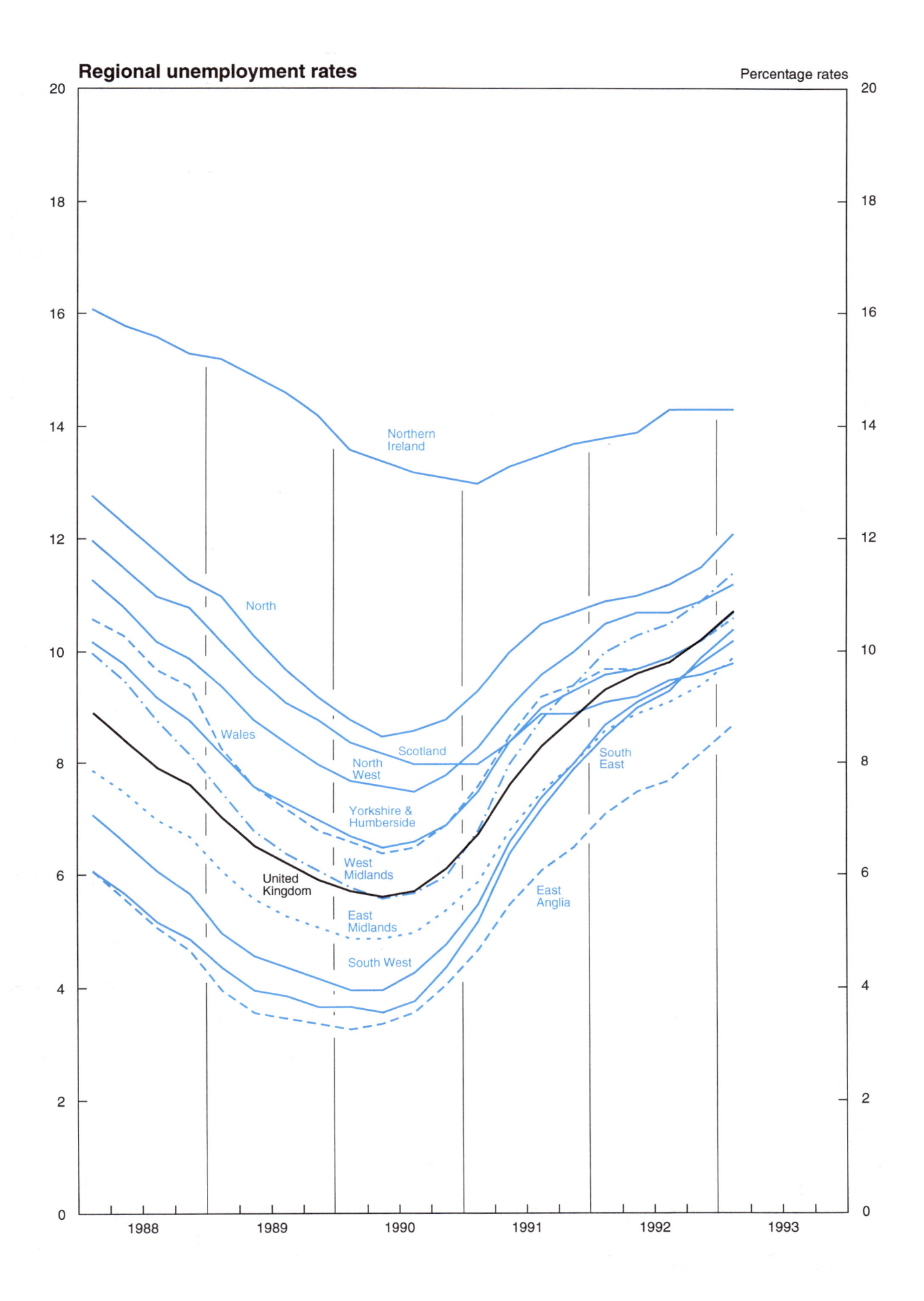

Regional unemployment rates

22 Labour Force Survey Economic activity[1]
Great Britain

Thousands, not seasonally adjusted

	In employment[2]					ILO unemployed	Total economically active	Economically inactive	All aged 16 and over
	Employees	Self-employed	On government employment and training programmes[3]	Unpaid family workers[4]	All[5]				
ALL									
	BASY	BATB	BATE	BATH	BATK	BATN	BATQ	BATT	BATW
Spring 1981	21 405	2 201	..	..	23 606	2 483[6]	26 089[6]	15 851[6]	41 940
Spring 1983	20 288	2 301	355	..	22 944	2 853[6]	25 797[6]	16 596[6]	42 394
Spring 1984	20 454	2 618	315	..	23 387	<u>2 916</u>	<u>26 304</u>	<u>16 371</u>	42 675
						3 094	26 481	16 194	
Spring 1985	20 629	2 714	396	..	23 739	2 968	26 708	16 244	42 952
Spring 1986	20 706	2 727	396	..	23 828	2 969	26 798	16 347	43 146
Spring 1987	20 762	2 997	488	..	24 247	2 879	27 126	16 303	43 429
Spring 1988	21 422	3 143	520	..	25 085	2 376	27 461	16 138	43 600
Spring 1989	22 055	3 426	481	..	25 962	1 978	27 941	15 804	43 745
Spring 1990	22 254	3 472	448	..	26 175	1 869	28 044	15 802	43 846
Spring 1991	21 876	3 318	408	..	25 601	2 302	27 903	16 000	43 903
Spring 1992	21 396	3 131	357	179	25 064	2 649	27 713	16 342	44 054
Summer 1992	21 485	3 135	330	176	25 127	2 797	27 923	16 156	44 079
Autumn 1992	21 353	3 091	344	179	24 967	2 801	27 768	16 331	44 099
Winter 1992	21 129	3 046	326	154	24 655	2 920	27 575	16 515	44 090
Spring 1993	21 185	3 103	337	148	24 773	2 804	27 577	16 568	44 145
Summer 1993	21 378	3 109	310	153	24 950	2 894	27 844	16 324	44 168
Estimated changes									
Spring 1993 - Summer 1993	193	7	-27	7	177	90	267	244	23
Per cent	*0.9*	*7*	*-7.9*	*7*	*0.7*	*3.2*	*1.0*	*-1.5*	*0.1*
MALE									
	BASZ	BATC	BATF	BATI	BATL	BATO	BATR	BATU	BATX
Spring 1981	12 348	1 745	..	..	14 093	1 560[6]	15 653[6]	4 434[6]	20 087
Spring 1983	11 601	1 751	212	..	13 565	1 815[6]	15 379[6]	4 952[6]	20 332
Spring 1984	11 537	1 978	195	..	13 710	<u>1 777</u>	<u>15 487</u>	<u>5 002</u>	20 489
						1 838	15 548	4 942	
Spring 1985	11 572	2 029	252	..	13 853	1 788	15 642	4 996	20 637
Spring 1986	11 491	2 047	268	..	13 806	1 786	15 592	5 155	20 748
Spring 1987	11 403	2 235	313	..	13 951	1 717	15 669	5 217	20 886
Spring 1988	11 728	2 358	327	..	14 413	1 398	15 811	5 168	20 980
Spring 1989	11 866	2 608	303	..	14 777	1 148	15 924	5 141	21 065
Spring 1990	11 943	2 628	289	..	14 860	1 091	15 950	5 183	21 133
Spring 1991	11 647	2 512	248	..	14 407	1 434	15 841	5 327	21 168
Spring 1992	11 248	2 353	236	53	13 890	1 785	15 676	5 579	21 255
Summer 1992	11 341	2 352	221	53	13 966	1 867	15 833	5 435	21 268
Autumn 1992	11 182	2 321	222	55	13 779	1 873	15 652	5 630	21 282
Winter 1992	11 012	2 295	207	46	13 560	1 981	15 541	5 741	21 282
Spring 1993	11 026	2 302	222	41	13 591	1 904	15 495	5 824	21 319
Summer 1993	11 173	2 318	210	46	13 748	1 923	15 671	5 662	21 333
Estimated changes									
Spring 1993 - Summer 1993	147	16	-12	7	157	19	176	-162	14
Per cent	*1.3*	*0.7*	*-5.3*	*7*	*1.2*	*1.0*	*1.1*	*-2.8*	*0.1*
FEMALE									
	BATA	BATD	BATG	BATJ	BATM	BATP	BATS	BATV	BATY
Spring 1981	9 057	455	..	..	9 512	923[6]	10 435[6]	11 417[6]	21 852
Spring 1983	8 687	550	143	..	9 379	1 039[6]	10 418[6]	11 644[6]	22 062
Spring 1984	8 918	639	120	..	9 678	<u>1 139</u>	<u>10 816</u>	<u>11 369</u>	22 186
						1 256	10 933	11 253	
Spring 1985	9 057	685	144	..	9 886	1 180	11 066	11 249	22 315
Spring 1986	9 215	680	128	..	10 023	1 182	11 205	11 192	22 398
Spring 1987	9 358	762	175	..	10 296	1 161	11 457	11 086	22 543
Spring 1988	9 694	785	193	..	10 672	978	11 650	10 970	22 620
Spring 1989	10 189	819	178	..	11 186	831	12 016	10 664	22 680
Spring 1990	10 311	845	159	..	11 315	779	12 094	10 620	22 713
Spring 1991	10 229	806	160	..	11 194	868	12 062	10 673	22 735
Spring 1992	10 148	778	121	126	11 174	863	12 037	10 762	22 799
Summer 1992	10 144	783	109	124	11 160	930	12 090	10 721	22 811
Autumn 1992	10 171	770	122	124	11 188	928	12 116	10 701	22 817
Winter 1992	10 117	751	119	108	11 095	939	12 034	10 774	22 808
Spring 1993	10 158	801	115	108	11 182	900	12 082	10 744	22 826
Summer 1993	10 205	790	100	107	11 201	971	12 173	10 662	22 835
Estimated changes									
Spring 1993 - Summer 1993	46	-11	-15	7	20	71	91	-82	7
Per cent	*0.5*	*-1.3*	*-13.1*	*7*	*0.2*	*7.9*	*0.8*	*-0.8*	*7*

1 Since 1984 the definitions used in the *Labour Force Survey (LFS)* have been fully in line with international recommendations. For details see "The quarterly Labour Force Survey: a new dimension to labour market statistics", *Employment Gazette*, October 1992, pp 483 - 490.
2 People in full time education who also did some paid work in the reference week have been classified as in employment since spring 1983.
3 Those on employment and training programmes have been classified as in employment since spring 1983.
4 Unpaid family workers have been classified as in employment since spring 1992.
5 Includes those who did not state whether they were employees or self-employed.
6 The Labour Force (LF) definition of unemployment and inactivity applies for these years. LF unemployment is based on a one week job search period, rather than four weeks with the ILO definition.
7 Less than 10 000 in cell: estimate not shown.

Source: Employment Department

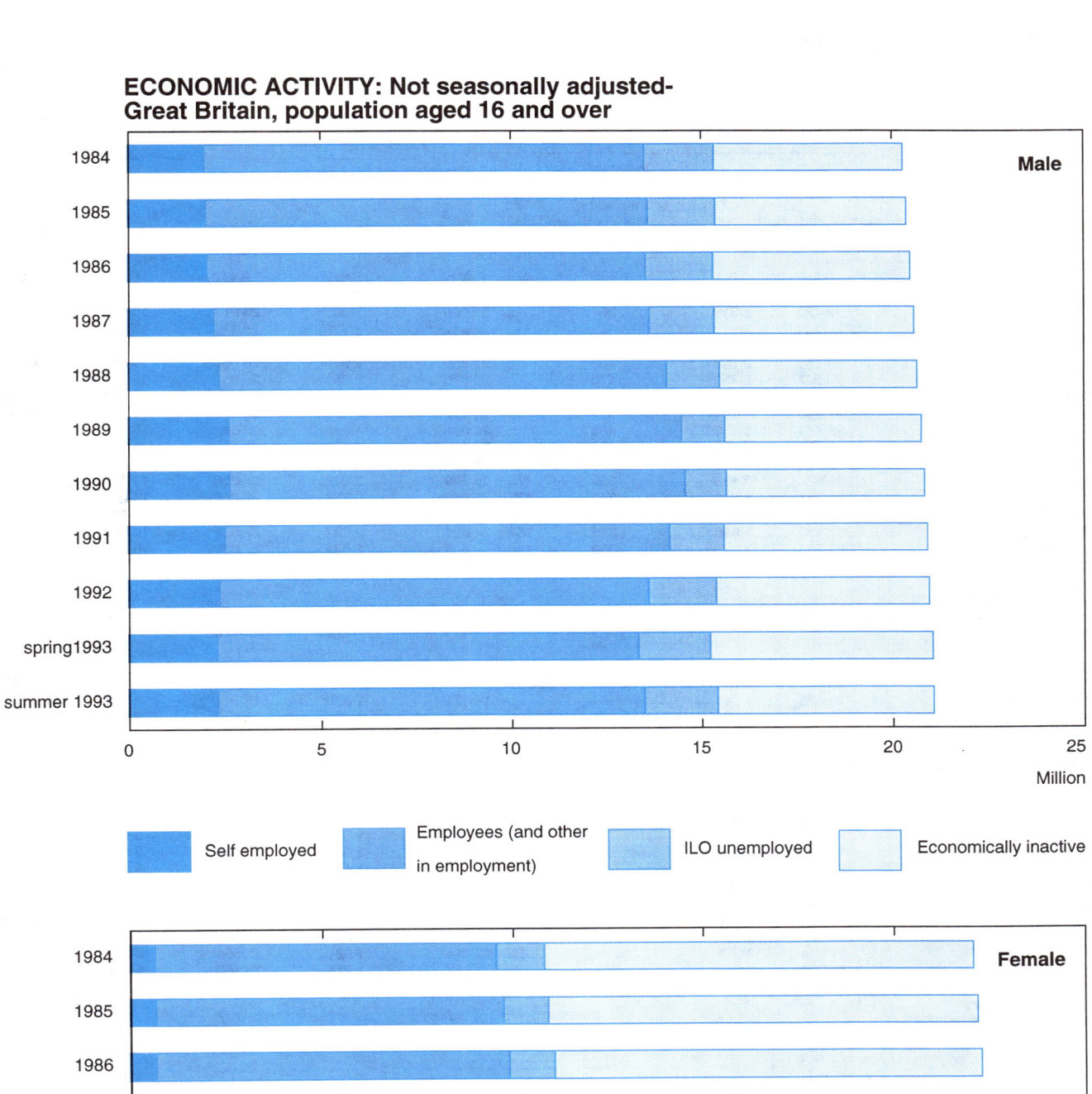

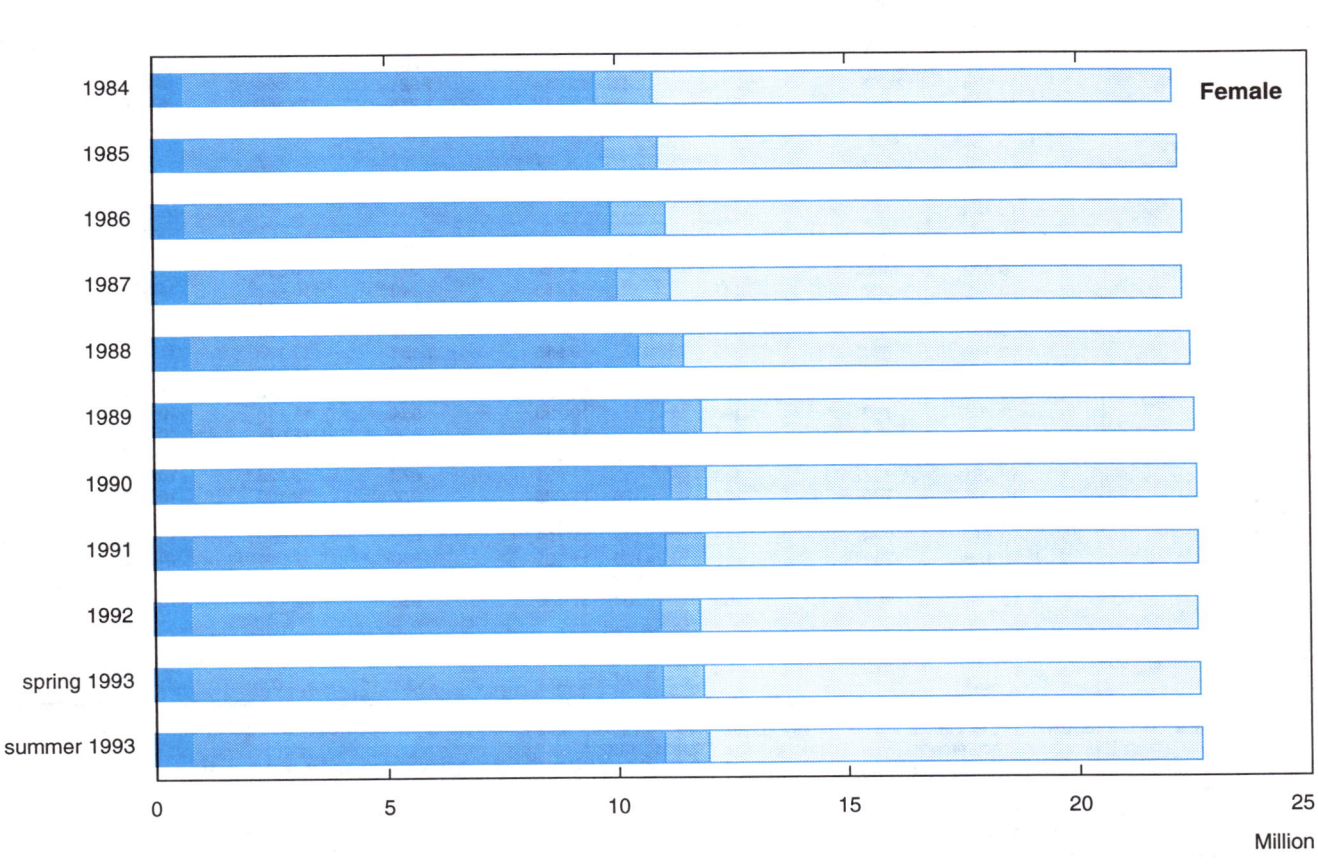

ECONOMIC ACTIVITY: Not seasonally adjusted – Great Britain, population aged 16 and over

Male

Female

Legend: Self employed | Employees (and other in employment) | ILO unemployed | Economically inactive

47

23 Labour Force Survey Economic activity[1]
Great Britain

Thousands, seasonally adjusted[8]

	In employment[2]					ILO unemployed	Total economically active	Economically inactive	All aged 16 and over
	Employees	Self-employed	On government employment and training programmes[3]	Unpaid family workers[4]	All[5]				
ALL									
	BAVS	BAVT	BAVU	BAVV	BAVW	BAVX	BAVY	BAVZ	BAWA
Spring 1981	21 550	2 211	–	..	23 760	2 494[6]	26 255[6]	15 690[6]	41 944
Spring 1983	20 420	2 310	368	..	23 098	2 865[6]	25 963[6]	16 435[6]	42 398
Spring 1984	20 587	2 627	328	..	23 542	2 928	26 470	16 210	42 680
						3 105	26 647	16 033	
Spring 1985	20 758	2 723	408	..	23 889	2 980	26 869	16 085	42 954
Spring 1986	20 827	2 739	410	..	23 976	2 981	26 957	16 191	43 148
Spring 1987	20 878	3 009	502	..	24 389	2 890	27 279	16 151	43 430
Spring 1988	21 535	3 154	534	..	25 222	2 385	27 607	15 993	43 600
Spring 1989	22 171	3 433	495	..	26 099	1 983	28 082	15 663	43 745
Spring 1990	22 379	3 477	462	..	26 318	1 871	28 189	15 658	43 847
Spring 1991	22 008	3 323	420	..	25 751	2 301	28 051	15 854	43 905
Spring 1992	21 524	3 138	369	179	25 209	2 649	27 858	16 199	44 057
Summer 1992	21 387	3 136	348	176	25 048	2 758	27 806	16 263	44 069
Autumn 1992	21 262	3 078	331	179	24 850	2 837	27 687	16 408	44 096
Winter 1992	21 183	3 046	312	154	24 694	2 931	27 625	16 461	44 086
Spring 1993	21 266	3 091	339	148	24 845	2 839	27 684	16 449	44 133
Summer 1993	21 250	3 100	326	153	24 829	2 865	27 693	16 461	44 154
Estimated changes									
Spring 1993 - Spring 1993	-16	7	-14	7	-16	26	10	12	22
Per cent	-0.1	7	-4.1	7	-0.1	0.9	0.0	0.1	0.0
MALE									
	BAWB	BAWC	BAWD	BAWE	BAWF	BAWG	BAWH	BAWI	BAWJ
Spring 1981	12 426	1 748	–	..	14 174	1 570[6]	15 744[6]	4 344[6]	20 088
Spring 1983	11 671	1 753	221	..	13 645	1 825[6]	15 470[6]	4 862[6]	20 332
Spring 1984	11 607	1 980	203	..	13 790	1 788	15 578	4 912	20 490
						1 848	15 639	4 851	
Spring 1985	11 639	2 032	260	..	13 931	1 798	15 730	4 908	20 637
Spring 1986	11 554	2 055	278	..	13 886	1 796	15 682	5 066	20 748
Spring 1987	11 462	2 246	324	..	14 032	1 724	15 756	5 130	20 886
Spring 1988	11 783	2 372	338	..	14 492	1 401	15 893	5 087	20 980
Spring 1989	11 924	2 620	314	..	14 858	1 146	16 004	5 061	21 065
Spring 1990	12 006	2 641	300	..	14 946	1 085	16 031	5 103	21 134
Spring 1991	11 716	2 527	257	..	14 500	1 424	15 924	5 247	21 170
Spring 1992	11 318	2 368	245	53	13 983	1 775	15 758	5 499	21 257
Summer 1992	11 260	2 351	230	53	13 894	1 850	15 743	5 522	21 265
Autumn 1992	11 152	2 300	216	55	13 722	1 915	15 637	5 639	21 277
Winter 1992	11 055	2 294	199	46	13 594	1 982	15 575	5 705	21 281
Spring 1993	11 074	2 305	224	41	13 644	1 921	15 564	5 747	21 311
Summer 1993	11 070	2 310	217	46	13 643	1 915	15 558	5 766	21 325
Estimated changes									
Spring 1993 - Summer 1993	7	7	7	7	7	7	7	20	13
Per cent	7	7	7	7	7	7	7	0.3	0.1
FEMALE									
	BAWK	BAWL	BAWM	BAWN	BAWO	BAWP	BAWQ	BAWR	BAWS
Spring 1981	9 123	463	–	..	9 586	924[6]	10 510[6]	11 346[6]	21 856
Spring 1983	8 749	557	147	..	9 453	1 040[6]	10 493[6]	11 573[6]	22 066
Spring 1984	8 980	647	125	..	9 751	1 140	10 891	11 298	22 190
						1 257	11 008	11 181	
Spring 1985	9 119	691	148	..	9 958	1 181	11 139	11 177	22 317
Spring 1986	9 273	684	132	..	10 090	1 186	11 275	11 125	22 400
Spring 1987	9 416	763	178	..	10 357	1 166	11 523	11 021	22 544
Spring 1988	9 752	782	196	..	10 730	984	11 714	10 906	22 620
Spring 1989	10 247	813	181	..	11 241	836	12 077	10 602	22 680
Spring 1990	10 373	836	163	..	11 372	785	12 158	10 556	22 713
Spring 1991	10 291	797	163	..	11 251	877	12 128	10 607	22 735
Spring 1992	10 206	770	124	126	11 226	874	12 100	10 701	22 801
Summer 1992	10 127	785	119	124	11 154	909	12 063	10 741	22 804
Autumn 1992	10 111	778	115	124	11 128	922	12 050	10 769	22 819
Winter 1992	10 128	752	113	108	11 101	949	12 050	10 755	22 805
Spring 1993	10 193	786	115	108	11 201	918	12 119	10 702	22 821
Summer 1993	10 180	791	109	107	11 186	950	12 135	10 695	22 830
Estimated changes									
Spring 1993 - Summer 1993	-13	7	7	7	-16	32	16	7	7
Per cent	-0.1	7	7	7	-0.1	3.4	0.1	7	7

1 Since 1984 the definitions used in the Labour Force Survey (LFS) have been fully in line with international recommendations. For details see "The quarterly Labour Force Survey; a new dimension to labour market statistics", Employment Gazette, October 1992, pp 483-490.
2 People in full time education who also did some paid work in the reference week have been classified as in employment since spring 1983.
3 Those on employment and training programmes have been classified as in employment since spring 1983.
4 Unpaid family workers have been classified as in employment since spring 1992.
5 Includes those who did not state whether they were employees or self-employed.
6 The Labour Force (LF) definition of unemployment and inactivity applies for these years. LF employment is based on a one week job search period, rather than four weeks with the ILO definition.
7 Less than 10 000 in cell: estimate not shown.
8 The seasonally adjusted estimates may be subject to revision as more quarterly data becomes available.

Source: Employment Department

24 Labour Force Survey
Economic activity[1] by age
Great Britain

Thousands, not seasonally adjusted

	All aged 16 and over			Age groups				50 - 64 (Male) 50 - 59 (Female)	65 and over (Male) 60 and over (Female)
	All	Male	Female	16 - 19	20 - 24	25 - 34	35 - 49		
In employment									
	BATK	BATL	BATM	BAUO	BAUT	BAUY	BAVD	BAVI	BAVN
Spring 1985	23 739	13 853	9 886	1 976	3 075	5 280	8 053	4 684	672
Spring 1986	23 828	13 806	10 023	1 927	3 086	5 412	8 166	4 598	640
Spring 1987	24 247	13 951	10 296	1 985	3 186	5 624	8 262	4 545	644
Spring 1988	25 085	14 413	10 672	2 072	3 227	5 973	8 570	4 575	668
Spring 1989	25 962	14 777	11 186	2 081	3 350	6 311	8 785	4 669	765
Spring 1990	26 175	14 860	11 315	1 917	3 264	6 563	8 950	4 717	764
Spring 1991	25 601	14 407	11 194	1 707	3 022	6 537	8 958	4 617	761
Spring 1992	25 064	13 890	11 174	1 505	2 826	6 471	8 932	4 535	794
Summer 1992	25 127	13 966	11 160	1 548	2 858	6 489	8 927	4 518	788
Autumn 1992	24 967	13 779	11 188	1 441	2 812	6 501	8 975	4 477	760
Winter 1992	24 655	13 560	11 095	1 370	2 720	6 454	8 909	4 464	737
Spring 1993	24 773	13 591	11 182	1 307	2 702	6 557	8 983	4 468	757
Summer 1993	24 950	13 748	11 201	1 387	2 753	6 597	8 992	4 469	751
ILO unemployed									
	BATN	BATO	BATP	BAUP	BAUU	BAUZ	BAVE	BAVJ	BAVO
Spring 1985	2 968	1 788	1 180	484	592	730	702	411	49
Spring 1986	2 969	1 786	1 182	495	607	754	682	406	46
Spring 1987	2 879	1 717	1 161	434	523	762	680	437	42
Spring 1988	2 376	1 398	978	326	437	621	551	401	40
Spring 1989	1 978	1 148	831	239	352	530	455	349	52
Spring 1990	1 869	1 091	779	250	325	501	444	314	35
Spring 1991	2 302	1 434	868	298	439	620	553	352	40
Spring 1992	2 649	1 785	863	296	494	729	684	414	31
Summer 1992	2 797	1 867	930	420	537	733	668	411	28
Autumn 1992	2 801	1 873	928	351	523	758	692	447	31
Winter 1992	2 920	1 981	939	322	541	793	752	484	28
Spring 1993	2 804	1 904	900	310	528	754	709	471	33
Summer 1993	2 894	1 923	971	418	562	741	709	441	23
Economically inactive									
	BATT	BATU	BATV	BAUQ	BAUV	BAVA	BAVF	BAVK	BAVP
Spring 1985	16 244	4 996	11 249	1 018	841	1 560	1 636	2 260	8 930
Spring 1986	16 347	5 155	11 192	971	854	1 552	1 664	2 273	9 034
Spring 1987	16 303	5 217	11 086	931	832	1 510	1 666	2 241	9 122
Spring 1988	16 138	5 168	10 970	881	822	1 477	1 584	2 232	9 142
Spring 1989	15 804	5 141	10 664	840	717	1 425	1 570	2 176	9 076
Spring 1990	15 802	5 183	10 620	859	727	1 417	1 519	2 156	9 125
Spring 1991	16 000	5 327	10 673	854	798	1 470	1 557	2 165	9 156
Spring 1992	16 342	5 579	10 762	1 011	899	1 534	1 555	2 194	9 148
Summer 1992	16 156	5 435	10 721	809	804	1 545	1 610	2 218	9 170
Autumn 1992	16 331	5 630	10 701	954	827	1 524	1 564	2 245	9 217
Winter 1992	16 515	5 741	10 774	1 021	872	1 553	1 592	2 239	9 236
Spring 1993	16 568	5 824	10 744	1 073	872	1 520	1 606	2 251	9 246
Summer 1993	16 324	5 662	10 662	858	758	1 514	1 626	2 299	9 270
Economic activity rate (per cent)[2]									
	BAUI	BAUJ	BAUK	BAUR	BAUW	BAVB	BAVG	BAVL	BAVQ
Spring 1985	62.2	75.8	49.6	70.7	81.3	79.4	84.3	69.3	7.5
Spring 1986	62.1	75.2	50.0	71.4	81.2	79.9	84.2	68.8	7.1
Spring 1987	62.5	75.0	50.8	72.2	81.7	80.9	84.3	69.0	7.0
Spring 1988	63.0	75.4	51.5	73.1	81.7	81.7	85.2	69.0	7.2
Spring 1989	63.9	75.6	53.0	73.4	83.8	82.8	85.5	69.8	8.3
Spring 1990	64.0	75.5	53.2	71.6	83.2	83.3	86.1	70.0	8.1
Spring 1991	63.6	74.8	53.1	70.1	81.3	83.0	85.9	69.6	8.0
Spring 1992	62.9	73.8	52.8	64.0	78.7	82.4	86.1	69.3	8.3
Summer 1992	63.3	74.4	53.0	70.9	80.9	82.4	85.6	69.0	8.2
Autumn 1992	63.0	73.5	53.1	65.2	80.1	82.6	86.1	68.7	7.9
Winter 1992	62.5	73.0	52.8	62.3	78.9	82.4	85.8	68.8	7.7
Spring 1993	62.5	72.7	52.9	60.1	78.7	82.8	85.8	68.7	7.9
Summer 1993	63.0	73.5	53.3	67.8	81.4	82.9	85.6	68.1	7.7
ILO unemployment rate (per cent)[3]									
	BAUL	BAUM	BAUN	BAUS	BAUX	BAVC	BAVH	BAVM	BAVR
Spring 1985	11.1	11.4	10.7	19.7	16.2	12.2	8.0	8.1	6.8
Spring 1986	11.1	11.5	10.6	20.4	16.4	12.2	7.7	8.1	6.7
Spring 1987	10.6	11.0	10.1	17.9	14.1	11.9	7.6	8.8	6.2
Spring 1988	8.7	8.8	8.4	13.6	11.9	9.4	6.0	8.1	5.6
Spring 1989	7.1	7.2	6.9	10.3	9.5	7.8	4.9	7.0	6.3
Spring 1990	6.7	6.8	6.4	11.5	9.1	7.1	4.7	6.2	4.3
Spring 1991	8.3	9.1	7.2	14.9	12.7	8.7	5.8	7.1	5.0
Spring 1992	9.6	11.4	7.2	16.4	14.9	10.1	7.1	8.4	3.8
Summer 1992	10.0	11.8	7.7	21.3	15.8	10.1	7.0	8.3	3.5
Autumn 1992	10.1	12.0	7.7	19.6	15.7	10.4	7.2	9.1	3.9
Winter 1992	10.6	12.7	7.8	19.0	16.6	10.9	7.8	9.8	3.7
Spring 1993	10.2	12.3	7.4	19.2	16.3	10.3	7.3	9.5	4.1
Summer 1993	10.4	12.3	8.0	23.1	17.0	10.1	7.3	9.0	3.0

1 See corresponding note to table 22.
2 The economic activity rate is the percentage of people aged 16 and over who are economically active.
3 The ILO unemployment rate is the percentage of economically active people who are unemployed on the ILO measure.

Source: Employment Department

25 Average earnings

	Average earnings (GB)[1]								Wages and salaries per unit of output 1990 = 100	
	Whole economy+	Underlying trend[2]	Production industries	Underlying trend[2]	Manufacturing industry	Underlying trend[2]	Service industries	Underlying trend[2]	Whole economy[3]	Manufacturing industry
1985 = 100	DNGA		DNGC		DNGE		DNGG		DJDO	DMGH
1986	107.9		108.0		107.7		107.7		74.5	85.1
1987	116.3		116.7		116.3		116.0		77.8	87.1
1988	126.4		126.5		126.2		126.2		83.1	89.4
1990 = 100	DNAB		DNAF		DNAD		DNDV			
1989	91.1		91.3		91.4		91.2		91.0	93.2
1990	100.0		100.0		100.0		100.0		100.0	100.0
1991	108.0		108.6		108.2		107.7		107.0	106.9
1992	114.6		115.8		115.3		114.1		111.7	108.6
1989 Q1	88.3		88.4		88.7		88.6		87.7	90.6
Q2	90.0		90.3		90.5		90.2		89.9	93.0
Q3	91.9		92.3		92.4		91.9		92.1	94.0
Q4	94.2		94.2		94.2		94.2		94.5	95.4
1990 Q1	96.5		96.6		96.6		96.6		96.6	97.2
Q2	99.1		98.8		98.8		99.2		98.8	98.6
Q3	101.2		101.3		101.3		101.2		101.6	100.9
Q4	103.1		103.2		103.2		103.0		103.0	103.3
1991 Q1	105.2		105.6		105.2		105.1		105.3	105.3
Q2	107.0		107.7		107.2		106.4		106.6	107.4
Q3	109.2		109.6		109.2		109.0		107.7	106.9
Q4	110.6		111.5		111.2		110.2		108.4	107.9
1992 Q1	113.4		114.7		114.2		112.9		112.0	110.2
Q2	113.7		114.3		113.6		113.4		112.1	108.4
Q3	114.9		116.1		115.9		114.5		111.1	108.3
Q4	116.4		118.1		117.6		115.7		111.5	107.4
1993 Q1	118.0		120.1		119.6		117.1		112.3	107.2
Q2	117.9		119.8		119.2		116.8		112.1	106.3
Q3	118.7		121.2		121.0		117.6		112.3	107.6
		DNEM		DNEN		DNEO		DNDX		
1991 Jul	107.8	7.75	108.3	8.50	108.1	8.25	107.6	7.50		105.8
Aug	109.8	7.75	110.0	8.25	109.8	8.00	109.6	7.50		107.6
Sep	110.0	7.75	110.6	8.00	109.8	8.00	109.8	7.50		107.3
Oct	110.2	7.50	111.0	8.50	110.8	8.00	110.0	7.25		108.2
Nov	111.0	7.50	111.7	8.25	111.3	8.00	111.0	7.25		107.2
Dec	110.5	7.25	111.9	8.00	111.6	7.75	109.5	7.00		108.4
1992 Jan	111.9	7.25	113.0	7.75	112.5	7.75	111.8	7.00		109.6
Feb	113.3	7.50	113.9	8.25	113.4	8.25	113.0	7.25		109.0
Mar	114.9	7.25	117.2	7.75	116.7	7.75	113.9	7.25		111.9
Apr	113.1	7.00	113.1	7.50	112.1	7.50	113.1	7.00		106.8
May	114.1	6.25	115.0	6.50	114.4	6.25	113.6	6.50		110.1
Jun	113.8	6.25	114.8	6.50	114.2	6.25	113.4	6.25		108.3
Jul	113.9	6.00	115.2	6.50	114.8	6.25	113.5	6.00		108.3
Aug	115.3	5.75	116.7	6.25	116.9	6.00	114.7	5.25		108.9
Sep	115.4	5.50	116.4	6.00	116.1	6.00	115.2	5.50		107.7
Oct	117.0	5.25	118.1	5.75	117.8	5.75	116.7	5.25		107.7
Nov	116.1	5.00	117.9	5.75	117.6	5.75	115.6	4.75		107.4
Dec	116.0	4.75	118.2	5.50	117.5	5.50	114.9	4.50		107.2
1993 Jan	117.0	4.75	118.6	5.25	118.1	5.25	116.7	4.50		106.4
Feb	118.2	4.50	119.6	5.00	119.2	5.00	117.5	4.25		106.3
Mar	118.7	4.00	122.2	5.00	121.6	5.00	117.1	3.75		108.9
Apr	117.6	4.00	118.9	5.00	118.0	5.00	116.8	3.25		105.4
May	118.3	3.75	120.4	5.00	119.9	5.00	117.0	3.00		105.6
Jun	117.8	3.75	120.2	5.00	119.6	5.00	116.5	2.75		107.9
Jul	118.3	3.75	121.0	4.75	120.5	4.75	117.3	2.75		107.1
Aug	118.9	3.25	121.0	4.50	121.1	4.50	117.7	2.75		107.8
Sep	118.8†	3.00	121.7	4.50	121.4	4.25	117.7†	2.25		107.9
Oct	119.4†	3.00	122.6	4.25†	122.3†	4.25	118.2†	2.25		108.1†
Nov	119.4	3.00	122.5	4.25	122.0	4.00	118.3	2.25		107.5

Note: For a detailed account of the revised Average Earnings Index please see the article in *Employment Gazette*, November 1989, p. 606 - 612.

1 The seasonal adjustment factors currently used are based on data up to January 1988.
2 Estimated to the nearest quarter of one percentage point. For the derivation of recent underlying changes see 'News Brief' item in *Employment Gazette*, September 1991.
3 The method for calculating whole economy unit wage costs is described in *Employment Gazette*, May 1986.

Sources: Department of Employment; Central Statistical Office

Earnings, wages, retail prices and output

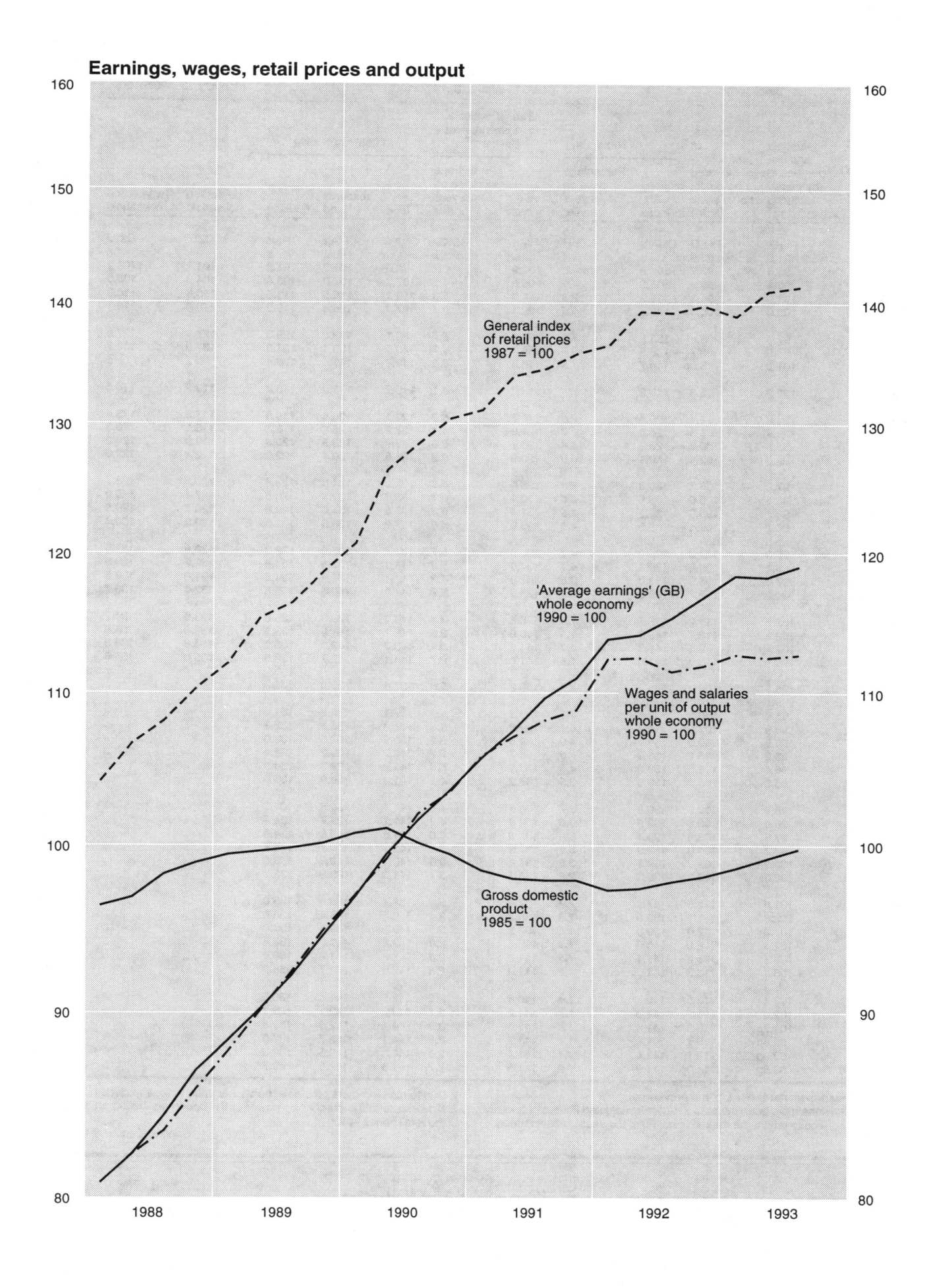

26 Prices

	Producer price index (1990=100)		Retail prices index (RPI) (NSA) (January 13, 1987=100)							Pensioner price index[2] (NSA) (January 13, 1987=100)		Purchasing power of the pound[3] (NSA) (1985=100)
	Materials and fuel purchased by manufacturing industry[1]	Output: all manufactured products: home sales (NSA)	All items		All items excluding mortgage interest payments		All items excluding			One-person household	Two-person household	
			Index	Percentage increase on a year earlier	Index	Percentage increase on a year earlier	food	seasonal food	housing			
	PLKZ	PLLU	CHAW	CZBH	CHMK	CDKQ	CHAY	CHAX	CHAZ	CZIF	CZIU	FJAK
1986	91.6	83.8	..	3.4	..	..	102.0	101.9	101.6	101.1	101.2	96
1987	93.5	86.7	101.9	4.2	101.9	..	102.0	101.9	101.6	101.1	101.2	92
1988	96.4	89.8	106.9	4.9	106.6	4.6	107.3	107.0	105.8	104.8	105.0	88
1989	101.5	94.1	115.2	7.8	112.9	5.9	116.1	115.5	111.5	110.6	110.9	81
1990	100.0	100.0	126.1	9.5	122.1	8.1	127.4	126.4	119.2	118.9	119.1	74
1991	97.7	105.4	133.5	5.9	130.3	6.7	135.1	133.8	128.3	127.4	127.8	70
1992	97.5r	108.7	138.5	3.7	136.4	4.7	140.5	139.1	134.3	131.8	132.7	67
1993	101.9p	113.0p	140.7	1.6	140.5	3.0	142.6	141.4	138.4	..	..	..
1989 Q4	102.2	95.8	118.3	7.6	115.2	6.1	119.2	118.6	113.7	113.2	113.4	79.0
1990 Q1	101.5	97.4	120.4	7.8	116.7	6.2	121.1	120.4	115.3	115.3	115.4	78.0
Q2	99.6	99.5	126.0	9.7	121.9	8.1	127.2	126.1	118.5	118.1	118.3	74.0
Q3	99.3	100.7	128.1	10.4	123.7	8.9	129.7	128.5	120.3	119.9	120.2	73.0
Q4	99.3	102.4	130.1	10.0	125.9	9.3	131.8	130.4	122.6	122.4	122.6	72.0
1991 Q1	97.8	103.7	130.8	8.6	126.6	8.5	132.2	131.0	123.4	123.8	123.7	71.0
Q2	98.3	105.6	133.6	6.0	130.1	6.7	135.0	133.8	128.5	127.4	128.0	70.0
Q3	98.1	105.9	134.2	4.8	131.4	6.2	135.8	134.6	129.8	128.5	128.9	70.0
Q4	96.7	106.4	135.5	4.2	133.0	5.6	137.2	135.8	131.5	129.9	130.4	69.0
1992 Q1	96.3	107.3	136.2	4.1	133.8	5.7	137.7	136.5	132.3	130.8	131.5	69.0
Q2	96.4	108.8	139.1	4.1	137.0	5.3	141.1	139.6	134.8	132.2	133.2	67.0
Q3	97.0	108.9	139.0	3.6	137.0	4.3	141.4	139.9	134.5	131.6	132.6	67.0
Q4	100.2r	109.7	139.6	3.0	137.9	3.7	141.9	140.4	135.6	132.6	133.7	67.0
1993 Q1	102.6	111.2	138.7	1.8	138.3	3.4	140.3	139.3	136.0	133.6	134.7	68.0
Q2	102.8	113.1	140.9	1.3	140.9	2.8	142.7	141.5	138.8	135.0	136.8	67.0
Q3	102.4p	113.5	141.3	1.7	141.2	3.1	143.3	142.1	139.1	134.8	136.8	66.0
Q4	99.8p	113.9p	141.8	1.6	141.6	2.7	144.1	142.7	139.5	135.0	136.8	..
1991 Dec	96.5	106.3	135.7	4.5	133.2	5.8	137.4	136.0	131.8	..	..	69.0
1992 Jan	95.9	106.8	135.6	4.1	133.1	5.6	137.1	135.9	131.6	..	..	69.0
Feb	96.9	107.2	136.3	4.1	133.8	5.6	137.8	136.6	132.3	..	..	69.0
Mar	96.0	108.0	136.7	4.0	134.5	5.7	138.2	137.0	133.0	..	..	69.0
Apr	96.5	108.6	138.8	4.3	136.7	5.7	140.7	139.2	134.4	..	..	68.0
May	96.6	108.8	139.3	4.3	137.1	5.3	141.2	139.7	134.9	..	..	67.0
Jun	96.2	108.9	139.3	3.9	137.2	4.8	141.3	139.9	135.0	..	..	67.0
Jul	96.7	108.9	138.8	3.7	136.7	4.4	141.1	139.6	134.3	..	..	68.0
Aug	96.6	108.8	138.9	3.6	136.9	4.2	141.2	139.7	134.4	..	..	68.0
Sep	97.6	108.9	139.4	3.6	137.3	4.0	141.8	140.3	134.9	..	..	67.0
Oct	99.2	109.3	139.9	3.6	137.8	3.8	142.3	140.7	135.5	..	..	67.0
Nov	100.9	109.8	139.7	3.0	137.9	3.6	142.1	140.5	135.6	..	..	67.0
Dec	100.6r	109.9	139.2	2.6	138.1	3.7	141.3	139.9	135.7	..	..	67.0
1993 Jan	101.6	110.6	137.9	1.7	137.4	3.2	139.7	138.6	135.0	..	..	68.0
Feb	102.8	111.1	138.8	1.8	138.3	3.4	140.5	139.4	136.0	..	..	68.0
Mar	103.3	112.0	139.3	1.9	139.2	3.5	140.8	139.8	137.0	..	..	68.0
Apr	102.5	112.9	140.6	1.3	140.6	2.9	142.5	141.3	138.4	..	..	67.0
May	102.7	113.2	141.1	1.3	141.0	2.8	142.8	141.6	139.0	..	..	67.0
Jun	103.1	113.3	141.0	1.2	141.0	2.8	142.9	141.7	138.9	..	..	67.0
Jul	103.1	113.5	140.7	1.4	140.6	2.9	142.6	141.5	138.5	..	..	67.0
Aug	102.8	113.5	141.3	1.7	141.2	3.1	143.2	142.1	139.1	..	..	66.0
Sep	101.2p	113.6	141.9	1.8	141.8	3.3	144.1	142.8	139.8	..	..	66.0
Oct	99.6p	113.7	141.8	1.4	141.7	2.8	144.1	142.7	139.6	..	..	66.0
Nov	99.9p	113.7p	141.6	1.4	141.4	2.5	144.0	142.5	139.3	..	..	66.0
Dec	99.8p	114.3p	141.9	1.9	141.8	2.7	144.3	142.8	139.7	..	..	66.0

Note: Figures marked with a 'p' are provisional.
1 Minor revisions have been made to seasonally adjusted figures previously published. These reflect the routine updating of the seasonal adjustment factor.
2 Due to measurement problems, pensioner price indices exclude housing costs.
3 Movements in the purchasing power of the pound are based on movements in the retail prices index.

Source: Central Statistical Office

CSO STATFAX
For the most up-to-date data on the retail prices and producer prices indexes, poll the following numbers from your fax machine:
0336 416037 (RPI), 0336 416042 (producer prices)
Calls charged at 36p per minute cheap rate, 48p per minute at all other times

Prices

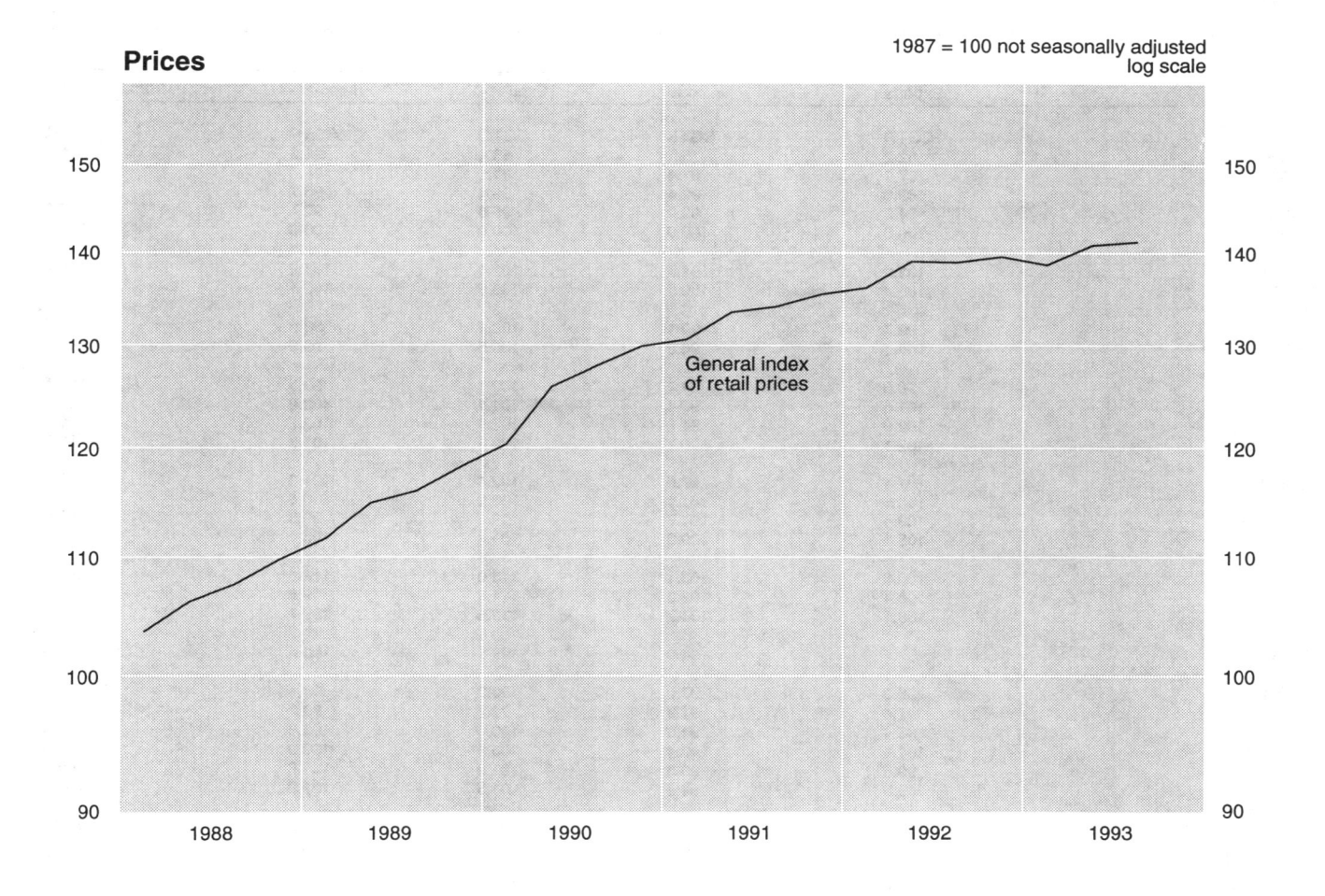

1987 = 100 not seasonally adjusted
log scale

General index of retail prices

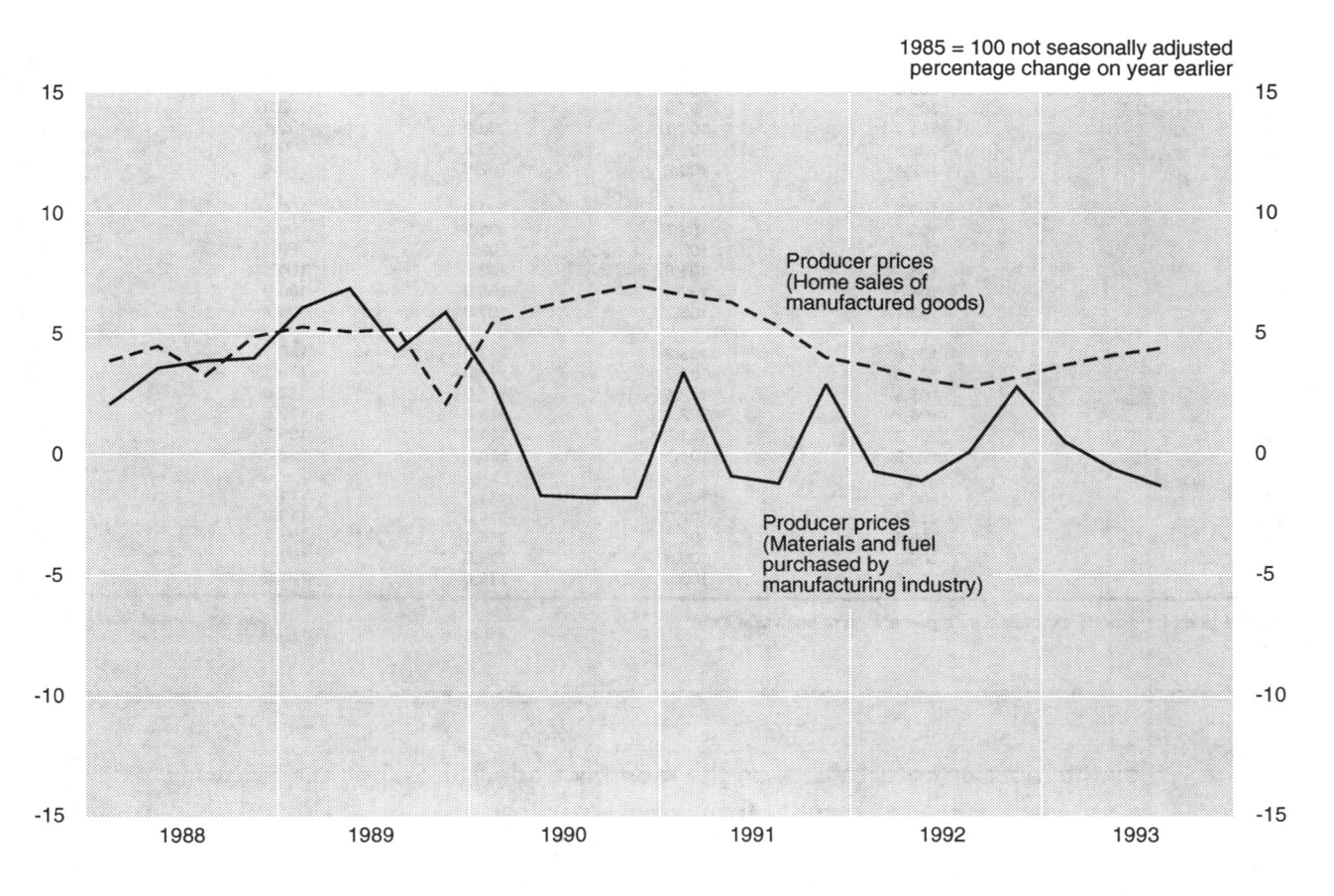

1985 = 100 not seasonally adjusted
percentage change on year earlier

Producer prices (Home sales of manufactured goods)

Producer prices (Materials and fuel purchased by manufacturing industry)

53

27 Visible trade (on a balance of payments basis)

1990 = 100

	Volume indices (SA)		Unit value indices (NSA)		
	Exports	Imports	Exports+	Imports+	Terms of trade[1]
	CGTR	CGTS	CGTO	CGTP	CGTQ
1986	82.2	75.5†	88.4	91.9	96.2
1987	87.1	81.4	91.5	94.6	96.7
1988	89.0	92.4	92.4	93.7	98.6
1989	94.2	99.9	96.6	97.7	98.9
1990	100.0	100.0	100.0	100.0	100.0
1991	101.2	94.7	101.4	101.2	100.2
1992	103.4	100.9	103.5	102.1	101.4
1990 Q3	99.7	99.1	100.1	98.3	101.8
Q4	100.1	96.8	100.5	99.9	100.6
1991 Q1	98.0	94.4	100.1	99.5	100.6
Q2	101.6	93.4	101.1	100.9	100.2
Q3	102.9	94.8	102.9	102.7	100.2
Q4	102.1	96.1	101.4	101.8	99.6
1992 Q1	101.4	97.5	102.4	101.3	101.1
Q2	103.5	101.1	103.2	100.6	102.6
Q3	103.4	101.7	102.8	99.8	103.0
Q4	105.4	103.3	105.4	106.7	98.8
1993 Q1	106.6†	103.1†	113.0†	112.1†	100.8†
Q2	106.4	102.6	111.6	109.6	101.8
Q3	108.1	104.7	113.8	109.7	103.7
1990 Dec	97.7	94.0	99.9	100.4	99.5
1991 Jan	98.3	97.2	100.3	99.4	100.9
Feb	97.4	91.3	99.7	99.2	100.5
Mar	98.4	94.6	100.4	99.8	100.6
Apr	100.1	92.4	100.9	100.9	100.0
May	99.3	93.8	101.0	100.6	100.4
Jun	105.3	94.1	101.5	101.2	100.3
Jul	102.6	92.2	103.4	103.2	100.2
Aug	104.9	96.1	103.5	102.6	100.9
Sep	101.2	96.1	101.7	102.4	99.3
Oct	100.4	94.7	101.2	102.0	99.2
Nov	100.8	96.0	101.4	102.1	99.3
Dec	105.1	97.5	101.6	101.4	100.2
1992 Jan	96.8	94.7	102.6	100.3	102.3
Feb	103.9	100.4	102.5	101.3	101.2
Mar	103.5	97.3	102.0	102.2	99.8
Apr	101.9	101.1	103.9	102.4	101.5
May	106.2	101.9	103.2	100.0	103.2
Jun	102.4	100.2	102.5	99.4	103.1
Jul	103.5	101.6	102.9	100.4	102.5
Aug	103.4	102.7	103.5	99.4	104.1
Sep	103.2	100.9	102.1	99.6	102.5
Oct	106.1	101.9	103.7	104.5	99.2
Nov	106.3	102.4	105.2	106.8	98.5
Dec	103.7	105.7	107.3	108.7	98.7
1993 Jan	106.0†	103.2†	111.9†	108.1	103.5†
Feb	108.3	103.7	111.8	115.1†	97.1
Mar	105.5	102.4	115.2	113.0	101.9
Apr	104.7	102.1	112.7	110.8	101.7
May	105.3	101.3	111.7	109.9	101.6
Jun	109.3	104.3	110.3	108.2	101.9
Jul	106.2	103.7	113.2	111.3	101.7
Aug	111.7	102.0	114.0	110.0	103.6
Sep	106.5	108.3	114.1	107.7	105.9
Oct	109.3	105.6	114.0	107.5	106.0
Nov	100.5	103.9	116.0	107.9	107.5

1 Unit value index for exports expressed as a percentage of unit value index for imports.

Source: Central Statistical Office.

CSO STATFAX

For the most up-to-date data on the monthly trade figures, poll the following number from your fax machine:

0336 416038

Calls charged at 36p per minute cheap rate, 48p per minute at all other times

Visible trade

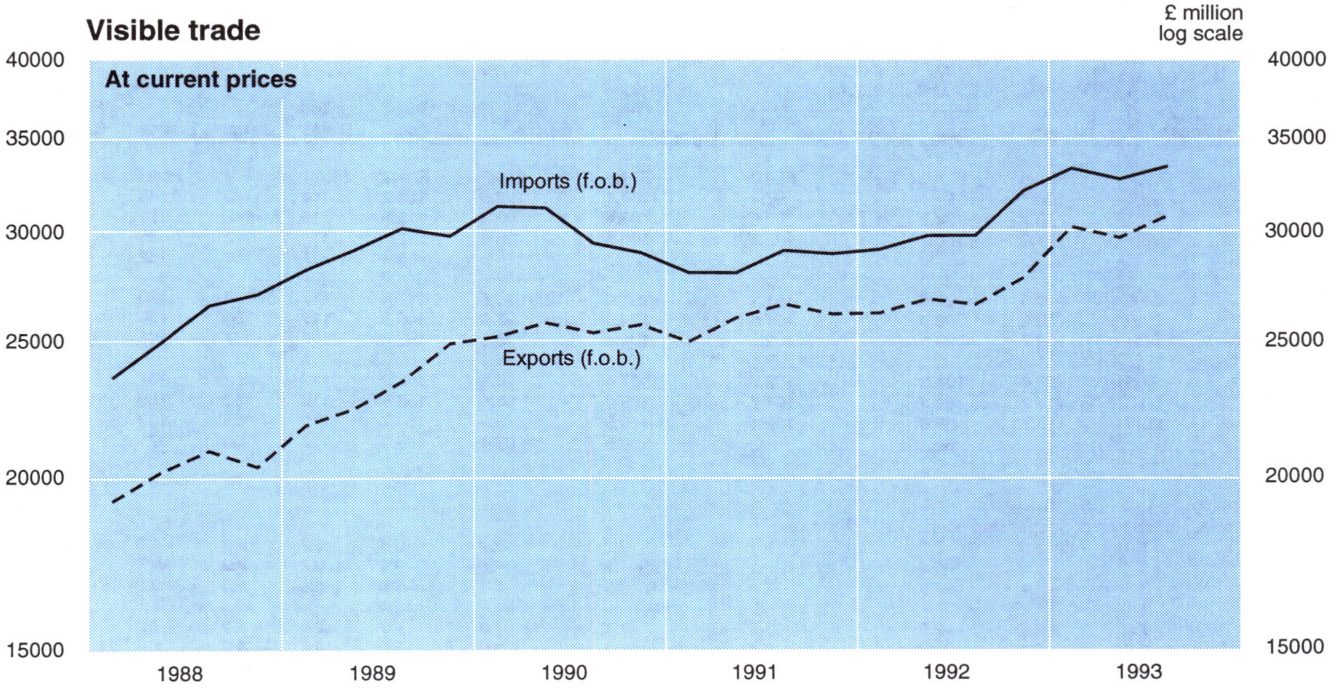
£ million
log scale
At current prices
40000
35000
30000
25000
20000
15000
Imports (f.o.b.)
Exports (f.o.b.)
1988
1989
1990
1991
1992
1993

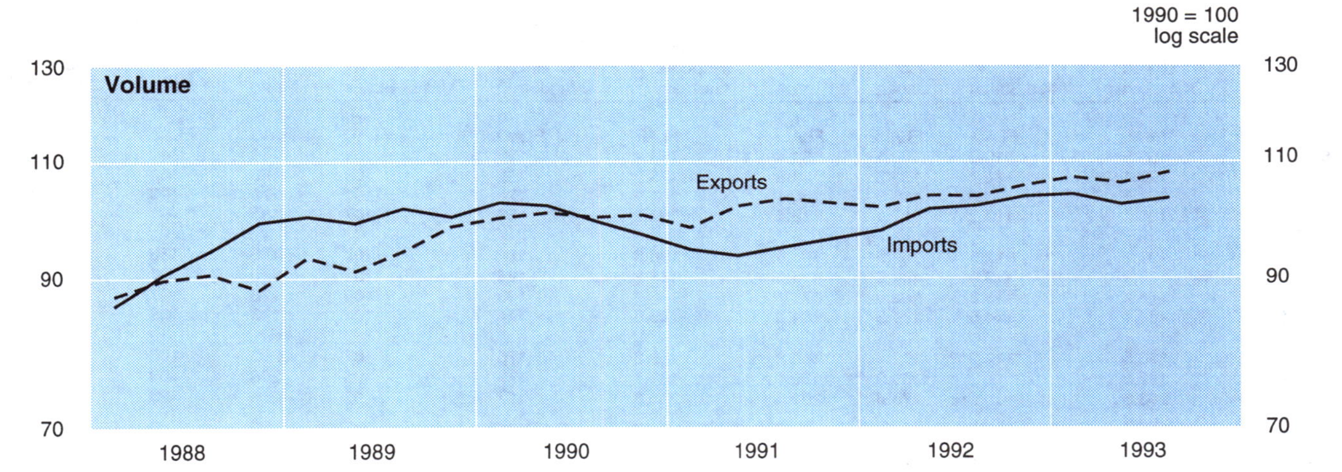
1990 = 100
log scale
Volume
130
110
90
70
Exports
Imports
1988
1989
1990
1991
1992
1993

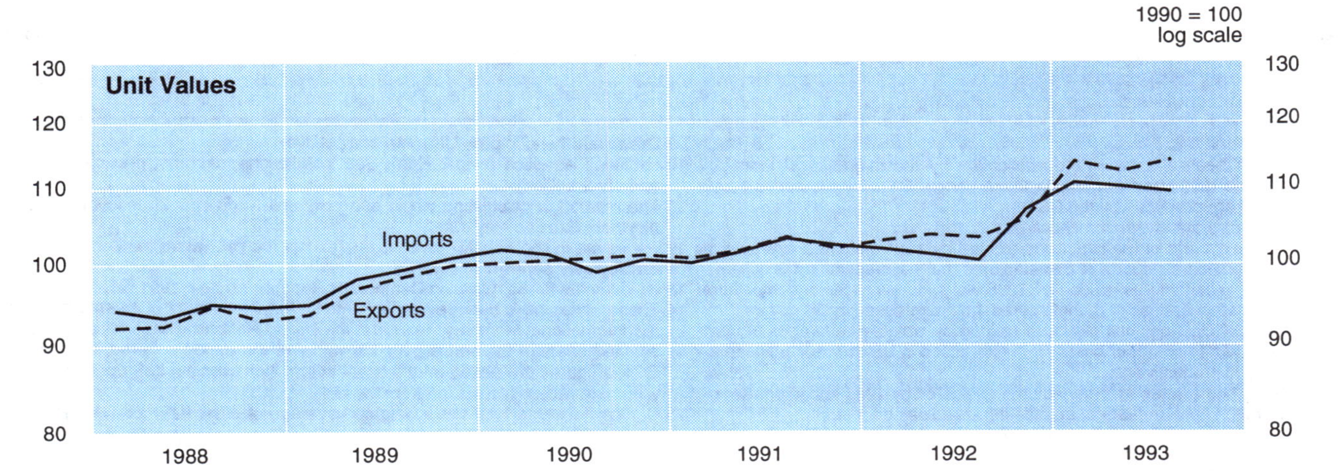
1990 = 100
log scale
Unit Values
130
120
110
100
90
80
Imports
Exports
1988
1989
1990
1991
1992
1993

28 Measures of UK competitiveness in trade in manufactures[1,2]

1985 = 100

	Summary measures						Export unit value index[3,14]				
	Relative export prices[4,9,14]	Relative producer prices[5,9]	IMF index of relative unit labour costs[3]		Import price competitiveness[7,9,10]	Relative profitability of exports[8,10]	United Kingdom	United States	Japan	France	Federal Republic of Germany[13]
			Actual[15]	Normalised[6,9,15]							
	FLAA	FLAB	FLAC	FLAD	FLAE	FLAF	FLAG	FLAH	FLAI	FLAJ	FLAK
1989	98.5	103.7	94.1	97.1	104.1	100.5	139.2	114	143	149	156
1990	98.6	110.3	98.2	99.5	105.6	99.3	155.5	116	142	171	180
1991	98.1	111.0	100.4	102.2	106.5	96.6	152.7	117	152	165	175
1992	..	..	..	..	..	..	150.4	117	154	162	172
1991 Q2	98.0	110.6	99.5	101.1	107.0	96.5	147.4	117	150	159	168
Q3	97.9	108.2	98.9	101.6	104.6	97.8	146.8	117	150	158	168
Q4	97.4	108.7	99.5	102.1	104.8	96.8	153.3	117	157	168	179
1992 Q1	97.5	113.4	101.0	102.7	107.4	96.3	153.9	117	162	167	177
Q2	98.3	116.2	99.8	101.7	109.2	96.5	156.5	118	162	169	179
Q3	96.6	115.7	98.8	102.4	109.5	96.2	164.7	119	165	182	199
Q4	..	..	84.2	..	100.6	98.4	138.0	118	166	171	187
1993 Q1	..	..	..	..	..	..	..	118	171	161	..
Percentage change, quarter on corresponding quarter of previous year											
1991 Q2	1.6	3.0	7.2	6.1	3.2	-3.9	0.4	1.7	10.3	-4.8	-4.0
Q3	-3.7	-5.3	-3.4	-2.1	-1.9	-1.6	-9.4	0.9	4.9	-9.7	-8.2
Q4	-3.3	-5.4	-4.6	-1.6	-3.9	0.1	-8.7	0.0	4.0	-9.2	-7.7
1992 Q1	-1.6	-2.6	-2.5	-1.3	-1.8	1.0	-5.6	0.0	5.2	-7.2	-6.8
Q2	0.3	5.1	0.3	0.6	2.1	0.0	6.2	0.9	8.0	6.3	6.5
Q3	-1.3	6.9	-0.1	0.8	4.7	-1.6	12.2	1.7	10.0	15.2	18.5
Q4	..	..	-15.4	..	-4.0	1.7	-10.0	0.9	5.7	1.8	4.5
1993 Q1	..	..	..	..	..	..	..	0.9	5.6	-3.6	..

	Producer price index[3]					Unit labour costs index[3,12]				
	United Kingdom	United States	Japan	France	Federal Republic of Germany[13]	United Kingdom[11]	United States	Japan	France	Federal Republic of Germany[13]
	FLAL	FLAM	FLAN	FLAO	FLAP	FLAQ	FLAR	FLAS	FLAT	FLAU
1989	150.5	110.0	158.1	151.4	158.2	136	101	166	140	175
1990	173.4	113.7	153.2	181.6	173.2	162	104	160	102	116
1991	181.5	113.6	165.9	180.1	184.0	170	107	179	103	119
1992	180.1	113.7	167.1	178.4	182.2	169	107	185	101	118
1991 Q1	192.2	112.8	167.5	193.0	196.8	182	107	176	113	126
Q2	175.2	113.9	161.9	171.6	174.8	164	107	179	100	114
Q3	174.2	113.3	162.8	171.4	175.7	163	106	176	97	113
Q4	184.4	114.5	171.5	184.3	188.5	174	107	193	106	125
1992 Q1	186.5	112.9	172.4	186.2	189.8	176	107	200	106	124
Q2	192.3	..	169.9	189.4	191.7	177	106	208	108	127
Q3	203.6	..	176.6	208.5	211.3	187	106	208	120	143
Q4	169.4	..	..	..	..	..	..	..	..	..
Percentage change, quarter on corresponding quarter of previous year										
1991 Q1	22.2	0.9	12.7	13.7	20.2	24.7	3.9	11.4	18.9	14.5
Q2	8.0	1.2	13.6	-1.0	5.3	10.1	2.9	17.0	1.0	0.0
Q3	-4.3	-0.4	6.9	-7.5	0.1	-4.7	2.9	11.4	-6.7	-4.2
Q4	-4.1	-1.7	1.4	-7.0	0.5	-5.9	1.9	9.0	-7.0	-0.8
1992 Q1	-3.0	0.1	2.9	-3.5	-3.6	-3.3	0.0	13.6	-6.2	-1.6
Q2	9.8	..	4.9	10.4	9.7	7.9	-0.9	16.2	8.0	11.4
Q3	16.9	..	8.5	21.6	20.3	14.7	0.0	18.2	23.7	26.5
Q4	-8.1	..	..	..	..	..	..	..	..	..

1 SITC Sections 5-8.
2 There has been a delay in the publication by the International Monetary Fund of the data used to compile these series. Data for the series FLAG and FLAQ are produced by the CSO.
3 All the indicies are shown in US dollars.
4 UVI of UK exports of manufactures divided by 1985 weighted averages of UVI of competitors' exports of manufactures, both expressed in US dollars.
5 UK PPI of manufactures divided by 1985 weighted averages of competitors' indicies of output prices of manufactures, both expressed in US dollars.
6 Index of UK ULC per unit of output divided by weighted averages of competitors' indicies of labour costs (both expressed in US dollars), adjusted for variations in productivity.
7 UK PPI of home sales of manufactures (weighted by 1985 import values) divided by the UVI of imports of manufactures, adjusted for tariffs.
8 UK UVI of exports of manufactures divided by UK producer prices of output of manufactures (weighted by 1985 export values). Upward trend implies improvement in profitability of export sales compared with home sales.
9 Downward trend implies UK more competitive.
10 Excludes erractics (ships, North Sea installations, aircrafts, precious stones, and silver bullion).
11 The method of calculating whole economy unit wage cost is described in Employment Gazette May 1986.
12 Series are in line with IMF ULC series (except the UK, where the Department of Employment series is used).
13 Includes the former German Democratic Republic as from 1991 Q1.
14 These series have been revised this month to take account of information from the International Monetary Fund and the United Nations. These revisions have affected some of the series over the whole of the period covered. From 1991 Q2 the figures are based on the latest information from the IMF updated in line with more recent information from the UN.
15 Compared with a total trade weighted average of other IMF countries in common currency terms.

Sources: Department of Trade and Industry; Department of Employment; International Monetary Fund

Measures of UK trade competitiveness

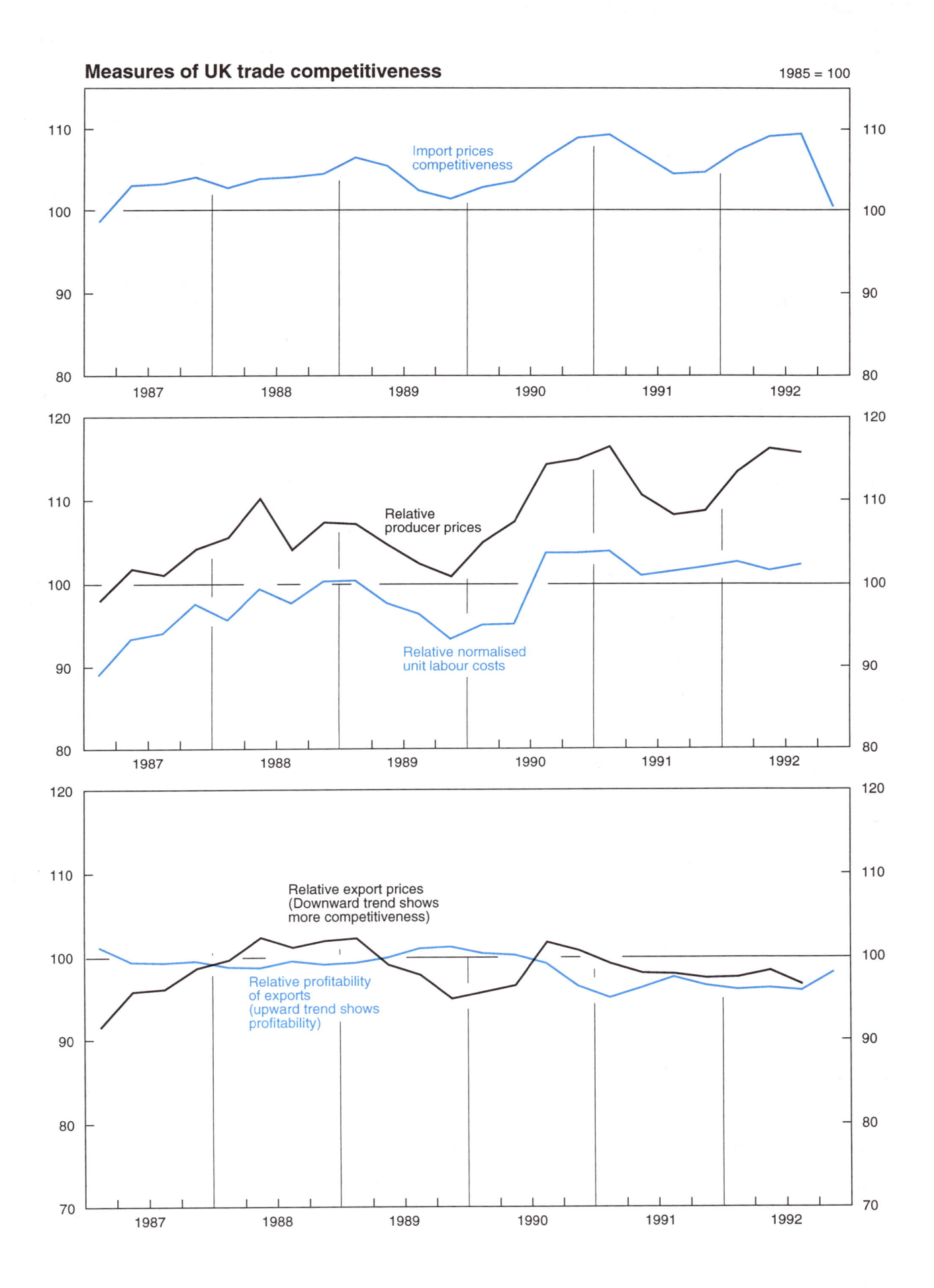

1985 = 100

29 Balance of payments: current account

£ million

	Visible trade			Invisibles						Current balance
	Exports (f.o.b.)+	Imports (f.o.b.)+	Balance	Credits	Debits	Balances				
						Services	IPD	Transfers	Total[1]	
	CGKG	CGHK	AIMA	CGKR	CGHT	AIMC	AIMD	AIME	AIMB	AIMF
1983	60 700	62 237	−1 537	65 392	60 326	3 829	2 831	−1 593	5 066	3 529
1984	70 265	75 601	−5 336	77 031	70 213	4 205	4 344	−1 731	6 817	1 482
1985	77 991	81 336	−3 345	79 593	74 010	6 398	2 296	−3 111	5 583	2 238
1986	72 627	82 186	−9 559	76 469	67 781	6 223	4 622	−2 157	8 688	−871
1987	79 153	90 735	−11 582	79 194	72 595	6 242	3 757	−3 400	6 599	−4 983
1988	80 346	101 826	−21 480	87 307	82 444	3 957	4 424	−3 518	4 863	−16 617
1989	92 154	116 837	−24 683	107 203	105 032	3 361	3 388	−4 578	2 171	−22 512
1990	101 718	120 527	−18 809	114 624	114 083	3 808	1 630	−4 897	541	−18 268
1991	103 413	113 697	−10 284	114 373	111 741	3 657	320	−1 345	2 632	−7 652
1992	107 047	120 453	−13 406	108 573	103 714	4 069	5 850	−5 060	4 859	−8 547
1988 Q3	20 817	26 465	−5 648	22 560	20 607	973	1 182	−202	1 953	−3 695
Q4	20 272	26 975	−6 703	22 789	22 157	872	1 143	−1 383	632	−6 071
1989 Q1	21 710	28 081	−6 371	25 362	24 213	728	1 127	−706	1 149	−5 222
Q2	22 303	28 995	−6 692	26 953	25 958	1 005	834	−844	995	−5 697
Q3	23 321	30 074	−6 753	26 438	26 307	824	703	−1 396	131	−6 622
Q4	24 820	29 687	−4 867	28 450	28 554	804	724	−1 632	−104	−4 971
1990 Q1	25 122	31 204	−6 082	28 177	28 197	1 147	−242	−925	−20	−6 102
Q2	25 706	31 113	−5 407	27 863	28 418	826	−78	−1 303	−555	−5 962
Q3	25 276	29 335	−4 059	28 751	27 817	913	1 132	−1 111	934	−3 125
Q4	25 614	28 875	−3 261	29 833	29 651	922	818	−1 558	182	−3 079
1991 Q1	24 915	27 952	−3 037	28 374	28 274	687	−448	−139	100	−2 937
Q2	25 914	27 939	−2 025	29 947	28 848	896	6	198	1 099	−926
Q3	26 507	28 985	−2 478	28 036	27 525	1 069	407	−965	511	−1 967
Q4	26 077	28 821	−2 744	28 016	27 094	1 005	355	−439	922	−1 822
1992 Q1	26 121	29 031	−2 910	26 971	26 136	1 069	916	−1 150	835	−2 075
Q2	26 737	29 704	−2 967	25 776	25 316	1 064	830	−1 434	460	−2 507
Q3	26 493	29 716	−3 223	26 688	25 130	943	2 075	−1 460	1 558	−1 665
Q4	27 696	32 002	−4 306	29 138	27 132	993	2 029	−1 016	2 006	−2 300
1993 Q1	29 988†	33 335†	−3 347†	29 503	29 110	1 490	214	−1 311	393	−2 954†
Q2	29 730	32 935	−3 205	27 872	27 164	998	876	−1 166	708	−2 497
Q3	30 791	33 656	−2 865	28 843	28 066	1 403	1 037	−1 663	777	−2 088
1991 Dec	8 909	9 696	−787	..	..	..	..	..	..	..
1992 Jan	8 309	9 412	−1 103	..	..	..	..	..	..	..
Feb	8 953	9 985	−1 032	..	..	..	..	..	..	..
Mar	8 859	9 634	−775	..	..	..	..	..	..	..
Apr	8 807	10 032	−1 225	..	..	..	..	..	..	..
May	9 159	9 978	−819	..	..	..	..	..	..	..
Jun	8 771	9 694	−923	..	..	..	..	..	..	..
Jul	8 846	9 943	−1 097	..	..	..	..	..	..	..
Aug	8 846	10 016	−1 170	..	..	..	..	..	..	..
Sep	8 801	9 757	−956	..	..	..	..	..	..	..
Oct	9 194	10 286	−1 092	..	..	..	..	..	..	..
Nov	9 307	10 620	−1 313	..	..	..	..	..	..	..
Dec	9 195	11 096	−1 901	..	..	..	..	..	..	..
1993 Jan	9 848†	10 947†	−1 099†	..	..	..	..	..	..	..
Feb	10 068	11 261	−1 193	..	..	..	..	..	..	..
Mar	10 072	11 127	−1 055	..	..	..	..	..	..	..
Apr	9 772	10 970	−1 198	..	..	..	..	..	..	..
May	9 834	10 854	−1 020	..	..	..	..	..	..	..
Jun	10 124	11 111	−987	..	..	..	..	..	..	..
Jul	10 022	11 196	−1 174	..	..	..	..	..	..	..
Aug	10 549	10 934	−385	..	..	..	..	..	..	..
Sep	10 220	11 526	−1 306	..	..	..	..	..	..	..
Oct	10 428	11 131	−703	..	..	..	..	..	..	..
Nov	9 853	10 888	−1 035	..	..	..	..	..	..	..

1 Monthly data is one third of the appropriate calendar quarter's estimate or projection.

Source: Central Statistical Office

CSO STATFAX

For the most up-to-date data on the balance of payments, poll the following number from your fax machine:

0336 416039

Calls charged at 36p per minute cheap rate, 48p per minute at all other times

Balance of payments

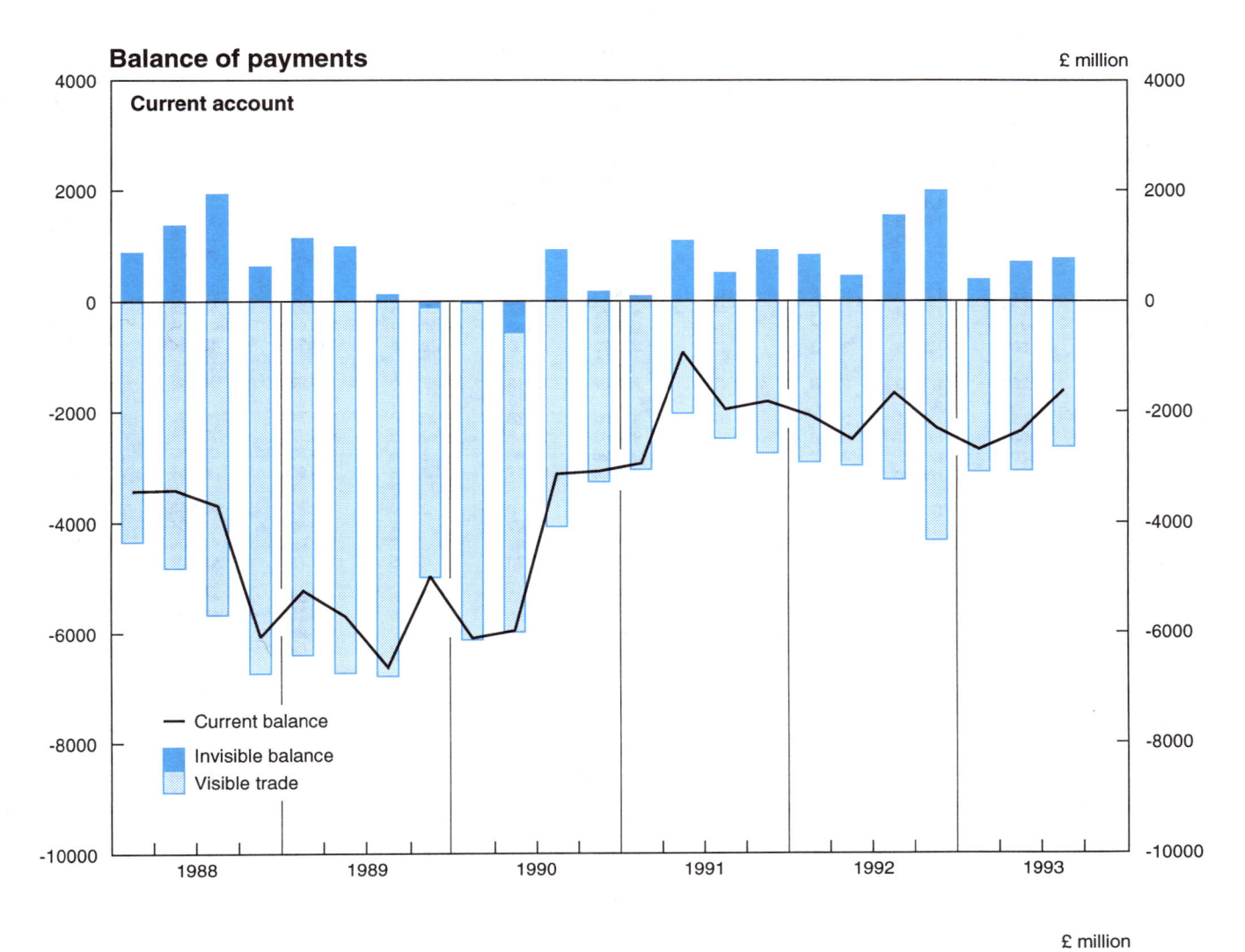

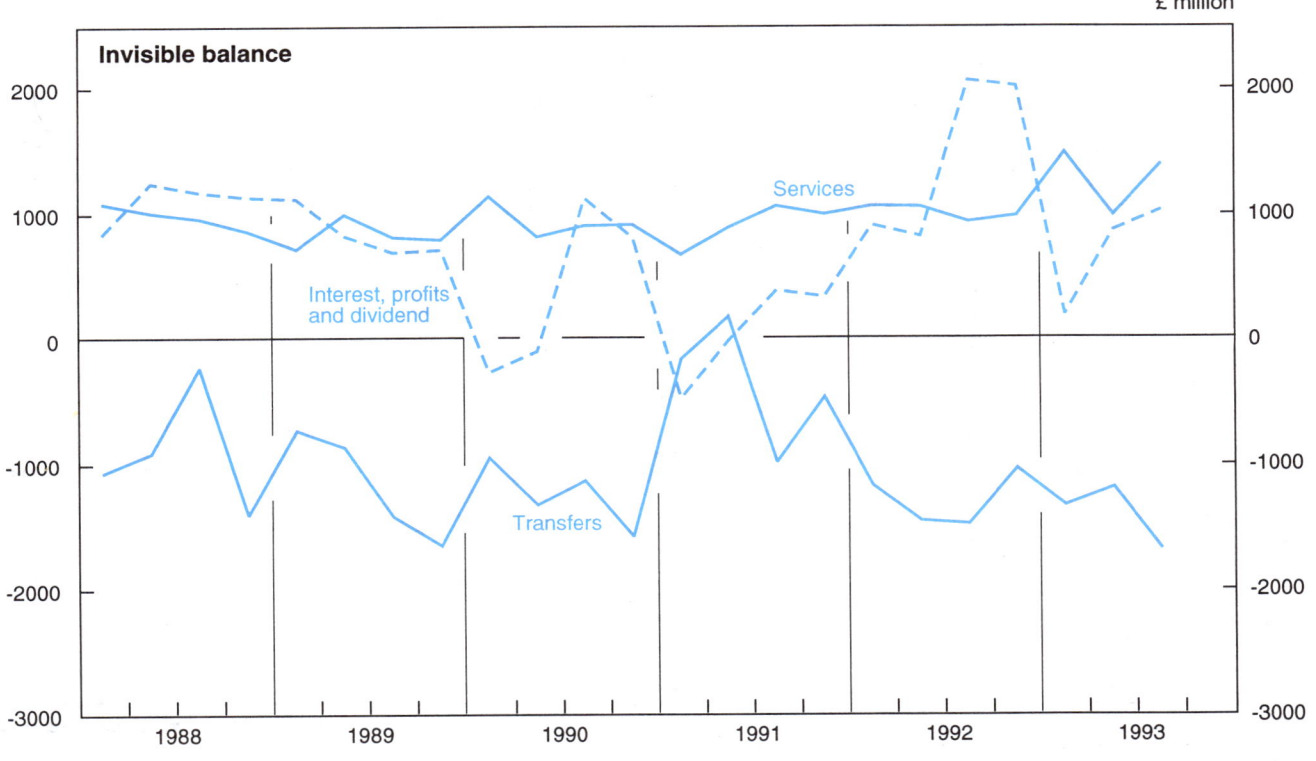

Current account

£ million

— Current balance
■ Invisible balance
▨ Visible trade

Invisible balance

£ million

Services

Interest, profits and dividend

Transfers

30 Sterling exchange rates and UK official reserves

Not seasonally adjusted

	Sterling exchange rate against major currencies[1]								UK official reserves[2] at end of period ($ million)	Sterling exchange rate index (average 1985=100)
	Japanese yen	US dollar	Swiss franc	European currency unit (ECU)	French franc	Italian lira	Deutsche-mark	Spanish peseta		
	AJFO	AJFA	AJFD	AJHW	AJFE	AJFF	AJFH	AJFM	AIPI	AJHV
1985	307.08	1.2976	3.155	1.6998	11.5495	2 463	3.784	219.56	15 543	100.0
1986	246.80	1.4672	2.635	1.4948	10.1569	2 186	3.183	205.31	21 923	91.5
1987	236.50	1.6392	2.439†	1.4200	9.8369	2 123	2.941	201.87	44 326	90.1
1988	227.98	1.7796	2.603	1.5060	10.5969	2 315	3.124	207.16	51 685	95.5
1989	225.66	1.6383	2.678	1.4886	10.4476	2 247	3.079	193.88	38 645	92.6
1990	257.38	1.7864	2.469	1.4000	9.6891	2 133	2.876	181.29	38 464	91.3
1991	237.56	1.7685	2.529	1.4284	9.9473	2 187	2.925	183.22	44 126	91.7
1992	223.72	1.7665	2.476	1.3620	9.3248	2 163	2.751	179.91	41 654	88.4
1993	166.73	1.5015	2.218	1.2845	8.5073	2 360	2.483	191.33	42 926	80.2
1989 Q4	226.76	1.5850	2.548	1.4090	9.7890	2 119	2.876	183.92	38 645	88.1
1990 Q1	245.05	1.6565	2.494†	1.3746	9.4982	2 078	2.800	180.71	39 295	88.1
Q2	260.04	1.6761	2.416	1.3708	9.4562	2 065	2.812	175.77	39 014	88.6
Q3	270.33	1.8617	2.487	1.4337	9.9425	2 190	2.965	183.53	39 060	94.2
Q4	254.23	1.9462	2.475	1.4194	9.8484	2 197	2.923	184.90	38 464	94.1
1991 Q1	255.26	1.9097	2.493	1.4200	9.9316	2 188	2.920	182.70	42 258	93.8
Q2	236.22	1.7094	2.517	1.4412	10.0290	2 197	2.961	183.52	44 264	91.4
Q3	229.80	1.6853	2.558	1.4371	9.9800	2 192	2.937	183.85	44 593	90.7
Q4	229.61	1.7733	2.544	1.4152	9.8504	2 170	2.885	182.79	44 126	90.9
1992 Q1	227.67	1.7721	2.575	1.4032	9.7501	2 155	2.865	180.88	45 027	90.6
Q2	235.40	1.8078	2.668	1.4219	9.8277	2 198	2.916	183.15	45 700	92.3
Q3	238.02	1.9049	2.483	1.3784	9.4465	2 154	2.787	181.23	42 677	90.9
Q4	194.23	1.5808	2.190	1.2482	8.3049	2 145	2.446	174.68	41 654	79.8
1993 Q1	178.38	1.4771	2.224	1.2397	8.1898	2 283	2.414	172.17	40 898	78.5
Q2	168.59	1.5340	2.241	1.2720	8.3783	2 306	2.484	186.28	41 897	80.2
Q3	159.00	1.5047	2.221	1.3148	8.7443	2 384	2.522	202.47	43 044	81.0
Q4	161.34	1.4914	2.189	1.3099	8.7019	2 463	2.510	203.67	42 926	81.0
1991 Jan	258.60	1.9348	2.459†	1.4200	9.9181	2 195	2.920	183.90	38 368	94.1
Feb	256.30	1.9654	2.491	1.4134	9.8994	2 182	2.908	181.86	41 794	94.2
Mar	250.55	1.8265	2.532	1.4265	9.9786	2 186	2.931	182.23	42 258	92.9
Apr	239.62	1.7502	2.519	1.4461	10.0645	2 207	2.979	183.83	43 591	92.3
May	238.25	1.7252	2.511	1.4452	10.0456	2 199	2.963	183.36	43 711	91.7
Jun	230.53	1.6499	2.523	1.4319	9.9742	2 185	2.940	183.36	44 264	90.2
Jul	227.46	1.6503	2.555	1.4359	10.0041	2 195	2.947	184.58	44 631	90.3
Aug	230.35	1.6841	2.560	1.4312	9.9779	2 195	2.936	183.39	44 691	90.7
Sep	231.80	1.7249	2.558	1.4442	9.9556	2 187	2.925	183.51	44 593	91.1
Oct	225.16	1.7226	2.547	1.4258	9.9248	2 176	2.911	183.55	44 252	90.5
Nov	230.50	1.7787	2.553	1.4133	9.8557	2 172	2.884	182.46	43 915	91.0
Dec	233.79	1.8258	2.532	1.4052	9.7592	2 160	2.856	182.26	44 126	91.2
1992 Jan	226.97	1.8127	2.539	1.4024	9.7433	2 152	2.856	181.05	44 586	90.8
Feb	226.85	1.7781	2.588	1.4074	9.7915	2 161	2.877	180.77	44 755	90.8
Mar	229.10	1.7238	2.602	1.4003	9.7221	2 152	2.865	180.74	45 027	90.1
Apr	234.50	1.7576	2.665	1.4133	9.7905	2 179	2.895	182.35	45 775	91.3
May	236.53	1.8109	2.697	1.4286	9.8702	2 209	2.936	183.47	45 804	92.8
Jun	235.27	1.8556	2.642	1.4231	9.8195	2 206	2.917	183.59	45 700	92.8
Jul	241.31	1.9186	2.559	1.4012	9.6503	2 167	2.860	182.00	45 750	92.5
Aug	245.33	1.9412	2.522	1.3852	9.5501	2 138	2.816	180.86	44 450	92.0
Sep	227.58	1.8559	2.365	1.3462	9.1261	2 159	2.683	180.55	42 677	88.2
Oct	200.70	1.6577	2.178	1.2549	8.3285	2 163	2.455	174.73	42 138	80.8
Nov	189.16	1.5275	2.182	1.2346	8.2010	2 083	2.424	173.81	42 087	78.3
Dec	192.55	1.5536	2.207	1.2538	8.3745	2 191	2.455	175.24	41 654	80.1
1993 Jan	191.58	1.5325	2.265	1.2632	8.3923	2 286	2.475	175.66	42 556	80.6
Feb	173.61	1.4386	2.184	1.2151	8.0010	2 228	2.362	168.91	43 452	76.8
Mar	171.05	1.4625	2.222	1.2406	8.1779	2 328	2.407	171.96	40 898	78.2
Apr	173.75	1.5472	2.255	1.2667	8.3444	2 370	2.468	178.81	41 658	80.5
May	170.77	1.5481	2.244	1.2730	8.3872	2 283	2.488	187.96	41 729	80.4
Jun	162.02	1.5099	2.227	1.2760	8.4015	2 269	2.496	191.63	41 897	79.6
Jul	161.16	1.4963	2.267	1.3184	8.7408	2 369	2.566	201.57	43 319	81.3
Aug	154.78	1.4911	2.234	1.3253	8.8478	2 391	2.529	206.96	43 163	81.0
Sep	160.88	1.5261	2.162	1.3013	8.6491	2 392	2.472	199.09	43 044	80.8
Oct	160.82	1.5037	2.166	1.2966	8.6394	2 405	2.463	198.47	43 551	80.4
Nov	159.66	1.4806	2.217	1.3124	8.7455	2 468	2.517	203.29	43 600	81.0
Dec	163.63†	1.4904†	2.182	1.3205†	8.7186†	2 514†	2.549†	209.27†	42 926	81.7
1994 Jan	166.35	1.4940	2.197	1.3412	8.8460	2 538	2.604	213.62	43 447	82.5

1 Average of daily Telegraphic Transfer rates in London.
2 Apart from transactions, the level of official reserves is affected by changes in the dollar valuation of gold, Special Drawing Rights and convertible currencies. Since end-March 1979 these rates have been revised annually. These valuation changes are described in detail in the description of Table 1.2I (10.3) in the *Financial Statistics Explanatory Handbook*, where the values of the annual changes are also shown.

Sources: Bank of England; HM Treasury

Sterling exchange rates

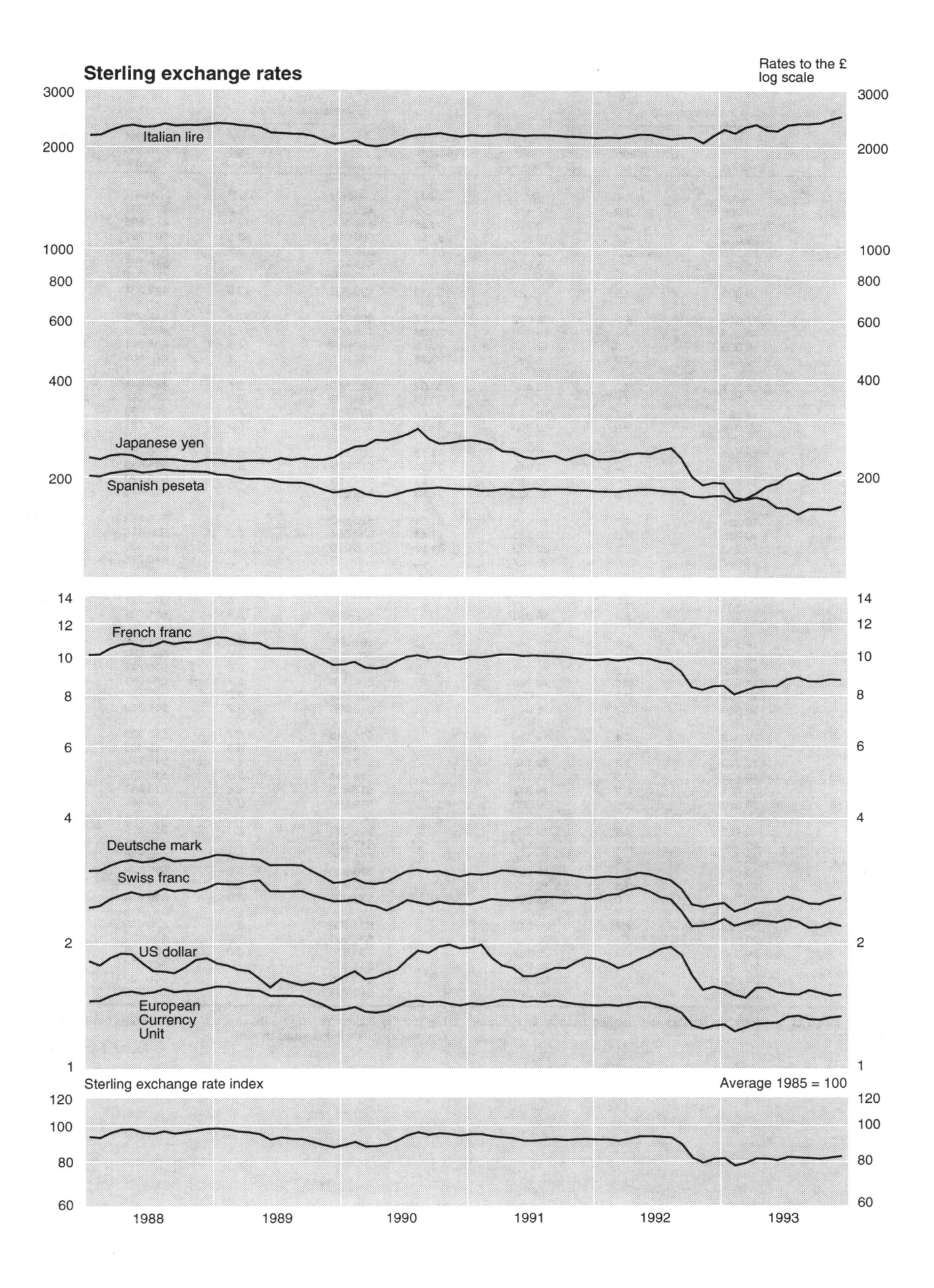

Rates to the £
log scale

(chart showing Italian lire, Japanese yen, Spanish peseta, French franc, Deutsche mark, Swiss franc, US dollar, European Currency Unit from 1988 to 1993)

Sterling exchange rate index — Average 1985 = 100

31 Monetary aggregates[1]

	M0				M4			
	Amount outstanding[2] (NSA)		Amount outstanding (£ million) +	Velocity of circulation: ratio	Amount outstanding (NSA)		Amount outstanding (£ million) +	Velocity of circulation: ratio
	£ million	Annual percentage change			£ million	Annual percentage change		
	AVAD	AVAK	AVAE	AVAM	AUYM	AUZP	AUYN	AUYU
1989	19 006	5.9	17 824	29.92	423 366	18.0	422 331	1.33
1990	19 493	5.4	18 297	30.35	474 255	12.1	473 605	1.23
1991	20 073	2.4	18 850	30.85	502 086	6.3	501 791	1.17
1992	20 570	2.2	19 380	31.28	519 282†	3.7	519 449†	1.16
1993	21 697	..	20 507	..	549 707	..	549 775	..
1989 Q4	19 006	5.5	17 824	30.18	423 366	18.0	422 331	1.29
1990 Q1	17 600	5.7	18 017	30.27	439 169	17.7	438 278	1.26
Q2	18 194	7.4	18 252	30.08	456 626	17.2	453 535	1.23
Q3	18 325	5.0	18 283	30.60	466 854	14.6	464 241	1.22
Q4	19 493	3.3	18 297	30.44	474 255	12.1	473 605	1.19
1991 Q1	18 161	3.2	18 452	30.52	482 953†	9.9	482 046†	1.18
Q2	18 581	1.5	18 631	30.83	493 123	8.0	489 654	1.18
Q3	18 757	2.1	18 713	30.92	497 761	6.5	495 689	1.17
Q4	20 073	2.8	18 850	31.15	502 086	6.3	501 791	1.17
1992 Q1	18 382	1.3	18 834	31.13	507 583	5.9	506 744	1.16
Q2	18 859	2.4	18 945	31.30	515 336	5.2	511 889	1.17
Q3	19 270	2.4	19 146	31.37	517 761	4.7	515 770	1.16
Q4	20 570	2.6	19 380	31.33	519 282	3.7	519 449	1.16
1993 Q1	19 281	4.7	19 716	31.34	525 842	3.6	525 153	1.18
Q2	19 795	4.3	19 791	31.44	532 554	3.3	529 574	1.18
Q3	20 262	5.1	20 122	31.52	538 370	4.0	536 035	1.18
Q4	21 697	..	20 507	..	549 707	..	549 775	..
Calendar month								
1991 Dec	20 073	3.0	18 850	..	502 086	6.3	501 791	..
1992 Jan	18 598	0.8	18 773	..	501 500†	6.3	504 656†	..
Feb	18 330	2.0	18 796	..	502 369	6.0	506 583	..
Mar	18 382	1.2	18 834	..	507 583	5.9	506 744	..
Apr	18 913	3.0	18 983	..	509 330	5.7	509 051	..
May	19 104	2.8	19 094	..	510 922	5.2	509 756	..
Jun	18 859	1.4	18 945	..	515 336	5.2	511 889	..
Jul	19 242	2.4	19 128	..	515 710	5.7	513 933	..
Aug	19 335	2.1	19 103	..	515 666	5.5	515 485	..
Sep	19 270	2.6	19 146	..	517 761	4.7	515 770	..
Oct	19 134	2.3	19 178	..	519 144	5.3	519 338	..
Nov	19 281	2.9	19 317	..	517 445	4.4	518 641	..
Dec	20 570	2.6	19 380	..	519 282	3.7	519 449	..
1993 Jan	19 452	4.6	19 525	..	515 800	3.1	519 879	..
Feb	19 196	4.7	19 368	..	517 421	3.3	522 135	..
Mar	19 281	4.9	19 716	..	525 842	3.6	525 153	..
Apr	19 874	5.1	19 398	..	526 916	3.5	526 546	..
May	19 641	2.8	19 747	..	530 432	3.8	528 949	..
Jun	19 795	5.0	19 791	..	532 554	3.3	529 574	..
Jul	20 132	4.7	20 018	..	534 508	3.6	532 479	..
Aug	20 316	5.2	20 069	..	534 909	3.7	534 454	..
Sep	20 262	5.3	20 122	..	538 370	4.0	536 035	..
Oct	20 164	..	20 212	..	541 492	..	541 528	..
Nov	20 257	..	20 294	..	543 175	..	544 002	..
Dec	21 697	..	20 507	..	549 707	..	549 775	..

1 A fuller range of monetary aggregates is published monthly in *Financial Statistics*.
2 The monthly figures for M0 give the average of the amounts outstanding each Wednesday during the calendar month.

Source: Bank of England

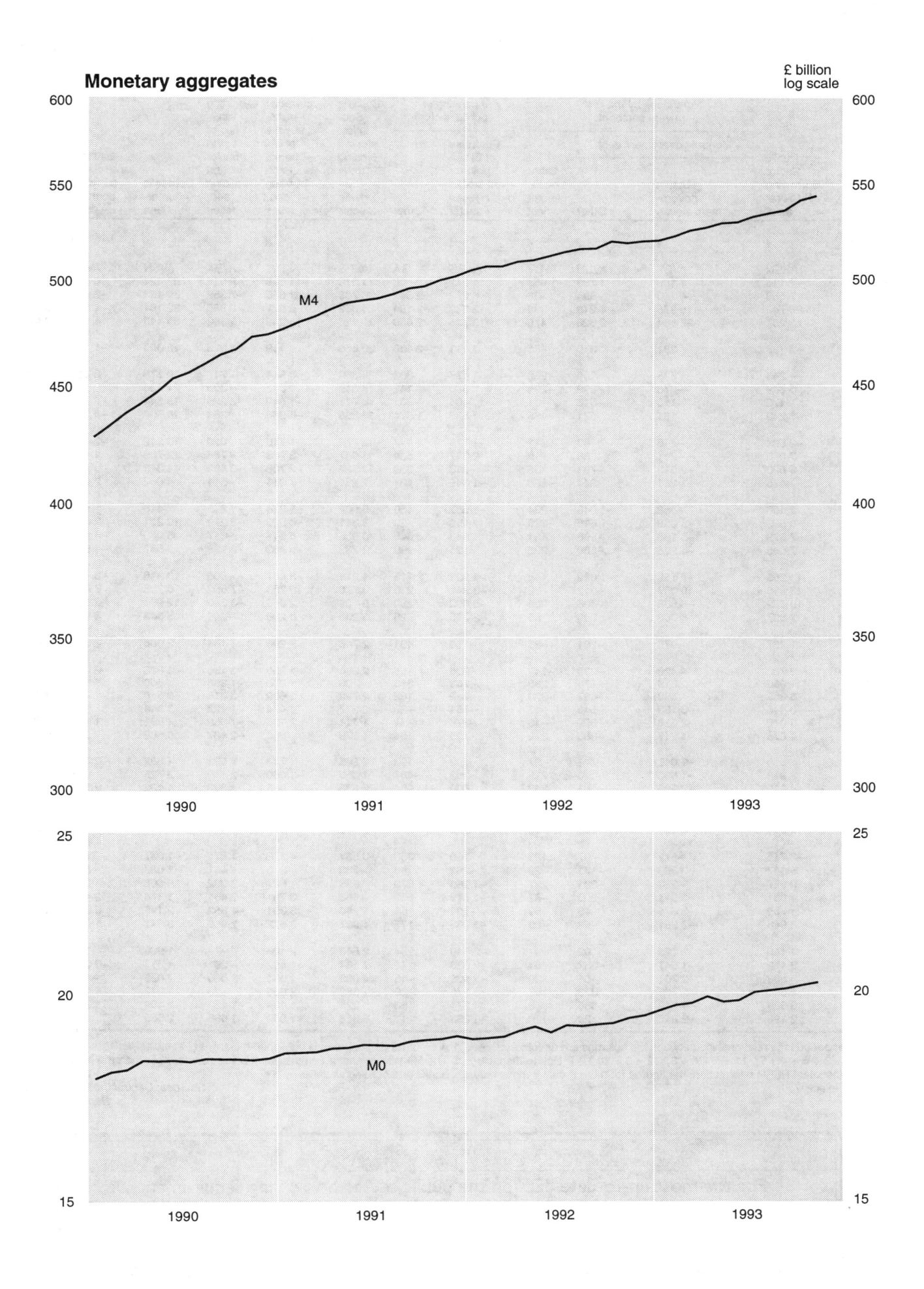

Monetary aggregates

£ billion
log scale

32 Counterparts to changes in money stock M4[1]

£ million, not seasonally adjusted

| | Public Sector Borrowing Requirement | Purchases by the M4[2] private sector of: | | | External and foreign currency financing of public sector | | Banks' and Building Societies' sterling lending to the M4 private sector | External and foreign currency transactions of UK banks and building societies | Net non-deposit sterling liabilities of the banks and building societies | Domestic counterparts | External and foreign currency counterparts | M4 |
| | | Central government debt | | Other public sector debt | Purchase of British government stocks by overseas sector | Other | | | | | | |
		British government stocks	Other									
	1	2	3	4	5	6	7	8	9	10	11	12
	ABEN	AVBY	AVBU	AVBV	-AARC	AQGA	AVBS	AVBW	AVBX	AVBN	AVBP	AUZI
1990	-2 116	1 160	-1 783	-1 056	4 242	-66	71 218	-11 009	-9 616	67 424	-6 535	51 273
1991	7 683	-4 283	-994	-36	-6 282	2 341	36 785	1 855	-7 359†	39 153	-2 077	29 717†
1992	28 743†	-16 978	-4 219	-389	-2 339	-9 186	24 852	6 971	-8 969†	32 184	-4 595	18 619†
1993	43 251	-27 564	-2 626	476	-13 736	2 650	21 926	15 242	-11 192	35 448	4 155	28 412
1989 Q4	-3 193	281	316	-65	1 111	-2 406	20 666	119	-1 328	18 005	-1 177	15 500
1990 Q1	-4 246	695	200	-262	1 477	303	23 390	-3 944	-1 717	19 778	-2 014	16 047
Q2	5 849	-278	-899	-295	883	-1 142	16 819	847	-4 308	21 196	587	17 475
Q3	-476	-118	-513	-61	494	-801	16 711	-1 549	-3 225	15 544	-1 856	10 463
Q4	-3 243	861	-571	-438	1 388	1 574	14 298	-6 363	-366	10 906	-3 252	7 288
1991 Q1	-2 582	-245	83	211	-1 773	1 047	12 775	-1 710	326†	10 242	-2 436	8 132†
Q2	7 050	-244	58	-15	-2 347	534	5 857	3 288	-3 765	12 706	1 475	10 416
Q3	3 690	-2 513	-791	36	-813	339	10 922	-2 739	-3 409	11 343	-3 213	4 721
Q4	-475	-1 281	-344	-268	-1 349	421	7 231	3 016	-511	4 862	2 097	6 448
1992 Q1	3 466	-648	-1 046	-234	-1 857	480	5 902	1 914	-1 245	7 446	537	6 737
Q2	10 593†	-6 958	-1 515	-326	-1 450	20	8 311	4 523	-5 279	10 271	3 094	8 086
Q3	7 679	-5 136	-998	461	843	-13 645	6 906†	6 517	-317	8 900†	-6 285	2 298
Q4	7 005	-4 236	-660	-290	125	3 959	3 733	-5 983	-2 128	5 567	-1 941	1 498
1993 Q1	11 269	-4 168	-1 099	148	-1 391	2 115	4 211	-3 867	-556	10 346	-3 144	6 646
Q2	13 366	-10 067†	-212†	-62	-3 942	230	3 770	10 753†	-7 052	6 795	7 038†	6 781
Q3	10 789	-6 566	-306	305	-6 003	280	8 739	2 058†	-3 340	12 961	-3 667	5 955
Q4	7 827	-6 763	-1 009	85	-2 395	25	5 206	6 298	-244	5 346	3 928	9 030
1991 Dec	1 267	-976	-281	-83	-160	461	2 746	2 296	141†	2 666	2 597	5 404†
1992 Jan	-3 782	-420	-233	-149	-236	-85	2 904	-1 750	3 130	-1 673	-2 083	-627
Feb	860	-618	-176	235	-763	383	205	1 995	-1 355	500	1 613	758
Mar	6 388	390	-637	-320	-849	182	2 792	1 669	-3 019	8 618	1 007	6 606
Apr	3 446†	-3 183	-540	-47	-461	-30	2 217	1 474	-1 122	1 944	965	1 787
May	3 072	-2 558†	-592	-43	-378	-54	1 714	2 189	-1 669	1 661†	1 601†	1 593
Jun	4 075	-1 217	-383	-236	-726	104	4 379	860	-2 487	6 665	528	4 706
Jul	675	-1 047	-711	-97	-602	-103	2 865†	-1 788	1 531	1 682	-2 549	664
Aug	2 992	-1 693	-140	215	1 262	-488	1 355	-1 660	-2 150	2 725	-947	-372
Sep	4 012	-2 396	-147	343	606	-13 054	2 685	9 965	303	4 492	-2 789	2 006
Oct	1 597	-1 603	-421	116	43	1 524	3 219	-3 606	381	2 914	-2 039	1 256
Nov	2 052	-272	-78	-101	-261	466	-282	-2 056	-1 187	1 324	-1 851	-1 714
Dec	3 356	-2 361	-161	-305	301	1 969	795	-321	-1 321	1 328	1 949	1 956
1993 Jan	-3 745	-572	-707	403	150	350	3 587	-4 178	1 374	-1 037	-3 678	-3 341
Feb	5 487	-3 363	-171	-28	-282†	86	-233	-316	451	1 688	-512	1 627
Mar	9 527	-233	-221	-227	-1 260	1 679	858	627	-2 382	9 696	1 046	8 360
Apr	4 661	-3 911	-203†	-82	-1 679	353	663	3 791†	-2 451	1 128	2 465	1 142
May	4 759	-3 875	43	59	-401	54	1 140	3 391	-1 652	2 126	3 044	3 518
Jun	3 946	-2 281	-52	-39	-1 865	-177	1 967	3 572	-2 950	3 541	1 530	2 121
Jul	1 449	-2 228	92	61	-2 540	254	2 546	2 406	-79	1 920	120	1 960
Aug	3 452	-1 547	-337	264	-2 026	71	2 184	-1 402	-261	4 016	-3 357	399
Sep	5 888	-2 791	-61	-20	-1 438	-45	4 009	1 054	-3 000	7 025	-430	3 596
Oct	2 590	-2 705	-373	197	-1 276	-39	1 668	2 936	123	1 377	1 621	3 121
Nov	3 039	-1 212	-656	8	274	53	225	1 404	-1 453	1 404	1 731	1 682
Dec	2 198	-2 846	20	-120	-1 393	11	3 313	1 959	1 086	2 565	577	4 227

For most periods the relationships between the columns are as follows: 10 = 1 + 2 + 3 + 4 + 7; 11 = 5 + 6 + 8; 12 = 9 + 10 + 11. Due to the inclusion of the latest PSBR information, the figures for more recent periods may not add exactly.

1 A wider range of figures is published monthly in *Financial Statistics*.
2 The M4 private sector comprises all UK residents other than the public sector, banks and building societies.

Sources: Central Statistical Office; Bank of England

CSO STATFAX

For the most up-to-date data on the public sector borrowing requirement, poll the following number from your fax machine:

0336 416040

Calls charged at 36p per minute cheap rate, 48p per minute at all other times

Counterparts to changes in money stock M4

£ million

- PSBR
- Net acquisitions of public sector debt by the M4 private sector*
- Banks' and Building societies sterling lending to M4 private sector*
- External and foreign currency counterparts
- Other
- —— Change in money stock sterling M4

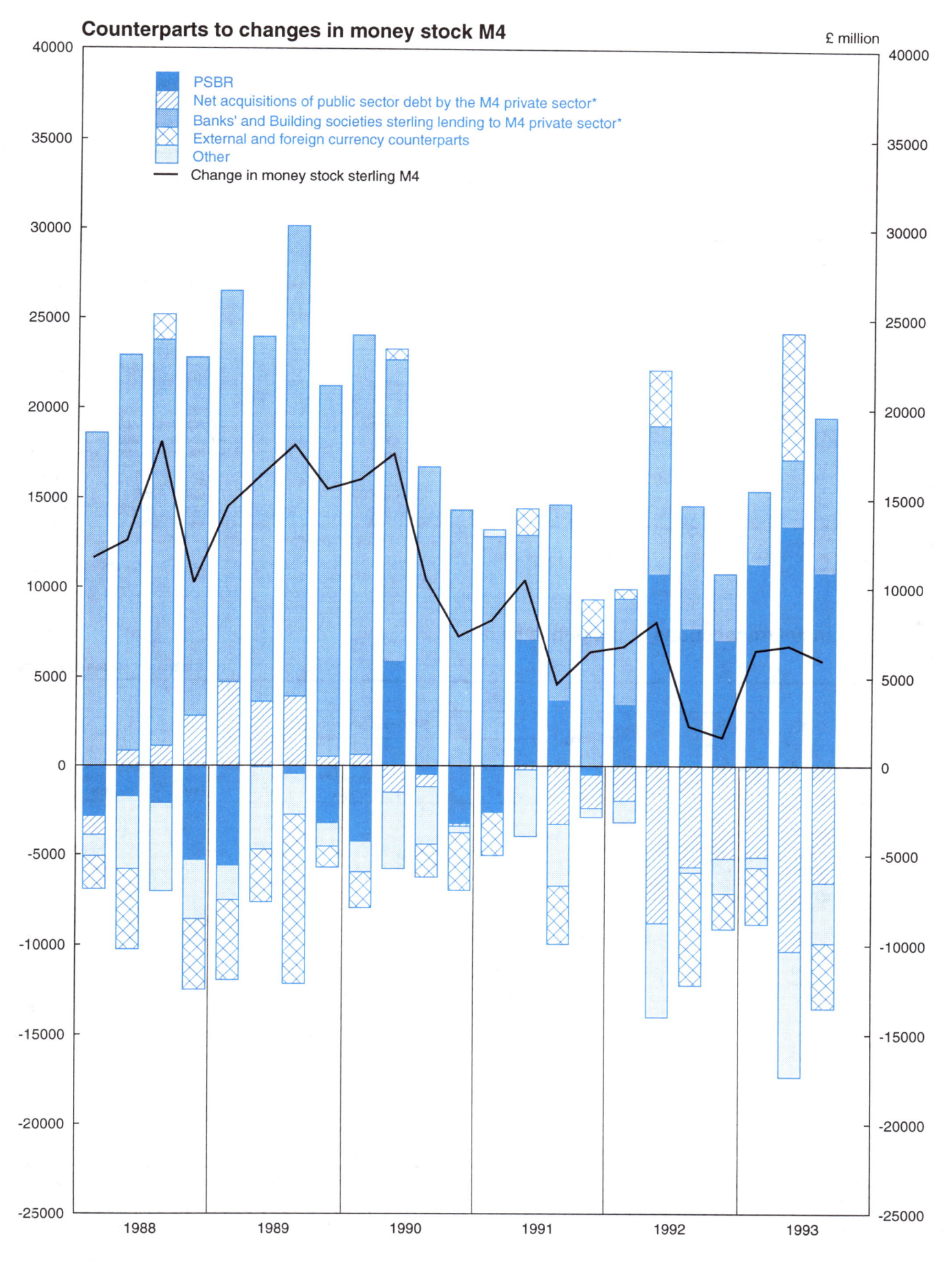

* Private sector other than banks and building societies

33 General government receipts and expenditure

£ million, not seasonally adjusted

	General government									
	Receipts[1]		Expenditure							
			Goods and services		Current and capital transfers					
	Taxes, social security contributions, community charge and royalties.	Trading income, rent, interest, etc	Final consumption	Gross domestic capital formation	Current grants and subsidies[2]	Capital transfers	Debt interest	Net lending etc[3]	Total	Public expenditure control total
	GTEA	ABKB	AAXI	ABKC	ABKD	AAYG	AAXL	ABAA	ABAB	ABBX
1989	188 480	14 628	101 796	9 419	64 093	4 233	18 867	−1 382	197 026	171 542
1990	203 247	14 396	112 934	12 815	69 602	10 148	18 708	−8 651	215 556	188 994
1991	208 238	13 873	124 205	12 324	76 227	7 935	16 965	−9 284	228 342	205 294
1992	209 871	13 649	132 715	12 549	91 126	7 643	17 118	−6 217	254 934	227 586
1991 Q3	51 437	3 692	31 533	2 792	19 634	1 714	4 231	−1 322	58 616	52 036
Q4	54 484	3 223	31 613	3 079	20 282	1 963	3 941	−3 371	57 465	52 671
1992 Q1	57 018	3 854	32 452	4 839	22 030	2 193	4 548	−1 123	64 939	57 919
Q2	47 812	3 049	33 543	2 146	22 679	1 613	3 599	−1 112	62 468	55 359
Q3	50 760	3 573	33 111	2 525	23 083	1 766	4 814	−2 832	62 467	56 410
Q4	54 281	3 173	33 609	3 039	23 334	2 071	4 157	−1 150	65 060	57 898
1993 Q1	55 871	3 756	33 797	5 246	25 400	3 020	5 330	−1 823	70 970	62 497
Q2	49 486	3 164	34 451	2 138	24 519	1 985	3 535	−899	65 729	58 600
Q3	53 338	3 623	34 279	2 447	24 457	1 852	5 219	−1 848	66 406	58 542

1 Excluding financial transactions.
2 Includes contributions received towards the UK's cost of the Gulf conflict from 1990 Q3 to 1992 Q1.
3 Net lending to public corporations, private sector and overseas; company securities.

Source: Central Statistical Office

34 Financial transactions of the public sector[1]

£ million, not seasonally adjusted

	Financial deficit[2]				Receipts						
				Net lending etc, to private sector and overseas[4]	Borrowing requirement[5]					Other financial transactions (net receipts)	Total
	General government[3]	Public corporations	Total		Central government (own account[6])	Local authorities	Public corporations+	Total	Seasonally adjusted total[7]		
	1	2	3	4	5	6	7	8	9	10	11
	-AABC	-AABD	-AABE	ABKG	ABEB	ABEG	ABEM	ABEN		ABKI	ABKH
1990	6 564	−4 746	1 818	−4 690	−1 109	3 903	−4 910	−2 116		−759	−2 872
1991	15 515	−752	14 763	−9 144	6 561	1 878	−756	7 683		−2 094	5 619
1992	37 631	−106	37 525	−7 464	33 709†	−5 595†	629†	28 743†		1 010	30 061
1993	..	..	..	..	46 114	−2 611	−218	43 251	ABFB	..	..
1991 Q4	3 129	−281	2 848	−3 373	−150	−5	−320	−475	1 976	−55	−525
1992 Q1	5 190	358	5 548	−1 349	1 738	1 165	563†	3 466†	6 048	565	4 199
Q2	12 719	−162	12 557	−1 790	10 467	23†	103†	10 593†	7 206	44	10 767
Q3	10 966	157	11 123	−3 160	9 096	−1 157	−260	7 679	6 296	322	7 963
Q4	8 756	−459	8 297	−1 165	12 408†	−5 626	223	7 005	9 501	79	7 132
1993 Q1	13 239	366	13 605	−1 897	10 396	886	−13	11 269	13 688	448	11 708
Q2	14 069	−583	13 486	−1 529	13 020	−99	445	13 366	9 828	−1 433	11 957
Q3	11 386	273	11 659	−1 920	12 144	−1 188	−167	10 789	9 424	−1 039	9 739
Q4	..	..	..	..	10 554	−2 210	−483	7 827	..	..	..
1993 Sep	..	..	..	..	6 197	−396	89†	5 888†	..	..	..
Oct	..	..	..	..	3 215	−490	−55	2 590	..	..	..
Nov	..	..	..	..	4 355†	−1 207	−63	3 039	..	..	..
Dec	..	..	..	..	2 984	−513	−365	2 198	..	..	..

The relationships between the columns are as follows: 1 + 2 = 3; 3 + 4 = 11; 5 + 6 + 7 = 8; 8 + 10 = 11.
1 Due to the inclusion of the latest PSBR figures this table may not be internally consistent.
2 The excess of current and capital expenditure over receipts.
3 Table 33, columns 3 to 7 *less* columns 1 and 2.
4 Including company securities. Lending is shown positively; repayment is shown negatively.
5 Redefined: see article in *Economic Trends*, No. 364, February 1984.
6 Excluding borrowing matched by on-lending to local authorities and public corporations.
7 Calendar year constrained.

Source: Central Statistical Office

Public expenditure and borrowing

£ billion
not seasonally adjusted

General government expenditure

Public expenditure control total

Public sector borrowing requirement

35 Summary capital accounts and financial surplus or deficit

£ million

	Public sector[1]			Financial companies and institutions			Industrial and commercial companies		
	Saving[2]	Capital transfers (net receipts)	Gross domestic capital formation[3]	Saving[2]	Capital transfers (net receipts)	Gross domestic capital formation[3]	Saving[2]	Capital transfers (net receipts)	Gross domestic capital formation[3]
	ABKJ	ABKK	ABKL	AAUM	AAUN	GGCX	AAUQ	AAUR	GGCW
1988	16 050	1 383	11 047	5 413	−141	6 527	45 956	−18	53 437
1989	18 683	1 779	15 160	7 468	−151	7 873	40 976	−872	61 821
1990	14 702	1 116	17 636	9 227	−100	6 793	37 027	−841	58 939
1991	2 075	−677	16 161	2 761	−100	6 409	40 042	−484	47 311
1992	−18 885	−1 795	16 845	6 453	−100	5 271	40 798	−163	47 393
1989 Q3	4 827	409	3 844	1 869	−38	1 978	8 522	−259	16 384
Q4	4 428	445	4 397	1 888	−38	2 036	10 239	−236	14 576
1990 Q1	4 791	279	4 437	1 543	−25	1 615	8 784	−192	15 661
Q2	4 603	272	4 051	2 565	−25	1 813	8 885	−219	15 613
Q3	4 091	287	4 499	3 013	−25	1 626	10 052	−240	15 757
Q4	1 217	278	4 649	2 106	−25	1 739	9 306	−190	11 908
1991 Q1	1 971	75	3 930	1 896	−25	1 809	8 443	−153	13 166
Q2	1 345	−91	3 986	338	−25	1 722	10 010	−123	11 053
Q3	−404	−213	4 197	209	−25	1 472	9 884	−103	10 965
Q4	−837	−448	4 048	318	−25	1 406	11 705	−105	12 127
1992 Q1	−1 617	−376	4 249	1 102	−25	1 461	8 482	−92	11 708
Q2	−4 878	−435	4 114	854	−25	1 355	9 799	−7	11 303
Q3	−6 187	−520	4 152	2 462	−25	1 304	10 795	−23	12 165
Q4	−6 203	−464	4 330	2 035	−25	1 151	11 722	−41	12 217
1993 Q1	−7 922	−1 093	4 872	1 090	−25	1 181	12 540	−31	11 425
Q2	−5 775	−654	4 036	1 855	−25	1 125	12 083	−19	12 607
Q3	−5 998	−622	3 966	1 694	−25	1 078	13 554	−28	11 800

	Personal sector			Financial surplus/deficit[4]					
	Saving[2]	Capital transfers (net receipts)	Gross domestic capital formation[3]	Public sector	Financial companies and institutions	Industrial and commercial companies	Personal sector	Overseas sector[5]	Balancing item[6]
	AAUU	AAUV	GGCV	AAVE	AAVF	AAVG	AAVH	AAVI	AAVJ
1988	18 202	−1 224	31 227	6 386	−1 255	−7 499	−14 249	16 617	−
1989	25 542	−756	30 327	5 302	−556	−21 717	−5 541	22 512	−
1990	32 565	−175	28 421	−1 818	2 334	−22 753	3 969	18 268	−
1991	41 012	1 261	24 106	−14 763	−3 748	−7 753	18 167	7 652	445
1992	55 125	2 058	23 119	−37 525	1 082	−6 758	34 064	8 547	590
1989 Q3	7 248	−112	6 882	1 392	−147	−8 121	254	6 622	−
Q4	6 732	−171	7 249	476	−186	−4 573	−688	4 971	−
1990 Q1	8 000	−62	7 507	633	−97	−7 069	431	6 102	−
Q2	6 852	−28	7 390	824	727	−6 947	−566	5 962	−
Q3	8 807	−22	7 206	−121	1 362	−5 945	1 579	3 125	−
Q4	8 906	−63	6 318	−3 154	342	−2 792	2 525	3 079	−
1991 Q1	9 337	103	5 757	−1 884	62	−4 876	3 683	2 937	78
Q2	10 448	239	6 407	−2 732	−1 409	−1 166	4 280	926	101
Q3	10 727	341	5 871	−4 814	−1 288	−1 184	5 197	1 967	122
Q4	10 500	578	6 071	−5 333	−1 113	−527	5 007	1 822	144
1992 Q1	12 957	493	5 702	−6 242	−384	−3 318	7 748	2 075	121
Q2	14 222	467	5 868	−9 427	−526	−1 511	8 821	2 507	136
Q3	14 422	568	5 691	−10 859	1 133	−1 393	9 299	1 665	155
Q4	13 524	530	5 858	−10 997	859	−536	8 196	2 300	178
1993 Q1	14 532	1 149	5 531	−13 887	−116	1 084	10 150	2 683	86
Q2	13 267	698	6 081	−10 465	705	−543	7 884	2 348	71
Q3	12 025	675	6 105	−10 586	591	1 726	6 595	1 613	61

1 Excluding financial transactions in writing-off debt.
2 Before providing for depreciation, stock appreciation and additions to reserves.
3 Comprises gross domestic fixed capital formation and increase in value of stocks and work in progress.
4 This balance is equal to saving *plus* capital transfers *less* gross domestic fixed capital formation, *less* increase in value of stocks and work in progress.
5 Equals, apart from the change in sign, the current balance of payments accounts, *plus* capital transfers.
6 For periods when the sector current and capital accounts are fully articulated, it is equal to the residual error in the national accounts.

Source: Central Statistical Office

Sector financial surplus/deficit

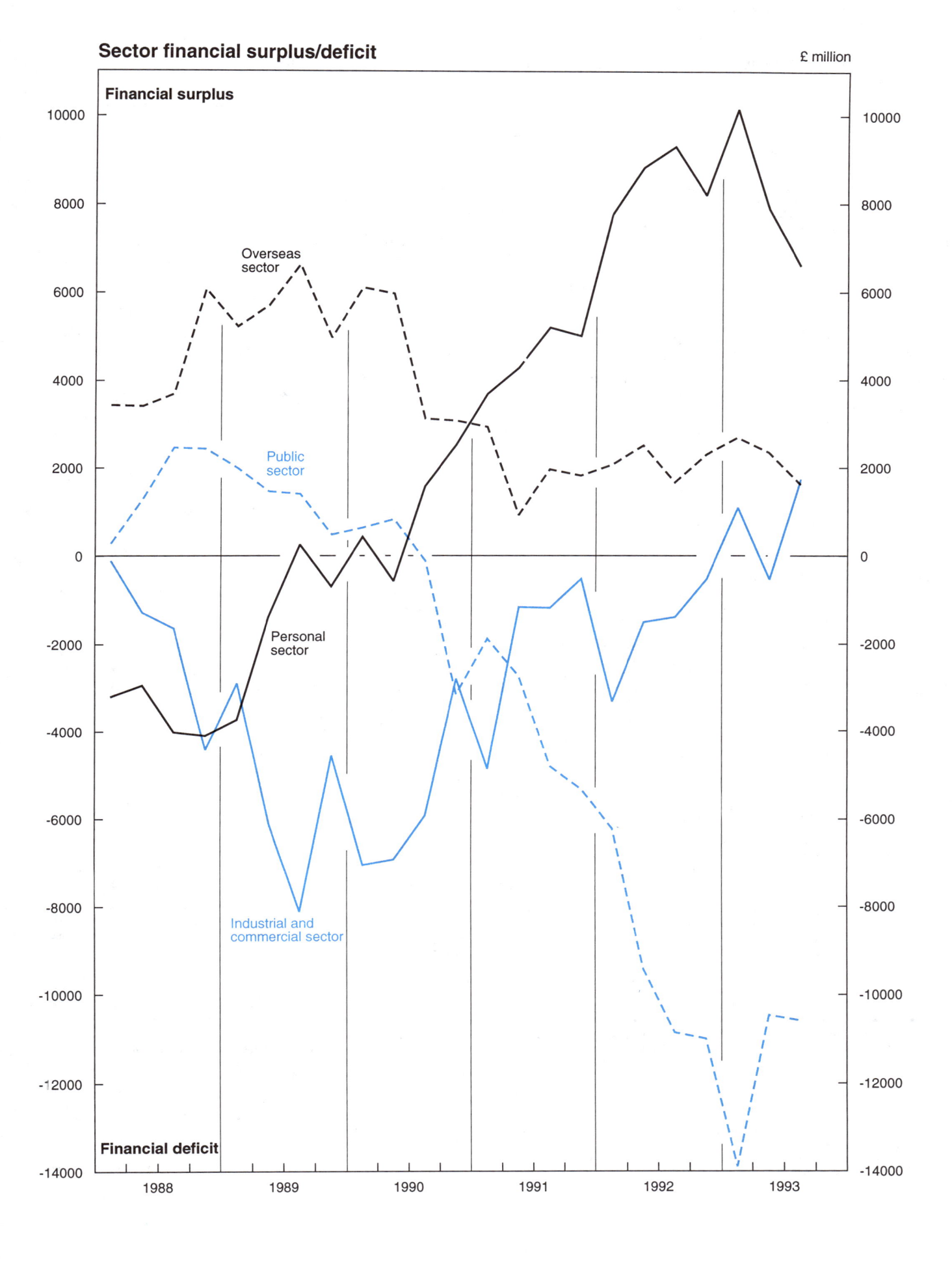

£ million

Financial surplus

- Overseas sector
- Public sector
- Personal sector
- Industrial and commercial sector

Financial deficit

36 Appropriation account of industrial and commercial companies[1]

£ million

	Income								Allocation of income				
	Income arising in the United Kingdom												
	Gross trading profits[3]												
	Net of stock appreciation			Stock appreciation	Before deducting stock appreciation	Rent and non-trading income	Income from abroad (net of taxes paid abroad)	Total income	Payments of dividends on ordinary and preference shares[4]	Payments of interest[5]	Profits due abroad (net of UK tax)	UK taxes on income (payments)[6]	Balance: Undistributed income[7]
	N. Sea oil companies	Other companies[2]	Total +[2]										
	CIDT	CIDU	AIAO	AIAP	AIAQ	AIAR	AIAS	AIAN	AIBA	AIAV	AIAW	AIAY	AAUQ
1983	15 683	26 057	41 740	3 619	45 359	4 988	6 706	57 053	5 343	9 487	4 631	10 867	26 725
1984	19 009	29 388	48 397	4 123	52 520	5 637	8 631	66 788	5 782	11 049	5 535	12 655	31 767
1985	18 514	38 955	57 469	2 155	59 624	6 878	8 565	75 067	6 099	12 934	6 403	14 934	34 697
1986	8 469	45 516	53 985	1 500	55 485	7 557	7 840	70 882	7 481	12 090	4 443	12 484	34 384
1987	9 554	52 196	61 750	4 148	65 898	8 053	11 366	85 317	9 441	13 211	6 891	13 179	42 595
1988	7 024	62 156	69 180	5 366	74 546	9 381	13 827	97 754	12 537	16 053	7 777	15 431	45 956
1989	6 806	67 086	73 892	6 203	80 095	12 538	18 124	110 757	16 212	25 896	8 635	19 038	40 976
1990	7 119	67 286	74 405	5 316	79 721	15 368	18 039	113 128	17 566	32 087	7 713	18 735	37 027
1991	6 478	71 585	78 063	2 098	80 161	13 856	15 010	109 027	18 363	29 793	5 440	15 389	40 042
1992	6 685	71 274	77 959	2 105	80 064	12 085	15 496	107 645	21 207	27 024	5 191	13 425	40 798
1985 Q3	4 196	9 871	14 067	122	14 189	1 705	2 108	18 002	1 649	3 075	1 362	3 838	8 078
Q4	4 220	10 398	14 618	495	15 113	1 730	1 586	18 429	1 707	3 139	1 572	3 674	8 337
1986 Q1	3 052	10 744	13 796	−401	13 395	1 843	1 643	16 881	1 676	3 074	968	3 580	7 583
Q2	1 796	11 205	13 001	−483	12 518	1 839	1 924	16 281	1 920	2 899	1 093	3 663	6 706
Q3	1 695	11 808	13 503	878	14 381	1 910	2 126	18 417	1 864	2 935	1 070	1 946	10 602
Q4	1 926	11 759	13 685	1 506	15 191	1 965	2 147	19 303	2 021	3 182	1 312	3 295	9 493
1987 Q1	2 377	12 566	14 943	838	15 781	1 996	2 760	20 537	2 348	3 208	1 756	2 660	10 565
Q2	2 477	12 868	15 345	1 071	16 416	1 942	2 874	21 232	2 289	3 212	1 642	3 324	10 765
Q3	2 531	13 674	16 205	1 155	17 360	2 027	2 902	22 289	2 348	3 404	1 755	3 735	11 047
Q4	2 169	13 088	15 257	1 084	16 341	2 088	2 830	21 259	2 456	3 387	1 738	3 460	10 218
1988 Q1	1 903	14 794	16 697	875	17 572	2 075	3 024	22 671	2 899	3 357	1 796	3 619	11 000
Q2	1 949	14 382	16 331	1 385	17 716	2 076	3 438	23 230	2 841	3 512	1 925	4 017	10 935
Q3	1 750	15 945	17 695	1 425	19 120	2 488	3 708	25 316	3 309	4 324	2 160	3 797	11 726
Q4	1 422	17 035	18 457	1 681	20 138	2 742	3 657	26 537	3 488	4 860	1 896	3 998	12 295
1989 Q1	1 470	17 109	18 579	1 753	20 332	2 805	4 338	27 475	3 576	5 469	2 065	4 123	12 242
Q2	1 754	16 235	17 989	1 831	19 820	3 004	4 896	27 720	4 613	6 155	2 332	4 647	9 973
Q3	1 768	16 747	18 515	1 151	19 666	3 213	4 054	26 933	4 067	6 747	1 966	5 631	8 522
Q4	1 814	16 995	18 809	1 468	20 277	3 516	4 836	28 629	3 956	7 525	2 272	4 637	10 239
1990 Q1	1 858	16 483	18 341	1 543	19 884	3 665	3 984	27 533	4 174	7 682	1 982	4 911	8 784
Q2	1 676	17 192	18 868	1 173	20 041	3 865	3 939	27 845	4 365	8 090	1 734	4 771	8 885
Q3	1 623	17 210	18 833	1 847	20 680	3 992	5 074	29 746	4 558	8 267	2 235	4 634	10 052
Q4	1 962	16 401	18 363	753	19 116	3 846	5 042	28 004	4 469	8 048	1 762	4 419	9 306
1991 Q1	1 692	17 121	18 813	691	19 504	3 678	3 408	26 590	4 447	8 253	1 281	4 166	8 443
Q2	1 475	17 818	19 293	665	19 958	3 475	3 889	27 322	4 506	7 561	1 346	3 899	10 010
Q3	1 654	17 657	19 311	412	19 723	3 465	3 770	26 958	4 825	7 114	1 399	3 736	9 884
Q4	1 657	18 989	20 646	330	20 976	3 238	3 943	28 157	4 585	6 865	1 414	3 588	11 705
1992 Q1	1 704	16 543	18 247	776	19 023	3 193	3 803	26 019	5 341	7 394	1 437	3 365	8 482
Q2	1 678	17 739	19 417	346	19 763	3 111	3 748	26 622	5 150	6 855	1 309	3 509	9 799
Q3	1 555	18 210	19 765	284	20 049	3 030	4 062	27 141	5 054	6 733	1 103	3 456	10 795
Q4	1 748	18 782	20 530	699	21 229	2 751	3 883	27 863	5 662	6 042	1 342	3 095	11 722
1993 Q1	1 802	19 257	21 059	656	21 715	2 518	4 108	28 341	5 126	5 686	1 920	3 069	12 540
Q2	1 997	19 503	21 500	483	21 983	2 439	4 034	28 456	6 269	5 287	1 463	3 354	12 083
Q3	2 031	20 704	22 735	308	23 043	2 487	4 005	29 535	5 252	5 249	1 932	3 548	13 554

1 Figures reflect privatisation of British Telecom with effect from 28 November 1984, British Gas from 3 December 1986, British Airways from 6 February 1987, Royal Ordnance from 22 April 1987, BAA from 16 July 1987, British Steel from 2 December 1988, water companies from 12 December 1989, electricity distribution companies from 11 December 1990, electricity generating companies from 12 March 1991 and Scottish electricity companies from 18 June 1991.
2 Gross trading profits of non-oil industrial and commercial companies include quarterly alignment adjustments. For details, see note 2 in Notes to editors section of 3rd quarter 1991 Industrial and commercial companies press notice, issued on 7 January 1992.
3 Before providing for depreciation.
4 Dividend payments on ordinary and preference shares are net of tax; the advance corporation tax in respect of these dividends is included in "UK taxes on income." Excludes payments by UK subsidiaries to their overseas parents.
5 Includes royalties and licence fees on oil and gas production and other current transfers. Franchise payments to ITC are also included from 1993.
6 Includes payments of corporation tax (including advance corporation tax) and petroleum revenue tax.
7 Includes unremitted profits from abroad; and is net of unremitted profits due abroad.

Source: Central Statistical Office

Industrial and commercial companies income and saving

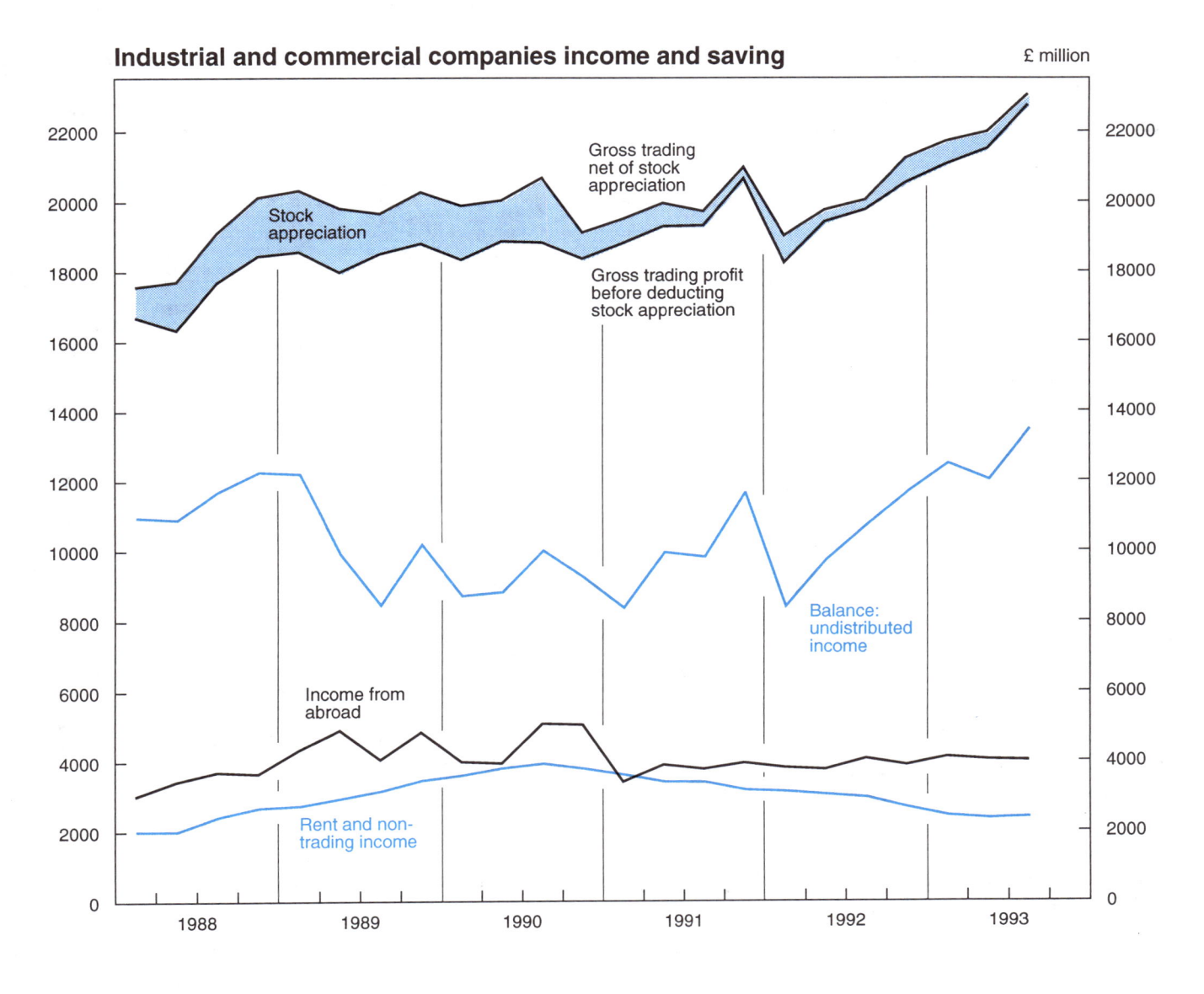

£ million

- Gross trading net of stock appreciation
- Stock appreciation
- Gross trading profit before deducting stock appreciation
- Balance: undistributed income
- Income from abroad
- Rent and non-trading income

Industrial and commercial companies income and saving

£ million

- Dividends and other interest payments
- UK taxes on income
- Profits due abroad

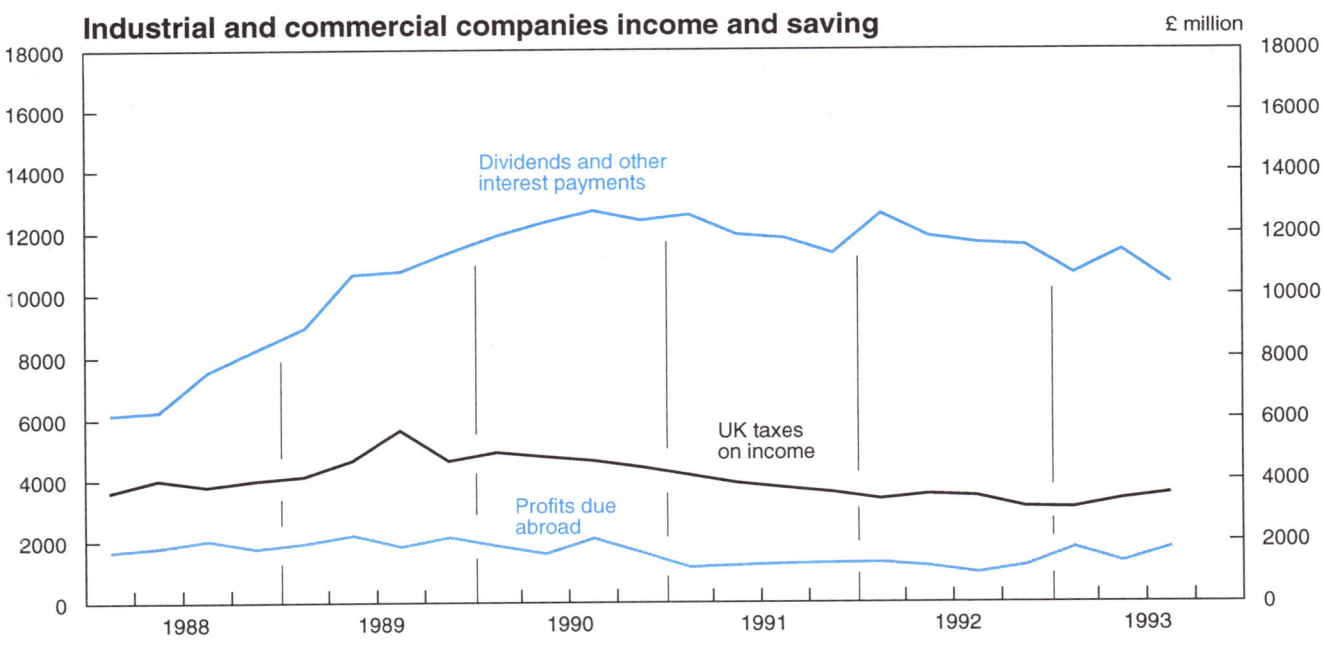

37 Capital account and financial surplus/deficit of industrial and commercial companies[1]

£ million

	Receipts					Expenditure				Balance: financial surplus/deficit
	Undistributed income	Stock appreciation	Undistributed income less stock appreciation	Capital transfers	Total receipts[2]	Gross domestic fixed capital formation	Value of physical increase in stocks and work in progress[3]	Taxes on capital and other capital transfers	Total expenditure	
	AAUQ	AIAP	FMBC	CIDZ	FMBA	AAUS	FMBG	FMBH	FMBF	AAVG
1989	40 976	6 203	34 773	561	35 334	52 538	3 080	1 433	57 051	−21 717
1990	37 027	5 316	31 711	513	32 224	54 729	−1 106	1 354	54 977	−22 753
1991	40 042	2 098	37 944	495	38 439	50 042	−4 829	979	46 192	−7 753
1992	40 798	2 105	38 693	491	39 184	47 403	−2 115	654	45 942	−6 758
1990 Q3	10 052	1 847	8 205	108	8 313	13 618	292	348	14 258	−5 945
Q4	9 306	753	8 553	125	8 678	13 155	−2 000	315	11 470	−2 792
1991 Q1	8 443	691	7 752	136	7 888	13 242	−767	289	12 764	−4 876
Q2	10 010	665	9 345	125	9 470	12 331	−1 943	248	10 636	−1 166
Q3	9 884	412	9 472	116	9 588	12 216	−1 663	219	10 772	−1 184
Q4	11 705	330	11 375	118	11 493	12 253	−456	223	12 020	−527
1992 Q1	8 482	776	7 706	112	7 818	11 983	−1 051	204	11 136	−3 318
Q2	9 799	346	9 453	125	9 578	11 693	−736	132	11 089	−1 511
Q3	10 795	284	10 511	124	10 635	11 736	145	147	12 028	−1 393
Q4	11 722	699	11 023	130	11 153	11 991	−473	171	11 689	−536
1993 Q1	12 540	656	11 884	112	11 996	11 789	−1 020	143	10 912	1 084
Q2	12 083	483	11 600	107	11 707	11 686	438	126	12 250	−543
Q3	13 554	308	13 246	110	13 356	12 048	−556	138	11 630	1 726

1 Figures reflect privatisation of British Telecom with effect from 28 November 1984, British Gas from 3 December 1986, British Airways from 6 February 1987, Royal Ordnance from 22 April 1987, BAA from 16 July 1987, British Steel from 2 December 1988, water companies from 12 December 1989, electricity distribution companies from 11 December 1990, electricity generating companies from 12 March 1991 and Scottish electricity companies from 18 June 1991.

2 After deducting stock appreciation but before providing for depreciation.
3 Includes quarterly alignment adjustments. For details, See note 2 in Notes to editors section of 3rd quarter 1991 Industrial and commercial companies press notice, issued on 7 January 1992.

Source: Central Statistical Office

38 Financial transactions including net borrowing requirement of industrial and commercial companies[1]

£ million

	Transactions leading to net borrowing requirement						Financing of net borrowing requirement[4]				Net borrowing requirement (NBR)
							Borrowing from		Financial assets		
	Financial surplus/ deficit	Net unremitted profits[2]	Net identified trade and other credit[3,4]	Investment in UK company securities[5]	Investment abroad	Balancing item	Banks[6]	Other	Liquid	Other	
	1	2	3	4	5	6	7	8	9	10	11
	AAVG	-AICX	-AIDL	-AICC	-AIDC	-AAOB	-AANA	-AICT	-AICU	-AICV	-AICW
1989	−21 717	−5 207	1 140	−17 945	−10 355	−528	33 952	37 007	−11 604	−4 743	54 612
1990	−22 753	−6 454	−484	−2 309	−1 048	−3 917	19 895	33 884	−8 170	−8 644	36 965
1991	−7 753	−5 252	819	−5 130	−4 216	−5 145	−918	34 885	−5 749	−1 541	26 677
1992	−6 758	−4 701	−1 184	−6 067	−3 077	−5 010	−2 312	22 148	2 317	4 644	26 797
			-ABKP			-AIDD	-AIDF	-AIDJ	-AIDG		-AIDI
1990 Q3	−5 945	−1 784	283	−48	−179	3 921	2 980	8 178	−4 069	−3 337	3 752
Q4	−2 792	−1 416	−1 325	−450	−2 231	−6 092	4 146	6 390	3 091	679	14 306
1991 Q1	−4 876	−1 609	−970	−1 762	−3 636	4 267	1 905	7 650	−234	−735	8 586
Q2	−1 166	−1 577	1 690	−1 173	−2 260	931	−1 707	11 934	−3 110	−3 562	3 555
Q3	−1 184	−1 364	−81	−595	−598	−4 050	−609	7 174	−679	1 986	7 872
Q4	−527	−702	180	−1 600	2 278	−6 293	−507	8 127	−1 726	770	6 664
1992 Q1	−3 318	−967	154	−3 149	−159	−2 250	−278	9 043	234	690	9 689
Q2	−1 511	−1 294	−82	−2 209	−1 467	−1 420	−156	5 912	1 168	1 059	7 983
Q3	−1 393	−1 117	−544	−276	482	659	−744	3 680	−673	−74	2 189
Q4	−536	−1 323	−712	−433	−1 933	−1 999	−1 134	3 513	1 588	2 969	6 936
1993 Q1	1 084	−1 408	1 663	−933	−1 423	768	−4 651	8 764	−1 390	−2 474	249
Q2	−543	−1 164	941	−863	−2 413	−2 684	−1 988	11 892	−302	−2 876	6 726
Q3	1 726	−1 068	1 075	60	−1 632	−2 909	−1 873	7 206	−1 970	−615	2 748

1 Inflows(+), outflows(-); relationships between columns:
 1 + 2 + 3 + 4 + 5 + 6 + 7 + 8 + 9 + 10 = zero; 7 + 8 + 9 + 10 = 11.
2 Retained in UK (+); retained abroad (-).
3 Includes accruals adjustment.
4 Seasonal adjustments include day-of-week adjustments. The quarterly figures therefore do not always sum to the annual totals.
5 Cash expenditure on subsidiaries and trade investments in the United Kingdom.
6 Includes Bank of England Issue Department transactions in commercial bills.

Source: Central Statistical Office

Industrial and commercial companies income and saving

£ million

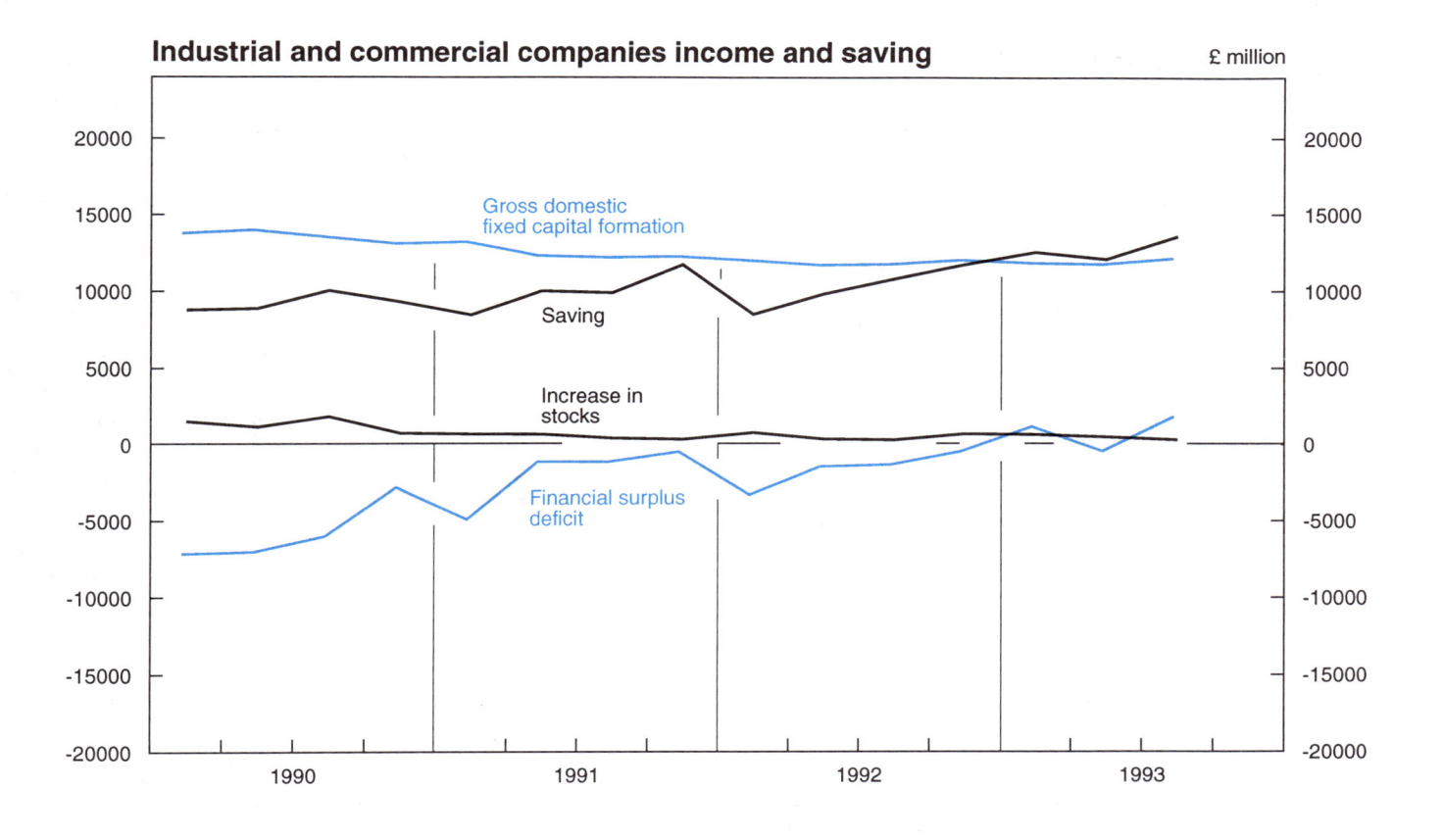

Gross domestic fixed capital formation

Saving

Increase in stocks

Financial surplus deficit

£ million

Net borrowing requirement

Other borrowing

Bank borrowing

Transactions in liquid assets

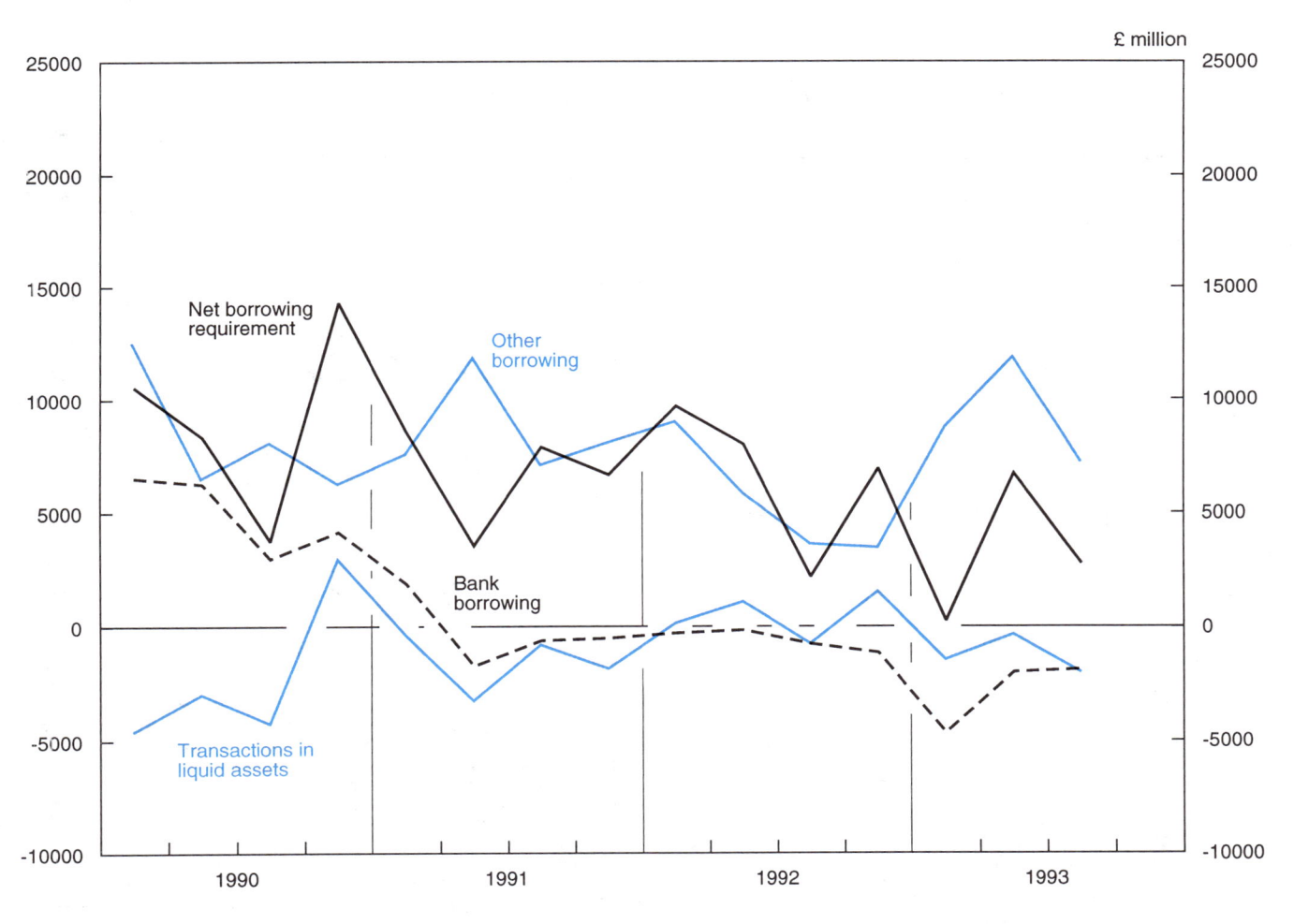

39 UK banks' lending to UK residents[1]

£ million

	Lending to public sector			Lending to private sector		
	Sterling	Other currencies	Total	Sterling	Other currencies	Total
Transactions	AEBT	VQAH	FPAA	VQAE	AECO	FPAD
1990	82	29	111	47 273	2 552	49 825
1991	−109	1	−108	15 290	9 105	24 395
1992	212[†]	4 433	4 645[†]	11 717	−2 599	9 118
1993	3 363	661	4 024	13 906	7 439	21 345
1990 Q1	409	−229	180	16 386	269	16 655
Q2	−218	79	−139	11 287	1 071	12 358
Q3	−430	11	−419	8 622	420	9 042
Q4	321	168	489	10 978	792	11 770
1991 Q1	−990[†]	−96	−1 086[†]	5 875	2 489	8 364
Q2	1 179	−1	1 178	1 942	1 426	3 368
Q3	690	−15	675	4 133	974	5 107
Q4	−988	113	−875	3 340	4 216	7 556
1992 Q1	−115	−191	−306	564	−988	−424
Q2	−299	−118	−417	5 726	−227	5 499
Q3	−1 666	4 140	2 474	3 187[†]	899	4 086[†]
Q4	2 292	602	2 894	2 240	−2 283	−43
1993 Q1	2 727	561	3 288	929	1 414	2 343
Q2	1 191	−168	1 023	2 692	1 983	4 675
Q3	548	59	607	5 863	605	6 468
Q4	−1 103	209	−894	4 422	3 437	7 859

1 Seasonally adjusted data are shown on a calendar year basis whereas data in Tables 32 and 33 are on a financial year basis. The quarterly figures do not necessarily add up to the (unadjusted) figures shown for the year as a whole. This is because as well as allowing for purely seasonal factors, the adjustments attempt to remove other distortions which do not necessarily cancel out over a year.

Source: Bank of England

40 UK banks' loans, advances and acceptances to UK residents[1,2]

£ million

	Manufacturing	Other production	Financial	Services	Persons	Total loans, advances and acceptances
Amounts outstanding	BALH	BALI	BALJ	BALK	BALL	BALG
1992 Aug	48 253	30 538	105 844	124 744	138 316	447 695
Nov	50 196	32 606	113 035	132 747	139 055	467 639
1993 Mar	47 431	31 379	118 039	130 358	140 755	467 962
Jun	45 211	30 390	121 655	128 717	143 188	469 162
Sep	44 160	30 706	124 352	126 470	146 498	472 186
Changes	FRAB	FRAC	FRAD	FRAE	FRAF	FRAA
1991 Feb	−301	996	4 467	2 573	1 228	9 750
May	−1 341	−547	3 393	−556	1 756	3 493
Aug	−1 745	−377	−743	−1 578	2 974	−682
Nov	−441	405	8 446	299	1 946	11 442
1992 Feb	269	87	2 522	−1 341	1 075	3 887
May	−1 803	248	1 613	−236	1 815	2 768
Aug	−338	326	414	−2 709	2 962	1 932
Nov	−632	813	1 903	4 693	688	8 448
1993 Mar	−2 888	−1 136	4 936	−2 319	2 112	2 186
Jun	−2 161	−957	3 711	−1 542	2 912	2 975
Sep	−1 144	295	2 498	−2 363	3 680	3 830

1 In these statistics lending flows are generally calculated as changes in reported amounts outstanding; they are thus potentially distorted by revaluations (eg write-offs). The Bank has used published data and certain other information provided by the banks to make adjustments to lending flows from 1986 to remove these distortions. These adjustments are believed to be broadly accurate on an annual basis but have been allocated to individual quarters purely by averaging the annual figure. Because the adjustments have not been carried through to all individual industrial categories, the sum of the individual categories does not add exactly to the total changes. The individual categories that have been adjusted for write-offs are *persons* and in the last quarter, 0.1bn of write-offs allocated between *other production* and *services*. Banks have recently begun to report revaluations quarterly - the write-off adjustments included in the last three periods are based upon these new reported figures.

2 For a more detailed breakdown of these figures see *Financial Statistics* Table 6.6. The analysis which is not seasonally adjusted covers loans, advances and acceptances and holdings of sterling commercial paper in both sterling and foreign currencies (changes in the latter being adjusted for exchange rate movements) provided by banks to their customers and therefore does not include funds placed through the local authority money market or funds lent to banks. Acceptances are not granted to persons.

3 At end-March 1993, the industrial analysis moved onto an end-calendar quarter basis. The analysis of the period to-end March 1993 therefore covers four months, and the changes are not directly comparable with those previously published.

Source: Bank of England

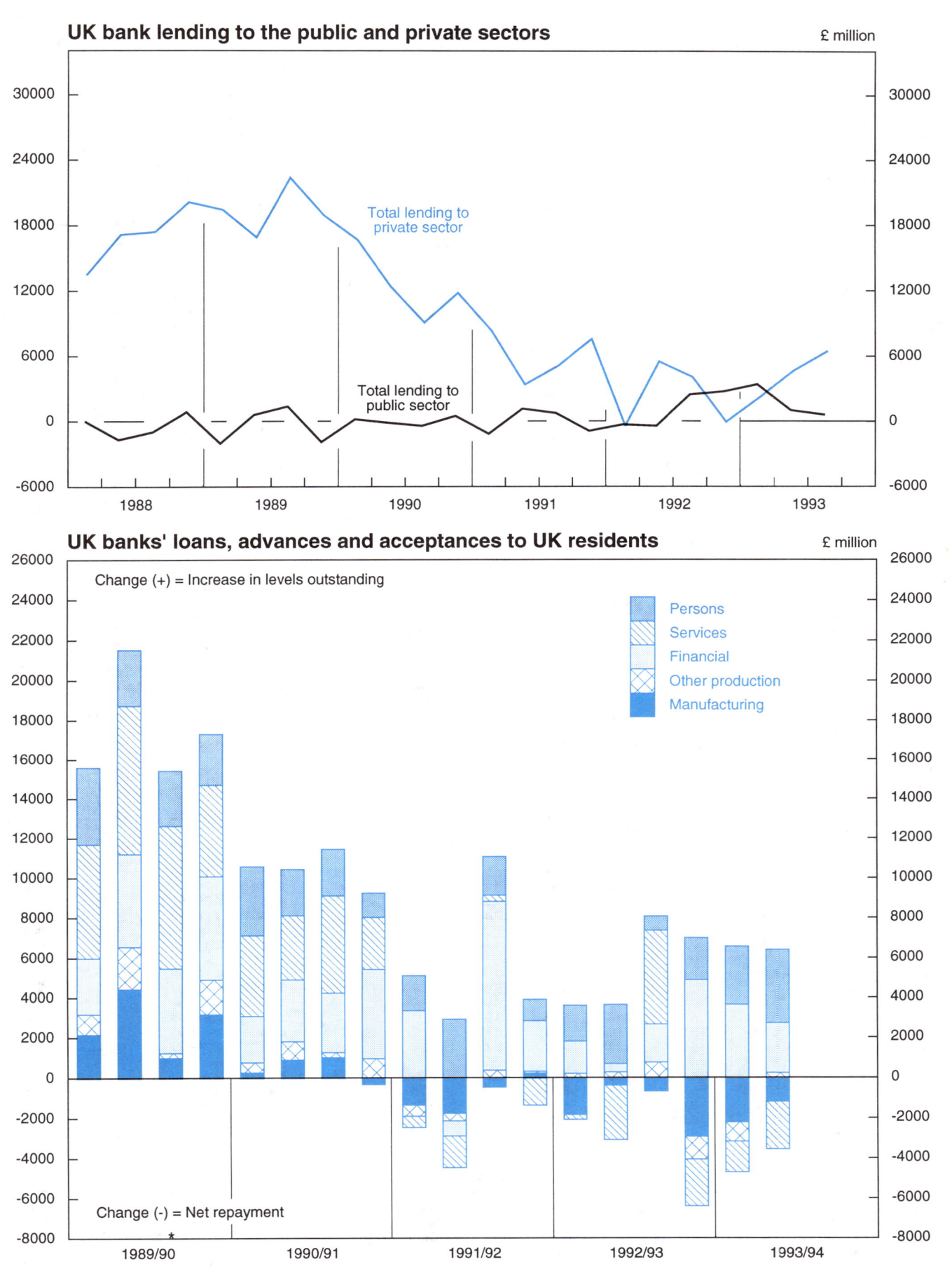

UK bank lending to the public and private sectors £ million

Total lending to private sector

Total lending to public sector

UK banks' loans, advances and acceptances to UK residents £ million

Change (+) = Increase in levels outstanding

- Persons
- Services
- Financial
- Other production
- Manufacturing

Change (−) = Net repayment

* See footnote[2] page 74 lower table

75

41 Interest rates, security prices and yields

Percentage rate

	Last Friday						Last working day	Average of working days			
	Treasury bill yield[1]	Deposits with local authorities - 3 months[2]	Selected retail banks: base rate	Inter-bank 3 months bid rate[3]	Inter-bank 3 months offer rate[3]	Sterling certificates of deposit 3 months bid rate	Sterling certificates of deposit 3 months offer rate	Euro-dollar 3 month rate	British government securities: long dated[4] - 20 years	Financial Times index of industrial ordinary shares 1 July 1935 = 100		
										Price index	Dividend yield	Earnings yield
	AJNC	AJOI		HSAJ	HSAK	HSAL	HSAM	AJIB	AJLX	AJMT	AJMU	AJMV
1990	13.50	13.94	14.00	14.00	14.00	13.81	13.88	7.50	11.08	1 749.43†	5.29†	11.70
1991	10.45	10.94	10.50	10.94	11.00	10.81	10.88	4.19	9.92	1 921.86	4.98	8.72
1992	6.44	7.13	7.00	7.13	7.19	6.88	6.91	3.32	9.13	1 951.91	4.68	6.75
1993	4.95	5.31	5.50	5.31	5.31	5.22	5.25	3.28	7.87†	2 287.94	4.10	5.26
1990 Jan	14.99	15.06	15.00	15.13	15.19	15.00	15.16	8.31	10.28	1 894.20	4.51	11.01
Feb	14.87	15.00	15.00	15.09	15.13	15.00	15.06	8.31	10.72	1 816.79	4.76	11.47
Mar	15.14	15.13	15.00	15.22	15.25	15.13	15.19	8.44	11.46	1 771.99	4.98	11.76
Apr	15.17	15.13	15.00	15.28	15.31	15.19	15.25	8.63	11.77	1 718.96	5.22	12.03
May	15.00	14.94	15.00	15.03	15.09	14.97	15.03	8.31	11.49	1 757.40	5.21	11.71
Jun	14.85	14.94	15.00	14.94	14.97	14.88	14.94	8.25	11.01	1 904.97	4.86	10.76
Jul	14.86	14.94	15.00	14.94	15.00	14.91	14.97	7.88	11.03	1 873.36	4.96	10.90
Aug	14.81	14.88	15.00	14.97	15.00	14.88	15.00	8.00	11.41	1 710.25	5.52	11.82
Sep	14.76	14.97	15.00	14.94	14.97	14.88	14.94	8.25	11.32	1 599.08	5.93	12.52
Oct	13.57	13.75	14.00	13.78	13.81	13.98	13.81	8.00	11.12	1 619.55	5.90	12.34
Nov	13.11	13.50	14.00	13.50	13.56	13.38	13.44	8.31	10.94	1 630.44	5.90	12.31
Dec	13.50	13.94	14.00	14.00	14.00	13.81	13.88	7.50	10.40	1 696.14†	5.67†	11.83
1991 Jan	13.23	13.88	14.00	13.97	13.97	13.75	13.88	7.00	10.22	1 653.17	5.82	12.07
Feb	12.44	12.75	13.00	12.75	12.88	12.75	12.81	6.81	9.89	1 803.59	5.33	11.07
Mar	11.90	12.88	12.50	12.38	12.44	12.25	12.31	6.31	10.06	1 953.94	4.96	9.25
Apr	11.49	11.44	12.00	11.78	11.81	11.66	11.72	6.00	9.99	1 983.19	4.87	8.80
May	11.04	11.38	11.50	11.38	11.41	11.25	11.28	6.00	10.15	1 952.19	4.91	8.68
Jun	11.04	11.63	11.50	11.31	11.37	11.13	11.19	6.13	10.34	1 951.73	4.88	8.57
Jul	10.72	11.06	11.00	11.13	11.13	10.94	11.00	6.00	10.10	1 953.22	4.84	8.47
Aug	10.33	10.81	11.00	10.78	10.81	10.63	10.69	5.63	9.89	2 027.33	4.68	7.81
Sep	9.94	10.62	10.50	10.19	10.25	10.13	10.19	5.62	9.54	2 053.95	4.64	7.49
Oct	10.24	10.50	10.50	10.50	10.56	10.41	10.44	5.19	9.62	1 979.08	4.74	7.48
Nov	10.34	10.63	10.50	10.59	10.63	10.50	10.53	4.93	9.68	1 920.39	5.03	7.46
Dec	10.45	10.94	10.50	10.94	11.00	10.81	10.88	4.19	9.56	1 830.52	5.03	7.54
1992 Jan	10.13	10.56	10.50	10.63	10.66	10.47	10.53	4.13	9.34	1 937.55	4.71	7.06
Feb	9.98	10.25	10.50	10.31	10.34	10.16	10.22	4.18	9.21	1 974.94	4.62	6.78
Mar	10.48	10.57	10.50	10.78	10.81	10.69	10.72	4.25	9.54	1 946.12	4.61	6.57
Apr	10.06	10.53	10.50	10.50	10.56	10.34	10.41	4.00	9.33	1 983.89	4.55	6.58
May	9.65	10.00	10.00	10.00	10.00	9.91	9.88	4.00	8.99	2 123.50	4.32	6.22
Jun	9.69	9.94	10.00	10.06	10.13	9.94	9.97	3.83	9.02	2 027.33	4.56	6.68
Jul	9.85	10.10	10.00	10.31	10.25	10.22	10.16	3.38	8.88	1 856.49	4.97	7.20
Aug	9.93	10.24	10.00	10.56	10.63	10.31	10.44	3.44	9.13	1 741.10	5.20	7.50
Sep	8.40	9.82	9.00	9.25	9.25	9.00	9.13	3.25	9.16	1 794.52	4.95	7.17
Oct	6.87	7.44	8.00	—†	7.63	7.44	7.50	3.57	9.24	1 899.13	4.73	6.80
Nov	6.56	7.19	7.00	7.25	7.31	7.03	7.09	3.94	8.84	2 023.15	4.55	6.38
Dec	6.44	7.13	7.00	7.13	7.19	6.88	6.91	3.32	8.84	2 115.20	4.40	6.03
1993 Jan	5.51	6.25	6.00	6.25	6.31	6.06	6.13	3.19	8.91	2 161.96	4.35	5.98
Feb	5.49	6.13	6.00	6.13	6.13	5.94	5.97	3.13	8.63	2 195.20	4.35	5.93
Mar	5.47	5.88	6.00	6.00	6.06	5.94	6.00	3.19	8.33	2 252.83	4.35	6.08
Apr	5.46	6.13	6.00	6.13	6.13	5.91	5.97	3.13	8.39	2 213.18	4.27	6.27
May	5.32	5.88	6.00	5.84	5.91	5.75	5.78	3.32	8.60	2 207.04	4.21	6.21
Jun	5.26	6.00	6.00	5.88	5.94	5.75	5.78	3.25	8.39	2 249.20	4.12	4.99
Jul	5.16	5.81	6.00	5.88	5.94	5.75	5.81	3.25	7.96	2 242.43	4.12	4.90
Aug	5.16	5.81	6.00	5.69	5.75	5.69	5.75	3.19	7.39	2 371.00	3.89	4.64
Sep	5.25	5.94	6.00	5.88	5.91	5.78	5.81	3.32	7.18	2 348.43	3.95	4.66
Oct	5.08	5.50	6.00	5.63	5.69	5.47	5.50	3.38	7.09	2 363.62	3.94	4.58
Nov	4.87	5.38	5.50	5.31	5.34	5.22	5.25	3.44	7.06	2 357.95	3.94	4.58
Dec	4.95	5.31	5.50	5.31	5.31	5.22	5.25	3.28	6.46†	2 492.46	3.73	4.25
1994 Jan	4.91	5.38	5.50	5.38	5.44	5.25	5.31	3.19	6.41	..	..	..

1 Average discount rate expressed as the rate at which interest is earned during the life of the bills.
2 For a minimum term of 3 months and thereafter at 7 days' notice.
3 Spread of rates over the day in the inter-bank sterling market; from June 1982 rates are the spread at 10.30 am.
4 Averages of Wednesdays until February 1980; from March 1980 figures are the average of all observations (3 a week); from January 1982 average of working days. Calculated gross redemption yields - see *Financial Statistics Explanatory Handbook*.

Sources: *Central Statistical Office;*
Building Societies Commission;
Institute of Actuaries;
Faculty of Actuaries;
Bank of England;
Financial Times;
HM Treasury

Interest rates, and security yields

42 A selection of asset prices

	Physical assets						Financial assets		
	Vehicles plant and machinery: producer price indices (1990 = 100)		Housing: DoE index of house prices (1990 = 100)			Average price of agricultural land in England (1985 = 100)[1]	British government stocks		Company securities: FT-Actuaries all ordinary shares (10 April 1962 = 100)
	Motor vehicles and their engines	Plant and machinery	New dwellings	Secondhand dwellings	All dwellings		Fixed interest (Dec 1975 =100)	Index linked (April 1982= 100)	
	PAES	PHVP	BAJF	BAJG	BAJH	BAJI	AJJY	AJJZ	AJMA
1982 Q4	..	..	39.7	38.7	39.1	99	128.82	108.45	378.63
1983 Q1	..	89.6	40.3	40.2	40.1	102	125.33	112.04	402.88
Q2	..	91.0	42.2	41.2	41.6	105	129.36	107.16	436.11
Q3	..	91.0	42.2	43.2	43.1	100	126.50	104.12	449.30
Q4	..	91.6	44.2	43.7	43.6	106	130.16	106.63	450.53
1984 Q1	91.0	93.0	44.7	43.7	44.1	109	130.30	105.17	499.26[†]
Q2	92.5	94.0	45.2	45.2	45.1	112	125.81	103.34	510.24
Q3	93.7	95.5	47.2	47.2	47.1	116	124.55	100.88	502.40
Q4	95.6	97.2	47.2	47.7	47.6	86	128.60	109.19	554.51
1985 Q1	97.5	99.4	48.7	47.7	47.6	115	125.60	109.64	613.75
Q2	99.2	101.0	48.7	49.7	49.6	107	127.79	110.27	625.55
Q3	100.8	101.0	49.7	51.2	50.7	96	130.95	111.15	619.96
Q4	102.5	100.0	51.7	52.2	52.2	109	130.46	109.86	668.64
1986 Q1	104.7	101.8	53.7	53.7	53.7	99	133.43	108.86	729.09
Q2	105.8	102.6	56.7	55.8	55.7	103	140.58	116.86	800.73
Q3	107.3	103.2	57.2	58.3	58.2	90	133.78	113.83	792.95
Q4	109.5	104.4	60.1	60.3	60.2	92	128.44	111.55	806.18
1987 Q1	112.2	106.5	61.1	61.8	61.7	91	136.02	119.28	943.82
Q2	114.2	106.6	64.6	64.8	64.7	81	140.54	118.13	1 063.65
Q3	115.3	106.6	67.6	67.8	67.7	86	132.50	113.63	1 174.51
Q4	117.3	106.5	71.1	71.8	71.7	90	137.38	114.36	916.60
1988 Q1	120.1	107.5	76.5	74.3	74.7	92	138.31	117.76	908.67
Q2	121.5	107.9	77.5	79.4	79.2	90	136.53	120.74	931.35
Q3	124.8	107.9	88.0	89.9	89.8	89	132.99	121.39	946.30
Q4	126.3	108.4	93.4	95.4	95.3	95	132.94	127.55	940.37
1989 Q1	129.9	110.7	101.4	96.9	97.3	98	132.67	131.92	1 037.42
Q2	130.2	112.6	101.4	101.0	100.8	103	130.11	132.93	1 089.48
Q3	132.6	114.3	102.9	104.5	104.3	109	130.86	138.63	1 182.76
Q4	134.9	115.1	98.4	103.0	102.3	117	128.18	139.05	1 131.51
1990 Q1	137.9	117.7	102.7	99.6	100.1	119	121.49	135.43	1 148.95
Q2	139.7	118.7	98.5	99.3	99.2	126	119.27	135.88	1 119.66
Q3	142.0	117.5	98.9	101.3	101.0	109	121.32	138.09	1 081.98
Q4	145.2	117.4	100.0	99.4	99.5	117	125.62	143.15	1 018.89
1991 Q1	148.8	119.6	96.8	98.3	98.1	106	130.11	145.37	1 099.00
Q2	150.7	119.9	95.4	98.1	97.7	115	129.52	147.19	1 206.59
Q3	151.2	119.8	100.9	99.4	99.6	97	132.00	147.89	1 239.48
Q4	151.3	118.9	95.9	99.2	98.7	92	132.83	149.59	1 204.14
1992 Q1	108.7	108.9	100.3	96.6	97.1	103	133.14	149.62	1 206.94
Q2	110.2	108.3	96.4	94.5	94.8	98	136.24	152.78	1 265.39
Q3	109.9	107.8	91.1	95.9	95.2	96	134.35	152.18	1 147.78
Q4	108.0	110.9	90.1	92.1	91.8	85	142.20	167.82	1 278.41
1993 Q1	112.5	115.2	91.9	91.6	91.6	94	144.18	171.70	1 384.00
Q2	113.7	..	93.4	91.2	91.5	102	143.44	173.73	1 403.58
Q3	114.7	–	95.1	94.2	94.3	81	150.07	181.20	1 472.28
Q4	115.9p	–	..	..	..	84	155.08	188.77	1 569.60

1 Prices of vacant possession land sold without buildings. Sales notified to the Inland Revenue in the period are thought to have taken place, on average, about nine months earlier.
2 Provisional.

Sources: Department of Environment;
Central Statistical Office;
MAFF

43 Number of property transactions in England and Wales[1,2]

Thousands

	Number of property transactions			Number of property transactions	
	Not seasonally adjusted	Seasonally adjusted[3]		Not seasonally adjusted	Seasonally adjusted[3]
	FTAP		1991 Nov	102	98†
1989	1 580		Dec	95	102
1990	1 398		1992 Jan	80	81
1991	1 306		Feb	74	93
1992	1 136		Mar	83	92
1993	1 196		Apr	86	90
			May	82	91
			Jun	97	90
		FTAQ	Jul	107	91
1989 Q4	378	369†	Aug	118	111
			Sep	143	131
1990 Q1	344	375	Oct	103	94
Q2	360	367	Nov	82	78
Q3	349	326	Dec	83	86
Q4	345	333	1993 Jan	78	84
1991 Q1	314	347	Feb	72	89
Q2	324	332	Mar	88	94
Q3	353	322	Apr	87	92
Q4	315	303	May	87	95
			Jun	105	99
1992 Q1	236	266			
Q2	265	271	Jul	114	101
Q3	367	333	Aug	113	106
Q4	268	258	Sep	120	106
			Oct	110	106
1993 Q1	239	267	Nov	119	109
Q2	279†	286	Dec	102	108
Q3	347	313			
Q4	331	323	1994 Jan	106	113

1 The figures are based on counts of the relevant administrative forms processed each month. Because of the time lags involved, the series above should be lagged one month to give a broad representation of transactions occurring in the month (details are given in the June 1991 edition of *Economic Trends*).

2 Over the period from 20 December 1991 to 19 August 1992, the stamp duty threshold was temporarily increased from £30 000 to £250 000. A stamp duty threshold of £60 000 has been operating following the March 1993 budget.

3 These figures have all been revised following a review of methodology; details are given in the February 1994 edition of *Economic Trends*.

More up to date figures can be obtained by phoning the CSO public inquiry service on 071-270 6363/6364 and quoting the 4 digit identifier (FTAP or FTAQ) given on the table. Figures can be obtained from the 21st (or the next working day after the 21st) of the month following the month to which they relate.

Source: Board of Inland Revenue

Cyclical indicators for the UK economy

Recent movements of the indices

The **longer leading index** is rising once again and is now approaching the high point in March 1993 after a period in the second and third quarters when it was fairly flat. The initial increase in the index from the second quarter of 1992 was mainly due to lower interest rates and a fall in the financial deficit of industrial and commercial companies; but the latest movement is mainly due to increases in business optimism, recorded in the January CBI Industrial Trends Survey, and in housebuilding starts in the last quarter of 1993.

The **shorter leading index** reached a trough in June 1991. Subsequently, it has generally been rising although it fell back during the third quarter of 1992. Recent rises reflect the continued strength of share prices, CBI reports of higher new orders, and an increase in the EC/Gallup index of consumer confidence in January.

The **coincident index** reached a trough in the second quarter of 1992. Since then it has maintained steady increases with all components, especially real M0, contributing to its growth for most months in 1993.

The **lagging index** reached a trough in the first quarter of 1993. It has subsequently shown a general rise mirroring improvements in labour market statistics.

Definitions

This section identifies peaks and troughs in the reference cycle of UK economic activity. In addition, it describes the movement in composite cyclical indicators constructed from economic series. These indicators have demonstrated an ability to identify in advance, concurrently and in retrospect, the peaks and troughs in economic activity. They do not measure the level of economic activity nor its growth rate.

The reference cycle in the UK economic activity is derived as the deviation of gross domestic product at constant factor cost from its long term trend value. The indicators forming each composite index have been chosen because they have had a consistent timing relationship to the reference chronology, and because there is an economic rationale to account for this relationship.

A composite index is formed by subtracting from each series the values of its long-term trend, then taking a simple average of the trend eliminated series after smoothing and scaling them to give cycles of similar amplitude and inverting them where appropriate.

Precise details on data availability for each of the component series used in the compilation of the indicators is shown on Table B.

Table A - Recent movements of the indicators

		Longer Leading (5 component series) DKBR	Shorter Leading (5 component series) DKBS	Coincident (6 component series) DKBP	Lagging (5 component series) DKBQ
1992	Jan	98.2	96.1	93.1	95.0
	Feb	98.1	96.4	92.8	94.7
	Mar	98.0	97.1	92.8	94.8
	Apr	98.2	98.5	92.7	94.9
	May	98.3	99.7	93.0	94.9
	June	99.1	94.3	94.7	98.3
	July	98.4	98.9	93.4	95.2
	Aug	98.5	95.3	94.5	94.7
	Sep	99.1	94.8	95.1	94.8
	Oct	100.5	95.6	95.5	95.3
	Nov	102.5	96.9	95.7	95.5
	Dec	103.9	98.7	96.2	94.9
1993	Jan	105.6	99.7	96.9	94.3
	Feb	106.6	100.2	97.6	94.0
	Mar	106.9	100.5	98.3	95.0
	Apr	106.9	101.3	99.1	95.2
	May	106.5	102.3	99.5	95.6
	June	106.1	103.5	100.3	95.9
	July	105.8	105.0	101.2	95.7
	Aug	105.8	106.6	102.0	96.0
	Sep	105.8	107.7	102.4	96.3
	Oct	105.9 (4)	107.7 (4)	103.1	96.2 (3)
	Nov	106.1 (4)	107.7 (4)	104.0	96.6 (3)
	Dec	106.3 (4)	108.8 (4)	104.6 (5)	N/A (1)
1994	Jan	106.6 (3)	110.2 (3)	N/A (2)	
	Feb				
	Mar				
	Apr				
	May				
	June				
	July				
	Aug				
	Sept				
	Oct				
	Nov				
	Dec				

1. A full explanation of the methodology used is given in *Economic Trends*, No 257, March 1975 and No 271, May 1976. Each month two charts of the composite indicators are published with, in the March, June, September and December issues, a further eight pages showing individual indicator series.

2. Values of the composite indices are published in order to show more precisely the shape of the graphs in recent months. The values are subject to revision each month, both because of revisions to the series from which they are formed and because of the nature of the trend-elimination process used in the calculation; the values of the indices have no intrinsic meaning but positive values indicate that an index is above its long-term trend and negative values indicate that it is below its long-term trend. The method of calculation for the indices means that they lie in the range 80 to 120. On the charts the parts of the curves which are liable to revision in the trend-elimination process are shown in pecked lines; where the composite indices are based on an incomplete set of indicators, the curves are shown as dotted lines. Additional tables giving the value of all series used are available from the CSO: Telephone 071-270 5970.

3. This table is based on monthly and quarterly data available to 7 February.

4. Bracketed figures show the number of series available where the index is incomplete.

5. The index numbers given here are for comparative purposes only and should not be regarded as accurate to the last digit shown.

6. Longer runs of the indices and their component series are available from the CSO Databank or on subscription from the CSO.

7. When a value for an index is first published it is usually based on incomplete information. Previous practice was to publish a provisional index value provided that at least two constituent series were available but this led to substantial revisions to the index as more data became available.

Cyclical indicators
Composite indices of indicator groups

Long term trend=100

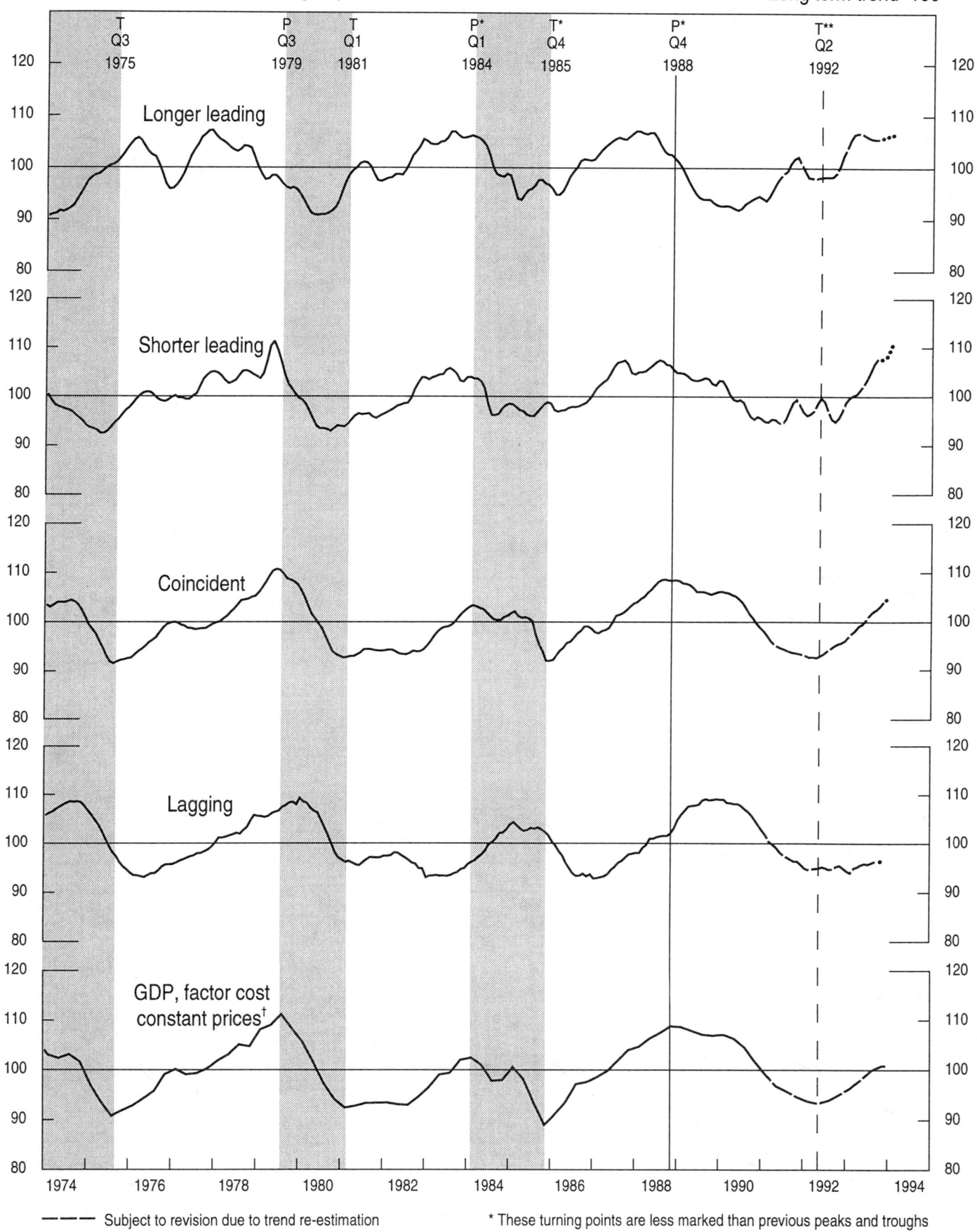

- – – – Subject to revision due to trend re-estimation
- ••••• Based on incomplete data
- † Strike adjusted
- * These turning points are less marked than previous peaks and troughs
- ** Provisional date

Cyclical indicators with leads and lags applied[1]

Composite indices of indicator groups

Long term trend=100

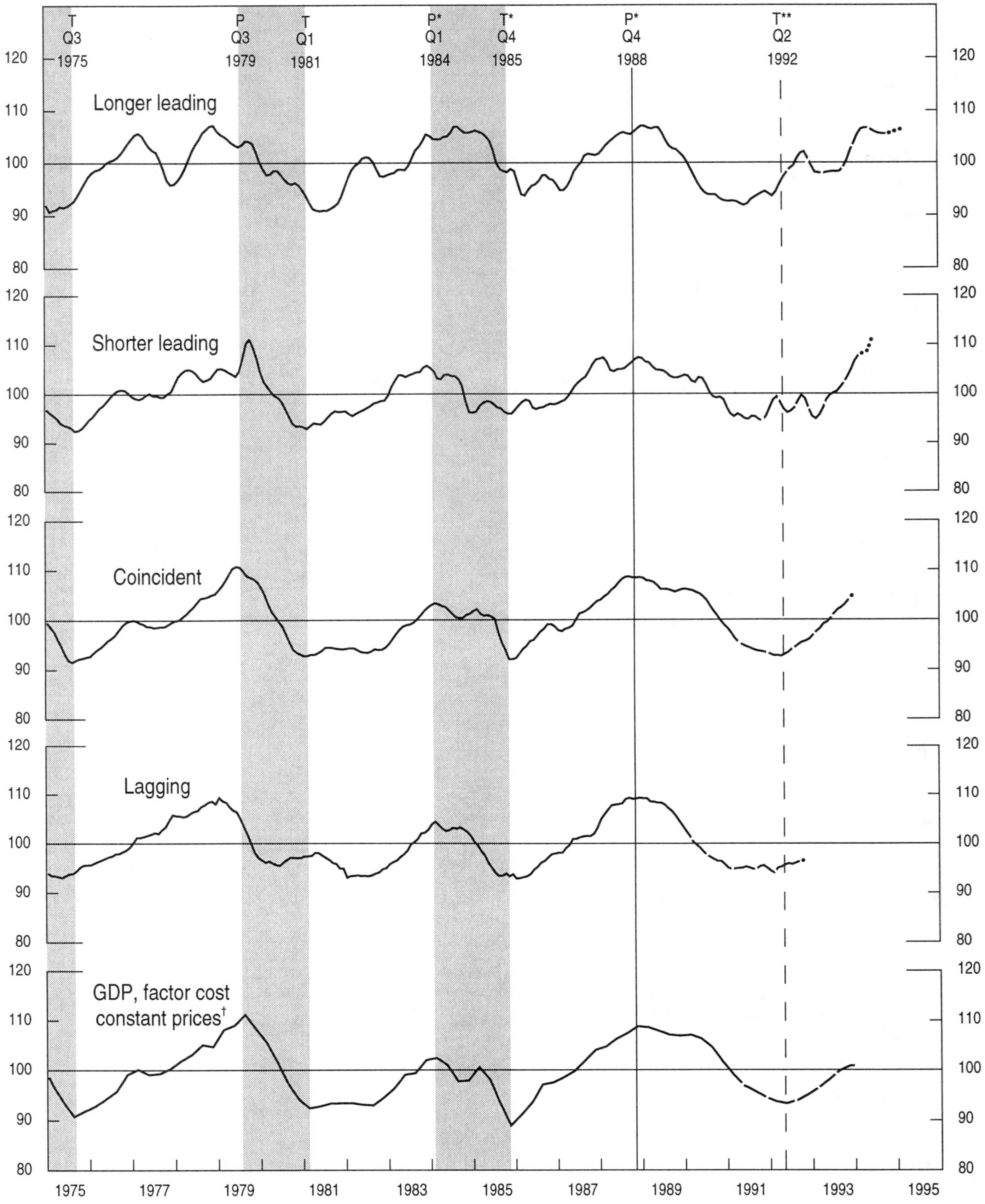

T Q3 1975
P Q3 1979
T Q1 1981
P* Q1 1984
T* Q4 1985
P* Q4 1988
T** Q2 1992
Longer leading
Shorter leading
Coincident
Lagging
GDP, factor cost constant prices†
120
110
100
90
80
1975
1977
1979
1981
1983
1985
1987
1989
1991
1993
1995

——— Subject to revision due to trend re-estimation

••••••• Based on incomplete data

† Strike adjusted

* These turning points are less marked than previous peaks and troughs

** Provisional date

1. The longer leading index has been advanced by 13 months, the shorter leading index has been advanced by 5 months and the lagging index has been moved back by 12 months. This allows a comparison based on past experience, of whether the indices are in step.

Table B - The indicators: their timing characteristics and data availability

Indicators		Latest data included	Timing relative to reference cycle dates[1] (-) leads (+) lags months		
			Median	Earliest	Latest
Longer leading					
Composite longer leading index	DKBR	January 1994	-13	-24	-5
Component series:					
Financial surplus/deficit, industrial and commercial companies, divided by GDP deflator (£m)	DKDJ	Q3 1993	-17	-33	12
CBI quarterly survey: change in optimism (percentage balance)	DKDK	January 1994	-13	-37	8
Rate of interest, 3 months prime bank bills	DKDH	January 1994	-14	-29	1
Total dwellings started, Great Britain (Thous)	DKBW	December 1993	-10	-43	2
Yield Curve	DKOD	January 1994	-21	-45	1
Shorter leading					
Composite shorter leading index	DKBS	January 1994	-5	-12	4
Component series:					
Consumer credit: change in total borrowing outstanding (£m, 1990 prices)	DKHK	Q3 1993	-6	-33	6
New car registrations (Thous)	DKBY	December 1993	-7	-26	7
CBI quarterly survey: change in new orders - past 4 months (percentage balance)	DKDM	January 1994	-6	-31	5
EC/Gallup Consumer confidence index	DKOF	January 1994	-5	-25	6
Financial Times - Actuaries 500 share index April 1962=100	DKDI	January 1994	-8	-20	8
Coincident					
Composite coincident index	DKBP	December 1993	-1	-6	12
Component series:					
GDP Factor Cost Constant prices, 1990=100[3]	DKOJ	Q4 1993	N/A	N/A	N/A
Output of the production industries (1990=100)[4]	DKOL	November 1993	1	-9	15
CBI quarterly survey: below capacity utilization (percentage)[2]	DKCE	January 1994	2	-10	17
Index of volume of retail sales (1990=100)	FAAM	December 1993	-3	-13	20
CBI quarterly survey: change in stocks of raw materials (percentage balance)[2]	DKDO	January 1994	2	-7	8
M0 divided by GDP deflator (£m, 1990 prices)	DKOH	December 1993	2	-1	33
Lagging					
Composite lagging index	DKBQ	November 1993	12	2	29
Component series:					
Adult Unemployment index (1990=100)[3]	DKDP	December 1993	7	1	32
Employment in manufacturing industries United Kingdom (thous)	DKDQ	November 1993	8	1	25
Investment in plant and machinery, manufacturing industry (£m, 1990 prices)	DKCK	Q3 1993	9	-3	33
Engineering industries, volume index for orders on hand (Average, 1990=100)	DKCJ	November 1993	9	-3	23
Level of stocks and work in progress, manufacturing industry (£m, 1990 prices)	DKCI	Q3 1993	9	3	30

All series seasonally adjusted, unless otherwise indicated.
[1] Assessed on performance up to last identified trough, second quarter of 1992.
[2] Not seasonally adjusted.
[3] See Standard Notes on Compilation.
[4] Strike adjusted.

Source: Central Statistical Office

Measures of variability of selected economic series[1]

| | Table | Period covered | Average percentage changes ||| $\bar{I}/\bar{C}$ | MCD or QCD | $\bar{I}/\bar{C}$ for MCD (or QCD) span |
			$\bar{CI}$	$\bar{I}$	$\bar{C}$			
Quarterly series								
National income and components at 1990 prices								
GDP, factor cost	2	Q1 1975 to Q2 1993	0.9	0.3	0.7	0.5	1	0.5
Consumers' expenditure	3,4,5	Q1 1980 to Q2 1993	1.0	0.5	0.8	0.6	1	0.6
Fixed capital formation								
Total	3,9	Q1 1975 to Q2 1992	2.5	1.4	1.7	0.8	1	0.8
Manufacturing industry	10	Q1 1975 to Q2 1992	4.0	2.1	2.8	0.7	1	0.7
Stockbuilding[2]								
Total	3,12	Q1 1975 to Q2 1992	536.6	389.0	320.8	1.2	2	0.5
Manufacturing	12	Q1 1975 to Q2 1992	357.7	241.3	198.7	1.2	2	0.6
Exports: goods and services	3	Q1 1975 to Q2 1992	2.3	1.6	1.4	1.1	2	0.5
Imports: goods and services	3	Q1 1975 to Q2 1992	2.9	1.6	2.1	0.8	1	0.8
Real personal disposable income	4	Q1 1975 to Q2 1992	1.4	0.9	0.9	1.0	1	1.0
Other national income series								
Gross trading profits of industrial and commercial companies	36	Q1 1975 to Q2 1992	6.0	3.3	4.3	0.8	1	0.8
Other quarterly series								
Construction output[3]	17	Q1 1975 to Q2 1992	2.1	1.2	1.5	0.8	1	0.8
Public sector borrowing requirement[4]	32	Q1 1980 to Q3 1992	1 955.4	1 335.2	1 024.8	1.3	2	0.7
Personal saving ratio[5]	4	Q1 1975 to Q2 1992	1.3	1.1	0.6	1.8	2	0.6
Monthly series								
Retail sales (volume per week)								
Food retailers	6	Jan 1971 to Nov 1993	0.7	0.7	0.2	2.9	3	0.9
Mixed retail businesses	6	Jan 1971 to Nov 1993	1.7	1.5	0.4	3.5	4	0.9
Clothing and footwear retailers	6	Jan 1971 to Nov 1993	1.9	1.8	0.5	3.3	4	0.8
Household goods retailers	6	Jan 1971 to Nov 1993	1.9	1.8	0.7	2.5	3	1.0
Other non-food retailers	6	Jan 1971 to Nov 1993	1.1	1.1	0.4	3.0	2	0.7
Cars: new registrations	6	Jan 1981 to Sep 1993	5.7	5.6	1.0	5.5	6	1.0
Housing starts[3]:								
Private enterprise	11	Jan 1980 to Jun 1992	8.3	8.1	1.4	6.0	6	1.1
Housing associations	11	Jan 1980 to Jun 1992	18.9	18.5	2.7	7.1	6	1.0
Local authorities	11	Jan 1980 to Jun 1992	14.9	15.3	3.0	5.1	6	1.0
Housing completions[3]:								
Private enterprise	11	Jan 1980 to Jun 1992	6.4	6.4	0.8	7.9	6	1.2
Housing associations	11	Jan 1980 to Jun 1992	17.0	17.0	1.6	10.4	6	1.7
Local authorities	11	Jan 1980 to Jun 1992	10.8	10.9	2.2	4.9	5	1.0
Index of industrial production:								
Production industries	1,15,16	Jan 1983 to Dec 1992	1.2	1.1	0.3	3.5	4	0.9
Manufacturing industries	15	Jan 1983 to Dec 1992	1.3	1.2	0.3	3.7	3	1.0
Passenger car production:								
Home market	18	Jan 1979 to Dec 1992	7.9	7.6	1.7	4.4	5	0.9
Export	18	Jan 1979 to Dec 1992	12.8	12.4	3.0	4.2	5	0.9
Commercial vehicle production:								
Home market	18	Jan 1979 to Dec 1992	9.2	8.5	3.0	2.9	4	0.8
Export	18	Jan 1979 to Dec 1992	11.5	10.9	2.7	4.0	5	0.9
Unemployed males - consistent series, 18 and over[6]	20	Jan 1971 to Dec 1992	18.5	4.8	17.6	0.3	1	0.3
Unemployed females - consistent series, 18 and over[6]	20	Jan 1971 to Dec 1992	7.0	1.8	6.8	0.3	1	0.3
Vacancies unfilled at job centres[6]	1,20	Apr 1978 to Sep 1992	4.4	2.2	3.4	0.6	1	0.6
Average earnings: whole economy	25	Jan 1988 to Jun 1992	0.8	0.4	0.7	0.6	1	0.6
Exports: value, f.o.b.[7]	27	Jan 1980 to Aug 1992	2.9	2.7	0.9	3.0	4	0.7
Imports: value, f.o.b.[7]	27	Jan 1980 to Aug 1992	2.7	2.5	1.0	2.5	3	0.8
Money stock - M0[8]	31	Jan 1971 to Apr 1993	0.7	0.5	0.6	0.8	1	0.8
Money stock - M4[8]	1,31	Jun 1982 to Apr 1993	1.0	0.2	1.0	0.2	1	0.2

1 For a fuller description of these measures see article 'Measuring variability in economic time series' in *Economic Trends*, No 226, August 1972.
The following are brief definitions of the measures.
$\bar{CI}$ is the average month to month (quarter to quarter for quarterly series) percentage change without regard to sign in the seasonally adjusted series.
$\bar{C}$ is the same for the trend component.
$\bar{I}$ is the same for the irregular component, obtained by dividing the trend component into the seasonally adjusted series, except for those series which are seasonally adjusted using an additive model, see footnotes 2,4,6 and 8.
$\bar{I}/\bar{C}$ is therefore a measure of the size of the relative irregularity of the seasonally adjusted series.
The average changes $\bar{I}$ and $\bar{C}$ can also be computed successively over spans of increasing numbers of months (quarters). MCD (QCD), months (quarters) for cyclical dominance, is the shortest span of months (quarters) for which $\bar{I}/\bar{C}$ is less than 1 and therefore represents the minimum period over which changes in the trend, on average, exceed the irregular movement.
MCD cannot exceed 6 even if $\bar{I}/\bar{C}$ exceeds 1 for 6-month periods.

2 The figures in the table were obtained from an additive analysis of stock changes so $\bar{CI}$, $\bar{I}$ and $\bar{C}$ are not percentage changes but differences in units of £ million. At present, seasonal adjustment of the published stocks series is performed multiplicatively on the level of stocks.
3 Series relate to Great Britain.
4 The seasonal adjustment is additive, so the figures for $\bar{CI}$, $\bar{I}$ and $\bar{C}$ are differences in units of £ million.
5 The figures in the tables were obtained from an additive analysis of the personal saving ratio so $\bar{CI}$, $\bar{I}$ and $\bar{C}$ are differences in percentage points.
6 Series relate to Great Britain and may be found in Tables 2.2 and 3.2 of *Employment Gazette*.
The seasonal adjustment is additive, so the figures for $\bar{CI}$, $\bar{I}$ and $\bar{C}$ are not percentage changes but differences in units of thousands.
7 The figures have been updated as described in an article in *Economic Trends*, No 320, June 1980.
8 As the irregular component for M0 and M4 is obtained by subtraction of the trend rather than by division, the figures for $\bar{CI}$, $\bar{I}$ and $\bar{C}$ are expressed as percentages of the trend level in the preceding month.

Source: Central Statistical Office

INTERNATIONAL ECONOMIC INDICATORS

(includes data up to 17 February 1994)

INTRODUCTION

The series presented here are taken from the Organisation of Economic Co-operation and Development's (OECD) Main Economic Indicators, except for the United Kingdom where several of the series are those most recently published. The series shown are for each of the G7 economies (United Kingdom, Germany, France, Italy, United States, Japan and Canada) and for the European Communities (EC) and OECD countries in aggregate.

2. The length and periodicity of the series have been chosen to show their movement over a number of years as well as the recent past. There is no attempt here to make cross country comparisons across cycles. Further, because the length and timing of these cycles varies across countries, comparisons of indicators over the same period should be treated with caution.

COMMENTARY

3. Between 1993 Q2 and 1993 Q3, Gross Domestic Product (GDP) at constant market prices grew in all the G7 economies except Italy. Growth was most rapid in the United States (0.8 per cent), the United Kingdom (0.7 per cent) and Germany (0.7 per cent). Between 1993 Q3 and 1993 Q4 growth accelerated in the United States to 1.4 per cent.

4. Annual growth in consumer prices in the United Kingdom rose from 1.9 per cent in December 1993 to 2.5 per cent in January 1994. Over the same period, consumer price inflation in Germany fell from 3.7 per cent to 3.5 per cent. Overall figures for the European Community show consumer price inflation fell from 3.5 per cent in July 1993 to 3.2 per cent in November 1993.

5. In the two countries where recovery has been well established, standardised unemployment rates fell - from 10.7 per cent in January 1993 to 9.9 per cent in December 1993 in the United Kingdom, and from 7.0 per cent to 6.3 per cent in the United States. Elsewhere - in continental Europe and Japan, unemployment has risen. In Germany, rates rose from 5.2 per cent in January 1993 to 6.3 per cent in November 1993, while in France they rose from 10.9 per cent to 12.0 per cent. In Japan, the unemployment rate rose from 2.3 per cent in January 1993 to 2.8 per cent in November 1993, but remained low compared with other G7 countries.

1 Gross domestic product at constant market prices: index numbers

1985 = 100

	United Kingdom[1]	Germany[2]	France	Italy	EC	United States	Japan[3]	Canada	Major 7	OECD
	FNAO	GABI	GABH	GABJ	GAEK	GAEH	GAEI	GAEG	GAEO	GAEJ
1980	90.5	94.3	92.7	93.3	93.0	88.2	83.2	86.7	88.7	88.9
1985	100.0	100.0	100.0	100.0	100.0	100.0	100.0	100.0	100.0	100.0
1986	104.4	102.3	102.5	102.9	102.9	102.9	102.7	103.3	102.9	102.9
1987	109.3	103.7	104.8	106.1	105.9	106.1	106.8	107.6	106.2	106.3
1988	114.8	107.5	109.5	110.5	110.3	110.3	113.5	113.0	111.0	111.0
1989	117.3	111.4	114.2	113.7	114.2	113.0	118.8	115.7	114.5	114.5
1990	117.8	118.0	117.1	116.1	117.7	114.4	124.6	115.6	117.2	117.4
1991	115.2	123.4	117.9	117.6	119.5	113.6	129.9	113.6	118.1	118.4
1992	114.5	124.9	119.5	118.7	120.3	116.5	131.4	114.4	120.1	120.3
1993	..	..	..	..	..	119.9	..	..	..	..
1990 Q4	116.5	120.4	117.3	116.4	118.4	113.7	127.1	114.3	117.3	117.7
1991 Q1	115.5	122.7	117.1	116.8	118.9	113.0	129.1	112.5	117.4	117.8
Q2	115.0	123.9	117.7	117.5	119.5	113.5	129.9	113.7	118.0	118.3
Q3	114.8	123.4	118.4	117.7	119.6	113.9	131.0	114.0	118.3	118.6
Q4	115.1	123.7	118.6	118.3	120.0	114.0	131.8	114.2	118.6	118.9
1992 Q1	114.0	125.4	119.6	118.9	120.5	115.0	132.6	114.2	119.5	119.8
Q2	114.3	125.4	119.6	119.3	120.5	115.8	132.2	114.2	119.9	120.1
Q3	114.7	124.9	119.7	118.6	120.3	116.8	132.1	114.3	120.2	120.4
Q4	115.1	123.7	119.2	118.0	119.9	118.4	132.0	115.0	120.8	120.9
1993 Q1	115.7	121.7	118.4	117.8	119.3	118.7	133.0	116.0	120.9	121.0
Q2	116.4	122.4	118.6	118.6	..	119.2	132.1	117.0	121.2	..
Q3	117.2	123.2	118.9	118.0	..	120.1	132.6	117.7	..	..
Q4	..	..	..	..	..	121.8	..	..	..	..
Percentage change, latest quarter on corresponding quarter of previous year										
1993 Q3	2.2	−1.4	−0.7	−0.5	..	2.8	0.4	3.0	..	..
Q4	..	..	..	..	..	2.9	..	..	..	..
Percentage change, latest quarter on previous quarter										
1993 Q3	0.7	0.7	0.3	−0.5	..	0.8	0.4	0.6	..	..
Q4	..	..	..	..	..	1.4	..	..	..	..

1 Estimates due to rebasing to 1990
2 Western Germany (Federal Republic of Germany before unification)
3 GNP

2 Consumer prices[1]
Percentage change on year earlier

	United Kingdom	Germany[2]	France	Italy	EC	United States	Japan	Canada	Major 7	OECD
1980	18.0	5.5	13.6	21.0	13.7	13.5	7.8	10.2	12.7	13.5
1985	6.1	2.2	5.8	8.6	6.1	3.5	2.0	4.0	4.0	4.9
1986	3.4	−0.1	2.7	6.1	3.7	1.9	0.6	4.2	2.1	3.0
1987	4.2	0.2	3.1	4.6	3.3	3.6	0.1	4.4	2.9	3.6
1988	4.9	1.3	2.6	5.0	3.6	4.1	0.7	4.0	3.3	4.3
1989	7.8	2.8	3.7	6.6	5.3	4.8	2.3	5.0	4.6	5.4
1990	9.5	2.7	3.4	6.0	5.6	5.5	3.1	4.8	5.0	5.8
1991	5.9	3.5	3.2	6.5	5.1	4.2	3.3	5.6	4.3	5.2
1992	3.7	4.0	2.4	5.3	4.3	3.0	1.7	1.5	3.1	4.0
1993	1.6	4.1	2.1	4.2	..	3.0	1.3	1.8	..	..
1992 Q4	3.0	3.6	1.9	4.8	3.8	3.0	1.0	1.8	2.8	3.7
1993 Q1	1.8	4.3	2.1	4.3	3.5	3.2	1.3	2.0	2.8	3.8
Q2	1.3	4.2	1.9	4.1	3.3	3.2	0.9	1.7	2.7	3.8
Q3	1.7	4.2	2.2	4.3	3.4	2.7	1.8	1.7	2.7	3.9
Q4	1.6	3.7	2.2	4.2	..	2.7	1.1	1.8	..	..
1993 Jan	1.7	4.4	2.1	4.2	3.5	3.3	1.3	2.1	2.9	3.8
Feb	1.8	4.2	2.0	4.4	3.4	3.3	1.4	2.3	2.9	3.8
Mar	1.9	4.2	2.2	4.2	3.4	3.1	1.2	1.9	2.8	3.7
Apr	1.3	4.3	2.0	4.2	3.3	3.2	0.9	1.8	2.7	3.8
May	1.3	4.2	2.0	4.0	3.3	3.2	0.9	1.8	2.7	3.8
Jun	1.2	4.2	1.9	4.1	3.2	3.0	0.9	1.6	2.6	3.8
Jul	1.4	4.3	2.1	4.4	3.5	2.8	1.9	1.6	2.7	4.0
Aug	1.7	4.2	2.2	4.5	3.4	2.7	1.9	1.7	2.7	4.0
Sep	1.8	4.0	2.3	4.2	3.4	2.7	1.5	1.9	2.6	3.9
Oct	1.4	3.9	2.2	4.3	3.3	2.8	1.3	1.9	2.6	3.9
Nov	1.4	3.6	2.2	4.2	3.2	2.7	0.9	1.9	2.4	3.8
Dec	1.9	3.7	2.1	4.0	..	2.7	1.0	1.7	..	..
1994 Jan	2.5	3.5	..	4.2	..	..	..	..	..	..

1 Components and coverage not uniform across countries
2 Western Germany (Federal Republic of Germany before unification)

3 Standardised unemployment rates: percentage of total labour force[1]

	United Kingdom	Germany[2]	France	Italy	EC[3]	United States	Japan	Canada	Major 7	OECD
	GABF	GABD	GABC	GABE	GADR	GADO	GADP	GADN	GAEQ	GADQ
1980	6.4	3.1	6.3	7.5	6.4	7.1	2.0	7.4	5.5	5.8
1985	11.2	7.1	10.3	9.6	10.9	7.1	2.6	10.4	7.2	7.8
1986	11.2	6.4	10.4	10.4	10.8	6.9	2.8	9.5	7.1	7.7
1987	10.3	6.2	10.5	10.9	10.6	6.1	2.8	8.8	6.7	7.3
1988	8.6	6.2	10.0	10.9	9.9	5.4	2.5	7.7	6.1	6.7
1989	7.2	5.6	9.4	10.9	9.0	5.2	2.2	7.5	5.7	6.2
1990	6.8	4.8	8.9	10.3	8.4	5.4	2.1	8.0	5.6	6.1
1991	8.7	4.2	9.5	9.8	8.7	6.6	2.1	10.2	6.3	6.8
1992	9.9	4.6	10.4	9.8	9.4	7.3	2.2	11.2	6.8	7.5
1993	10.3	..	..	..	..	6.7	..	11.1	..	..
1992 Q4	10.4	4.9	10.7	9.3	9.7	7.2	2.3	11.5	6.9	7.6
1993 Q1	10.5	5.3	11.0	9.0	10.2	6.9	2.3	10.9	6.8	7.7
Q2	10.3	5.6	11.5	10.6	10.6	6.9	2.4	11.3	7.0	7.8
Q3	10.4	5.9	11.7	10.3	10.8	6.7	2.5	11.3	6.9	7.9
Q4	10.0	..	..	..	..	6.4	..	11.0	..	..
1992 Dec	10.6	5.0	10.9	−	9.8	7.2	2.4	11.4	6.9	7.6
1993 Jan	10.7	5.2	10.9	9.0	10.0	7.0	2.3	11.0	6.8	7.6
Feb	10.5	5.3	11.0	−	10.2	6.9	2.3	10.8	6.8	7.7
Mar	10.4	5.5	11.2	−	10.4	6.9	2.3	11.0	6.9	7.7
Apr	10.3	5.6	11.4	10.6	10.5	6.9	2.3	11.3	7.0	7.8
May	10.3	5.6	11.5	−	10.6	6.9	2.5	11.3	7.0	7.8
Jun	10.3	5.7	11.6	−	10.7	6.8	2.5	11.3	7.0	7.9
Jul	10.4	5.8	11.7	10.3	10.8	6.7	2.5	11.5	7.0	7.9
Aug	10.4	5.9	11.7	..	10.8	6.7	2.5	11.3	6.9	7.9
Sep	10.4	6.1	11.8	..	10.9	6.6	2.6	11.1	6.9	7.9
Oct	10.2	6.2	12.0	..	10.9	6.6	2.7	..	7.0	7.9
Nov	10.0	6.3	12.0	..	10.9	6.4	2.8	..	6.9	..
Dec	9.9	..	..	..	..	6.3	..	..	..	..

1 Uses an ILO based measure of those without work, currently available for work, actively seeking work or waiting to start a job already obtained
2 Western Germany (Federal Republic of Germany before unification)
3 Excludes Denmark, Greece and Luxembourg

4 Balance of payments current account as percentage of GDP

	United Kingdom	Germany[1,2]	France	Italy	United States[1]	Japan[1]	Canada
1980	1.3	−1.7	−0.6	−2.3	0.1	−1.0	−0.6
1985	0.8	2.7	−0.1	−0.9	−3.1	3.6	−0.6
1986	−	4.5	0.3	0.4	−3.5	4.3	−2.3
1987	−1.1	4.1	−0.6	−0.2	−3.7	3.6	−2.1
1988	−3.4	4.2	−0.5	−0.7	−2.6	2.7	−2.6
1989	−4.2	4.9	−0.5	−1.2	−1.9	2.0	−3.6
1990	−3.1	3.1	−0.8	−1.3	−1.7	1.2	−3.9
1991	−1.1	−1.3	−0.5	−1.9	−0.1	2.1	−4.3
1992	−2.0	−1.4	0.3	−2.2	−1.1	3.2	−4.0
1992 Q3	−1.5	−0.5	−	−0.5	−1.2	3.2	−3.1
Q4	−2.6	−0.3	0.2	−0.4	−1.5	3.4	−3.3
1993 Q1	−2.0	−0.3	0.1	−0.3	−1.4	3.7	−4.7
Q2	−1.7	−0.2	0.3	0.3	−1.7	2.9	−3.2
Q3	−1.3	−0.6	..	..	−1.7	2.9	−3.1

1 Balance as percentage of GNP
2 Western Germany (Federal Republic of Germany before unification)

5 Total industrial production: index numbers

1985 = 100

	United Kingdom[1]	Germany[2]	France	Italy	EC	United States	Japan[3]	Canada[4]	Major 7	OECD[5]
	DVZI	HFGA	HFFZ	HFGB	GACY	HFGD	HFGC	HFFY	GAES	GACX
1980	92.6	97.3	101.9	103.6	97.2	89.1	84.4	86.2	91.0	91.3
1985	100.0	100.3	100.0	100.0	100.0	100.0	100.0	100.0	100.0	100.0
1986	102.4	102.2	100.9	103.6	102.2	100.9	99.8	99.3	101.1	101.2
1987	106.5	102.6	102.8	107.6	104.8	106.0	103.3	104.1	104.9	104.9
1988	111.6	106.3	107.7	114.1	109.3	110.7	113.7	109.6	110.7	110.5
1989	114.0	111.4	112.1	117.6	113.5	112.4	120.3	109.5	114.1	114.1
1990	113.6	117.1	114.2	117.6	115.7	112.4	125.3	106.0	115.7	115.8
1991	109.1	120.7	114.1	115.4	115.5	110.3	127.7	102.2	115.0	115.1
1992	108.6	118.4	113.0	114.8	114.4	112.9	120.4	102.6	114.4	114.5
1993	111.6	..	..	..	..	..	..	..	..	..
1992 Q4	109.8	112.9	110.6	112.0	111.6	114.7	117.1	104.1	113.7	113.6
1993 Q1	109.9	109.5	108.5	113.3	110.5	116.3	117.8	106.0	114.2	114.0
Q2	110.8	109.5	..	109.9	110.0	116.9	115.9	106.8	113.9	113.7
Q3	112.2	110.3	..	110.9	111.1	117.7	115.7	107.8	114.6	114.7
Q4	113.5	..	..	..	..	..	..	..	..	..
1992 Dec	108.9	110.1	108.0	107.6	109.2	115.4	116.3	104.6	113.0	112.8
1993 Jan	109.3	109.8	108.0	113.4	109.8	115.8	115.9	104.8	113.5	113.2
Feb	110.6	108.4	110.8	114.1	110.8	116.4	117.2	105.8	114.2	114.1
Mar	109.7	110.4	109.8	112.4	110.9	116.6	120.3	107.3	115.0	114.7
Apr	109.9	109.0	109.2	107.6	109.1	116.9	117.1	106.4	113.9	113.5
May	111.8	109.9	109.3	112.3	110.8	116.7	114.3	106.1	113.8	113.8
Jun	110.7	109.6	109.2	109.7	110.0	117.1	116.2	108.0	114.1	113.8
Jul	112.2	108.8	109.9	112.3	110.9	117.4	115.6	107.0	114.4	114.5
Aug	112.0	111.1	109.9	110.3	111.3	117.6	114.6	107.8	114.4	114.6
Sep	112.2	111.1	109.9	110.1	111.0	118.0	117.0	108.7	115.0	115.0
Oct	113.6	110.2	109.5	..	..	118.9	110.9	108.6	..	..
Nov	113.9	108.3	..	..	..	119.9	113.1	..	..	..
Dec	113.2	..	..	..	..	..	..	..	..	..

Percentage change: average of latest three months on that of corresponding period of previous year

	United Kingdom	Germany	France	Italy	EC	United States	Japan	Canada	Major 7	OECD
1993 Nov	2.7	−5.0	..	..	..	4.6	−4.5	..	..	..
Dec	..	..	..	..	..	..	..	..	..	..

Percentage change: average of latest three months on previous three months

	United Kingdom	Germany	France	Italy	EC	United States	Japan	Canada	Major 7	OECD
1993 Nov	1.2	0.0	..	..	..	1.3	−1.6	..	..	..
Dec	..	..	..	..	..	..	..	..	..	..

1 Estimates due to rebasing to 1990
2 Western Germany (Federal Republic of Germany before unification)
3 Not adjusted for unequal number of working days in a month
4 GDP in industry at factor cost and 1986 prices
5 Some countries excluded from area total

6 Producer prices (manufacturing)
Percentage change on a year earlier

	United Kingdom	Germany[1]	France[2]	Italy	EC	United States	Japan	Canada	Major 7	OECD
1980	12.8	7.1	9.2	..	11.3	13.4	14.8	13.4	13.2	13.2
1985	5.3	2.0	4.4	7.8	5.0	0.8	-0.8	2.8	2.0	2.9
1986	4.2	-2.4	-2.8	0.2	-0.8	-1.4	-4.7	0.9	-1.5	-1.1
1987	3.7	-0.4	0.6	3.0	1.3	2.1	-2.9	2.8	1.1	1.5
1988	4.3	1.6	5.1	3.5	3.5	2.5	-0.2	4.4	2.5	3.5
1989	4.7	3.4	5.4	5.9	5.0	5.1	2.1	1.9	4.4	5.3
1990	5.8	1.5	-1.1	4.2	2.4	4.9	1.6	0.3	3.3	3.9
1991	5.4	2.1	-1.3	3.3	2.3	2.1	1.0	-1.0	2.0	2.6
1992	3.5	1.6	-1.6	1.9	1.1	1.2	-0.8	0.5	0.7	1.7
1993	3.9	0.1	..	..	..	1.2	..	..	..	..
1993 Q1	3.2	0.8	-2.3	3.1	1.2	2.0	-1.1	4.0	1.3	2.5
Q2	3.7	0.0	-3.3	3.9	0.9	2.0	-1.5	3.3	1.1	2.6
Q3	3.9	-0.3	-3.4	4.3	1.2	0.8	-1.8	3.1	0.5	2.5
Q4	4.0	-0.2	..	..	..	0.3	..	..	..	..
1992 Dec	3.3	1.0		2.5	1.0	1.5	-1.2	3.6	0.9	2.1
1993 Jan	3.3	1.0		2.8	1.2	2.0	-1.1	4.4	1.3	2.5
Feb	3.2	0.7		2.9	1.1	2.0	-1.0	3.8	1.2	2.5
Mar	3.2	0.6		3.5	1.1	2.0	-1.2	3.8	1.2	2.6
Apr	3.5	0.3		3.7	0.9	2.5	-1.2	3.9	1.4	2.8
May	3.7	-0.1		3.9	0.9	2.1	-1.5	3.2	1.1	2.7
Jun	3.8	-0.3		4.1	0.9	1.3	-1.5	2.9	0.8	2.4
Jul	4.0	-0.2		4.2	1.2	1.3	-1.7	2.8	0.8	2.7
Aug	3.9	-0.2		4.4	1.3	0.5	-1.8	3.4	0.4	2.4
Sep	4.0	-0.5		4.3	1.2	0.5	-2.0	3.0	0.4	2.3
Oct	4.0	-0.3		4.1	1.5	0.3	-2.1	2.9	0.4	2.3
Nov	3.6	-0.2		..	..	0.3	-2.1	2.9	..	..
Dec	4.0	-0.1		..	..	0.3	..	..	..	..

1 Western Germany (Federal Republic of Germany before unification).
2 Producer prices in intermediate goods

7 Total employment: index numbers[1]

1985 = 100

	United Kingdom[2]	Germany[3,4]	France[4]	Italy	EC	United States[4]	Japan	Canada[4]	Major 7	OECD
	DMBC	GAAR	GAAU	GAAS	GADW	GADT	GADU	GADS	GAEU	GADV
1980	103.6	102	101.1	100	..	93	95	95	..	..
1985	100.0	100	100.0	100	100	100	100	100	100	100
1986	100.2	101	100.5	101	101	102	101	103	101	101
1987	102.0	102	100.9	100	102	105	102	106	103	103
1988	105.2	103	102.0	102	104	107	104	109	105	105
1989	107.8	104	103.5	101	106	109	106	111	107	107
1990	108.6	107	104.6	103	107	110	108	112	108	109
1991	105.5	109	104.8	104	108	109	110	110	108	108
1992	102.7	110	104.3	103	106	110	111	109	108	108
1992 Q2	103.5	110	104.7	105	107	110	112	109	109	109
Q3	102.2	110	104.7	104	106	111	112	112	109	109
Q4	101.2	110	103.4	102	105	110	111	109	108	108
1993 Q1	100.9	108	103.2	100	104	109	109	107	107	107
Q2	101.0	108	103.5	98	104	111	112	111	109	108
Q3	101.3	..	..	99	104	113	112	113	109	109
1993 Jul	..	107	..	99	104	113	112	114	112.3	109
Aug	..	107	..	..	104	113	112	114	111.6	109
Sep	..	108	103.0	..	..	112	112	112	112.6	108
Oct	..	108	..	..	..	112	112	111	112.3	..
Nov	..	107	..	..	..	113	112	110	..	..

Percentage change, latest quarter on that of corresponding period of previous year

| 1993 Q2 | -2.4 | -1.8 | -1.1 | -6.7 | -2.8 | 0.9 | 0.0 | 1.8 | 0.0 | -0.9 |
| Q3 | -0.9 | .. | .. | -4.8 | -1.9 | 1.8 | 0.0 | 0.9 | 0.0 | 0.0 |

Percentage change latest quarter on previous quarter

| 1993 Q2 | 0.1 | 0.0 | 0.3 | -2.0 | 0.0 | 1.8 | 2.8 | 3.7 | 1.9 | 0.9 |
| Q3 | 0.3 | .. | .. | 1.0 | 0.0 | 1.8 | 0.0 | 1.8 | 0.0 | 0.9 |

1 Not seasonally adjusted except for the United Kingdom
2 Estimates due to rebasing to 1990
3 Western Germany (Federal Republic of Germany before unification)
4 Excludes members of armed forces

8 Average wage earnings in manufacturing[1]
Percentage change on a year earlier

	United Kingdom[2]	Germany[3]	France	Italy	EC	United States	Japan	Canada	Major 7	OECD
1980	17.8	6.5	15.2	18.6	12.4	8.6	7.5	10.9	9.0	10.9
1985	9.1	4.2	5.7	11.2	7.6	4.2	3.1	4.2	5.3	7.4
1986	7.7	4.0	3.9	4.9	5.5	2.0	1.4	3.0	3.0	3.7
1987	8.0	3.8	3.2	6.4	5.5	2.0	1.7	2.9	2.9	5.4
1988	8.5	4.6	3.1	6.1	5.5	2.9	4.6	3.8	4.7	3.7
1989	8.8	3.5	3.8	6.1	6.0	2.8	5.8	5.5	4.5	5.0
1990	9.3	5.1	4.5	7.2	6.6	3.6	5.4	5.2	5.2	5.7
1991	8.2	5.7	4.3	9.8	7.6	2.6	3.5	4.9	4.9	5.2
1992	6.6	6.2	3.6	5.4	7.8	2.6	1.0	3.9	3.9	4.0
1993	..	..	2.6	..	..	2.5	..	..	..	..
1993 Q1	4.7	..	3.4	2.8	3.4	2.5	-0.5	3.0	2.4	3.1
Q2	5.0	..	2.6	3.1	3.2	2.5	0.7	1.5	3.1	3.0
Q3	4.4	..	2.3	4.1	4.4	2.5	0.4	2.3	3.0	2.9
Q4	..	..	2.2	..	..	3.3	..	..	..	..
1992 Dec	5.4	..	..	2.4	5.4	2.5	-1.0	3.8	1.8	2.4
1993 Jan	5.0	..	3.4	2.8	4.8	3.4	-3.6	3.8	1.6	2.3
Feb	5.1	..	..	2.8	4.7	2.5	1.3	3.8	3.3	3.9
Mar	4.2	..	..	2.7	4.7	2.5	1.0	2.3	3.2	3.9
Apr	5.3	..	2.6	2.6	4.7	2.5	2.0	2.3	3.2	3.9
May	4.8	..	..	2.6	4.6	2.5	2.3	1.5	3.2	3.1
Jun	4.8	..	..	4.1	4.6	2.5	-0.9	2.3	2.8	2.8
Jul	5.0	..	2.3	4.1	4.6	2.5	-1.2	3.1	2.7	2.7
Aug	3.6	..	..	4.1	3.9	2.5	2.3	1.5	3.1	3.8
Sep	4.5	..	..	4.2	4.6	2.5	1.5	2.3	3.2	3.1
Oct	..	..	2.2	3.9	..	2.5	0.6	1.5	3.2	..
Nov	..	..	..	..	..	3.3	0.9	..	..	..
Dec	..	..	..	..	..	3.3	..	..	..	..

1 Definitions of coverage and treatment vary among countries
2 Figures for Great Britain refer to weekly earnings; others are hourly
3 Western Germany (Federal Republic of Germany before unification)

9 Retail Sales (volume): index numbers

1985 = 100

	United Kingdom[2]	Germany[1]	France	Italy	EC	United States	Japan	Canada	Major 7	OECD
	FAAM	GADD	GADC	GADE	GADH	GADA	GADB	GACZ	GAEW	GADG
1980	86.4	103.0	101.0	83.1	94.6	84.0	103.2	83.6	89.9	90.7
1985	100.0	100.0	100.0	100.0	99.9	100.0	99.9	100.0	100.0	100.0
1986	105.3	103.4	102.4	106.8	104.4	105.5	101.5	104.6	104.5	104.4
1987	110.6	107.5	104.5	112.0	108.6	108.3	107.1	110.3	108.3	108.0
1988	117.5	111.1	108.0	109.5	111.7	112.6	111.4	114.6	112.0	111.7
1989	119.9	114.1	109.5	117.1	116.1	115.6	115.8	114.5	115.4	115.2
1990	120.8	123.7	110.1	114.4	119.2	116.5	121.7	112.0	117.3	117.4
1991	119.4	130.7	109.7	111.3	120.2	114.2	124.2	100.4	116.3	116.6
1992	120.2	128.6	108.9	117.0	120.5	117.8	120.8	101.6	117.8	117.8
1993	124.4	..	..	..	..	..	..	..	..	..
1993 Q3	124.9	125.0	110.3	..	118.1	124.3	114.4	105.5	119.9	119.1
Q4	125.8	..	..	..	..	..	..	..	..	..
1993 Apr	123.3	124.5	112.4	120.0	120.6	121.5	115.9	104.8	119.5	118.8
May	122.9	119.7	104.6	111.6	115.8	122.6	114.8	104.8	118.2	117.4
Jun	124.8	121.3	113.4	..	116.7	123.5	114.9	104.1	118.7	118.1
Jul	124.5	122.6	111.0	..	117.9	124.0	114.1	105.2	119.4	118.7
Aug	124.9	125.9	107.8	..	117.5	124.7	114.1	105.7	119.7	118.9
Sep	125.2	126.5	112.1	..	119.1	125.0	114.9	105.7	120.5	119.7
Oct	125.6	122.2	108.7	..	..	126.2	..	105.8	121.1	..
Nov	126.1	..	107.4	..	..	..	..	..	..	..
Dec	126.0	..	..	..	..	..	..	..	..	..
1994 Jan	126.8	..	..	..	..	..	..	..	..	..

Percentage change average of latest three months on that of corresponding period of previous year

| 1993 Dec | 3.7 | .. | .. | .. | .. | .. | .. | .. | .. | .. |
| 1994 Jan | .. | .. | .. | .. | .. | .. | .. | .. | .. | .. |

Percentage change average of latest three months on previous three months

| 1993 Dec | 0.7 | .. | .. | .. | .. | .. | .. | .. | .. | .. |
| 1994 Jan | .. | .. | .. | .. | .. | .. | .. | .. | .. | .. |

1 Western Germany (Federal Republic of Germany before unification)
2 Estimates due to rebasing to 1990

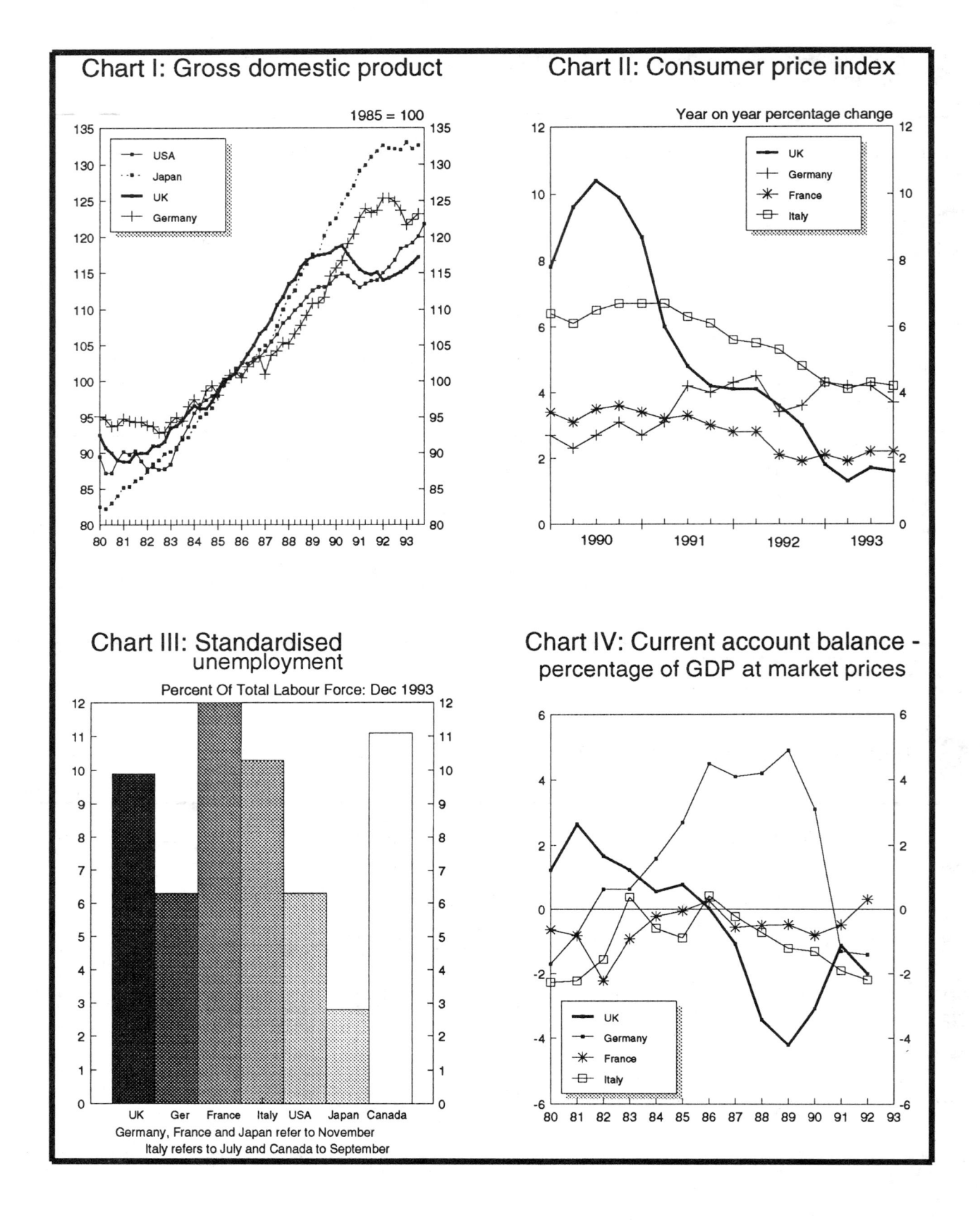

Chart I: Gross domestic product
1985 = 100

- USA
- Japan
- UK
- Germany

Chart II: Consumer price index
Year on year percentage change

- UK
- Germany
- France
- Italy

Chart III: Standardised unemployment
Percent Of Total Labour Force: Dec 1993

UK, Ger, France, Italy, USA, Japan, Canada

Germany, France and Japan refer to November
Italy refers to July and Canada to September

Chart IV: Current account balance - percentage of GDP at market prices

- UK
- Germany
- France
- Italy

Chart V: Industrial production

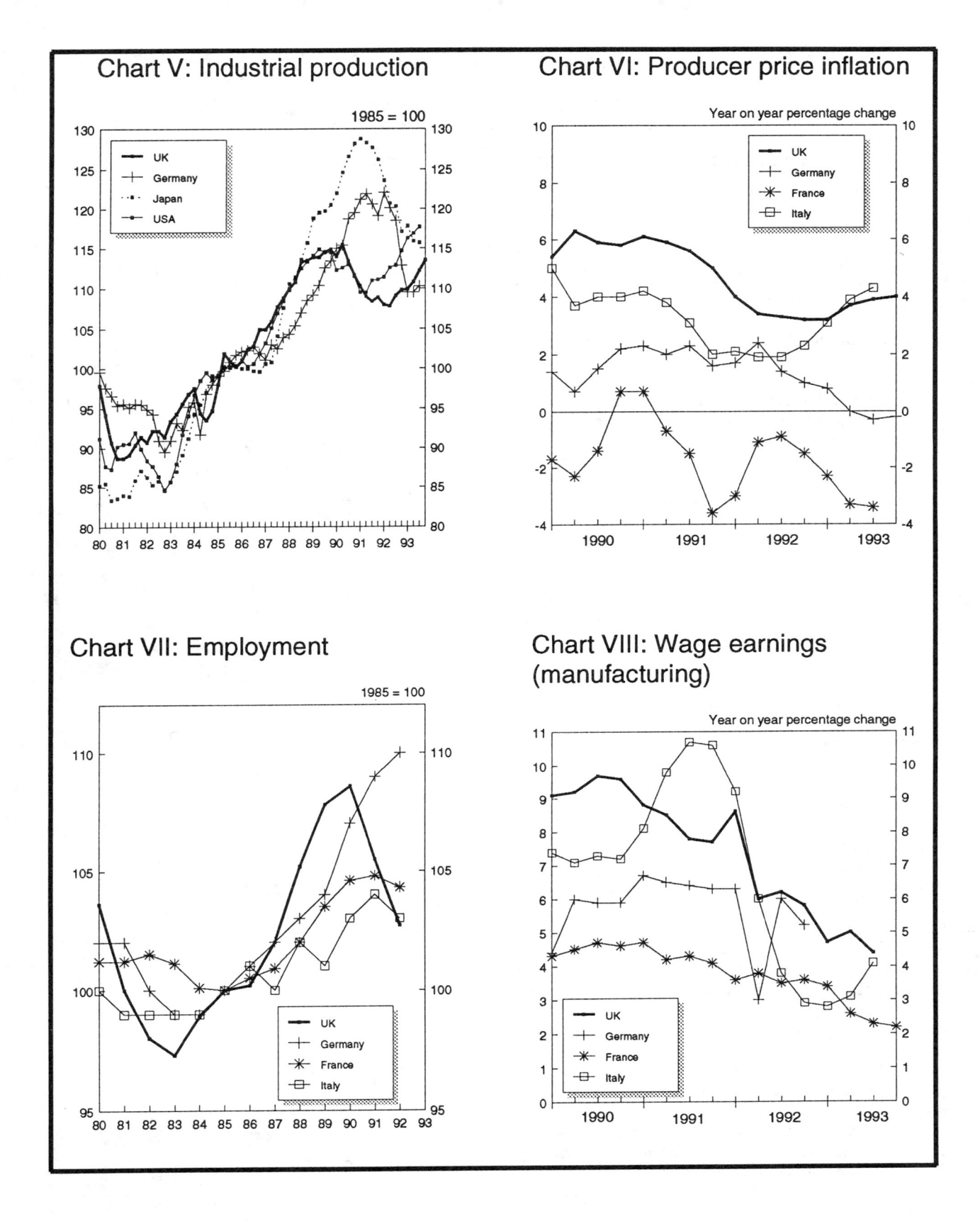

Chart VI: Producer price inflation

Chart VII: Employment

Chart VIII: Wage earnings (manufacturing)

TAXES AND SOCIAL SECURITY CONTRIBUTIONS:
AN INTERNATIONAL COMPARISON 1981 - 1991

Introduction

This article will examine the following: **first**, the overall amount taken by total taxes and social security contributions as a percentage of gross national product (GNP) at factor cost, and gross domestic product (GDP) at market prices; **second**, the distribution over categories of tax; and **third**, the percentage of household income taken.

2. This year's article will focus on the largest economies within the OECD, commonly known as the group of seven countries (G7). The G7 countries are the United Kingdom, Germany, France, Italy, Japan, United States and Canada. As a consequence this approach marks a departure from previous articles in this series where the coverage has been more extensive. However, the data for all 20 OECD countries that were shown in previous articles is contained in the tables that follow this commentary.

3. Comparisons between countries is complicated by the varying length and depth of economic cycles. This affects to varying degrees: the level of tax and social security contributions; the level of GNP and GDP; the distribution of tax; and the level of household disposable income. Caution should therefore be employed when interpreting these results. There are also other means of financing government expenditure, such as charging for services and borrowing.

Overall comparisons

Taxes and social security contributions as a proportion of total economic activity

4. In 1991, taxes and social security contributions, as a percentage of GNP, varied from 44 per cent in France to 29 per cent in the United States. Between 1981 and 1991 most G7 countries had increases in the proportion taken in taxes and social security contributions. The notable exceptions were the United Kingdom - which had the only significant fall, Germany and the United States - where they remained roughly constant. The largest rise occurred in Italy where tax and social security contributions, relative to GNP, rose from 32 per cent in 1981 to 40 per cent in 1991. Chart 1 shows the variation in tax and social security as percentage of GNP in 1981 and 1991.

5. The order is changed when social security contributions are excluded from the comparison of tax systems in the G7 economies in 1991. France and Germany rely relatively more on social security contributions than other countries, and thereby fall from the countries with the two highest tax burdens (including social security contributions), as a percentage of GNP, to joint fourth if social security contributions are excluded from the comparison. Japan and the United States had the lowest tax as a percentage of GNP, both including and excluding social security contributions. Chart 2 shows the effect of excluding social security contributions from the comparison.

6. The exclusion of social security contributions does not affect the direction of change in tax as a percentage of GNP between 1981 and 1991. It rose in all countries except the United Kingdom, the United States and Germany, over this period.

Chart 1
Taxes and social security contributions as a percentage of GNP at factor cost

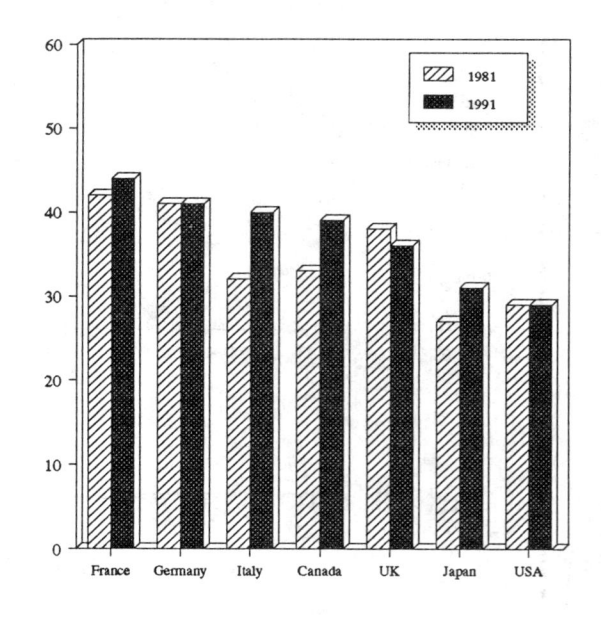

Chart 2
Taxes as a percentage of GNP at factor cost

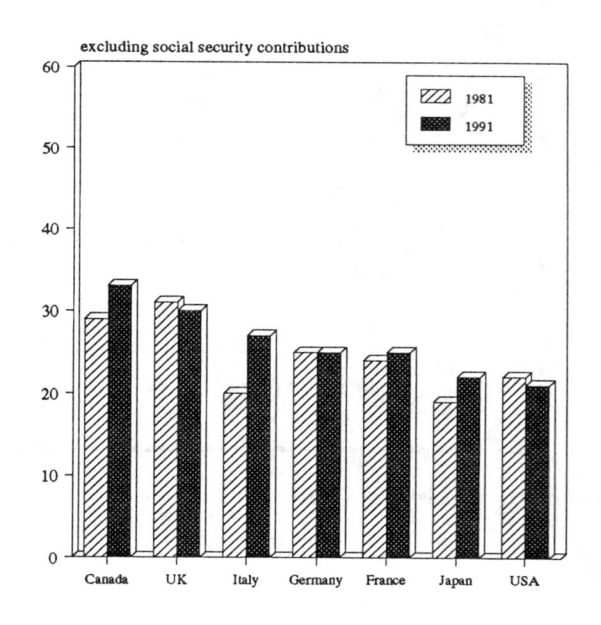

7. Changing the measure of national income to GDP does not have a significant effect on the percentage of national income taken in taxes and social security contributions. The only G7 country where there was any significant difference in 1991 was Canada, where

Economic Trends No.484 February 1994. Crown copyright 1994.

taxes and social security contributions were equivalent to 37 per cent of GDP compared with 39 per cent on the GNP basis. This was due to an outflow of net income from abroad equivalent to over 3 per cent of GDP. The inter-country comparison on the basis of GDP is shown in chart 3.

Chart 3
Taxes and social security contributions as a percentage of GDP at market prices

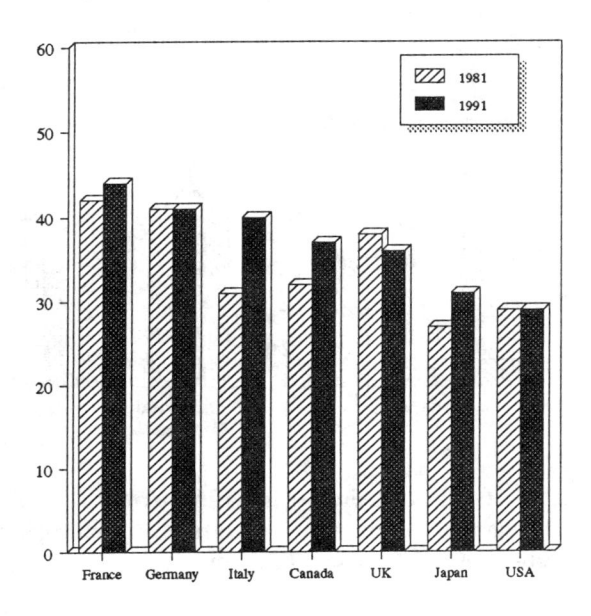

Chart 4
Direct taxes on households as a percentage of total taxes and social security contributions

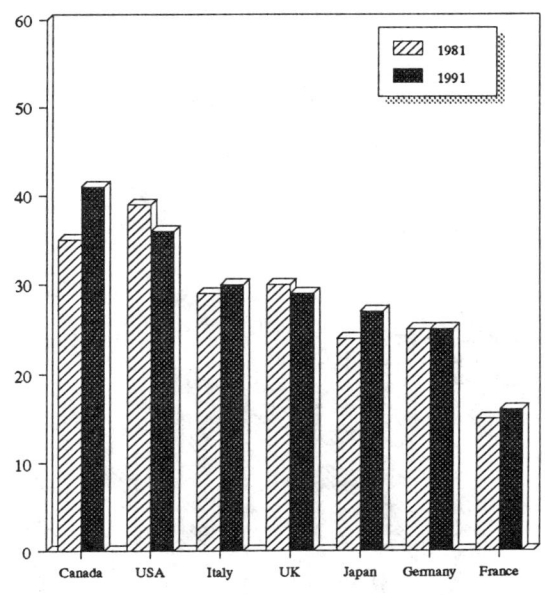

Chart 5
Direct taxes on corporate income as a percentage of total taxes and social security contributions

Distribution over categories of tax

Direct taxes on households as a share of total taxes and social security contributions

8. In Canada and the United States, direct taxes on households raised the largest proportion of taxation revenue (including social security contributions). As chart 4 shows, the only countries where direct taxation on households as a percentage of total taxes and social security contributions fell were the United States and the United Kingdom, between 1981 and 1991. The largest rise occurred in Canada, where the percentage rose from 35 per cent in 1981 to 41 per cent in 1991, resulting in the largest proportion of tax raised through direct taxation on households in the G7 economies.

Direct taxes on corporate income as a share of total taxes and social security contributions

9. As chart 5 shows, the proportion of taxation raised in direct taxation on corporate income by 1991 was below 10 per cent in all countries except Japan. Despite a fall of 1 percentage point between 1981 and 1991, Japan's rate at 17 per cent of tax raised, was nearly twice as much as the country ranked second - the United Kingdom. The proportion raised through direct taxation on corporate income remained fairly constant in most countries. The only country where there was a significant change in the proportion of tax raised through corporation tax was Canada, where the proportion raised was halved from 12 per cent in 1981 to 6 per cent in 1991. This represented a significant shift in the balance of taxation from corporations to the households.

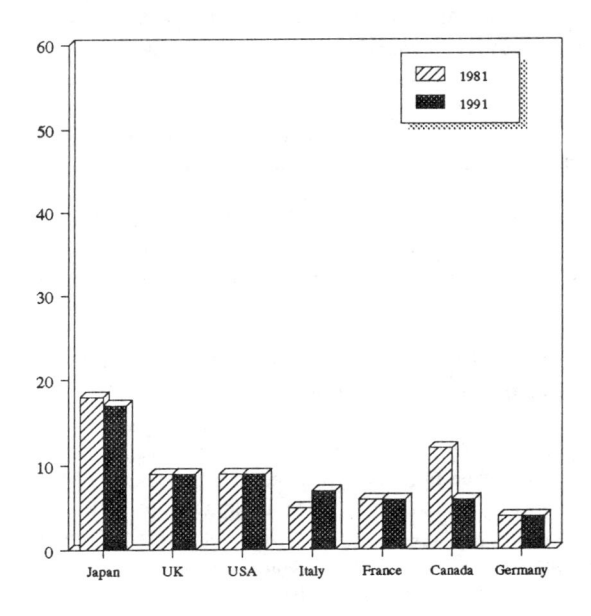

Indirect taxes as a share of total taxes and social security contributions

10. Indirect taxation, as a proportion of tax and social security contributions, fell in the majority of countries. The most pronounced fall was in Japan, where it fell from 28 per cent in 1981 to 25 per cent in 1991. This represented a slight shift in the burden of taxation in Japan from indirect to direct taxation. Although most countries rely on indirect taxes for a significant

proportion of tax revenue (including social security contributions), the United Kingdom was the only country where indirect taxes raise more than any other form of taxation, including social security contributions. Chart 6 shows the varying reliance on indirect taxes.

Chart 6
Indirect taxes as percentage of total taxes and social security contributions

Chart 7
Social security contributions as a percentage of total taxes and social security contributions

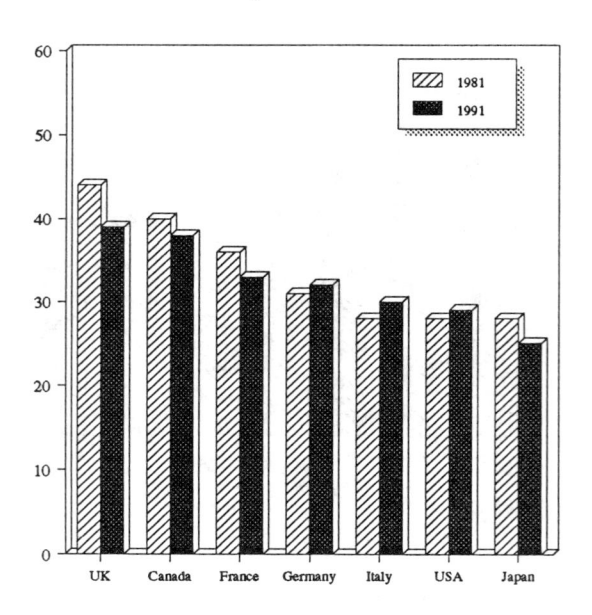

Value added tax as a share of total taxes and social security contributions

11. In the G7 countries in 1991, VAT as a percentage of tax and social security contributions ranged from 19 per cent in the United Kingdom to 4 per cent in Japan. The United Kingdom had the largest rise in VAT as a percentage of taxes and social security contributions, it rose by 7 percentage points between 1981 and 1991. (There has been a growth in the number of countries that levy VAT. In the attached tables, Australia, Switzerland and the United States are the only countries out of the 20 that did not levy VAT in 1991).

Social security contributions as a share of total taxes and social security contributions

12. The majority of countries raise more from social security contributions than from any other individual category of tax. France, Germany, Italy and Japan all raise the largest proportion of taxation revenue via social security contributions. France was the most dependent on social security contributions with 44 per cent of taxation revenue raised by this form of taxation in 1991. Between 1981 and 1991 the only country where social security contributions fell significantly as a percentage of taxation was Italy. The United States had the largest rise in the proportion raised through social security contributions over this period; it rose from 22 per cent of taxation revenue in 1981 to 27 per cent in 1991. Chart 7 shows the varying contribution social security makes to the tax systems of the G7 economies.

Taxes on capital as a share of total taxes and social security contributions

13. The proportion of tax and social security contributions raised through taxes on capital remained low in all countries. Rates in 1991 varied from a tenth of 1 per cent in Italy, to just under two per cent in Japan.

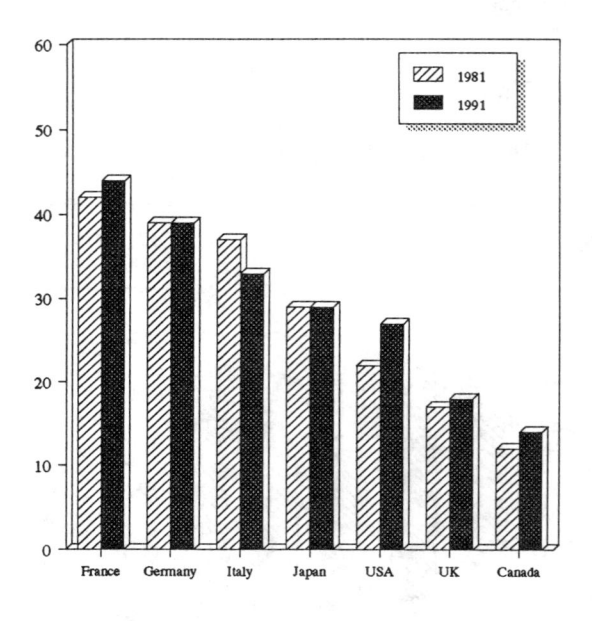

Direct taxes on households, including employers' social security contributions and the community charge, as a percentage of total personal income

14. Direct taxes, including employers' social security contributions and the community charge, as a percentage of total personal income ranged from 28 per cent in Germany to 19 per cent in Japan in 1991. The percentage rose in all countries except the United Kingdom and the United States between 1981 and 1991. In both countries the rises in total personal income outpaced rises in direct taxes on households over this period. The United Kingdom moved from having the joint third highest tax take, as a proportion of personal income, in 1981 to the second lowest in 1991. Chart 8 shows the variation in direct taxes as a percentage of households' income.

Chart 8
Direct taxes on households as a percentage of total personal income

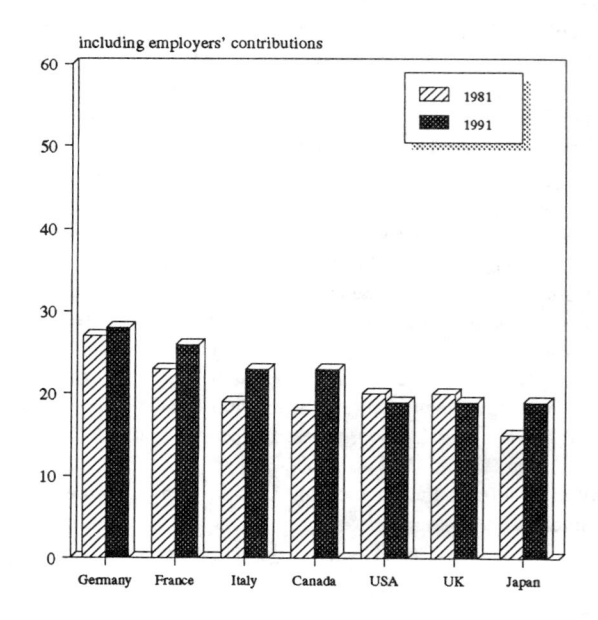

15. Excluding employers' contributions reduces the amount of household income taken through direct taxes by between 3 and 10 percentage points in 1991. All countries except the United States and the United Kingdom had increases in the proportion of personal income paid in direct taxes between 1981 and 1991 on this basis. Chart 9 shows the lower percentage taken if employers' contributions are excluded. Italy is not shown as there were no figures on the breakdown of social security contributions between employers and employees.

Chart 9
Direct taxes as percentage of total personal income [1]

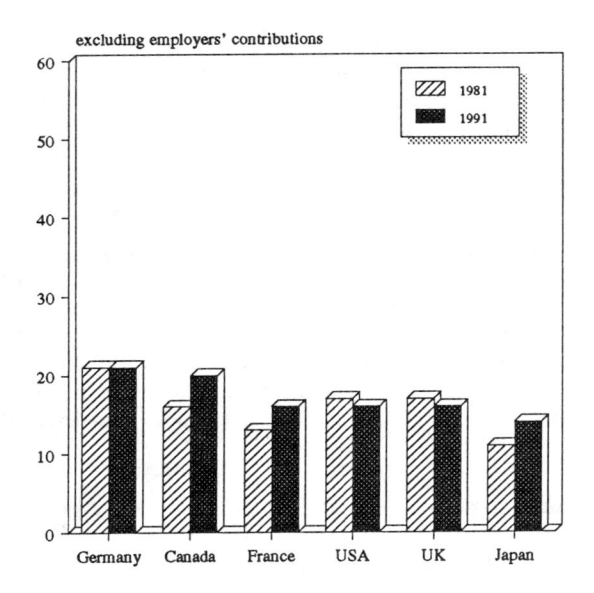

excluding employers' contributions

1. Data is unavailable for employers' contributions in Italy from 1989.

Table A : Total receipts from taxes and social security contributions as a percentage of GDP at market prices: preliminary estimates for 1992.

	Percentages 1991	1992	Differences between 1991 and 1992
Sweden	50.3	50.4	0.1
Denmark	48.2	48.9	0.7
Netherlands	47.2	46.7	-0.5
Norway	47.0	46.7	-0.3
Belgium	42.0	45.4	-3.4
France	43.9	43.7	-0.2
Austria	42.0	43.6	1.6
Italy	40.5	42.4	0.9
Germany	36.6	40.0	0.4
Ireland	37.9	38.0	0.1
Finland	37.9	37.7	-0.2
Spain	34.6	35.9	-1.3
United Kingdom	36.2	35.8	-0.4
Switzerland	31.4	32.2	-0.2

Preliminary estimates for 1992

16. For some member countries of OECD, provisional data for 1992 are available in the latest edition of *OECD Revenue Statistics*. While these figures are not on the same basis as those in the rest of the article a number of points can be made.

17. Figures on total receipts of taxes and social security as a percentage of GDP are shown in table A opposite. Figures for non-European countries in the G7 were unavailable in 1991 and 1992. Of the countries available, Germany and Italy had large rises between 1991 and 1992. In Germany there was a rise of 3.4 percentage points while Italy had a rise of 1.9 percentage points. France and the United Kingdom had small falls over this period.

Technical notes

1. Limitations of the comparisons

The comparisons made in this article indicate only broadly the relative importance of taxation in different countries. There are various factors which should be kept in mind:

- Total taxation, the composition of taxes, and the burden of taxes on household income, reflect differences between countries in their economic and financial structures and in the degree of government involvement in providing services and financial support (for example, medical care and retirement pensions).

- Comparisons are also affected by the methods governments choose to achieve their aims, for example: government tax receipts may be reduced through a system of tax relief, or a gross system may be adopted under which money is collected in taxes and then handed back as cash grants.

- The extent to which governments finance their expenditure by borrowing or from taxation varies between countries, and over time, and has an effect on the ratios of taxes to the gross national product.

- Including or excluding social security contributions can have a marked effect on comparisons between countries.

The figures shown here relate to total tax yields in each country: they reveal nothing about the incidence of tax on different groups.

2. Sources

The figures in the tables for direct taxes, indirect taxes and social security contributions are based on returns supplied to the OECD by national statistical offices and summarised in *OECD National Accounts 1979 - 1991, Detailed Tables, Volume Two*. These returns are made on the accounting conventions of the international organisations, which differ from those established in the United Kingdom; consequently the estimates made are not in all cases identical to those given in the CSO's own publications. Taxes on capital - which in the OECD national accounts presentation are included indistinguishably in capital transfers - have been derived from *Revenue Statistics of OECD Member Countries 1966 - 1992*. Figures for value added tax have also been obtained from this publication.

In this article, national accounts data have been used as the prime source, because the figures will be the more consistent with other statistics which are frequently derived from the national accounts publication.

3. Differences between OECD National Accounts Statistics and OECD Revenue Statistics

There are a few minor differences between the definitions of taxes and social security contributions used in revenue statistics and those used in the national accounts returns.

The main differences are in the time of recording the transactions. Hence revenue statistics use a cash based system (that is transactions at the time the public authority receives the money), while national accounts are accrual based (entries occur when a transaction is due to be paid).

4. Differences between the United Kingdom system of national accounts, the Former SNA and the Present SNA

The national accounts returns to OECD are based as far as possible on the System of National Accounts introduced by the United Nations in 1968 (the "Present SNA"). However, two countries - Greece and Switzerland - still provide figures on the basis of the previous system (the "Former SNA"). The figures on one basis are not strictly comparable with those on the other but the difference in definitions has little effect on the comparisons made in this article.

The main differences between the United Kingdom system and the international systems are summarised in Table C. United Kingdom figures in this article on a "national accounts" basis have been converted to the Present SNA.

5. The Community charge

The community charge was introduced in Scotland from April 1989 and in England and Wales from April 1990 to replace domestic rates. The community charge has been classed as a non-discretionary transfer to general government in line with its treatment in the UK National Accounts. As domestic rates were classified as an indirect tax, the different classification will cause distortion in the results for the United Kingdom between 1989 and 1992.

6. Other issues

Detailed figures for each country from 1981 are given in the Appendix.

All mention of Germany in the text, charts and appendix tables refer to *western* Germany (Federal Republic of Germany before the unification of Germany).

Table C shown on the following page, provides in alphabetical order of country, the percentages scored both on an OECD National Accounts basis and on a Revenue Statistics basis. In the table, there are small differences in ranking for a number of the countries shown.

Table B : Total taxes and social security contributions : percentage of GNP and ranking

	1981				1986				1991			
	National Accounts		Revenue Statistics		National Accounts		Revenue Statistics		National Accounts		Revenue Statistics	
	Per Cent	Rank	Per Cent	Rank	Per Cent	Rank	Per Cent	Rank	Per Cent	Rank	Per Cent	Rank
Australia	33.5	14	33.5	14	36.5	16	36.4	16	..	..	34.4	17
Austria	50.0	4	49.6	4	50.3	6	49.9	6	..	..	49.1	7
Belgium	50.0	4	49.6	4	52.3	4	52.1	4	49.8	6	49.6	6
Canada	37.2	13	40.0	12	39.0	13	40.2	13	44.5	9	45.2	10
Denmark	55.7	3	55.6	3	64.1	1	61.0	1	59.0	2	59.0	2
Finland	39.0	12	39.6	13	43.6	11	44.5	9	45.5	8	43.8	13
France	47.6	7	47.6	7	50.3	6	50.4	5	50.6	5	50.8	5
Germany	46.4	8	42.3	9	45.3	9	41.7	12	46.3	7	46.9	9
Greece	29.6	18	31.6	16	40.8	12	42.3	11	42.6	11	44.6	11
Ireland	44.3	9	41.6	10	52.1	5	49.1	8	..	..	47.0	8
Italy	33.4	15	33.4	15	37.6	15	38.7	15	44.1	10	44.3	12
Japan	28.6	20	28.3	19	30.2	19	30.6	19	33.3	13	33.2	18
Luxembourg	40.1	11	40.0	11	38.9	14	39.0	14	..	..	40.1	15
Netherlands	49.7	6	49.4	6	49.6	8	49.2	7	52.8	4	52.0	4
Norway	56.6	1	48.7	2	56.9	3	59.1	3	53.6	3	54.2	3
Spain	28.7	19	27.2	20	19.8	20	33.9	17	..	..	38.2	16
Sweden	56.6	1	56.9	1	60.4	2	61.7	2	63.0	1	63.1	1
Switzerland	30.1	17	30.8	18	32.6	17	32.9	18	31.4	15	31.2	20
U.K.[1]	43.7	10	42.4	8	43.8	10	43.5	10	40.2	12	41.8	14
U.S.A.	31.1	16	31.1	17	30.6	18	30.4	20	31.5	14	31.9	19

.. Not available

[1] Includes the community charge

Table C : Definitions : UK system of national account, former SNA and present SNA

	UK system	Former SNA	Present SNA
Definition of gross national product at factor cost			
i. Net property income from abroad			
a. Unremitted profits	Included	Excluded	Excluded
b. Profits remitted abroad	Measured after deduction of tax	Measured before deduction of tax	Measured before deduction of tax
ii. Rent income of public authorities (other than from dwellings)	Includes only capital consumption in place of imputed rents	Includes imputed rents before deduction interest and depreciation	Includes only capital consumption in place of imputed rents
Definition of taxes			
Direct taxes are taxes on income and indirect taxes are taxes on expenditure			
There are the following differences in treatment:-			
Motor vehicle licence duties paid by households	Indirect	Indirect	Direct
Taxes on capital gains[1]	Capital	Capital	Direct
Compulsory fees, fines and penalties	Non-tax	Indirect	Non-tax[2]

[1] For the United Kingdom, the betterment levy (introduced in 1967) and the development land tax (introduced in 1977) both representing a charge on the development value of land - are classified and treatment in the same way as taxes on capital gains.

[2] Only compulsory fees paid by household are excluded; similar payments by business are treated as indirect taxes.

1 Taxes and social security contributions as a percentage of gross national product at factor cost

Percentages

	1981	1982	1983	1984	1985	1986	1987	1988	1989	1990	1991
Australia[1]	29.8	30.2	29.3	31.0	31.1	32.0	32.2	32.0	32.1	32.3	..
Austria	43.2	42.2	41.9	43.1	43.9	43.6	43.1	42.7	41.7	41.9	..
Belgium	45.8	47.7	47.7	48.7	48.9	48.1	48.3	46.8	45.0	45.7	45.4
Canada	33.3	33.8	32.9	33.0	33.1	34.6	35.3	35.7	35.7	37.7	38.8
Denmark	46.8	46.3	48.2	49.7	51.2	53.0	53.7	53.7	52.8	50.6	50.4
Finland	34.9	34.4	34.4	35.9	37.2	38.5	36.2	37.6	37.5	38.7	40.0
France	41.8	42.8	43.7	44.8	44.7	44.0	44.6	43.9	43.8	43.8	44.2
Germany	41.3	41.5	40.9	41.0	41.4	40.7	40.9	40.6	40.9	39.3	41.1
Greece[2]	26.9	30.9	32.4	33.4	33.7	36.0	36.1	34.4	32.2	34.4	36.7
Irish Republic	39.3	42.0	44.2	46.0	45.4	46.0	45.6	47.9	44.8	44.2	..
Italy	31.5	33.6	35.0	34.8	34.9	35.5	36.2	36.7	38.3	39.2	40.1
Japan	26.8	27.1	27.3	27.7	28.2	28.3	29.8	30.1	30.4	31.5	31.1
Luxembourg	37.0	34.0	35.6	34.9	35.5	35.0	..	..	..	..	..
Netherlands	45.2	45.4	46.5	44.9	44.6	45.3	48.3	48.8	45.5	45.4	47.7
Norway	50.5	50.4	49.8	49.3	50.8	48.9	49.9	49.8	48.2	48.2	47.8
Spain	27.1	27.1	29.1	29.5	28.9	29.9	32.1	32.2	34.1	33.8	..
Sweden	51.0	50.4	51.8	51.6	51.3	53.0	57.3	55.8	57.9	57.9	54.7
Switzerland[2]	28.5	29.0	29.5	29.9	29.9	30.8	30.5	30.8	30.1	30.3	30.0
United Kingdom[3]	37.7	38.2	37.9	37.9	37.7	37.5	37.2	37.3	36.9	37.1	36.3
United States	28.7	28.0	27.6	27.6	28.1	28.3	29.2	28.7	29.1	29.1	29.0

1 Fiscal years beginning on 1 July of year indicated.
2 Former SNA.
3 Includes the community charge.

Source: Data derived from OECD statistics

2 Taxes as a percentage of gross national product at factor cost

Percentages

	1981	1982	1983	1984	1985	1986	1987	1988	1989	1990	1991
Australia[1]	29.8	30.2	29.3	31.0	31.1	32.0	32.2	32.0	32.1	32.3	30.5
Austria	30.5	29.8	29.7	30.8	31.4	31.1	30.6	30.3	29.4	29.6	..
Belgium	31.8	33.6	32.9	33.1	32.9	31.9	32.0	30.9	29.5	30.0	29.4
Canada	29.3	29.7	28.6	28.6	28.6	29.9	30.5	30.8	31.1	32.7	33.3
Denmark	45.8	45.0	46.3	47.7	49.2	51.3	51.6	52.2	51.3	49.0	48.9
Finland	30.2	29.8	29.9	31.0	31.7	33.1	31.1	32.8	32.8	33.7	34.0
France	24.1	24.5	24.8	25.5	25.3	25.1	25.4	24.9	24.6	24.5	24.8
Germany	25.2	24.9	24.8	25.0	25.2	24.5	24.6	24.4	25.0	23.6	25.1
Greece[2]	18.1	20.9	21.6	22.3	22.2	24.9	25.3	23.9	22.0	24.7	25.6
Irish Republic	36.0	38.7	41.1	43.0	41.8	42.7	42.4	44.5	42.7	40.8	..
Italy	20.0	21.2	22.4	22.8	22.8	23.0	23.8	24.4	25.7	26.1	26.8
Japan	19.0	19.1	19.2	19.6	20.0	20.0	21.3	21.7	22.1	22.3	22.0
Luxembourg	26.0	24.3	26.5	25.9	26.6	26.1	..	..	..	..	..
Netherlands	26.9	26.2	25.2	24.6	24.6	25.9	27.8	28.1	26.6	28.3	29.9
Norway	38.3	37.9	37.7	37.8	39.1	35.6	35.5	35.8	35.5	35.7	35.3
Spain	14.8	14.8	16.6	17.5	16.8	17.9	20.1	20.3	21.8	21.4	..
Sweden	36.0	36.4	38.0	38.2	38.5	39.6	43.7	41.7	43.2	42.2	39.0
Switzerland[2]	19.9	20.2	20.4	20.6	20.6	21.4	21.0	21.4	20.7	20.8	20.4
United Kingdom[3]	31.4	31.7	31.0	31.0	31.0	30.7	30.4	30.4	30.4	30.7	29.9
United States	22.3	21.5	21.0	20.8	21.1	21.2	22.0	21.3	21.7	21.6	21.3

1 Fiscal years beginning on 1 July of year indicated.
2 Former SNA.
3 Includes the community charge.

Source: Data derived from OECD statistics

3 Taxes and social security contributions by category as a percentage of gross national product at factor cost

Percentages

| | Direct taxes ||||||| Indirect taxes ||||||
| | Households[1] ||| Corporations ||| Total ||| of which: VAT |||
	1981	1986	1991	1981	1986	1991	1981	1986	1991	1981	1986	1991
Australia[1]	13.7	14.9	12.6	3.4	2.9	4.4	12.7	14.2	13.5	..	..	..
Austria	11.9	12.6	12.0	0.7	1.6	2.2	16.7	16.6	16.2	8.6	8.9	8.6
Belgium	16.3	16.4	14.0	2.5	3.2	2.8	12.7	12.1	12.2	7.9	7.3	7.3
Canada	11.7	13.1	16.0	4.1	3.3	2.3	13.4	13.3	14.9	..	..	2.9
Denmark	..	..	..	..	..	..	19.0	20.5	18.1	10.7	10.3	9.3
Finland	14.6	16.4	16.1	1.6	1.6	2.1	13.9	15.0	15.6	..	..	9.4
France	6.2	6.6	6.9	2.4	2.7	2.5	15.1	15.5	14.8	8.7	8.4	7.8
Germany[2]	10.5	10.1	10.3	1.7	2.1	1.7	12.9	12.2	13.0	6.4	5.7	6.8
Greece[3]	3.6	4.6	4.4	1.0	1.5	1.7	13.1	18.4	19.0	..	..	..
Irish Republic	..	..	..	..	..	..	18.2	20.5	18.7	5.7	9.0	8.3
Italy	9.5	10.5	11.7	1.5	2.5	3.0	9.0	10.0	12.1	4.7	5.3	5.8
Japan	6.6	6.8	8.3	4.7	5.3	5.4	7.6	7.5	7.7	..	..	1.4
Luxembourg	..	..	..	..	..	..	11.5	12.3	13.1	4.3	4.7	5.3
Netherlands[2]	11.7	9.9	13.3	3.1	3.3	3.6	11.8	12.5	12.8	6.9	7.4	7.4
Norway	12.5	11.7	13.6	8.2	4.0	4.4	17.6	19.8	17.3	8.8	10.0	8.4
Spain	5.5	6.1	..	1.8	0.6	..	7.4	10.9	10.7	..	4.6	5.5
Sweden	20.3	20.5	19.5	1.1	1.8	0.9	14.5	17.2	18.5	6.9	7.2	9.1
Switzerland[3]	11.9	12.4	12.2	1.3	1.5	1.4	6.5	6.8	6.0	..	..	..
United Kingdom	11.4	10.5	10.7	3.4	4.0	3.2	16.4	16.0	14.3	4.5	5.9	6.7
United States	11.2	10.3	10.4	2.6	2.5	2.2	8.1	8.1	8.4	..	..	..

| | Taxes on capital ||| Social security contributions |||||| Community charge |
| | ||| Total ||| of which: Paid by employers ||| |
	1981	1986	1991	1981	1986	1991	1981	1986	1991	1991
Australia[1]	0.1	..	..	..	..	..	..	..	..	
Austria	0.1	0.1	..	12.7	12.5	12.5	9.7	9.8	9.8	
Belgium	0.4	0.3	0.3	14.0	16.1	16.0	8.5	9.6	..	
Canada	0.1	0.2	0.2	4.0	4.7	5.4	2.4	2.9	3.1	
Denmark	0.2	0.3	0.3	1.0	1.7	1.6	..	..	..	
Finland	0.1	0.1	0.2	9.4	10.7	12.1	10.4	10.5	12.8	
France	0.3	0.3	0.6	17.7	18.9	19.4	11.8	12.0	11.9	
Germany	0.1	0.1	0.1	16.2	16.2	16.0	7.6	7.6	7.5	
Greece[3]	0.4	0.4	0.5	8.9	11.0	11.1	..	..	..	
Irish Republic	0.1	0.1	0.2	7.4	8.3	..	..	..	..	
Italy	0.1	0.1	0.1	11.5	12.5	13.3	8.6	8.8	..	
Japan	0.2	0.4	0.6	7.8	8.3	9.1	4.0	4.4	4.7	
Luxembourg	0.1	0.1	0.1	10.9	8.9	..	..	..	..	
Netherlands	0.2	0.2	0.2	18.4	19.4	17.8	9.0	8.8	3.7	
Norway	–	0.1	0.1	12.2	13.4	12.5	..	..	..	
Spain	0.2	0.3	0.4	12.3	12.0	..	12.1	11.4	..	
Sweden	0.1	0.1	0.1	15.1	13.4	15.7	14.5	12.9	15.2	
Switzerland[3]	0.2	0.6	0.7	8.6	9.4	9.6	3.0	3.1	3.2	
United Kingdom	0.2	0.3	0.2	6.2	6.8	6.4	3.5	3.5	3.8	1.4
United States	0.3	0.2	0.3	6.4	7.2	7.7	3.4	3.7	3.8	

1 Fiscal years beginning on 1 July of year indicated.
2 Households includes unincorporated businesses, except for Germany and the Netherlands.
3 Former SNA.

Source: Data derived from OECD statistics

4 Taxes and social security contributions by category as a percentage of total taxes[1] and social security contributions

Percentages

	1981	1982	1983	1984	1985	1986	1987	1988	1989	1990	1991
AUSTRALIA [2]											
Direct taxes:											
Paid by households[3]	45.8	45.1	44.3	44.9	45.2	46.5	45.0	45.5	44.1	42.8	..
Paid by corporations	11.4	10.1	8.9	9.3	9.4	9.1	10.3	10.7	12.7	14.1	..
Total	57.2	55.2	53.2	54.2	54.6	55.6	55.3	56.2	56.8	56.9	..
Indirect taxes	42.6	44.6	46.7	45.7	45.4	44.4	44.7	43.8	43.2	43.0	..
Taxes on capital	0.3	0.1	0.1	–	–	–	–	–	–	–	..
Social security contributions	..	..	..	..	..	..	..	..	..	..	..
AUSTRIA											
Direct taxes:											
Paid by households[3]	27.5	27.5	27.4	27.7	28.5	28.8	28.0	28.2	26.2	27.2	..
Paid by corporations	4.4	4.0	4.0	4.1	4.4	4.3	4.1	4.1	4.8	4.8	..
Total	31.9	31.5	31.4	31.8	32.9	33.1	32.1	32.3	31.0	32.0	..
Indirect taxes	38.4	38.9	39.3	39.6	38.4	38.1	38.7	38.5	39.2	38.4	..
of which: VAT	20.0	19.8	20.5	21.5	20.7	20.5	20.7	20.5	21.0	20.6	..
Taxes on capital	0.2	0.2	0.2	0.1	0.2	0.2	0.2	0.2	0.2	0.1	..
Social security contributions	29.5	29.4	29.1	28.5	28.5	28.6	29.0	29.0	29.6	29.5	..
BELGIUM											
Direct taxes:											
Paid by households[3]	35.6	36.4	35.2	35.1	34.7	34.1	33.1	32.4	31.1	31.3	30.9
Paid by corporations	5.4	6.2	5.9	6.2	6.5	6.6	6.6	6.9	6.7	6.5	6.1
Total	41.0	42.6	41.1	41.3	41.2	40.7	39.7	39.3	37.8	37.8	37.0
Indirect taxes	27.6	27.1	27.4	26.1	25.5	25.1	25.9	26.2	27.3	27.1	27.0
of which: VAT	17.4	16.4	16.4	15.8	15.4	15.1	15.3	15.8	16.2	15.9	16.0
Taxes on capital	0.8	0.7	0.6	0.6	0.6	0.6	0.6	0.6	0.6	0.7	0.7
Social security contributions	30.6	29.6	30.9	32.0	32.7	33.6	33.8	33.9	34.3	34.4	35.3
of which: paid by employers	18.7	16.9	17.4	18.2	19.2	20.0	20.2	20.5	21.0	20.6	..
CANADA											
Direct taxes:											
Paid by households[3]	35.1	36.8	36.8	35.9	36.2	37.9	38.2	38.6	38.7	42.3	41.3
Paid by corporations	12.2	10.6	10.4	11.4	10.9	9.7	9.7	9.3	9.0	7.7	6.0
Total	47.3	47.4	47.2	47.3	47.2	47.6	47.9	47.9	47.7	50.0	47.3
Indirect taxes	40.4	39.7	39.0	38.9	38.5	38.3	38.2	38.1	39.1	36.2	38.3
of which: VAT	..	..	..	..	..	..	..	..	..	1.4	7.4
Taxes on capital	0.3	0.5	0.6	0.6	0.6	0.5	0.5	0.4	0.4	0.4	0.4
Social security contributions	12.0	12.3	13.3	13.2	13.7	13.6	13.4	13.6	12.7	13.4	14.0
of which: paid by employers	7.2	7.1	7.9	8.0	8.3	8.3	8.0	8.1	7.7	7.8	8.0
DENMARK											
Direct taxes:[6]											
Paid by households[3]	..	..	..	..	..	..	..	..	..	..	..
Paid by corporations	..	..	..	..	..	..	..	..	..	..	..
Total	56.8	57.0	57.3	57.6	58.2	57.7	57.9	59.8	60.6	59.9	60.5
Indirect taxes	40.6	39.7	38.4	38.0	37.4	38.7	37.7	36.9	36.1	36.3	35.9
of which: VAT	22.8	22.3	21.1	20.6	20.0	19.4	18.9	18.2	18.1	18.5	18.4
Taxes on capital	0.4	0.4	0.4	0.4	0.5	0.5	0.6	0.6	0.5	0.6	0.5
Social security contributions	2.2	2.9	3.9	4.0	3.9	3.1	3.8	2.7	2.8	3.2	3.1
FINLAND											
Direct taxes:											
Paid by households[3]	41.9	41.5	41.7	41.4	41.8	42.7	40.9	41.9	41.2	41.5	40.2
Paid by corporations	4.6	4.7	4.9	4.3	3.9	4.1	3.3	3.8	4.0	5.4	5.2
Total	46.5	46.2	46.6	45.7	45.7	46.8	44.2	45.7	45.3	46.9	45.4
Indirect taxes	39.9	40.2	40.1	40.3	39.2	39.0	41.4	41.0	41.9	39.9	38.9
of which: VAT	19.3	19.3	19.3	20.5	20.3	20.5	23.7	23.1	24.0	23.0	22.0
Taxes on capital	0.2	0.3	0.3	0.3	0.3	0.3	0.4	0.4	0.4	0.4	0.5
Social security contributions	13.4	13.3	13.0	13.7	14.8	13.9	14.0	12.9	12.4	12.8	15.2

100

4 Taxes and social security contributions by category as a percentage of total taxes[1] and social security contributions

continued

Percentages

	1981	1982	1983	1984	1985	1986	1987	1988	1989	1990	1991
FRANCE											
Direct taxes:											
Paid by households[3]	14.8	14.7	15.4	15.4	14.9	14.9	14.6	13.9	13.7	13.8	15.6
Paid by corporations	5.8	5.9	5.2	5.5	5.6	6.2	6.4	6.6	6.9	6.6	5.6
Total	20.6	20.6	20.6	20.9	20.5	21.1	21.0	20.5	20.6	20.4	21.2
Indirect taxes	36.2	36.1	35.5	35.4	35.6	35.3	35.2	35.4	34.7	34.4	33.4
of which: VAT	20.9	21.0	20.3	19.6	19.7	19.2	19.2	19.3	18.9	18.5	17.6
Taxes on capital	0.8	0.6	0.6	0.6	0.6	0.7	0.8	0.9	0.9	1.0	1.5
Social security contributions	42.4	42.7	43.3	43.1	43.3	42.9	43.0	43.2	43.8	44.2	43.9
of which: paid by employers	28.3	28.2	28.3	27.6	27.8	27.3	27.0	26.5	26.9	27.1	27.0
GERMANY											
Direct taxes:											
Paid by households[4]	25.3	25.0	24.7	24.5	24.9	24.9	25.6	25.1	25.7	23.8	25.1
Paid by corporations	4.2	4.3	4.6	4.9	5.4	5.2	4.5	4.8	4.9	4.4	4.1
Total	29.5	29.3	29.3	29.4	30.3	30.1	30.1	29.9	30.6	28.2	29.2
Indirect taxes	31.2	30.5	31.2	31.3	30.3	30.0	29.8	30.0	30.4	31.6	31.7
of which: VAT	15.4	14.8	15.4	15.3	14.5	14.1	14.5	14.4	14.3	15.4	16.6
Taxes on capital	0.2	0.2	0.2	0.2	0.2	0.2	0.3	0.3	0.2	0.3	0.2
Social security contributions	39.1	40.0	39.3	39.1	39.2	39.7	39.8	39.8	38.8	39.9	38.9
of which: paid by employers	18.4	18.8	18.5	18.4	18.5	18.7	18.7	18.8	18.3	18.8	18.3
GREECE [5]											
Direct taxes:											
Paid by households[3]	13.3	14.6	13.7	14.4	13.5	12.9	12.4	13.5	12.2	12.7	12.0
Paid by corporations	3.7	4.0	3.0	3.4	3.3	4.2	4.5	3.9	4.3	5.1	4.7
Total	17.0	18.6	16.7	17.8	16.8	17.1	16.9	17.4	16.5	17.8	16.7
Indirect taxes	48.7	47.4	48.7	47.8	48.3	51.1	52.0	51.0	50.6	52.6	51.8
of which: VAT	..	..	..	..	..	..	22.3	23.3	25.5	26.5	25.6
Taxes on capital	1.4	1.7	1.4	1.1	1.0	1.1	1.1	1.2	1.2	1.3	1.2
Social security contributions	32.9	32.3	33.2	33.3	33.9	30.7	30.0	30.4	31.7	28.3	30.3
IRISH REPUBLIC											
Direct taxes:[6]											
Paid by households[3]	..	..	..	..	..	..	..	..	..	..	..
Paid by corporations	..	..	..	..	..	..	..	..	..	..	..
Total	34.6	34.0	34.1	35.5	35.7	37.0	38.0	39.4	35.6	37.3	..
Indirect taxes	46.3	46.3	46.5	45.8	45.4	44.7	44.0	42.9	46.0	43.9	..
of which: VAT	14.5	18.2	19.9	20.1	19.4	19.7	19.0	19.8	20.4	19.4	..
Taxes on capital	0.3	0.3	0.3	0.3	0.3	0.3	0.3	0.3	0.3	0.4	..
Social security contributions	18.8	19.4	19.1	18.4	18.6	18.0	17.7	17.4	18.1	18.4	..
ITALY											
Direct taxes:											
Paid by households[3]	30.1	30.1	30.0	30.7	31.1	29.5	28.7	30.3	29.3	29.2	29.2
Paid by corporations	4.8	5.3	5.6	5.7	6.4	7.0	8.3	6.3	8.3	8.1	7.4
Total	34.9	35.4	35.6	36.4	37.5	36.5	37.0	36.6	37.6	37.3	36.6
Indirect taxes	28.4	27.5	28.2	28.8	27.7	28.1	28.6	29.7	29.2	29.3	30.1
of which: VAT	15.0	14.4	14.8	15.2	14.4	15.0	14.7	15.3	14.0	14.9	14.4
Taxes on capital	0.2	0.2	0.2	0.2	0.2	0.3	0.2	0.2	0.2	0.1	0.1
Social security contributions	36.5	36.9	36.0	34.6	34.6	35.1	34.2	33.5	33.0	33.3	33.2
of which: paid by employers	27.4	26.6	25.8	24.6	24.7	24.9	23.9	23.6	..	..	..
JAPAN											
Direct taxes:											
Paid by households[3]	24.5	24.6	25.3	24.4	23.4	24.2	24.0	23.4	23.0	24.8	26.7
Paid by corporations	17.5	17.2	17.1	18.0	19.0	18.6	18.7	19.6	21.4	18.6	17.4
Total	42.0	41.8	42.4	42.4	42.4	42.8	42.7	43.0	44.4	43.4	44.1
Indirect taxes	28.2	27.8	26.8	27.4	27.5	26.5	27.2	27.5	26.4	26.2	24.8
of which: VAT	..	..	..	..	..	..	..	..	3.4	4.3	4.4
Taxes on capital	0.8	0.9	1.0	1.1	1.2	1.5	1.7	1.6	1.7	1.4	1.8
Social security contributions	29.0	29.5	29.8	29.1	28.9	29.2	28.4	27.9	27.5	29.0	29.3
of which: paid by employers	14.8	15.1	15.1	14.8	14.8	15.4	14.7	14.5	14.6	14.9	15.2

4. Taxes and social security contributions by category as a percentage of total taxes[1] and social security contributions

continued
Percentages

	1981	1982	1983	1984	1985	1986	1987	1988	1989	1990	1991
LUXEMBOURG											
Direct taxes:[6]											
Paid by households[3]	..	..	..	..	..	..	..	..	..	..	..
Paid by corporations	..	..	..	..	..	..	..	..	..	..	..
Total	39.0	38.8	39.9	39.1	40.5	39.0	..	..	..	..	..
Indirect taxes	31.1	32.4	34.4	34.6	34.2	35.2	..	..	..	..	..
of which: VAT	11.7	12.2	12.0	13.2	12.9	13.4	..	..	..	..	..
Taxes on capital	0.3	0.4	0.3	0.3	0.3	0.3	..	..	..	..	..
Social security contributions	29.6	28.4	25.4	26.0	25.0	25.5	..	..	..	..	..
NETHERLANDS											
Direct taxes:											
Paid by households[4]	25.9	25.1	22.6	22.2	20.8	21.8	21.2	22.0	23.0	26.3	27.8
Paid by corporations	6.8	6.6	6.0	5.6	6.8	7.3	8.1	7.7	7.6	7.9	7.6
Total	32.7	31.7	28.6	27.8	27.6	29.1	29.3	29.7	30.6	34.2	35.4
Indirect taxes	26.2	25.5	25.2	26.7	27.1	27.6	27.7	27.4	27.4	27.7	26.7
of which: VAT	15.3	14.7	14.5	15.4	15.9	16.3	16.1	16.2	16.1	16.2	15.4
Taxes on capital	0.5	0.4	0.4	0.4	0.4	0.5	0.5	0.5	0.5	0.5	0.5
Social security contributions	40.6	42.4	45.8	45.1	44.9	42.8	42.5	42.4	41.5	37.6	37.4
of which: paid by employers	19.8	19.4	19.4	19.3	19.3	19.5	17.0	16.6	16.2	8.0	7.7
NORWAY											
Direct taxes:											
Paid by households[3]	24.7	24.2	22.8	22.5	21.2	23.9	25.1	28.5	29.0	28.2	28.4
Paid by corporations	16.3	15.9	16.8	18.0	19.2	8.2	6.9	5.6	7.9	10.0	9.1
Total	41.0	40.1	39.6	40.5	40.4	32.1	32.0	34.1	36.9	38.2	37.5
Indirect taxes	34.7	35.1	36.0	36.1	36.5	40.5	39.0	37.6	36.6	35.9	36.2
of which: VAT	17.5	17.7	17.6	16.8	17.4	20.4	20.2	19.7	18.5	18.1	17.6
Taxes on capital	0.1	0.1	0.1	0.1	0.1	0.1	0.1	0.2	0.2	0.1	0.1
Social security contributions	24.2	24.7	24.3	23.3	23.0	27.3	28.9	28.1	26.3	25.8	26.2
of which: paid by employers	15.1	15.4	14.9	14.4	13.7	15.8	16.2	17.2	16.8	16.4	16.5
SPAIN											
Direct taxes:											
Paid by households[3]	20.3	18.7	20.3	21.6	22.7	20.5	23.8	24.6	25.4	25.2	..
Paid by corporations	6.5	6.7	6.7	6.5	1.2	2.0	3.5	2.9	5.4	5.2	..
Total	26.8	25.3	27.0	28.1	23.9	22.5	27.3	27.5	30.8	30.4	..
Indirect taxes	27.1	28.8	29.2	30.4	33.1	36.4	34.0	34.3	32.2	31.8	..
of which: VAT	..	..	..	..	..	15.2	16.4	16.9	16.7	16.2	..
Taxes on capital	0.7	0.6	0.7	0.9	1.1	1.2	1.2	1.3	1.2	1.1	..
Social security contributions	45.4	45.3	43.1	40.6	41.8	40.0	37.5	36.9	35.9	36.7	..
of which: paid by employers	44.6	44.2	41.3	37.8	39.2	38.0	..	..	..	..	..
SWEDEN											
Direct taxes:											
Paid by households[3]	39.8	40.9	39.5	38.8	38.7	38.6	37.6	39.7	39.8	38.3	35.6
Paid by corporations	2.1	2.7	3.5	3.6	3.1	3.3	4.7	4.7	4.9	3.6	1.7
Total	26.8	25.3	27.0	28.1	40.9	37.1	43.5	43.4	47.7	47.7	37.3
Indirect taxes	28.4	28.5	30.1	31.4	32.9	32.5	30.8	30.1	29.6	30.8	33.8
of which: VAT	13.6	13.2	13.4	13.3	14.0	13.6	13.2	13.4	13.4	14.8	16.7
Taxes on capital	0.2	0.2	0.2	0.2	0.3	0.2	3.0	0.2	0.2	0.2	0.2
Social security contributions	29.5	27.7	26.6	26.0	25.0	25.4	23.9	25.3	25.5	27.1	28.7
of which: paid by employers	28.4	26.6	25.5	24.8	23.8	24.3	22.9	24.3	24.3	25.9	27.8
SWITZERLAND[5]											
Direct taxes:											
Paid by households[3]	41.7	41.8	41.3	41.5	40.5	40.4	39.4	39.3	38.9	40.0	40.8
Paid by corporations	4.5	4.7	4.8	4.5	4.5	5.0	4.9	5.2	4.8	5.1	4.8
Total	46.2	46.5	46.1	46.0	45.0	45.4	44.3	44.5	43.7	45.1	45.6
Indirect taxes	22.9	22.4	22.4	22.0	21.9	22.1	22.6	22.0	22.2	20.8	20.1
Taxes on capital	0.7	0.8	0.8	0.8	1.9	2.1	2.2	2.8	2.9	3.0	2.2
Social security contributions	30.2	30.3	30.7	31.3	31.1	30.4	30.9	30.7	31.2	31.1	32.1
of which: paid by employers	10.7	10.6	10.5	10.5	10.3	10.1	10.2	10.2	10.3	10.3	10.5

4 Taxes and social security contributions by category as a percentage of total taxes[1] and social security contributions

continued
Percentages

	1981	1982	1983	1984	1985	1986	1987	1988	1989	1990	1991
UNITED KINGDOM											
Direct taxes:											
Paid by households[3]	30.2	29.6	28.8	28.0	27.8	27.9	27.2	27.3	27.6	29.4	29.4
Paid by corporations	9.1	10.1	10.7	11.7	12.6	10.6	10.6	10.8	12.3	11.0	8.9
Total	39.3	39.7	39.5	39.7	40.4	38.5	37.8	38.1	39.9	40.4	38.3
Indirect taxes	43.6	42.8	41.9	41.6	40.9	42.7	43.2	42.9	41.6	37.4	39.4
of which: VAT	12.1	13.7	13.8	14.7	15.7	15.7	15.8	16.8	16.7	17.1	19.2
Taxes on capital	0.5	0.5	0.6	0.6	0.7	0.7	0.7	0.6	0.6	0.7	0.6
Social security contributions	16.6	17.0	18.0	18.1	18.0	18.1	18.3	18.4	17.5	17.2	17.8
of which: paid by employers	9.2	8.8	9.1	9.1	9.1	9.4	9.5	9.6	9.5	10.0	10.4
Community charge	..	..	..	..	..	..	..	..	0.4	4.4	4.0
UNITED STATES											
Direct taxes:											
Paid by households[3]	39.2	39.7	37.3	36.1	36.8	36.3	37.1	36.0	37.2	36.9	35.8
Paid by corporations	9.2	7.1	8.2	9.0	8.5	8.9	9.7	9.9	9.3	8.6	7.6
Total	48.4	46.8	45.5	45.1	45.3	45.2	46.8	45.9	46.5	45.5	43.4
Indirect taxes	28.3	28.6	29.6	29.5	29.0	28.7	27.8	27.5	27.2	27.7	29.2
Taxes on capital	1.0	1.2	0.9	0.8	0.8	0.8	0.8	0.8	0.8	1.0	0.9
Social security contributions	22.3	23.4	24.0	24.6	24.9	25.3	24.6	25.8	25.5	25.8	26.5
of which: paid by employers	11.8	12.3	12.7	13.3	13.0	13.1	12.6	13.1	12.7	12.9	13.2

1 All minor discrepancies in total direct taxes are due to rounding.
2 Fiscal years beginning on 1 July of year indicated.
3 Households include unincorporated businesses.
4 Unincorporated businesses are included with corporations not households.
5 Former SNA.
6 Components of direct taxation were not separately identified

Source: Data derived from OECD statistics

5 Direct taxes on households[1], community charge and social security contributions as a percentage of total personal income in 1981, 1986 and 1991

Percentages

	Direct taxes			Community charge	Social security contributions			Total		
	1981	1986	1991	1991	1981	1986	1991	1981	1986	1991
a. Including employers' contributions										
Australia[2]	15.6	16.7	13.9		..	..	..	15.6	16.7	..
Austria	12.7	13.1	12.4		13.7	13.0	12.9	26.4	26.2	25.3
Belgium	13.7	14.1	12.1		11.8	13.9	13.8	25.5	28.0	25.9
Canada	13.8	15.0	17.2		4.7	5.4	5.8	18.5	20.4	23.0
Finland	16.6	18.2	16.2		5.3	5.9	6.1	21.9	24.1	22.3
France	6.0	6.5	6.8		17.3	18.7	19.1	23.4	25.2	25.9
Germany[1]	10.4	10.5	10.8		16.1	16.8	16.7	26.5	27.3	27.5
Greece	3.7	4.7	4.2		9.2	11.1	10.6	12.9	15.8	14.8
Italy	8.7	9.7	10.6		10.5	11.6	12.0	19.2	21.3	22.6
Japan	6.9	7.3	8.9		8.2	8.8	9.8	15.1	16.2	18.7
Netherlands[1]	11.4	9.7	12.2		17.9	19.1	16.4	29.3	28.9	28.6
Norway	15.4	13.7	15.0		15.0	15.6	13.8	30.4	29.3	28.8
Spain	5.5	6.4	..		12.2	12.6	..	17.7	19.0	..
Sweden	19.6	20.7	18.6		14.5	13.6	15.0	34.1	34.2	33.5
Switzerland[3]	13.3	14.0	13.4		9.7	10.5	10.6	23.0	24.5	23.9
United Kingdom	12.8	11.7	11.1	1.5	7.0	7.6	6.7	19.8	19.3	19.3
United States	12.5	11.2	11.1		7.1	7.8	8.2	19.6	19.0	19.4
b. Excluding employers' contributions										
Australia[2]	15.6	16.7	..		..	..	..	15.6	16.7	..
Austria	..	..	..							
Belgium	14.8	15.4	..		4.9	6.1	..	19.7	21.5	..
Canada	14.2	15.5	17.8		1.9	2.2	2.6	16.1	17.7	20.3
France	6.8	7.4	7.7		6.5	7.8	8.3	13.4	15.1	16.0
Finland	..	..	..							
Germany[1]	11.3	11.4	11.7		9.2	9.6	9.6	20.5	21.1	21.3
Greece	..	..	..							
Italy	9.4	10.6	..		2.9	3.7	..	12.3	14.2	..
Japan	7.2	7.7	9.4		4.2	4.4	4.9	11.4	12.1	14.4
Netherlands[1]	12.5	10.7	12.6		10.0	11.4	13.5	22.6	22.1	26.1
Norway	17.0	15.0	16.4		6.2	7.2	5.6	23.2	22.3	22.0
Spain	6.2	7.3	..		..	..	..	6.2	7.3	..
Sweden	22.7	23.8	21.7		0.6	0.7	0.6	23.4	24.4	22.3
Switzerland[3]	13.8	14.5	13.9		6.5	7.3	7.4	20.3	21.8	21.2
United Kingdom	13.3	12.1	11.6	1.6	3.3	3.8	2.9	16.6	16.0	16.1
United States	13.0	11.7	11.6		3.5	3.9	4.3	16.5	15.6	15.9

1 Households include unincorporated businesses, except for the Germany and the Netherlands.
2 Fiscal years beginning on 1 July of year indicated.
3 Former SNA.
4 Luxembourg and the Irish republic are excluded as data is not compiled

Source: Data derived from OECD statistics

TESTING FOR BIAS IN INITIAL ESTIMATES OF THE COMPONENTS OF GDP

U M Rizki, Central Statistical Office

Introduction

This article updates the results published in February 1993 and continues the series of articles analyzing the revisions data to test for bias in the initial estimates of main economic indicators. The last article published in May 1993 suggested that quarterly estimates of year on year growth rates of gross domestic product (GDP) published in the 10 years ending Q4 1992, showed some evidence of bias in initial estimates produced three years earlier. The present article analyses the revisions to growth rates of the components of GDP, when examined in terms of income, expenditure, and output in order to identify which of the individual components contributed to the bias in the aggregated measure of GDP.

It should, however, be stressed that since this article is looking at long term revisions the latest figures which can be covered relate to estimates of growth rates into 1989. The analysis in this article, therefore, could not take full account of some significant recent improvements made particularly to the methodology and in the identification of new data sources, incorporated into the initial estimates of quarterly growths from 1989 onwards. The expected improvements in the results due to these measures and also from the statutory requirements on the respondents to supply the relevant data to CSO, would only be seen in the short term revisions, which are not covered in this article.

Estimates of the components of expenditure, income and output are published in a quarterly article on national accounts in *Economic Trends*. The data for the first to the thirteenth estimate of each item and for each of the 40 quarters, analyzed in this article, have been taken from successive quarterly issues. The analysis covers published data for the 10 years from 1983 to end 1992, as in the May 1993 article. The dates refer to the publication of the thirteenth estimate, as before.

Methods of Testing for Bias

The methods used for the present analysis are the same as described in the articles published in the earlier issues of *Economic Trends*. Revisions series for each item were arrived at by taking the difference between the first and the thirteenth estimates of percentage growth rates over four quarters. The same definition of bias is used here as in the last article; an indicator is considered to be biased if its mean revision is significantly (in a statistical sense) different from zero. The following procedure was adopted.

a) To test the hypothesis of mean revision equals zero, the Student's t-test was applied, in the first instance, to each series. A 'significant' t-value would indicate bias. However, this test requires the revisions to follow a normal (Gaussian) distribution. The Wilcoxon signed-rank test, which is a non parametric test and which requires no assumption about the underlying distribution, was also applied to all the series. Strictly speaking this test examines whether the median (rather than the mean) is different from zero.

b) All series were tested for serial correlation. Where a significant coefficient for correlation was associated with a significant t-value, a Cochrane-Orcutt transformation was performed before re-applying the t-test.

c) As in the last article, all the series were examined for the effect of business cycles. The series of revisions were regressed on a dummy variable with 1 denoting the expansion and -1 denoting the contraction phase of the economy.

Conclusions

The main purpose of this article is to update last year's analysis by adding the data for 1992 and to examine the results to see if any improvements have been made to the revision practices. This is done for the whole 10 and the recent 5 year periods.

Although results based on just one year of new data cannot be conclusive, the analysis in this article shows that the average revisions were smaller in a majority of cases examined over both the two periods ending in December 1992.

Despite the lowering of the average revisions to the growth rates of total GDP expenditure components and of consumers' expenditure, the t-value in each case remained significant[1]. The average revisions to the growth rates of GDFCF were higher and t-values significant for both the 10 and recent 5 year periods. Similarly total GDP income components and other income showed significant t-values for both periods. The components of output that showed significant t-values were total output, output of AFF, manufacturing, distribution and other services, but for the 10 year period only. This showed that a tendency to bias still exists in the initial estimates of these variables and all of which, except the output of distribution industry, on average were revised upwards.

Significant serial correlation was observed in consumers' expenditure and GDFCF, in total GDP income components and other income and in total output components, AFF, distribution and other services. A Cochrane-Orcutt transformation reduced the significant t-value to non significant levels in all these cases except for consumers' expenditure in current prices, total expenditure in constant prices and total output.

The regression of initial estimates on economic cycles showed that during the ten year period to 1989, when there were two expansion (Q4'81 to Q2'84 and Q3'86 to Q2'89) and two contraction (Q1'80 to Q3'81 and Q3'84 to Q2'86) periods, the phase of business cycles in the expansion phases has significant effect on the underestimation of the growth rates relating to total expenditure, consumers' expenditure and GDFCF in current and constant prices. The same phase effect was identified for total income, income from employment, other income, total output and the output of manufacturing industry. The contraction phase had no effect on the under or overestimation of any of the variables. The business cycle effect on the underestimation of all these variables was more pronounced in the expansion phase of the recent 5 year period 1985 to 1989.

---

1 The significance level of a test for bias is a measure of how unlikely the test results would be if the process were really unbiased. For example when we say that the 10 year mean revision to GDP (0.43) is highly significantly different from zero we mean that if the long-run average revision were really zero, the chance that a sample of 40 revisions would have a mean differing from zero by 0.43 or more is 1% or less.

'Economic Trends' No. 484 February 1994 © Crown copyright 1994

It must be emphasised again that because of the long term nature of the revisions the recent improvements made to the methodology would not have affected the initial estimates made before 1988, but have influenced the revisions. The total effect of the new methodology would not be apparent for some years.

Results and Discussion of individual items

The results are summarised in Tables 1 to 6 in the annex. First the total of the relevant components is examined, e.g. the total of the GDP expenditure components. Then the components are examined separately. Also included in the annex are separate graphs for each indicator, showing the magnitude of individual revisions over the whole ten year period.

Components of Total Expenditure

Mean revision to the growth rates of total GDP expenditure components at current prices was down to 0.9 percent compared to 1.1 per cent over the previous 10 year period ending December 1991. However, it remained at 1.3 percent for the latter 5 year periods. The corresponding figures in constant prices were 0.70 from 0.78 in the 10 year period but up to 1.17 from 1.08 percent in the recent 5 year period. The t-values for all four means remained highly significant. However, the serial correlations were also significant and after Cochrane-Orcutt transformation on the 10 year data the t-values were reduced; falling to non significant levels at current prices but remaining significant, at constant prices.

A regression on the business cycle variable showed significant upward revisions to the initial estimates made particularly in the expansion phase of the recent 5 year period (publication dates: 1988 to 1992).

The components which contributed most to the revisions to the total expenditure were, as in the previous 10 year analysis, **consumers' expenditure and gross domestic fixed capital formation (GDFCF)**. These two items together account for more than 60% of total GDP expenditure components. The t-values for the mean revisions over the 10 year period, for the two items, were still highly significant in both current and constant prices. The same results were obtained by the Wilcoxon test. In all cases these revisions increased the initial estimates. The main reason for these significantly upward mean revisions were some very large and consistently positive changes to consumers' expenditure, and higher revisions still to GDFCF during the recent years of the 10 year period.

The mean revision to consumers' expenditure in current prices was an increase of 0.7 percentage points in the whole 10 year period but rising to 1.07 per cent in the second 5 year span. At constant prices these upward revisions were 0.39 and 0.69 percentage points respectively. The corresponding figures for GDFCF were 2.38 and 3.84 at current prices and 2.16 and 3.78 percentage points at constant prices.

The serial correlation was significant for both consumers' expenditure and GDFCF. A Cochrane-Orcutt transformation over the 10 year period reduced the t-values for GDFCF, in both current and constant prices, to non-significant levels. The t-value for consumers' expenditure remained significant in current prices but was reduced to a non-significant level for constant prices.

A regression on the business cycle variable showed a non-significant effect of the phase of the cycle for consumers' expenditure for the 10 year and the first 5 year periods in both price measures. However, in the second 5 year period, the initial estimates of consumers' expenditure indicated a downward bias in the expansion phase of the business cycle. There were significant phase effects for GDFCF in both price measures and for all time spans. The main contributing factor to the significant effects in the final 5 years is the number of high positive revisions to both consumers' expenditure and GDFCF in this period. Of the 20 observations of the revisions to consumers' expenditure in this 5 year period, which contains 8 contraction and 12 expansion quarters of the economic cycles, only 3 revision in current prices and 5 in constant prices were negative and the other 17 and 15 respectively were positive. For GDFCF, which was prone to very high revisions, the range of revisions in this period was -4.24 to 9.73 per cent (4 negative and 16 positive) in current prices and -2.29 to 8.88 per cent (3 negative and 17 positive) in constant prices.

General government final consumption (GGFC) represents the total of Local Authority and Central Government current expenditure on goods and services. The average revisions to the year on year growth of GGFC at current prices were reduced from 0.65 and 0.53 percentage points for the 10 year and the latter 5 year periods to 0.28 and 0.25 respectively. The corresponding revisions at constant prices were changed from -0.11 and 0.11 to -0.17 and 0.07 for the 10 and 5 year periods respectively. The t-values in all four cases were not significant. A regression on the business cycle variable showed a non-significant effect of the economic phases in each case.

Exports are added to the total domestic expenditure to get total final expenditure, while **imports** are subtracted from the final expenditure to arrive at the GDP estimate. The t-values for the average revisions to the growth rates of both exports and imports remained non significant for both the current and constant price measures. However, a regression on the business cycle variable showed a slightly significant effect in the expansion phase for the current price measure of imports in the 10 year and the first 5 year periods but not for the latter 5 year period.

Components of Total Incomes

The mean revision to the year on year growth rate of **total GDP income components** was an increase of .42 percentage points over the 10 year period and an increase of 0.75 per cent in the latter 5 year period. The t-values were significant in both periods. The indication of the downward bias in the initial estimates, was more pronounced during the expansion phases of the business cycles.

The components which contributed most to the overall mean revision were **other income (sum of income from self employment and rent)** and **gross trading profits of companies**. However, the t-values were significant only for the revisions to other incomes and not for company profits. The non-significant t-value in the latter case was due to a high standard deviation which was in turn the result of a very wide range of revisions, mostly made in the latter 5 years of the ten year period. The range of revisions to the growth rates of company profit in the latter 5 years was between -8.82 and 19.74 (6 negative and 14 positive).

Both components showed high serial correlation. A Cochrane-Orcutt analysis reduced the t-value for other income to a non-significant level.

A regression on the business cycle variable over the 10 year data showed a significant phase effect for other income but not for company profits.

The mean revision to **income from employment** over the 10 year period was not significant. This result was confirmed by the Wilcoxon signed-rank test. However, during the expansion phases of the business cycles the average revisions to the growth rates were higher and significant; 0.54 (standard error, 0.18) and 0.64 (standard error, 0.26) percentage points respectively for the 10 year and the latter 5 year periods.

The other total GDP income components are **gross trading surpluses of public corporations and general government** and **non trading capital consumption** along with **stock appreciation** which is a negative item. These components have not been included in this study.

Components of Output

Output by industry is measured and published only as index numbers, at constant prices. The mean revision over the 10 years to the annual growth rates of the **aggregate output** of all industries was reduced from 0.63 in the last 10 year span to the current average of 0.49 percentage points. However the t-value remained significant, and this was confirmed by the Wilcoxon test to show that an element of bias still exists.

The average over the latter 5 year period was also reduced to 0.12 percentage points with the t-value remaining non-significant. The data showed high serial correlation over the 10 year period but small and non-significant correlation in the latter 5 year period. A Cochrane-Orcutt analysis reduced the level of significance over the 10 year period but it still remained significant.

The regression on the business cycle variable showed that there was a tendency to underestimate the growth rates during the expansion phases in the 10 and the first 5 year periods. No phase effects were observed in the latter 5 years.

The components of output which contributed most to the overall mean revision were, as in the Feb 93 article, **agriculture, forestry and fishing, manufacturing and other services**). The t-values for all these components were highly significant. AFF and other services showed high serial correlations, but a Cochrane-Orcutt analysis reduced the t-values for both these components to non-significant levels.

A regression of data on the business cycle variable showed significant effect in the expansion phase for manufacturing over the 10 and the first 5 year periods, for AFF and other services over the first 5 year period and for none of these components in the latter 5 years.

Among the other component of output - **construction, distribution hotels and catering, and transport and communications** - only distribution showed a slightly significant t-value, i.e a small indication of bias. But distribution data showed a high serial correlation and when a Cochrane-Orcutt transformation was applied to adjust for the serial correlation the t-value became non-significant.

There was phase effects in the contraction period over the 10 year period for distribution, hotels and catering (overestimation) and for other services (underestimation). Over the first 5 year period, significant phase effect in the contraction phase was also observed for AFF, manufacturing, construction and other services - all underestimation and for distribution, hotel and catering (overestimation).

The analysis covered data of initial estimates made up to 1989. The recent improvements made to the methodology of compiling the national accounts should reduce these biases. Further monitoring to verify this will be reported in July this year in an update to this article. In addition an analysis which will update the results of the article published in May 1993 will be published in the April 1994 issue of *Economic Trends*.

TABLE 1: REVISIONS ANALYSIS: EXPENDITURE COMPONENTS AT CURRENT PRICES 1983 - 1992 REVISION REFERENCE: THREE YEARS AFTER THE FIRST PUBLICATION YEAR ON YEAR GROWTH RATE (PER CENT)

Indicator	No. of yrs	No. of obs.	Mean rev.	Std dev.	SE of Mean	t-value	Wilcoxon Z	% of + rev	% of - rev	Coefficient of serial correlation	Range of revision values
Total GDP expenditure components	10	40	0.92	1.68	0.27	3.40 **	3.22 **	72.5	27.5	0.53 **	4.91 to -2.86
	5	20	1.30	1.61	0.36	3.51 **		85	15	0.43 **	4.76 to -2.86
Consumer expenditure	10	40	0.72	1.04	0.17	4.32 **	3.69 **	70	30	0.46 **	3.38 to -0.85
	5	20	1.07	1.02	0.23	4.55 **		85	15	0.46 **	2.98 to -0.85
General govmnt final consumption	10	40	0.28	1.50	0.24	1.18	1.34	55	45	0.32 *	3.01 to -3.84
	5	20	0.25	1.37	0.31	0.80		55	45	0.39 *	3.01 to -1.93
Gross domestic fixed capital formation	10	40	2.38	3.92	0.62	3.79 **	3.23 **	67.5	32.5	0.62 **	9.73 to -4.24
	5	20	3.84	3.62	0.81	4.62 **		80	20	0.52 **	9.73 to -4.24
Exports	10	40	-0.05	0.82	0.13	-0.37	0.65	45	55	0.11	2.28 to -1.54
	5	20	-0.25	0.79	0.18	-1.37		30	70	-0.18	1.51 to -1.54
Imports	10	40	0.27	1.07	0.17	1.60	1.43	57.5	42.5	0.25	2.91 to -2.56
	5	20	0.20	1.03	0.23	0.85		60	40	0.08	2.08 to -2.56

NOTE: Ten year period runs from April '83 to Jan '93.
Five year period runs from April '88 to Jan '93.
These dates relate to the publication dates; e.g. revision published in Q4 1992 would relate to Q3 1992.

Wilcoxon Z is the equivalent normal score of the Wilcoxon test.

* = significant at the 5% level; ** = significant at the 1% level.

TABLE 2: REVISIONS ANALYSIS: EXPENDITURE COMPONENTS AT CONSTANT PRICES 1983 - 1992
REVISION REFERENCE: THREE YEARS AFTER THE FIRST PUBLICATION
YEAR ON YEAR GROWTH RATE (PER CENT)

Indicator	No. of yrs	No. of obs.	Mean rev.	Std dev.	SE of Mean	t-value	Wilcoxon Z	% of + rev	% of + rev	Coefficient of serial correlation	Range of revision values
Total GDP expenditure components	10	40	0.70	1.19	0.19	3.66 **	3.42 **	75	25	0.24	4.39 to -1.96
	5	20	1.17	1.17	0.26	4.38 **		85	15	0.14	4.39 to -0.71
Consumer expenditure	10	40	0.39	0.92	0.14	2.63 *	2.40 *	65	35	0.38 *	2.85 to -1.25
	5	20	0.69	0.99	0.22	3.01 **		75	25	0.29	2.85 to -1.25
General govmnt final consumption	10	40	-0.17	1.11	0.18	-0.94	1.09	35	65	0.10	2.56 to -2.06
	5	20	0.07	1.32	0.30	0.23		40	60	0.18	2.56 to -2.06
Gross domestic fixed capital formation	10	40	2.16	4.03	0.64	3.35 **	2.98 **	70	30	0.61 **	8.88 to -5.09
	5	20	3.78	3.31	0.74	4.98 **		85	15	0.39 *	8.88 to -2.29
Exports	10	40	-0.00	1.17	0.18	-0.00	0.25	50	50	0.33 *	3.17 to -2.37
	5	20	0.01	1.26	0.28	0.05		45	55	0.29	3.17 to -2.29
Imports	10	40	-0.26	1.59	0.25	-1.01	0.81	45	55	0.51 **	2.46 to -4.12
	5	20	0.01	1.28	0.29	0.03		45	55	0.22	2.46 to -2.87

NOTE: Ten year period runs from April '83 to Jan '93.
Five year period runs from April '88 to Jan '93.
These dates relate to the publication dates; e.g. revision published in Q4 1992 would relate to Q3 1992.

Wilcoxon Z is the equivalent normal score of the Wilcoxon test.

* = significant at the 5% level; ** = significant at the 1% level.

TABLE 3: REVISIONS ANALYSIS: INCOME COMPONENTS AT CURRENT PRICES 1983 - 1992
REVISION REFERENCE: THREE YEARS AFTER THE FIRST PUBLICATION
YEAR ON YEAR GROWTH RATE (PER CENT)

Indicator	No. of yrs	No. of obs.	Mean rev.	Std dev.	SE of Mean	t-value	Wilcoxon Z	% of + rev	% of - rev	Coefficient of serial correlation	Range of revision values
Total GDP income components	10	40	0.42	1.26	0.20	2.06 *	2.24 *	62.5	37.5	0.34 *	3.98 to -2.40
	5	20	0.75	0.93	0.21	3.54 **		75.0	25.0	0.25	2.45 to -0.91
Income from employment	10	40	0.22	0.89	0.14	1.51	1.22	55.0	45.0	0.62 **	1.95 to -1.47
	5	20	0.24	0.93	0.21	1.10		45.0	55.0	0.65 **	1.95 to -0.89
Gross trading profits of companies	10	40	1.39	7.35	1.16	1.18	0.84	55.0	45.0	0.26	22.82 to -12.34
	5	20	3.06	6.84	1.53	1.95		70.0	30.0	0.31 *	19.47 to -8.82
Other income	10	40	1.40	2.41	0.38	3.63 **	3.22 **	70.0	30.0	0.63 **	6.89 to -3.26
	5	20	1.83	2.63	0.59	3.03 **		75.0	25.0	0.66 **	6.89 to -3.26

NOTE: Ten year period runs from April '83 to Jan '93.
Five year period runs from April '88 to Jan '93.
These dates relate to the publication dates; e.g. revision published in Q4 1992 would relate to Q3 1992.

Wilcoxon Z is the equivalent normal score of the Wilcoxon test.

* = significant at the 5% level; ** = significant at the 1% level.

TABLE 4: REVISIONS ANALYSIS: OUTPUT COMPONENTS AT CONSTANT PRICES 1983 - 1992 REVISION REFERENCE: THREE YEARS AFTER THE FIRST PUBLICATION YEAR ON YEAR GROWTH RATE (PER CENT)

Indicator	No. of yrs	No. of obs.	Mean rev.	Std dev.	SE of Mean	t-value	Wilcoxon Z	% of + rev	% of - rev	Coefficient of serial correlation	Range of revision values
Total GDP output components	10	40	0.49	0.64	0.10	4.81 **	3.97 **	80	20	0.66 **	1.39 to -1.24
	5	20	0.12	0.51	0.11	0.99		70	30	0.21	0.81 to -1.24
Agriculture, forestry and fishing	10	40	2.12	5.75	0.91	2.30 *	1.98	62.5	37.5	0.77 **	16.96 to -8.33
	5	20	-1.07	4.30	0.96	-1.08		40	60	0.86 **	6.56 to -8.33
Manufacturing	10	40	0.62	1.01	0.16	3.82 **	3.71 **	80	20	0.22	2.76 to -2.35
	5	20	0.30	0.98	0.22	1.34		70.0	30.0	0.16	2.07 to -2.35
Construction	10	40	0.43	1.88	0.30	1.44	1.28	57.5	42.5	0.33 *	3.96 to -4.23
	5	20	0.02	2.17	0.49	0.03		45	55	0.49 **	3.96 to -4.23
Distribution, hotels and catering	10	40	-0.67	2.06	0.33	-2.01 *	1.32	45.0	52.5	0.70 **	1.90 to -7.57
	5	20	0.03	1.22	0.27	0.10		55	40	0.29	1.77 to -2.54
Transport and communication	10	40	0.11	2.00	0.32	0.34	0.55	55.0	42.5	0.25	4.24 to -5.34
	5	20	0.52	2.16	0.48	1.06		65.0	35.0	0.11	4.24 to -3.61
Other services	10	40	0.79	1.32	0.21	3.73 **	3.49 **	77.5	22.5	0.68 **	3.86 to -1.87
	5	20	-0.20	0.84	0.19	-1.05		55.0	45.0	0.32 *	0.93 to -1.87

NOTE: Ten year period runs from April '83 to Jan '93.
Five year period runs from April '88 to Jan '93.
These dates relate to the publication dates; e.g. revision published in Q4 1992 would relate to Q3 1992.

Wilcoxon Z is the equivalent normal score of the Wilcoxon test.

* = significant at the 5% level; ** = significant at the 1% level.

TABLE 5: RESULTS OF STUDENT'S T-TEST AFTER COCHRANE-ORCUTT TRANSFORMATION
(Revisions after 3 Years to growth rates - 1983 to 1992)

	Before transformation		After transformation	
	t-value	ρ	t-value	ρ
Expenditure (current prices)				
Total	3.40	0.53	1.49	-0.05
Consumer expenditure	4.32	0.46	2.20	-0.05
Gross domestic fixed capital formation	3.79	0.62	1.62	0.03
Expenditure (constant prices)				
Total	3.66	0.24	2.64	-0.02
Consumer expenditure	2.63	0.38	1.32	0.06
Gross domestic fixed capital formation	3.35	0.61	1.36	0.00
Income (current prices)				
Total	2.06	0.34	1.65	-0.00
Other income	3.63	0.63	1.45	0.01
Output (constant prices)				
Total	4.81	0.66	2.36	0.06
Agriculture, forestry and fishing	2.30	0.77	0.43	0.12
Distributions, hotels and catering	-2.01	0.70	-0.90	0.13
Other services	3.73	0.68	1.42	-0.05

TABLE 6: SUMMARY OF TESTS FOR CYCLICAL VARIATION

Series	Overall mean	1983 to 1992 Expansion phase mean	1983 to 1992 Expansion phase t-value	1983 to 1992 Contraction phase mean	1983 to 1992 Contraction phase t-value	Overall mean	1983 to 1987 Expansion phase mean	1983 to 1987 Expansion phase t-value	1983 to 1987 Contraction phase mean	1983 to 1987 Contraction phase t-value	Overall mean	1988 to 1992 Expansion phase mean	1988 to 1992 Expansion phase t-value	1988 to 1992 Contraction phase mean	1988 to 1992 Contraction phase t-value
Expenditure (current prices)															
Total	0.92	1.12	2.92	0.61	1.58	0.53	0.16	0.30	1.09	2.00	1.30	2.08	4.90	0.13	0.30
Consumer expenditure	0.72	0.83	3.46	0.56	2.36	0.38	0.30	0.94	0.49	1.54	1.07	1.36	4.27	0.64	2.01
General government final consumption	0.28	0.42	1.23	0.07	0.21	0.31	0.51	0.94	0.02	0.04	0.25	0.34	0.74	0.12	0.27
Gross domestic fixed capital formation	2.38	4.01	5.18	-0.08	-0.10	0.91	2.26	2.06	-1.12	-1.02	3.84	5.76	6.43	0.96	1.08
Exports	-0.05	0.08	0.43	-0.24	-1.30	0.15	0.44	1.77	-0.28	-1.15	-0.25	-0.28	-1.06	-0.20	-0.78
Imports	0.27	0.57	2.45	-0.17	-0.72	0.35	0.74	2.20	-0.24	-0.71	0.20	0.40	1.20	-0.10	-0.29
Expenditure (constant prices)															
Total	0.70	0.94	3.49	0.35	1.29	0.23	0.27	0.77	0.17	0.48	1.17	1.60	4.68	0.52	1.53
Consumer expenditure	0.39	0.52	2.49	0.19	0.89	0.09	0.31	1.37	-0.25	-1.11	0.69	0.73	2.21	0.62	1.89
General government final consumption	-0.17	-0.20	-0.79	-0.11	-0.44	-0.40	-0.42	-1.58	-0.37	-1.39	0.07	0.02	0.04	0.15	0.34
Gross domestic fixed capital formation	2.16	3.89	4.94	-0.43	-0.55	0.54	2.33	2.05	-2.13	-1.88	3.78	5.46	6.43	1.27	1.50
Exports	-0.00	0.19	0.73	-0.29	-1.10	-0.01	0.42	1.35	-0.67	-2.13	0.01	-0.04	-0.09	0.09	0.22
Imports	-0.26	0.22	0.66	-0.98	-2.88	-0.52	0.14	0.27	-1.53	-2.80	0.01	0.30	0.75	-0.44	-1.08
Income (current prices)															
Total	0.42	0.73	2.63	-0.05	-0.20	0.08	0.44	0.94	-0.46	-0.99	0.75	1.02	3.56	0.35	1.23
Income from employment	0.22	0.54	2.96	-0.28	-1.51	0.20	0.45	1.66	-0.19	-0.69	0.24	0.64	2.47	-0.37	-1.43
Gross trading profits of companies	1.39	1.54	0.91	1.17	0.69	-0.27	1.23	0.50	-2.52	-1.03	3.06	1.86	0.84	4.86	2.20
Other income	1.40	2.27	4.58	0.09	0.18	0.97	1.27	1.82	0.52	0.74	1.83	3.27	5.19	-0.34	-0.54
Output (constant prices)															
Total	0.49	0.51	3.44	0.47	3.17	0.87	1.05	6.47	0.61	3.77	0.12	-0.03	-0.18	0.33	2.11
Agriculture, forestry and fishing	2.12	2.51	1.89	1.54	1.16	5.31	5.04	2.88	5.71	3.26	-1.07	-0.03	-0.02	-2.63	-1.94
Manufacturing	0.62	0.73	3.17	0.45	1.93	0.94	1.10	3.55	0.68	2.20	0.30	0.46	0.26	0.00	0.00
Construction	0.43	0.55	1.26	0.27	0.62	0.85	0.72	1.49	1.05	2.16	0.02	0.37	0.52	-0.51	-0.73
Distribution, hotels and catering	-0.67	-0.28	-0.59	-1.25	-2.70	-1.36	-0.26	-0.37	-3.02	-4.37	0.03	-0.29	-0.77	0.51	1.34
Transport and communications	0.11	0.42	0.94	-0.37	-0.81	-0.31	-0.29	-0.48	-0.34	-0.58	0.52	1.13	1.69	-0.39	-0.59
Other services	0.79	0.59	1.96	1.09	3.63	1.78	1.54	5.55	2.14	7.70	-0.20	-0.37	-1.35	0.04	0.15

Total GDP expenditure components at current prices
four quarter per cent change
revisions after three years
quarter of publication for revised estimate

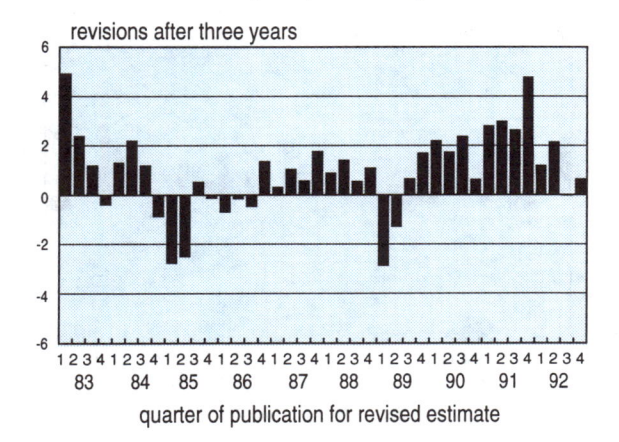

Consumer expenditure at current prices
four quarter per cent change
revisions after three years
quarter of publication for revised estimate

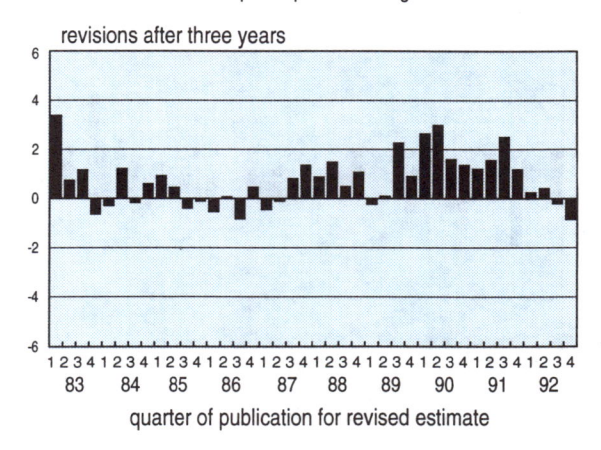

Government final consumption at current prices
four quarter per cent change
revisions after three years
quarter of publication for revised estimate

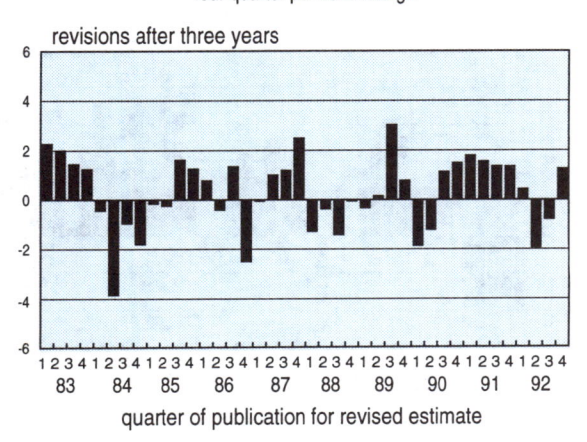

GDFCF at current prices
four quarter per cent change
revisions after three years
quarter of publication for revised estimate

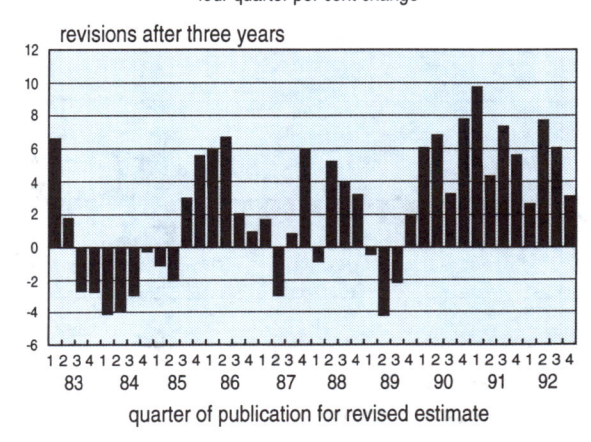

Exports at current prices
four quarter per cent change
revisions after three years
quarter of publication for revised estimate

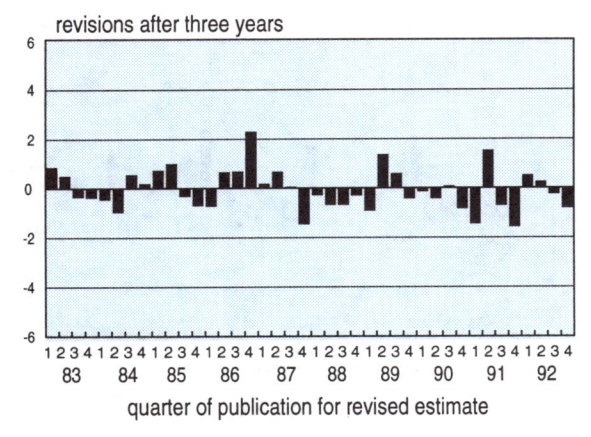

Imports at current prices
four quarter per cent change
revisions after three years
quarter of publication for revised estimate

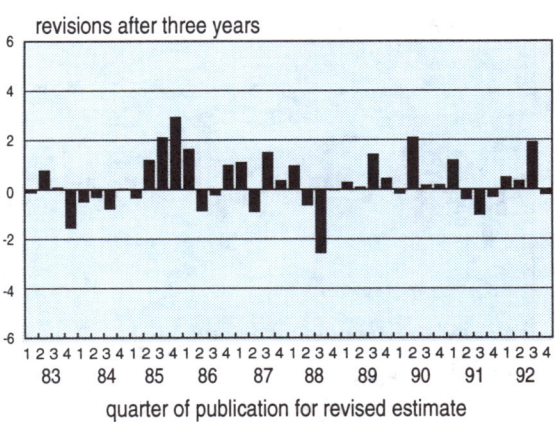

Total GDP expenditure components at constant prices
four quarter per cent change

revisions after three years

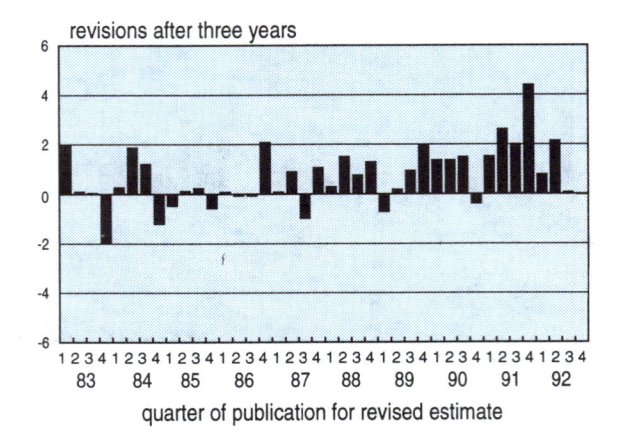

Consumers' expenditure at constant prices
four quarter per cent change

revisions after three years

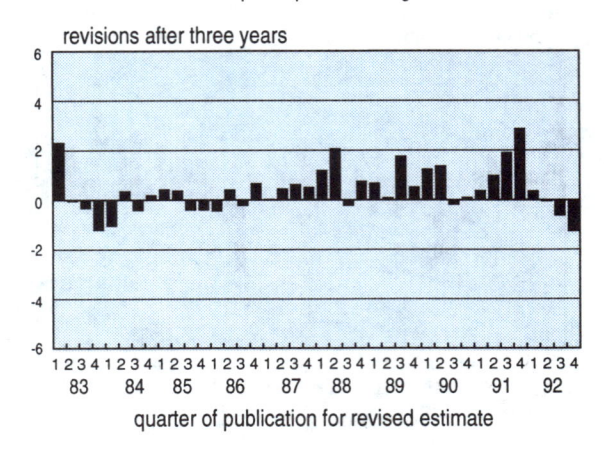

Government final consumption at constant prices
four quarter per cent change

revisions after three years

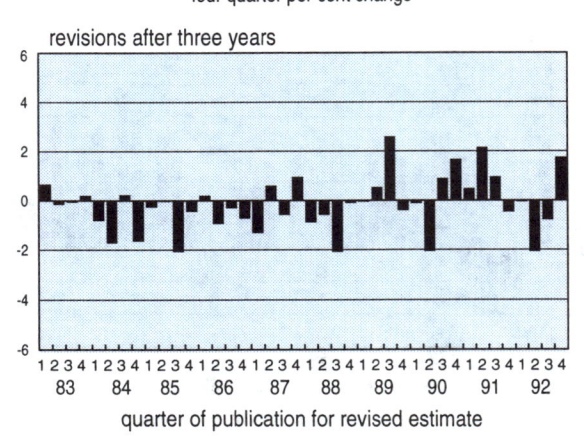

GDFCF at constant prices
four quarter per cent change

revisions after three years

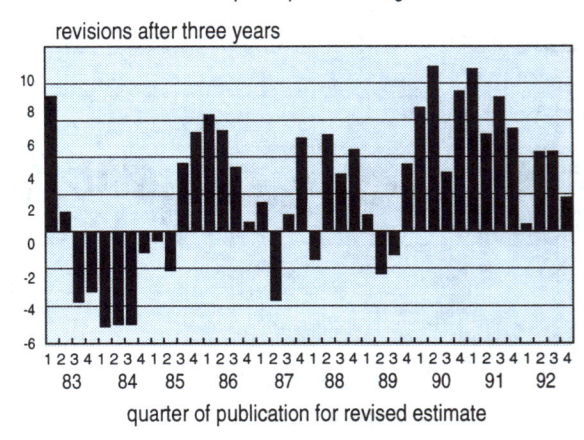

Exports at constant prices
four quarter per cent change

revisions after three years

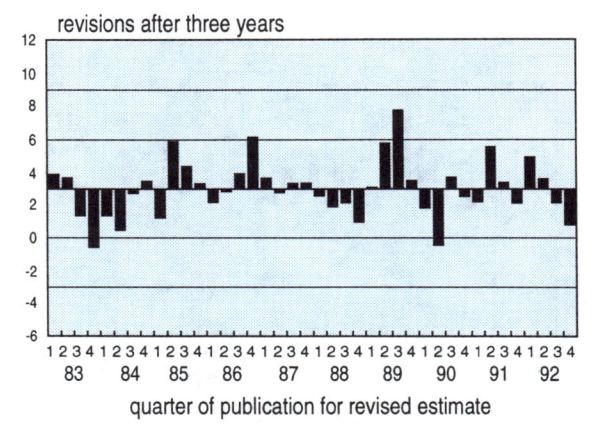

Imports at constant prices
four quarter per cent change

revisions after three years

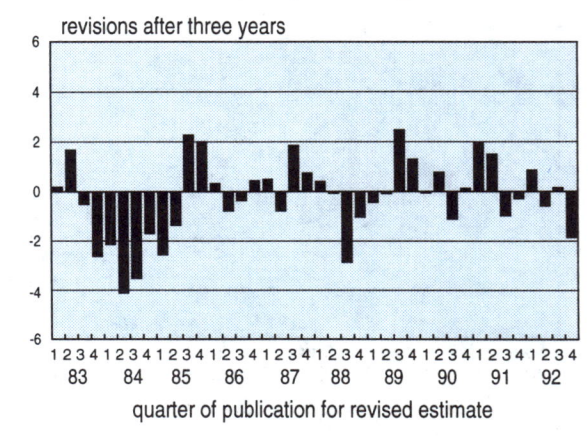

Total GDP income components at current prices
four quarter per cent change

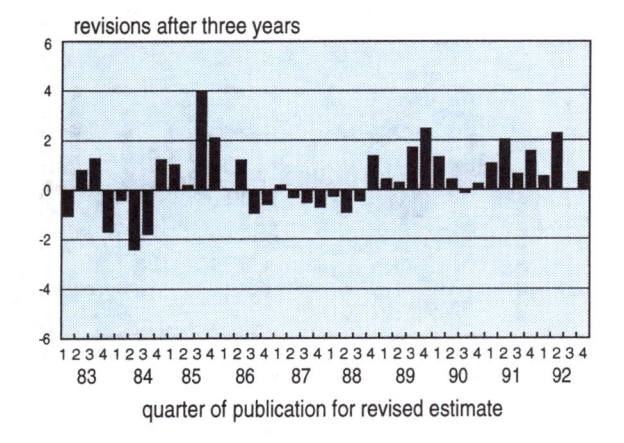

Income from employment
four quarter per cent change

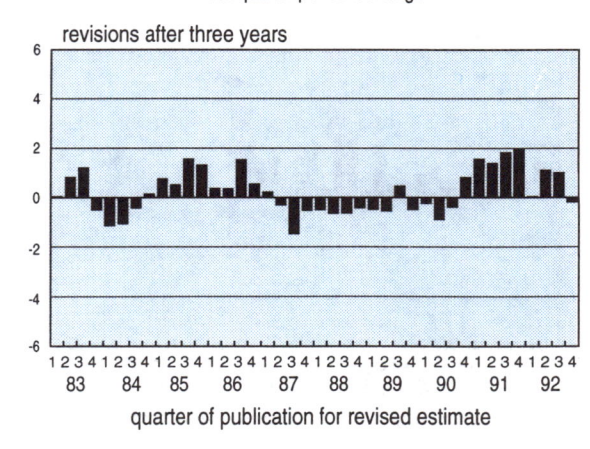

Gross trading profits of companies
four quarter per cent change

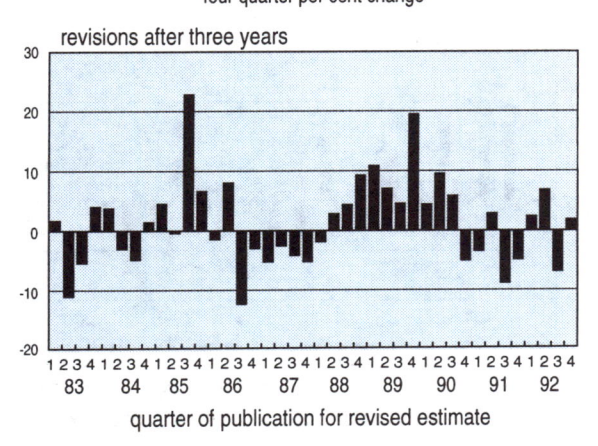

Other income
four quarter per cent change

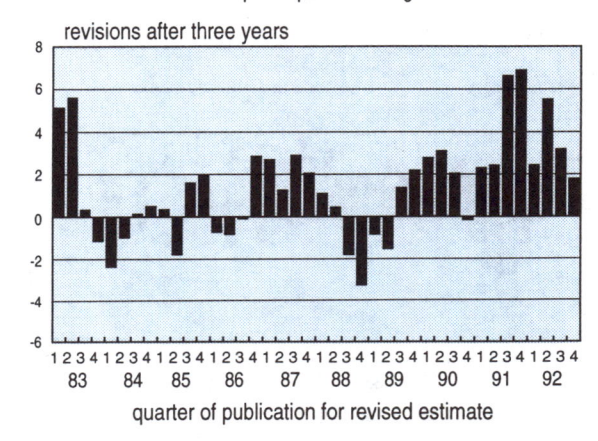

Total GDP output components at constant prices
four quarter per cent change

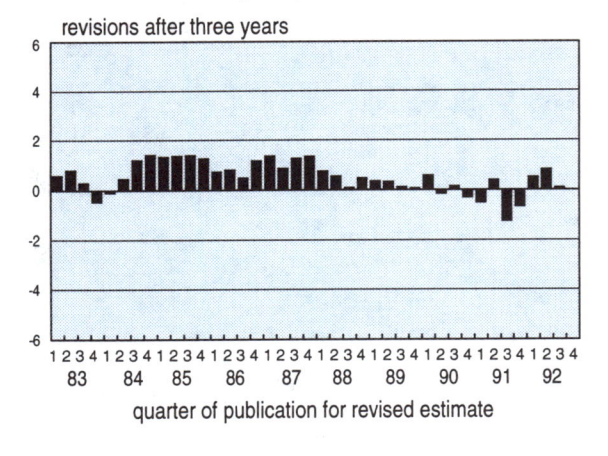

Agriculture, forestry and fishing
four quarter per cent change

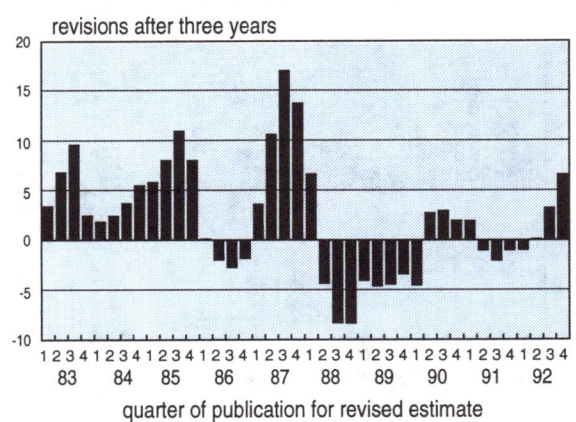

Manufacturing
four quarter per cent change

revisions after three years

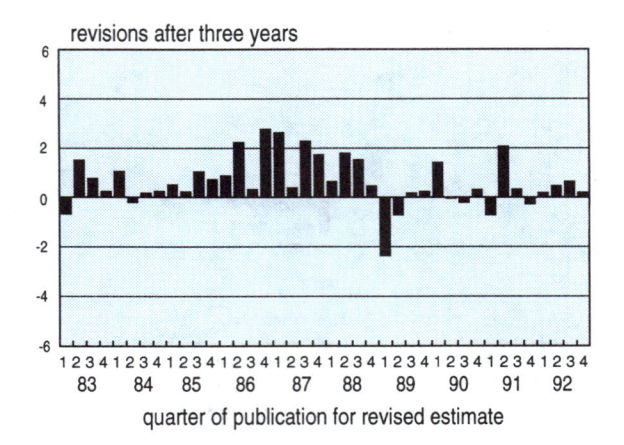

Transport and communication
four quarter per cent change

revisions after three years

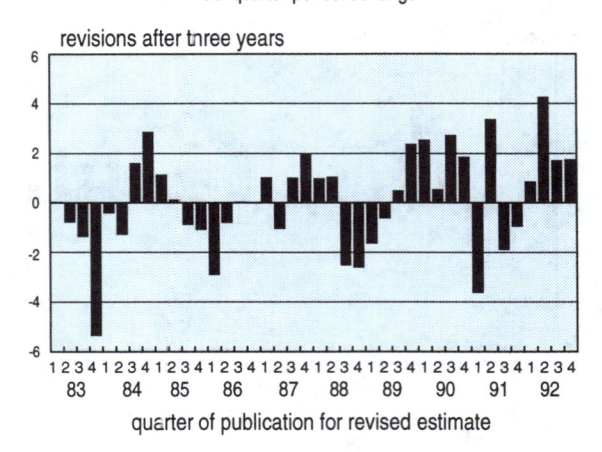

Distribution, hotels and catering
four quarter per cent change

revisions after three years

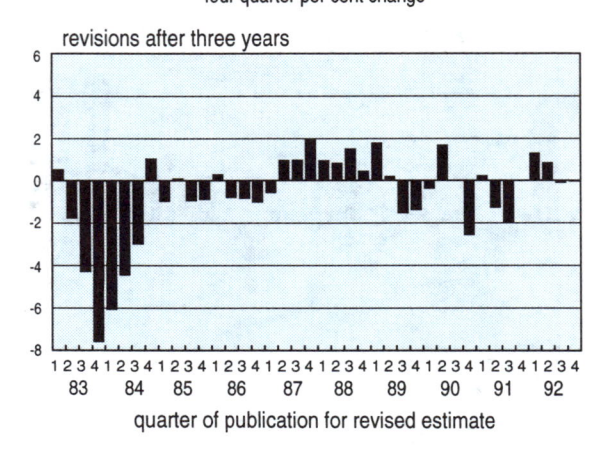

Construction
four quarter per cent change

revisions after three years

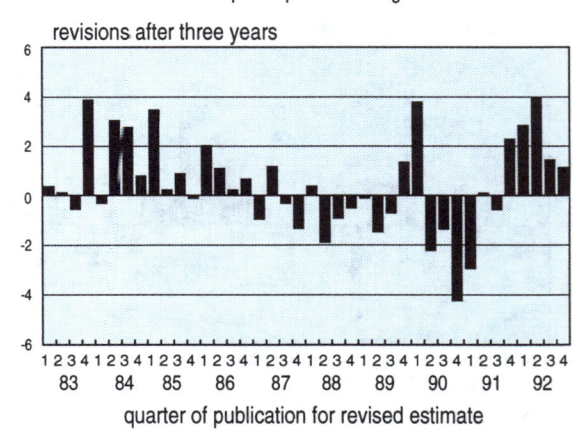

Other services
four quarter per cent change

revisions after three years

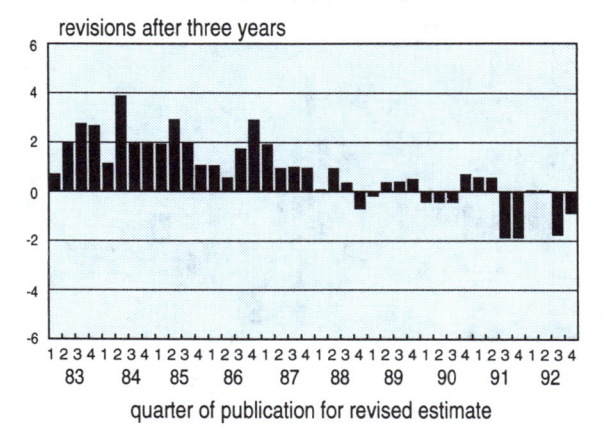

SEASONAL ADJUSTMENT OF THE NUMBER OF PROPERTY TRANSACTIONS IN ENGLAND AND WALES

Frank Kane and Mark Wardell,
Statistics and Economics Office, Inland Revenue

Introduction

The seasonally adjusted series of property transactions was first introduced into *'Economic Trends'* in the June 1991 edition in an article by Paul Heggs and Alan Holmans[1]. Since that article was published, there have been a number of potential distortions to the series. An obvious example is the temporary raising of the stamp duty threshold to £250,000 from December 1991 to August 1992, sometimes referred to as the stamp duty 'holiday'; other examples are given later in the article. It was therefore necessary to investigate the methodology to check whether these potential distortions had had an adverse effect upon the seasonal adjustment of the series.

Particulars Delivered (PDs)

A PD form must be completed on any transaction involving freehold land or property or when a lease of greater than seven years is granted. The series is based upon a count of the numbers of PDs processed by either the Stamp Office or the District Land Registry each month.

The series is an important indicator of the state of the property market, since it covers the majority of transactions and not just properties purchased with a mortgage. The PD series lags completions by an average of one month so, for example, the September number refers mainly to completions in August. Further details of PDs can be found in the original *'Economic Trends'* article.

The property market is very seasonal. It tends to be at its peak in the second and third quarters of the calendar year, i.e. in the spring and summer. Publication of only the unadjusted series would not, therefore, give a clear indication of the state of the market. The seasonal adjustment of the series is an attempt to analyse past monthly changes in order to separate changes due to the seasonality of the series and changes due to the underlying trend.

Seasonal Adjustment of Series

The program used to make the seasonal adjustment is X-11, which was devised by the US Bureau of Census. It assumes that in any time series, data is composed of three elements - a trend cycle (C), a seasonal component (S) and an irregular component (I). For economic time series it is common to assume a multiplicative relationship, i.e. CxSxI. By using a sequence of moving averages the three components can be estimated. Full details of the methodology of X-11 are available from Mr M A Baxter, SMQ Branch, Central Statistical Office, Room 54/2, Great George Street, London SW1P 3AQ.

During the process, extreme high or low values of the product of the seasonal and irregular components are averaged out so that unusual figures do not unduly influence the calculation of the seasonal factors. The set of seasonal factors for each month (the S values) are constructed in order to estimate and take out the seasonal component in the series. High seasonal factors for a particular month indicate that the unadjusted series is usually high.

Examination of the old seasonally adjusted series in Chart 1 shows how the property market has fluctuated since 1977. From the early 1980s, it shows a gradual increase in property transactions as home

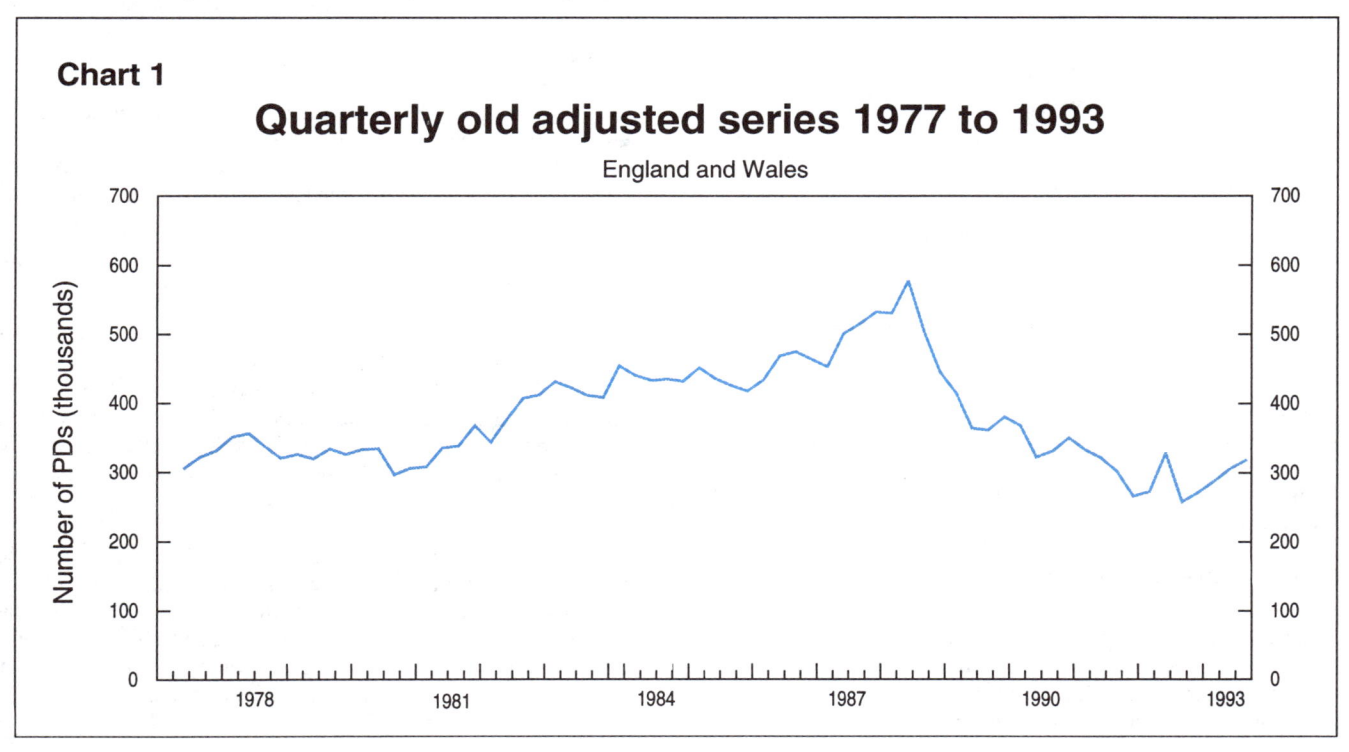

Chart 1
Quarterly old adjusted series 1977 to 1993
England and Wales

'Economic Trends' No. 484 February 1994 © Crown copyright 1994

ownership increased followed by the boom of the mid to late 1980s, which peaked in mid 1988. Property transactions fell off rapidly at the end of the 1980s and the early 1990s. There was a concentration of activity in mid 1992 around the end of the temporary raising of the stamp duty threshold. This has been followed by a moderate increase in transactions in 1993.

Problems with the series

When X-11 is run it produces a number of measurements and statistical tests that help to determine how effective the estimated seasonal adjustment is. One problem that was identified with the old adjustment process was moving seasonality. This occurs when the estimated seasonal factors change very rapidly over time for particular months. The X-11 analysis of variance F-test for moving seasonality was significant. The main problem with moving seasonality is that it can result in large revisions to seasonal factors in the recent past. From an examination of the seasonal factors in table 1, which shows the change in factors between 1988 and 1993, it can be seen that the seasonal factors for January, August and September changed by 9%, 7% and 6% respectively. It is worth noting that prior to this period there was no sign of significant moving seasonality.

Another problem was the months to cyclical dominance (MCD). This measures the length of time in months that it takes the trend component to dominate the irregular component. It shows how many months it takes to get a clear indication of the trend. In the old adjustment the MCD was 6 months. This in effect meant that to ascertain the recent trend correctly it was necessary to compare the seasonally adjusted series of the latest six months with the previous six months. A smaller MCD is desirable in that a measure of the trend is available for a more recent period and turning points are more quickly estimated.

It was also noticed that, particularly for 1992, there were a number of values that were being flagged as extreme, in addition to January, August and September. These are likely to have also been caused by the stamp duty 'holiday'.

Analysis of the adjustment

The problems with the MCD and moving seasonality in the adjustment were thought to have been caused by a number of events in the property market. These were:

(1) the temporary rise in the stamp duty threshold to £250,000 between December 1991 and August 1992;

(2) the impact of increasing the stamp duty threshold to £60,000 in the March 1993 Budget;

(3) the Autumn Statement package of 1992, which enabled housing associations to purchase suitable empty properties;

(4) the ending of multiple MIRAS applications for one property in the summer of 1988; and

(5) more generally, the effect of trading days, Easter and other public holidays.

Effects of the stamp duty 'holiday'

Examination of the old seasonal factors and the seasonally adjusted series shows that for some months, particularly those at the beginning and the end of the 'holiday', January, August and September, there appears to be a certain amount of distortion. This problem was identified as significant moving seasonality. This means that the seasonally adjusted series had become a less reliable indicator of trends in the property market.

This problem of moving seasonality suggests that further adjustments, in addition to the averaging out of extreme values discussed earlier are required. One option within X-11 is to replace the unusual values with interpolated values. This option ignores the irregular component in calculating the seasonal and trend cycle for the flagged months. The three most extreme values in 1992, January, August and September were interpolated. This had the effect of reducing the moving seasonality from the series caused by the 'holiday', as shown by a non-significant F-test.

Other events

The raising of the stamp duty threshold to £60,000 in the March 1993 Budget does not seem to have had a significant impact upon the seasonal factors. This is backed up by the fact that there was no significant evidence of moving seasonality after allowance for the 'holiday'. If the unadjusted series had become unusually high for some months, as occurred with the 'holiday', then there could have been an impact on the seasonal factors. However, this was not apparent in the months following the change.

The Autumn Statement package of 1992 increased the money that was available to housing associations to purchase properties. It is likely that this boosted transactions by about 23,000. However, as with the raising of the threshold, it is likely that this effect was spread over a number of months and not just concentrated in a few. Hence, there is no ascertainable impact on the seasonality of the series.

The ending of multiple MIRAS relief for one property at the beginning of August 1988, which coincided with the top of the boom, does not seem to be having any significant impact on the seasonal pattern of the current series. Interpolation of the August 1988 figure has no noticeable effect on the current series. This is due to the fact that in the seasonal adjustment for the current year greater weight is placed upon data for the previous two years than on earlier data.

The above analysis of past events shows that interpolation of the most extreme 1992 values has led to an alignment of the seasonal factors with their historical values and a reduction in the moving seasonality caused by the 'holiday'. None of the other potential distortions outlined above have had a significant impact on the seasonal adjustment process. However, the MCD was still high at six months. One way of reducing this is to see whether the irregular component can be partly explained by the number of trading days in the month.

Trading days and public holidays

With X-11 it is possible to take into account the number of trading days within a month and even to assign different weights for different days if it is known that there are differing levels of activity on different days. The PD series is a count of documents processed, and as processing is only done on working days of the week and not at weekends, assigning positive weights to working days of the week and zero weights to weekends seemed logical.

As a result of assigning weights to days in this way, part of the irregular component of the series was explained. This led to a reduction in the MCD from six months to three months, meaning that a comparison of only three months data is needed to ascertain the trend. With the inclusion of trading day effects, an extra trading day component (TD) enters the multiplicative relationship described at the start of the article and the series is represented as $C \times S \times I \times TD$.

Public holidays do not have an effect on the adjustment process since they are fixed and are automatically taken account of by X-11. However, Easter is a potential problem, since the date changes each year and can fall in either March or April. According to the Stamp Office if Easter falls at the beginning or middle of the month then the work can be caught up and there would be no significant effect upon the series. The only problem would be if Easter fell at the end of the month. However, examination of Easter dates for the past few years shows that only 1991 had an Easter date at the end of the month and in this case only one day. This does not seem to have had a significant impact upon the adjustment as the seasonal factor for March 1991 is little different from the value in surrounding years.

Extreme values

Another measure to improve the adjustment process was to raise the upper limit that determines how many of the extreme values are replaced by averages. It was felt that after using the interpolation option, the upper limit could be increased so that more of the actual data for recent years is used. This had the effect of reducing the MCD slightly.

New seasonal adjustment process

The analysis of the PD series described above has led to a number of changes to be made to the adjustment process. The new adjustment process incorporates interpolated values for the most affected 'holiday' months in 1992, a trading day adjustment and a higher limit to deal with other outliers. The revised seasonal factors are given in table 2, the complete new seasonally adjusted series can be seen in table 3 and the latest figures in table 43 of this edition of 'Economic Trends'. It can be seen that the revised seasonal factors are more stable, the large changes in the old adjustment factors for January, August and September (see table 1) have been eliminated.

Chart 2 gives a comparison between the new seasonally adjusted series and the unadjusted series since 1988. Chart 3 shows the old and the new seasonally adjusted series for 1992 and 1993. Both show the effect of the 'holiday' in 1992 and the most recent trend of a modest pick up in 1993. However, the line of the new adjusted series is smoother than the old and allows the underlying trend to be seen more clearly. Because of the lower MCD and the reduction of moving seasonality, future changes in the trend can be detected much earlier by the new adjustment process.

Summary

The count of the PDs takes into account all land and property transactions in England and Wales, apart from short term leases. It therefore provides a good indicator of the state of the property market, bearing in mind that on average, the series lags completion dates by a month.

A review of the methodology underlying the seasonal adjustment process was prompted by recent events such as the stamp duty 'holiday'.

Interpolation of the months most affected by the 'holiday' has led to the seasonal factors moving more in line with their historical values and the reduction of the moving seasonality caused by the 'holiday'.

The months to cyclical dominance (MCD) has been decreased from six to three months, after taking into account trading day effects. This means that direct three month upon three month comparisons can now be made to detect changes in the underlying trend.

As a result of these changes, the seasonal factors used to adjust the series have become more stable and the revised adjusted series allows the underlying trend to be detected more quickly.

Reference

(1) P Heggs and A Holmans, 'Number of Property Transactions in England and Wales', *Economic Trends* June 1991

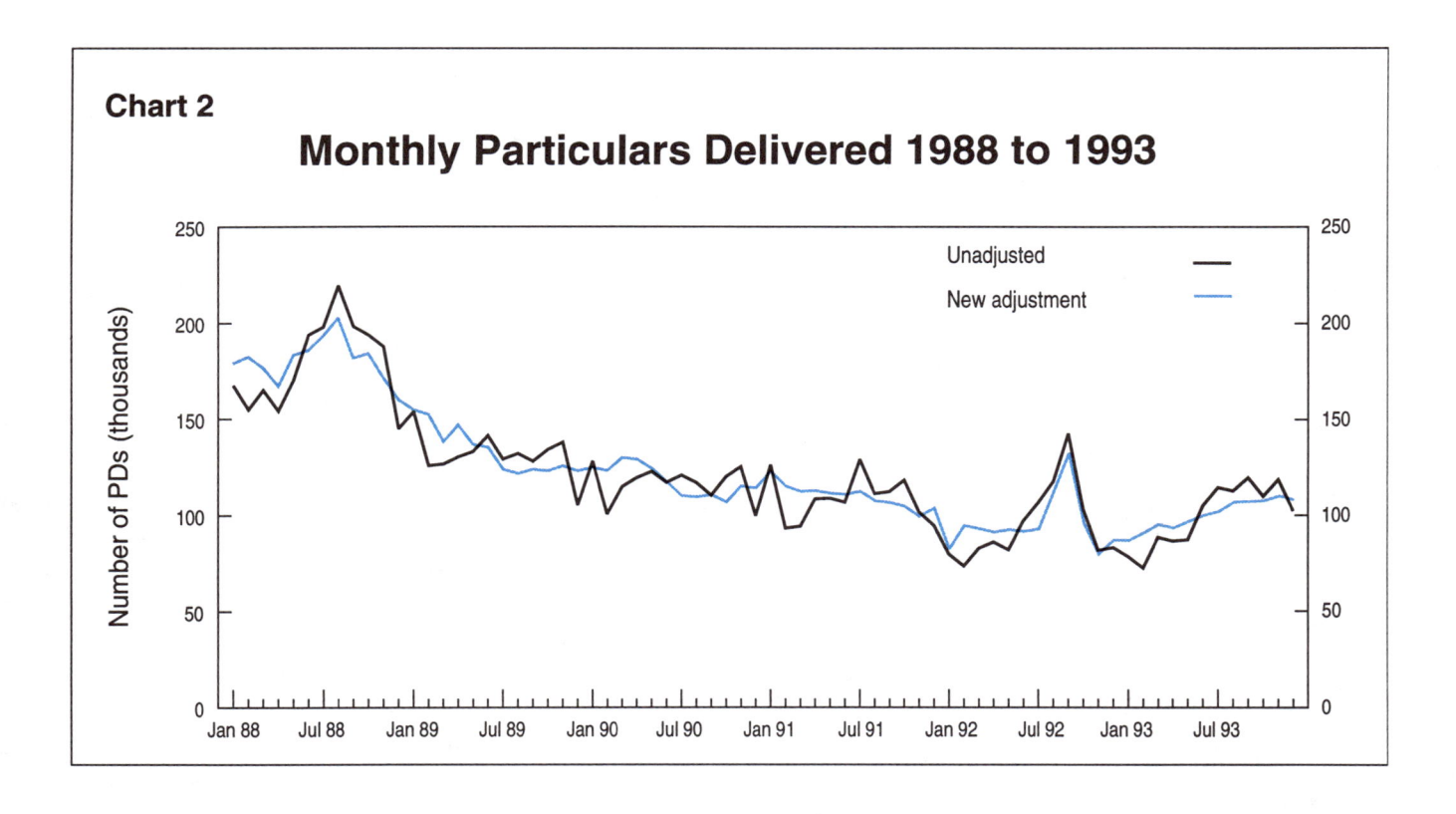

Chart 2

Monthly Particulars Delivered 1988 to 1993

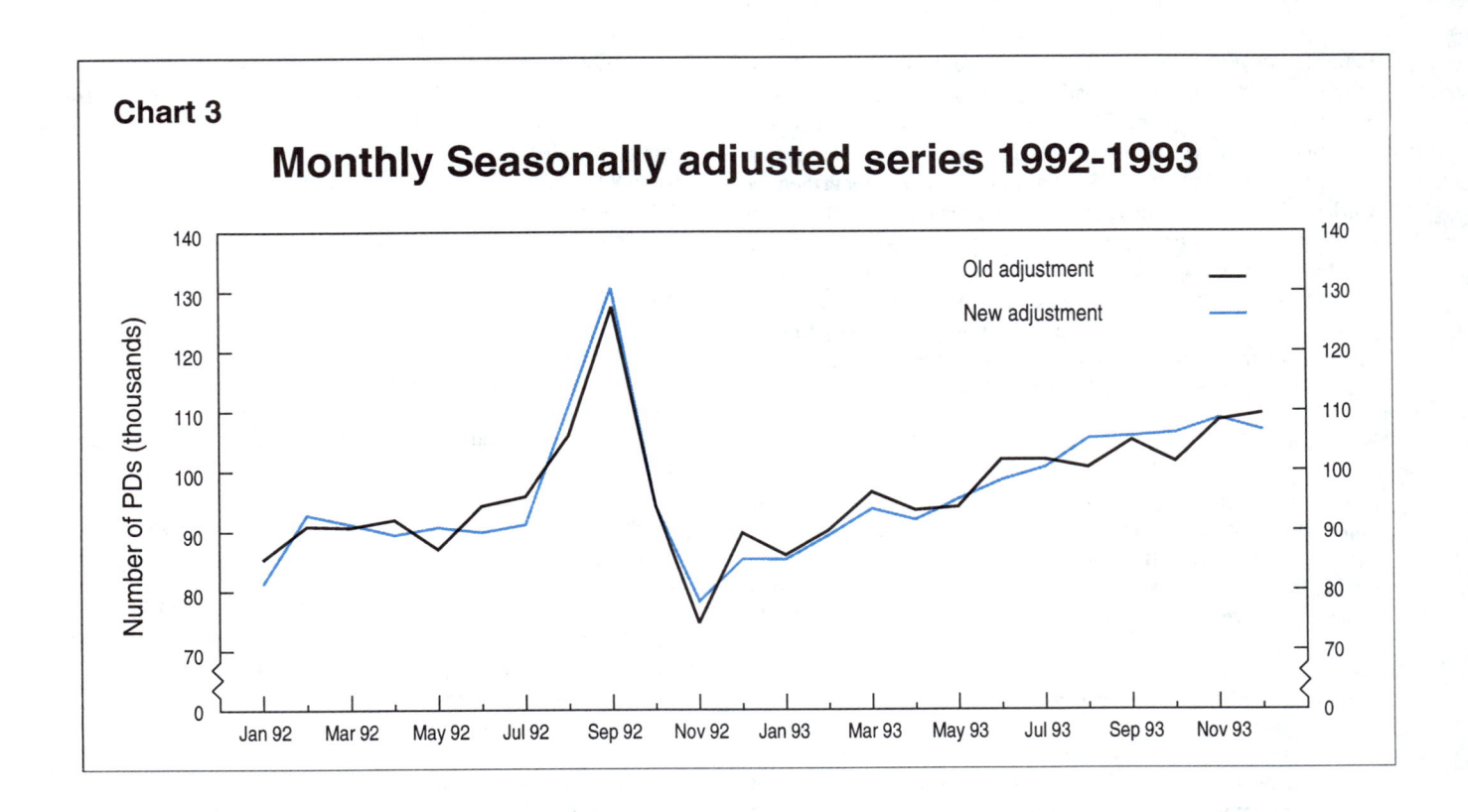

Chart 3

Monthly Seasonally adjusted series 1992-1993

Seasonal adjustment of Particulars Delivered series for England and Wales

Table 1: Seasonal factors of PD series-old adjustment

	JAN	FEB	MAR	APR	MAY	JUN	JUL	AUG	SEP	OCT	NOV	DEC
1988	100	85	91	94	95	103	108	105	108	113	109	92
1989	99	84	91	94	96	103	107	106	108	112	110	91
1990	97	83	91	95	96	103	108	108	108	112	110	91
1991	95	82	91	94	96	103	110	110	110	110	110	92
1992	94	81	91	94	94	103	111	111	112	110	110	93
1993	91	81	92	93	93	103	112	112	114	108	109	93

Table 2: Seasonal factors of PD series-new adjustment

	JAN	FEB	MAR	APR	MAY	JUN	JUL	AUG	SEP	OCT	NOV	DEC
1988	101	84	90	96	94	102	110	105	107	111	108	92
1989	101	83	90	96	95	103	111	105	107	111	108	92
1990	100	83	90	95	96	104	111	105	108	110	107	93
1991	99	82	90	94	96	104	112	105	109	110	107	93
1992	99	81	91	93	96	104	113	106	109	110	106	93
1993	98	81	91	92	96	104	114	107	110	110	106	93

Table 3: New seasonally adjusted series of PDs

Number: thousands

	JAN	FEB	MAR	APR	MAY	JUN	JUL	AUG	SEP	OCT	NOV	DEC	TOTAL
1977	n/a	n/a	n/a	97	104	99	107	108	109	109	111	117	960
1978	116	118	115	123	113	114	117	115	110	107	112	107	1369
1979	106	110	108	87	115	111	107	110	123	114	107	105	1303
1980	113	112	109	123	98	107	102	96	99	102	100	105	1266
1981	102	101	106	106	112	112	108	119	113	116	128	121	1344
1982	115	113	117	123	124	126	140	132	133	135	138	139	1536
1983	136	141	153	143	141	136	138	138	137	139	133	140	1674
1984	148	154	151	142	144	154	145	146	146	144	146	143	1763
1985	142	146	146	150	153	149	145	144	143	140	142	143	1742
1986	150	145	125	147	142	145	148	155	160	161	158	157	1793
1987	155	153	157	140	157	157	168	163	165	168	170	175	1928
1988	177	181	175	166	182	184	192	201	180	183	170	159	2149
1989	153	151	137	146	136	134	123	121	123	122	125	122	1592
1990	124	122	129	128	123	116	109	108	109	106	114	113	1401
1991	122	114	111	112	110	110	111	106	105	103	98	102	1305
1992	81	93	92	90	91	90	91	111	131	94	78	86	1128
1993	85	89	94	92	95	99	101	106	106	106	109	107	1189

Index of sources

United Kingdom balance of payments: United Kingdom national accounts. In addition to the series indexed below, further detailed statistics are included in the regular quarterly publication *UK Economic Accounts.*

	Table	Source	Further statistics (Where available)
Asset prices	42	Central Statistical Office Department of the Environment MAFF	
Average earnings	1, 25	Department of Employment	Monthly Digest of Statistics Employment Gazette
Balance of payments (current balance)	29	Central Statistical Office	Financial Statistics Quarterly articles in UK Economic Accounts
Banking		Bank of England	Financial Statistics
Banking loans, advances and acceptances	38, 39, 40		
British government securities (long dated)			
20 years yield	41	Bank of England	
Building societies			Financial Statistics
Advances on new dwellings	11	Building Societies Association	
Average prices of new dwellings on mortgage (see also Housing)	11	Department of the Environment	
Commitments on new dwellings	11	Building Societies Association	
Capital account summary, analysis by sector	35	Central Statistical Office	Financial Statistics
Car registrations and production (see also Motor vehicles)	6, 18	Central Statistical Office Department of Transport	
CBI Intentions Inquiry (see also Fixed investment)	10	Confederation of British Industry	
Coal (see also Energy)	14	Department of Trade and Industry	
Commercial vehicles, production (see also Motor vehicles)	18	Central Statistical Office	
Companies		Central Statistical Office	Financial Statistics
Financial companies and institutions			
Capital account, financial surplus/deficit	35		
Saving	35		
Gross trading profits	36		
In relation to total domestic income	7		Monthly Digest of Statistics
Industrial and commercial companies	35, 36, 37, 38		Financial Statistics
Appropriation account	36		
Capital account, financial surplus/deficit	37		
Dividends, interest and current transfer payments	36		
Fixed investment	38		
Income	36		
Net borrowing requirement	38		
Saving	35		
Security prices and yields (see also Interest rates)	41		
Stock appreciation	38		
Taxes	38		
Construction industry			Housing and Construction Statistics
Index of output (see also Industrial production)	16	Central Statistical Office	
Orders received	10, 11, 17	Department of the Environment	
Output	17	Department of the Environment	
Consumer credit	1, 6	Central Statistical Office	Financial Statistics

Consumers' expenditure		Central Statistical Office	Monthly Digest of Statistics
Component categories	5		
In relation to personal income	4		
In relation to total final expenditure	7		
Per head	8		
Counterparts to changes in M4	32	Bank of England	Financial Statistics
Credit business (see also Hire purchase)	6	Central Statistical Office	
Current balance (see also Balance of payments)	29	Central Statistical Office	
Cyclical indicators (also see article on page 78)	1	Central Statistical Office	
Distributive trades		Central Statistical Office	Monthy Digest of Statistics
Output (see also Retail sales; Stocks)	16		
Dividends, interest and current transfer payments	36	Central Statistical Office	
Domestic income (see also Incomes)	7	Central Statistical Office	
Dwellings (see also Housing)	11	Central Statistical Office Department of the Environment	
Earnings (average)	1, 25	Department of Employment	Monthly Digest of Statistics Employment Gazette
Electricity (see also Energy)	14	Department of Trade and Industry	
Employed labour force	19, 20, 22, 23, 24	Central Statistical Office Department of Employment	Monthly Digest of Statistics Employment Gazette
Employees in employment		Department of Employment	Monthly Digest of Statistics
All industries and services and manufacturing	1, 20, 22, 23, 24	Employment Gazette	
Energy	14	Department of Trade and Industry	
Consumers' expenditure on energy products	5	Central Statistical Office	Monthly Digest of Statistics
Output index for energy and water supply	15		Monthly Digest of Statistics United Kingdom Energy Statistics
Primary fuel input: total, coal, petroleum, natural gas and primary electricity	14	Department of Trade and Industry	Energy Trends
Engineering industries		Central Statistical Office	Monthly Digest of Statistics Business Bulletin
Sales and orders: total, home market and export	1, 17		
Eurodollar-3-month rate (see also Interest rates)	41	Bank of England	
Exchange rates	1, 30	Bank of England	Financial Statistics
Expenditure (see also Total final expenditure)	3, 7	Central Statistical Office	
Exports		Central Statistical Office	Monthly Digest of Statistics Business Bulletin
Of goods	1		
Unit value index	27	Central Statistical Office	Monthly Review of External Trade Statistics
Unit value index for manufactures (international comparisons)	28	Department of Trade and Industry	
Value	1, 29	Central Statistical Office	
Volume index	27		
Of goods and services	3, 7		
Of passenger cars, commercial vehicles	18		
Orders; engineering industries	17		
Relative prices (as measure of trade competitiveness)	28	Department of Trade and Industry	Monthly Review of External Trade Statistics
Relative profitability (as measure of trade competitiveness	28		
Final expenditure (see also Total final expenditure)	3, 7	Central Statistical Office	
Financial companies (see also Companies)	35	Central Statistical Office	
Fixed investment		Central Statistical Office	
By industrial and commercial companies (see also Companies)	38		

By sector and by type of asset	9		Monthly Digest of Statistics
Dwellings (see also Housing)	9, 11	Central Statistical Office Department of the Environment	Business Bulletin
In relation to total final expenditure	3, 7	Central Statistical Office	Monthly Digest of Statistics
Manufacturing industry			
CBI Intentions Inquiry		Confederation of British Industry	Industrial Trends Survey
Contractors' orders for private industrial work	10	Department of the Environment	Housing and Construction Statistics
In plant and machinery, new buildings and work	10	Central Statistical Office	Monthly Digest of Statistics
Gas (see also Energy)	14	Department of Trade and Industry	
General government consumption of goods and services	3, 7	Central Statistical Office	Monthly Digest of Statistics
Receipts and expenditure	33		Financial Statistics
Gross domestic fixed capital formation (see also Fixed investment)	7, 9, 36	Central Statistical Office	
Gross domestic product	2	Central Statistical Office	Monthly Digest of Statistics
And components of final expenditure	3		
At factor cost	1, 8		
In relation to output	16		
In relation to stocks	13		
Per head	8		
Gross national product per head		Central Statistical Office	
At factor cost	8		
Per head	8		
Gross trading profits of companies (see also Companies)	36		
Hire purchase debt	6	Central Statistical Office	Monthly Digest of Statistics Business Bulletin Financial Statistics
Housing			
Average price of new dwellings mortgages approved	11	Department of the Environment	Housing and Construction Statistics
Commitments and advances on new dwellings	11		Financial Statistics
Consumers' expenditure on housing	5	Central Statistical Office	Monthly Digest of Statistics
Fixed investment in dwellings	9, 11		
Orders received by contractors for new houses	11	Department of the Environment	Monthly Digest of Statistics
Starts and completions	1, 11		Housing and Construction Statistics
Imports			
Of goods	1	Central Statistical Office	Monthly Digest of Statistics
Unit value index	1, 27		Business Bulletin
Value	29		
Volume index	27		
Of goods and services in relation to total final expenditure	3		Monthly Digest of Statistics
Price competitiveness	28	Department of Trade and Industry	
Incomes		Central Statistical Office	Monthly Digest of Statistics
Company income (see also Companies)	36		
Income from employment as a percentage of total domestic income (see also Wages: Earnings)	7		
Personal disposable income	4		
Per head	8		
Personal income before tax	4		
Total domestic income	7		
Industrial and commercial companies (see also Companies)	35, 36, 37, 38		

Industrial production: index of output	1, 15	Central Statistical Office	Monthly Digest of Statistics
By market sector	15		
By selected industries	15		
In relation to output	16		
In relation to stocks (manufacturing industries)	13		
Inter-bank 3-month rate (see also Interest rates)	41	Bank of England	
Interest rates	41	Central Statistical Office	Financial Statistics
British government securities long-dated (20 years) yield		Bank of England	
Building Societies Association recommended share rate		HM Treasury Building Societies Association *Financial Times*	
Eurodollar 3-month rate		Institute of Actuaries	
Financial Times index of industrial ordinary shares		Faculty of Actuaries	
Inter-bank 3-month rate			
Local authorities 3-month deposit rate			
Selected retail banks base rate and 7-day deposits			
Sterling certificates of deposit 3-month rate			
Treasury bill yield			
Invisibles (see also Balance of payments)	29	Central Statistical Office	
Labour Force Survey	22,23,24	Employment Department	Employment Gazette
Local authorities 3-month deposit rate (see also Interest rates)	41	Bank of England	
Manufacturing industry (see Banking; Employees in employment; Fixed investment; Industrial production; Output per person employed; Output per person hour; Stocks; Wages and salaries)			
Money stock	1, 31,42	Bank of England	Financial Statistics
Motor vehicles			
New car registrations	1, 6	Department of Transport	Monthly Digest of Statistics
Production of passenger cars and commercial vehicles: total and for export	1, 18	Central Statistical Office	Business Bulletin
National disposable income	2	Central Statistical Office	
Official reserves	30	HM Treasury	Financial Statistics Monthly Digest of Statistics
Orders received			
By construction industry (see also Construction)	17	Central Statistical Office	
By contractors for private industrial work	10	Department of the Environment	Housing and Construction Statistics
By engineering industries (see also Engineering)	17		
Output		Central Statistical Office	
By construction industry (see also Construction)	1, 16, 17	Department of the Environment	
By engineering industries (see also Engineering)	17	Central Statistical office	
Index numbers by industry groups	16		Monthly Digest of Statistics
Manufacturing industries	15		
Per person employed	19		
Per person hour: manufacturing industry	19		
Production industries	15		
Overseas trade (see Exports; Imports; Visible trade)			
Personal disposable income	4, 8	Central Statistical Office	Monthly Digest of Statistics
Personal income before tax	4	Central Statistical Office	Monthly Digest of Statistics
Petroleum (see also Energy)	14	Department of Trade and Industry	

Population			
Estimates *per capita*, income, product and spending	8	Central Statistical Office	Not published elsewhere
Prices			
Asset prices	42	Central Statistical Office Department of the Environment MAFF	
Average price of new dwellings on mortgage (see also Housing)	11	Department of the Environment	
Pensioner price indices	26	Central Statistical Office	Employment Gazette
Producer price index: input and output	1, 26	Department of Trade and Industry	Monthly Digest of Statistics Business Bulletin
Producer price index (international comparisons)	28	Department of Trade and Industry	
Relative wholesale prices (as measure of trade competitiveness)	28	Department of Trade and Industry	
Retail price index	1, 26	Central Statistical Office	Monthly Digest of Statistics Employment Gazette
Tax and price index	1	Central Statistical Office	
Private sector			
Capital account, financial surplus/deficit	35	Central Statistical Office	Financial Statistics
Gross fixed investment	7, 9		Monthly Digest of Statistics
Housing starts and completions (see also Housing)	11		Housing and Construction
Statistics			
Producer price index (see also Prices)	1,26	Central Statistical Office	
Production (see Industrial production; Motor vehicles; Output; Steel)		Central Statistical Office	
Productivity: output per person employed, output per hour in manufacturing industries	1,19	Central Statistical Office Department of Employment	Monthly Digest of Statistics
Profits (see also Companies)	36	Central Statistical Office	
Property Transactions	43	Board of Inland Revenue	
Public sector			Financial Statistics
Borrowing requirement	32,35	Bank of England Central Statistical Office	
Expenditure	33		
Capital account, financial surplus/deficit	35		
Fixed investment	7, 9		
Housing starts and completions (see also Housing)	11	Department of the Environment	Housing and Construction
Statistics			
Receipts	33	Central Statistical Office	
Purchasing power of the pound	26	Central Statistical Office	
Regional unemployment rates (see also Unemployment)	21	Department of Employment	
Rent and non-trading income; industrial and commercial companies	36	Central Statistical Office	
Retail price index (see also Prices)	1, 26	Central Statistical Office	
Retail sales			
Value index numbers	6	Central Statistical Office	Monthly Digest of Statistics Business Bulletin
Volume index numbers	1, 6		
Ratio of distributors' stocks to retail sales	13		
Salaries (see also Wages and salaries)	25	Central Statistical Office	
Saving, company (see also Companies)	35	Central Statistical Office	
Savings ratio, personal	4	Central Statistical Office	Monthly Digest of Statistics

Selected retail banks rates (see also Interest rates)	41	Bank of England	
Services (see also Balance of payments)	26	Central Statistical Office	
Steel, production and consumption	18	British Independent Steel Producer Association	Monthly Digest of Statistics
Sterling certificates of deposit (see also Interest rates)	41	Bank of England	
Sterling			
Exchange rate index	1, 30	HM Treasury	Financial Statistics
Exchange rates against major currencies	30	Bank of England	
Stock appreciation, company sector (see also Companies)	36	Central Statistical Office	
Stocks			
Changes by industry groups	12	Central Statistical Office	Monthly Digest of Statistics Business Bulletin
Ratios: total stocks to GDP(E), manufactured stocks to manufacturing production, distributors' stocks to retail sales	13		
Total changes in relation to GDP(E)	3		Monthly Digest of Statistics
Taxes		Central Statistical Office	Financial Statistics
On capital	33		
On income	33		
On expenditure	33		
Payment of taxes by companies	36, 37		
Terms of trade	1, 25	Central Statistical Office	Monthly Digest of Statistics Business Bulletin
Total domestic income (see also Incomes)	7	Central Statistical Office	
Total final expenditure on goods and services	3, 7	Central Statistical Office	Monthly Digest of Statistics
Trade competitiveness measures	28	Department of Trade and Industry Central Statistical Office International Monetary Fund	Monthly Review of External Trade Statistics International Financial Statistics
Transfers (see also Balance of payments)	29	Central Statistical Office	
Treasury bill yield (see also Interest rates)	41	Bank of England	
Undistributed income: industrial and commercial companies	36, 37	Central Statistical Office	
Unemployment		Department of Employment	Monthly Digest of Statistics Employment Gazette
Regional unemployment rates	21		
Total unemployed	1, 20, 22, 23, 24		
Unfilled vacancies	1, 20	Department of Employment	Monthly Digest of Statistics Employment Gazette
Unit labour costs (international comparisons)	28	International Monetary Fund	International Financial Statistics
Unit values of exports and imports (see also Exports; Imports)	27	Central Statistical Office	
Vacancies notified and remaining unfilled	1, 20	Department of Employment	
Visible trade (see also Exports; Imports)	1, 27, 29	Central Statistical Office	Monthly Digest of Statistics Business Bulletin
Wages and salaries			
In relation to personal income before tax	4	Central Statistical Office	Monthly Digest of Statistics
Per unit of output	25		Monthly Digest of Statistics Employment Gazette
Workforce	20	Department of Employment	Employment Gazette Monthly Digest of Statistics

ISBN 0 11 620633 0
ISSN 0013-0400

Release dates of economic statistics as at 28 February

Issued by the Central Statistical Office on behalf of the Government Statistical Service and other organisations as a guide to publication dates of major economic series. The final columns list the next three announced release dates after 28 February. Exceptionally, there may be some delays due to unavoidable statistical problems. Enquiries about release of individual series should be made at source.

The CSO Bulletin series has been discontinued. In most cases the data are now being published in new or existing First Releases or News Releases.

Series	Release method	Source	Last	Mar	Apr	May
Acquisitions and mergers within the UK (Q)	FR	CSO	15 Feb			17 May
Advance energy statistics (M)	SB	DTI	1 Feb	1 Mar	7 Apr	4 May
Agriculture in the UK (A)	AV	MAFF		24 Mar		
Balance of payments (Q)	FR	CSO	20 Dec	24 Mar		
Balance of payments advance annual estimates (A)	PN	CSO	5 Aug			
Balance of payments (CSO Pink Book)	AV	CSO	9 Sept			
Balance of trade with countries outside the EC(M)[3]	FR	CSO	25 Feb	21 Mar	25 Apr	23 May
Balance of visible trade (M)[3]	FR	CSO	11 Feb	11 Mar		
Bank of England Quarterly Bulletin	QV	Bank of England	8 Feb			
Bankruptcy Statistics (Q)	PN	LCD	11 Feb			
Banks registered in the UK: consolidated external claims (H)	PN	Bank of England	3 Nov			
Bill turnover statistics (M)	PN	Bank of England	4 Feb	4 Mar	6 Apr	6 May
Bricks and cement production and deliveries (Q)	PN	DOE	26 Jan		27 Apr	
Building societies monthly figures	PN	BSA	18 Feb	18 Mar	22 Apr	20 May
Capital expenditure	NR	CSO	22 Feb			25 May
Capital issues and redemptions (M)	PN	Bank of England	11 Feb			
CBI Industrial trends survey	PN	CB	24 Jan		26 Apr	
CBI Monthly Trends Enquiry	PN	CBI	25 Feb	25 Mar		27 May
CBI survey of distributive trades (M)	PN	CBI	15 Feb	15 Mar		17 May
Census of Employment (A)	EG	ED	8 Apr			
Company liquidity (Q)	FR	CSO	14 Dec	15 Mar		
Construction - new orders (provisional)(M)	PN	DOE	15 Feb	15 Mar	19 Apr	17 May
Construction output (provisional)(Q)	PN	DOE	10 Dec	11 Mar		
Credit business (M)	FR	CSO	7 Feb	7 Mar	11 Apr	9 May
Cross border acquisitions & mergers (Q)	FR	CSO	16 Dec	21 Mar		
Cyclical indicators for the UK economy	FR	CSO	8 Feb	8 Mar	8 Apr	6 May
Details of employment, unemployment, earnings, prices and other indicators	EG	ED	13 Jan	10 Feb	10 Mar	7 Apr
Digest of United Kingdom energy statistics	AV	DTI	29 July			
Earnings and hours of agricultural and horticultural workers in England & Wales (Q)	PN	MAFF		24 Mar		
Economic Trends	MV	CSO	28 Feb	31 Mar	29 Apr	
Electronics industry in Scotland (A)	SB	Scottish Office	24 Feb			
Energy trends (M)	SB	DTI	24 Feb	31 Mar	28 Apr	26 May
Engineering sales and orders at current and constant prices (M)	FR	CSO	24 Feb	24 Mar	21 Apr	26 May
Family Expenditure Survey	FR	CSO	4 Aug			
Family Spending	AV	CSO	3 Sept			
Farm incomes in the UK (FY)	AV	MAFF		24 Mar		
Farm incomes (A)	PN	MAFF	31 Jan			
Farm rents in Wales (A)	PN	Welsh Office	16 Feb			
Financial Statistics	MV	CSO	17 Feb	17 Mar		
Finished steel consumption and stock changes (Q)	CSOB	CSO	19 Apr †			
Great Britain cinema exhibitors	NR	CSO		25 Mar		
Gross domestic expenditure on research and development (A)	FR	CSO	31 Mar	4 Mar		
Gross Domestic Product (preliminary estimate) (Q)[1]	FR	CSO	21 Jan		25 Apr	
Gross Domestic Product (including analyses of expenditure, income and output components) (Q)[1]	PN	CSO	12 Mar[1]			
Half-yearly update to seasonal adjustment of monetary aggregates (H)	PN	Bank of England	15 Oct		19 Apr	

See footnotes on page 130

Series	Release method	Source	Release dates			
			Last	Mar	Apr	May
House renovations (Q)	PN	DOE	10 Jan		7 Apr	
Housing starts and completions (M)	PN	DOE	7 Feb	7 Mar	7 Apr	10 May
Index of production	FR	CSO	15 Feb	8 Mar	7 Apr	11 May
Index of production and construction for Wales (Q)	PN	Welsh Office	12 Jan		13 Apr	
Index of production for Scotland (Q)	PN	Scottish Office	9 Feb			
Industrial and commercial companies (Q)[2]	PN	CSO	12 Mar[2]			
Inland Revenue Statistics	AV	Inland Revenue	9 July			
Insolvency statistics (Q)	PN	BCC *	11 Feb			
Institutional investment (Q)	FR	CSO	22 Dec	23 Mar		
International banking statistics (Q)	PN	Bank of England	21 Dec	23 Mar		
Labour Force Survey (Q) (formerly annual, now published quarterly)	PN	ED	16 Dec	16 Mar		
Labour market statistics: unemployment and unfilled vacancies(provisional); average earnings indices (provisional); employment, hours, productivity and unit wage costs; industrial disputes (M)	PN	ED	16 Feb	16 Mar	20 Apr	18 May
Lending for house purchase (M)[5]	PN	Bank of England	4 Feb	4 Mar	6 Apr	6 May
Long-term unemployment (quarterly analysis of unemployment by age and duration)	PN	ED	16 Feb			18 May
Machine tools (M)	NR	CSO	17 Feb	17 Mar	14 Apr	19 May
Major British banking groups' monthly statement	PN	BBA	18 Feb	18 Mar	22 Apr	20 May
Major British banking groups' mortgage lending (M)	PN	BBA	28 Feb	28 Mar		3 May
Major British banking groups' quarterly analysis of lending[4]	PN	BBA	4 Feb			6 May
Monetary statistics (including bank and building society balance sheets) (M)	PN	Bank of England	4 Feb	4 Mar	6 Apr	6 May
Monthly Digest of Statistics	MV	CSO	28 Feb	31 Mar	29 Apr	
Mortgage possession statistics (Q)	PN	LCD	26 Jan			
National Accounts advance annual estimates (A)	PN	CSO	20 Dec			
National Accounts (CSO Blue Book)	AV	CSO	16 Sept			
National Food Survey : household food consumption (Q)	PN	MAFF	13 Dec	14 Mar		
National Savings results (M)	PN	Dpt for National Savings	12 Feb	12 Mar	16 Apr	14 May
New Earnings Survey						
Part A: Streamlined and summary analyses; description of the survey	PN+AV	ED	30 Sept			
Part B: Analyses by agreement	AV	ED	14 Oct			
Part C: Analyses by industry	AV	ED	28 Oct			
Part D: Analyses by occupation	AV	ED	11 Nov			
Part E: Analyses by region; analyses by age group	AV	ED	25 Nov			
Part F: Distribution of hours; joint distribution of earnings and hours;analyses of earnings and hours for part-time women employees	AV	ED	9 Dec			
New vehicle registrations (M)	PN	DTp	24 Feb	24 Mar		
Official operations in the money market (M)	PN	Bank of England	4 Feb	4 Mar	6 Apr	6 May
Official reserves (M)	PN	HMT	2 Feb	2 Mar	6 Apr	4 May
Overseas direct investment (A)	FR	CSO	28 Apr	28 Mar		
Overseas earnings of the City (A)	PN	British Invisibles	16 Aug			
Overseas travel and tourism (M)	FR	CSO	2 Feb	2 Mar		4 May
Personal income, expenditure & saving (Q)[2]	PN	CSO				
Producer price index numbers (M)	FR	CSO	14 Feb	14 Mar	18 Apr	16 May
Profitability of UK companies (A)	FR	CSO	30 Sept			
Provisional estimates of M4 and counterparts(M)	PN	Bank of England	18 Feb	18 Mar	22 Apr	20 May
Provisional figures of vehicle production (M)	PN	SMMT	17 Feb	17 Mar	21 Apr	19 May
Public sector borrowing requirement (M)	FR	HMT/CSO	16 Feb	16 Mar	20 Apr	18 May
Quarterly analysis of bank lending[4]	PN	Bank of England	11 Feb			

See footnotes on page 130

Series	Release method	Source	Release dates			
			Last	Mar	Apr	May
Regional Trends	AV	CSO	10 June			
Retail prices index (M)	FR	CSO	16 Feb	23 Mar	15 Apr	18 May
Retail sales (M)	FR	CSO	16 Feb	16 Mar	21 Apr	19 May
Social Trends	AV	CSO	28 Jan			
Sterling certificates of deposit (M)	PN	Bank of England	4 Feb	4 Mar	6 Apr	6 May
Sterling commercial paper (M)	PN	Bank of England	4 Feb	4 Mar	6 Apr	
Stocks and work in progress (Q)	NR	CSO	22 Feb [6]	24 Mar [7]		25 May
Trade figures (non-EC) (M)	FR	CSO	25 Feb	21 Mar	25 Apr	23 May
UK Economic Accounts	QV	CSO	17 Jan		15 Apr	
UK National Accounts[2]	FR	CSO	20 Dec	24 Mar		
UK output, income and expenditure (Q)[2]	FR	CSO	22 Feb			25 May
UK Spending on Research and Development (A)	FR	CSO		4 Mar		
Usable steel production (M)	FR	BISPA	11 Feb	11 Mar	15 Apr	13 May
VAT registrations and deregistrations (A)	PN	DTI	17 Aug			
Workforce in employment: revisions (A)	PN	ED	12 Mar	16 Mar		

BBA	=	British Bankers Association	071 623 4001 ext 3175
BCC	=	British Chambers of Commerce	071 222 1555
BISPA	=	British Iron & Steel Producers' Assoc.	071 581 0231/5
		(Statistics from ISSB Ltd	081 686 9050)
BSA	=	Building Societies Association	071 437 0655
CBI	=	Confederation of British Industry	071 379 7400
CML	=	Council of Mortgage Lenders	071 437 0655
CSO	=	Central Statistical Office	071 270 6363/6364
DOE	=	Department of the Environment	071 276 3496
DTp	=	Department of Transport	071 276 8208
DTI	=	Department of Trade and Industry	071 215 5000
ED	=	Employment Department	071 270 6969
HMT	=	HM Treasury	071 270 4860/5238
LCD	=	Lord Chancellors' Department	071 270 8740
MAFF	=	Ministry of Agriculture, Fisheries and Food	071 270 8562
SMMT	=	Society of Motor Manufacturers and Traders	071 235 7000
Bank of England			071 601 4878
British Invisibles			071 600 1198
Department for National Savings			071 605 9461
Inland Revenue			071 438 7370
Scottish Office			041 248 2855
Welsh Office			071 270 0566

* Figures compiled by the Department of Trade and Industry to whom inquiries about the data should be addressed.
† Series temporarily in abeyance pending receipt of INTRASTAT data. See note 4.

1. The two former CSO GDP press notices have been replaced by three quarterly first releases: Gross Domestic Product (preliminary estimate), giving a breakdown by broad aggregates in terms of the SIC, is published approximately one month earlier than the previous provisional estimate; UK output, income and expenditure, published about one month later, includes the main analysis previously published in the second quarterly press notice; and UK National Accounts, about one month later, includes the information from the personal income and expenditure, and industrial and commercial companies press notices, which have been discontinued.
2. This press notice has been discontinued: see footnote 1.
3. For the time being, as a result of the introduction of the European Single Market and the INTRASTAT system of recording trade within the EU, whole world trade figures are being published considerably in arrears and not in full detail. Provisional trade figures for the third quarter 1993 were first published on 10 December and monthly figures up to October on 10 January.
4. Reporting period for these statistics now coincides with calendar quarters.
5. Previously published quarterly by the Council of Mortgage Lenders as 'Mortgage Lending'.
6. Provisional.
7. Revised.

AV	= Annual Volume		(A)	= Annually
CSOB	= CSO Bulletin		(FY)	= Financial year figures
EG	= Employment Gazette		(H)	= Half-yearly
FR	= First Release		(M)	= Monthly
MV	= Monthly Volume		(Q)	= Quarterly
NR	= News Release			
PN	= Press Notice			
QV	= Quarterly Volume			
SB	= Statistical Bulletin			

Central Statistical Office

THE CSO BLUE BOOK

Concerned with macro-economics?
Have you considered CSO's Blue Book?
If not, you should.

The Blue Book - or United Kingdom National Accounts - is the main annual publication for national accounts statistics.

Detailed estimates of national output, income and expenditure. All for £15.50.

From HMSO and through good booksellers.

United Kingdom National Accounts

Published for the Central Statistical Office by HMSO.
Price £15.50 net
ISBN 0 11 620598 9

THE CSO PINK BOOK

Question: What is our trade with the rest of the European Community?

Question: How much does the UK earn from its investment?

Question: What are the UK's overseas assets and liabilities?

If you need to know answers to questions like these you need the CSO's *Pink Book United Kingdom Balance of Payments*

The *Pink Book* is the reference book for balance of payments statistics.

Detailed information on visible trade, invisibles and capital transactions.

Data for the last 11 years. Summary figures for earlier years. Notes and definitions.

From HMSO and through good booksellers.

United Kingdom Balance of Payments

Published for the Central Statistical Office by HMSO.
Price £13.25 net
ISBN 0 11 620597 0